Luminous

ALSO BY MIKE KING:

Mountain Calls
(Stochastic Press, 2017)

The Beauty of Judaism on Film
(Stochastic Press, 2017)

Enigma's Coda
(Stochastic Press, 2016)

Quakernomics: An Ethical Capitalism
(Anthem Press, 2014)

The Angel of Har Megiddo: A novel of the US-Israel-Palestine conflict
(Stochastic Press, 2012)

Postsecularism: The Hidden Challenge to Religious Extremism
(James Clarke & Co., 2009)

The American Cinema of Excess: Extremes of the National Mind on Film
(Stochastic Press, 2016 / McFarland & Company, 2009)

Secularism: The Hidden Origins of Disbelief
(James Clarke & Co., 2007)

Other writings are archived at www.jnani.org/mrking/writings and
www.stochasticpress.com/papers.html

LUMINOUS

The Spiritual Life on Film

MIKE KING

Foreword by Linus Roache

Text copyright © 2018 Mike King

All rights reserved. No part of this book may be reproduced or transmitted in any form or by any means, electronic or mechanical, including photocopying, recording, or by an information storage and retrieval system – except by a reviewer who may quote brief passages in a review – without permission in writing from the author.

mike@jnani.org

Version 2.0 © 2018

This book is also available in Kindle format.

ISBN-13: 978-0-9956480-4-3

ISBN-10: 0995648042

London: Stochastic Press
www.stochasticpress.com

Table of contents

Foreword by Linus Roache	1
Preface	3
Introduction	5
1. Spiritual Aesthetics, Nature and the Romantic	23
2. The Esoteric, the New Age and Neoplatonism	36
3. Dying, Suicide and Bereavement	65
4. Ghosts, Angels and the Afterlife	81
5. Reincarnation and Resurrection	92
6. Spiritual Chaos and Rubber Reality	110
7. Wisdom, Teachers and Disciples	123
8. Priests, Monks, Nuns and Spiritual Community	133
9. Spiritual Practice, Discipline and the Martial Arts	148
10. Violence, Compassion, Forgiveness and Atonement	168
11. East vs. West	192
12. Secular vs. Spiritual	208
Conclusions: A Luminous Cinema of the Spirit	237
Filmography	241
Appendix: Sixty Must-See Films for the Spiritual Life	247
Chapter Notes	253
Bibliography	261
Index	265

Note on the Stochastic edition

In order to retain formatting and page numbers I have made every attempt in typesetting this edition to follow the excellent work of McFarland & Company. However there is a little drift here and there from the original edition, but usually no more than a paragraph. Hence I ask the reader's forgiveness when using the index because a few words may have drifted to the end of the previous page or the beginning of the next.

I would also like to thank the staff at McFarland & Company for their encouragement and editing professionalism with the original edition.

Foreword
by Linus Roache

When a book speaks authentically to something you are passionate about then you find yourself reading it immersed in the joy of real interest and revelation, and that is exactly what this book was like for me.

I have been blessed to have two great passions and vocations in my life. At a very early age I was drawn towards the mystery of the spiritual life with a desire to understand the ultimate reality, meaning and purpose of existence. A big aspiration for a teenager but one that has led me to take enormous risks and embark on many adventures. It is still a passion burning very brightly in me to this day. Also at a very early age I was drawn to the powerful experience of live theater and movies that transported me into the deeper dimensions of life, humanity and the secrets of the cosmos. I wanted to be a part of this magical art, which led me to pur sue a career as an actor and now a fledgling movie producer. As I am sure it is true for many of you who are about to read this book, these movie experiences can sometimes be profound moments that can be life changing as they compel and encourage us toward the power and potential of transformation. Like light shone in darkness they can reveal things that we might never see on our own. Mike King tells us: "For a film to succeed at all it has to engage the audience; for film to be memorable it has to move the audience; and for a film to be luminous it has to have the potential for spiritual transformation."

What King has done in this wonderful book is actively seek out and share the qualities that make a movie illuminating, transformational or, as he so beautifully says, "luminous." By doing this he elevates the value and role that movies play as one of the greatest and most influential art forms in the world today. He walks readers meticulously through the many ways in which a movie can be "luminous" and he has done an enormous amount of research to make his case. Indeed, he surprised me with a bigger "must-see" list than I thought was possible for someone who has watched films as avidly I have, and with this particular interest in them.

Not only does this book prove to be a rich cornucopia of movies with spiritual depth but it also serves as a fascinating insight into the many different dimensions of the spiritual and religious experience and what that might mean to us today. In this way King expands the horizons of our understanding of the nature of spiritual experience itself. He finds it lurking in places that others might have missed and in movies readers will have definitely overlooked. So while they might be reading about how the art of movie making has either succeeded or failed to convey that which is transcendent, he helps his readers to be more rigorous in discerning what is truly illuminating and even enlightening in the first place.

In my understanding great art always reflects that which is transcendent and ungraspable and simultaneously moves us closer to the infinite source of our own nature. It goes beyond the mind and touches the soul and reaches the essence of who we are. In short, it shows and moves us to be who we are. Sometimes in life one can suddenly see the infinite in a night sky or a child's smile or in the vulnerable eyes of another human being, but a movie is a constructed and made experience, built frame by frame to touch and move viewers. It is a fine and complex art, and like a Swiss watchmaker King is able to reveal the inner workings of this great craft as a vehicle for spirit and illuminates its power for transformation.

Linus Roache is an actor. His movie credits include *Priest*, *Pandaemonium*, *Wings of a Dove*, *Blind Flight*, *Siam Sunset* and *Batman Begins*. His television credits include *The Gathering Storm* and *RFK* (2003 Golden Globe nomination). He is most recently known in the U.S. for his portrayal of ADA Michael Cutter on NBC's *Law & Order*.

Preface

This book is intended as a companion to the spiritual life. To be more precise, it is intended to be a companion to watching films as an *adjunct* to the spiritual life. By "spiritual life" I mean the pursuit of the sacred, or truth, or unconditional love, or any similar thing, either within a religious tradition or without one, or, as in my own case, as the grateful participant in many traditions. By "adjunct" I mean something supplementary to, but illuminating of, such sources as religious texts, teachers, and traditions, or the wisdom found within non-religious sources or ancient tribal cultures. Films above all are shared experiences, and, as traditional communities and their foundational stories become fragmented and lost in the broader adoption of secular values, films can become a new source of collective experience.

I watched more than 500 films in the preparation of this book—a process which naturally took some years—and hence the nature of it evolved over time. It was originally intended as a comprehensive survey of religion-spirituality and film, and is still, I believe, the first volume to attempt that. But the surprise for me in completing the project lay firstly in realizing the extent to which the spiritual life on film so often becomes defined in terms of moral questions. Secondly, I discovered that the book became in effect an interfaith project. Spiritual films allow us to explore the meaning of real-life ethical challenges and at the same time allow us to peer deep into the grandeur and beauty of spiritual traditions quite remote from our own experience.

It became impossible to avoid spoilers in this book. This is because in many cases the dramatic denouement of the film involved the revealing of some truth or the resolution of a moral challenge, the discussion of which was needed to demonstrate the spiritual or religious significance of the film. I hope that this does not detract from the pleasure of subsequent viewing. At the same time the sheer number of films has meant that they are introduced without ceremony, as are the many film critics and scholars whose opinions I reference. To help the reader there is a detailed filmography which lists the director(s) and year of release of each film. The chapter notes and bibliography identify the many critics and other sources I have drawn on. Apart from that I have mostly not had space to place these writers in context or justify why I chose to cite them.

The book leads naturally to a selected listing of sixty "must-see" films for the spiritual life. Although the inclusion of each film often has a lengthy justification in the text, the ultimate choice of sixty out of four hundred is undoubtedly personal and may seem to be idiosyncratic at times. This is perhaps inevitable, but I hope that readers will discover a *method* here that has a clear rationale, and can be used and adapted to construct similar lists for different contexts. Whether taken as it is, or somehow adapted, I hope my list will be useful for those who want to run a film club with a spiritual-religious and interfaith purpose, as I have been doing for a while in my hometown. The lengthy discussions at the end of each film have been for me just as rewarding as the research and writing side of the project. I have been left with no doubt: Film can take us deeper into the spiritual life.

I have many people to thank who helped me prepare this book. It started as a university research project, and so firstly I have to thank my then-department at London Metropolitan University for allocating the initial research funding for it out of a departmental Arts and Humanities Research Board grant. I would like to thank Dr. Lila Moore and Moe Dodson for their early work on the project, and also countless individuals who suggested a "spiritual" film I had not heard of, many of which turned out to be gems. Finally thanks go to my wife, Heather, who viewed many of the candidate films with me, including some that were undoubtedly a trial to watch.

Introduction

Film is quite simply an astonishing medium. It is one of a cluster of technological media that grew up after the centrality of religion had faded from public life, and so was free to serve whatever purpose it chose. In its long history, more than one hundred years, it rarely set out directly to convey in a positive sense the drama of the lived spiritual life, but, within the truly vast outpourings of cinematic production, there are some important films that do. Even the skeptical films can tell us much, because hidden behind the bluster or satire there is a sense of what is missing. The lived religious or spiritual life, while seeking balance and sometimes attaining it, also has moments of great and unique drama to it. By conveying this drama through the immersive experience of the big screen and big sound film has a transformative potential. It makes us laugh or cry, but at a deeper level it can shake us to the core, and the religious life—when properly understood—is precisely about the core of who we are.

When two such different fields as film and religion are brought together—in what is called an "inter-discipline"—the point in the first instance is to allow each to inform the other. What can we learn about the spiritual life through the film camera lens? What can we learn about film through the lens of spirituality and religion? The first question suggests that a film can do things that a book for example cannot. The spiritual life is enriched or transformed by reading the written word, so in what different or specific way is it enriched or transformed by film? The second question requires a critique to be constructed about film from a spiritual or religious worldview: What can filmmakers learn about the meaning and impact of their works when viewed from a spiritual perspective? Put more simply: film critiques religion; religion critiques film. But within this there will be a matter of emphasis and in this book the emphasis is on using film as an exploration of the lived religious or spiritual life. Hence it is firstly an *advocacy* of the spiritual life, a necessary endeavor because the context of filmmaking is an essentially secular one. It is also an advocacy of film, a celebration of it as the most important medium in which our global culture shares the experience of what it is to be human, dramatizing to each other our differences. In a sense, then, this is an interfaith project.

By making the lived spiritual or religious life the starting point for this work, a number of other possible approaches are discarded, although not entirely. For example, one could start from the point of view of belief, in which case one would examine films for the symbols of faith tradition and depth of their treatment. Or one could pursue the theme of comparative religion, for which there is much good material, though some surprising absences: there is very little for example on the devotional life, and very little that conveys the subtleties and splendors of Islam. Instead, by focusing on films relevant to the lived spiritual life, the issue becomes: Can the viewer potentially deepen their own spiritual practice through these films? Is there even a possibility for spiritual transformation here?

A wide range of films have been examined by other writers on film and religion, as we shall see, under the heading of a single term like "shamanic," "Gnostic," or even "Buddhist." Each one of these approaches yields valuable insights, but also very often fails to make distinct the peculiarities of each spiritual tradition. Here, a much wider range of concepts are used to examine the specific issues of the religious life portrayed on film. To give two examples: the film *Groundhog Day* will be examined through the issue of moral development, while the film *The Kite Runner* will be examined through the issue of atonement. It doesn't matter that for *Groundhog Day* the context is broadly secular and for *The Kite Runner* the context is broadly Islamic. The former film drew a wide range of positive responses from faith tradition, none of which were triggered by the discovery of the obvious outer symbols of their faith, while the latter film is about the regret for harm done to a faithful friend, and the convoluted journey of recompense. Who has not done or said something they later regretted? Hence these become universal themes of the spirit, whether or not an explicitly recognizable spiritual path or tradition is evoked in the narrative. One could attempt a shamanic, Gnostic, or even Buddhist reading of the two films, but this would be to overlay them with the religious ideas of traditions far removed from their contexts.

The book divides its filmic sources into twelve "pools" in a thematic way, so as to cover all the areas well-represented in film. These different themes will become the starting point for discovery, rather than any one religious viewpoint, idea, or symbol. Nearly four hundred films will be either touched upon or allowed to speak in some detail, thus building up a comprehensive vision of what film offers the spiritual life.

In searching for the films most relevant to the lived spiritual life the idea of the "luminous" emerges. Across all the religious and spiritual traditions metaphors of light are common, as they are in the secular world, to indicate a moment of insight or understanding. Hence a special meaning of the word "luminous" will be proposed here to convey a film, or a moment in a film, which contains within its dramatic presentation both the potential for spiritual transformation and the aesthetic mastery of light in the moving image. Such films or filmic moments stand at the pinnacle of achievement in religion and film. The search is on to find them.

Spirituality, Religion, and Life

First, some details of the approach need to be spelled out, including the way that some rather contested terms are used here. To start with, the terms "spirituality" and "religion" will be used more or less interchangeably in this book, though for many people they suggest quite different things, or at least a difference in emphasis. It would seem that for people who are skeptical of religion or perhaps hostile to it in some way—and also for many people who are simply struggling with their feelings about it—the word "religion" is unconsciously prefaced by the word "organized." It is the church they do not like. Hence "organized religion" is often disparaged, but one rarely finds a person commending *disorganized* or spontaneously-felt religion, at least not using those terms exactly. Rather, we may hear the assertion "religion bad, spirituality good." Those that broadly disown religion but value spirituality can probably be described as New Age to some degree in their outlook. The feminist writer Elizabeth Debold, for example, epitomizes this New Age view in an influential essay, "Spiritual But Not Religious."[1] Citing what she calls "the New Age's most beloved prophets," including Deepak Chopra, Eckhart Tolle, and Barbara Marx Hubbard, she puts forward the central tenet of the New Age, that "we are in the process of a global transformation of consciousness." Her question is how this is to be understood outside of conventional religion, her point being that those who pursue this idea are spiritual not religious. She is an advocate of the spiritual life, but is aware that "the very *idea* of religion may evoke a sense of stricture, empty ritual, and blind adherence to precepts that are out of step with our time." But when we look at the sources that a New Age writer like Chopra draws on, they turn out to be great *religious* figures, such as Meister Eckhart, who was both a mystic and a skillful regional organizer of church affairs. Spirituality has many roots in organized religion.

Hence it is ultimately not easy to pin down the difference between religion and spirituality beyond the fact that the term "religion" carries negative connotations to some people— including New Agers—where "spirituality" does not. Does the assumed prefix "organized" really help? Perhaps, but even then it is notable that Quakers, for example, have almost nothing of the conventional organization of religion, while spirituality can be highly organized in some guru-led contexts—including that of Debold's own guru, the American spiritual teacher Andrew Cohen. "Spirituality" in turn has negative connotations for some religionists, implying a pick-and-choose approach, often summed up in the rather scornful term "self-religion." So, while acknowledging that some people reject "religious," as Debold does, and others reject "spiritual," in this book—attempting as it does to speak equally to religious, New Age and secular audiences—the terms will be used somewhat interchangeably. It will be up to the reader to be generous: where they read "spiritual" can they admit that "religious" could be intended, or vice versa?

While distinguishing between spirituality and religion is not so easy, some definition of spirituality-religion must be ventured. Hence the following offering:

> At the core of the religious and spiritual life is a *profound connectedness*. Its opposite is an *anguished alienation*.

The phrase "profound connectedness" clearly has no meaning in a strictly materialist worldview, even though science can talk about ecosystems, sociopolitical entities, or at the quantum level about the interchange of fundamental particles as forms of connection. This is not to deny that a meditation on the physical connectedness of objects in general and living systems in particular is fruitful. Primo Levi, who trained as a chemist, famously ends one essay in a short contemplation of the fact that a carbon atom from the cross of Jesus is very likely present in the charcoal-based ink used in the last full stop of the last sentence of his text. All very good. But "profound connectedness" in the spiritual or religious sense requires a vision of self that is not limited to the body and its boundary of skin, or to the biochemistry of it. The self that is capable of a profound connectedness is more the self encapsulated in old-fashioned words that belong to religion—and belonged to philosophy before its estrangement from religion—such as "soul," "being," "spirit" and so on. Profound connectedness also carries connotations of the sacred. One could say that the apprehension of the universe in terms of wholes rather than parts is the key indicator of the sacred.

The opposite of a profound connectedness, an anguished alienation, is again not to be confined to a materialist interpretation. We may accept Marx's notion that laboring within a means of production imposed on us is alienating, but this is not the immediate meaning of "alienation" used here; rather it is an alienation from existence itself, or an alienation from self. The struggle against such alienation is even then not necessarily a spiritual or religious journey, as the Prozac literature illustrates.[2] Neither is an anguished alienation a prerequisite for the lived spiritual life; it is just a way of indicating that the journey *towards* profound connectedness is also *away* from a specific form of alienation. And the spiritual or religious life does not always appear as a journey: one finds that some deeply spiritual or religious individuals live a life of continuous serenity. But this would provide little material for a filmic treatment, because where is the drama in that? Let us confess: if we love film, we love a drama.

To anticipate a couple of films discussed later, in *Enlightenment Guaranteed* one of the protagonists learns that Zen is "going beyond the separate sense of self." "All of life is a coming home," says the voice of Robin Williams in the opening of the film *Patch Adams*. In the idea of a profound connectedness, in which the anguished sense of separation is transcended, and in which destination there is a sense of "coming home," there lies the essence of the religious drama. At the same time, it suggests that in scholarship of mysticism we might turn to illuminate our understanding of the spiritual and the religious, rather than to theologians. Going back less than a hundred years we find that the educated person often "read the mystics," and whatever they made of them, they read them in good faith. In Bertrand Russell's *Mysticism and Logic*, he readily admits he has no mystical experience himself but is prepared to find the mystics genuine.[3] In Somerset Maugham's novel *The Razor's Edge* (of which two film versions were made and are discussed later), the author demonstrates a comprehensive acquaintance with the mystical literature, while maintaining something of an amused distance from it. Jean-Paul Sartre read the mystics—according to Simone de Beauvoir—and his cynical treatment of Teresa of Avila in *Saint Genet* is the outcome.[4] Today such a natural interest in the mystics has passed mostly out of secular culture—and mostly out of theology—to be pursued, and, it has to be said, often bowdlerized, in the New Age.

"Mysticism" as a term has become debased, or simply broadened over the years to include much of what might be called charlatanry, or at the very least sensationalist and shallow experience-seeking. Alternatively it might be read into certain texts and films. Jeffrey F. Keuss shows in this extract that he would cast the net of mysticism too wide:

> One aspect of Kubrick not fully addressed however is that he was deeply concerned with the religious aspects of life as well. While not overtly playing his cards in any dogmatic pronouncements, reading the films of Kubrick shows a director who invokes an experience of the numinous and the predestined, what theologian Rudolf Otto would call the experience of the holy, the *mysterium tremendum et fascinans*. It is a mystical experience, an ecstasy at the end of things, that continually threatens to consume or immerse the subjects of his films and ultimately draws us as viewers into this experience of the holy as well.[5]

If one took as examples *Stanley Kubrick's 2001: A Space Odyssey* and *Eyes Wide Shut*, then "an ecstasy at the end of things" is certainly more than hinted at in these films, but none of them really draw us into the holy, as Keuss suggests. Hegel's great dictum "by the little which now satisfies Spirit, we can measure the extent of its loss," was even by the early nineteenth century registering the waning of the spiritual life.[6] One might say that his dictum covers all the attempts to read the spiritual or religious into films which, by the standards of earlier times at least, satisfy "Spirit" so little. At the same time, however, such films may well measure our loss. Keuss is right to point us to auteur film directors like Kubrick, and we will certainly investigate whether the oeuvres of such directors are spiritual. It is often hinted at here and there, and may flare up brilliantly in places where we least expect it. A director like Martin Scorsese is operating in an intensely secular context, so his films *The Last Temptation of Christ* and *Kundun* appear starkly religious. But his work must be understood against the backdrop of a world in which religion had mostly been vanquished as mere superstition. Keuss tells us this about Kubrick and *2001: A Space Odyssey*:

> Upon its initial release, the Vatican contacted Kubrick and invited him to come for a special showing of the film. Christiane Kubrick said that, as the images of the film filled the ancient wall of St. Peter's where the movie was being viewed, Stanley smiled and said "now I am beginning to understand my religion—this is an agnostic prayer, a plea for the 'something' that must be out there somewhere."[7]

But Kubrick's *2001: A Space Odyssey* is not really an "agnostic prayer" in the proper sense of prayer, because the "something out there" has been translated into merely physical terms. The vacuum of outer space may contain a "something"—but if it is an alien being, then there is no reason to suppose that it is any greater in Spirit than a human being, even if its technology is superior. And no psychedelic dream-sequence, with which the film ends, can conjure through chance juxtaposition the meaning of religion. To clutch at straws is not to pray: instead, true prayer involves the whole being of a person in a longing for profound connectedness. "Agnosia" simply means to not know, so prayer as a kind of searching is often agnostic, and we will find many films where that searching is directed to more fruitful ends for the spiritual life than science-fiction aliens.

A spiritual or religious life, then, is one where, even if momentarily, something much larger enters that broadens the narrow horizon of the conventional self, and in which there is some striving, or at least yearning, for that expanded perception of self and its relation to others and the universe. The mystics tell us that such an experience of profound connectedness is at the heart of all religious and spiritual systems. However, much writing and other engagement with spirituality and religion is at the level of doctrine: i.e., what is believed and the justifications for those beliefs. This is true of theologians, philosophers, and contemporary writers on either side of the atheism debate. Not so much attention, however, is given to the spiritual or religious *life*, meaning the attempt to live an ordinary life that at the same time embodies something of the sacred and the moral, one that embodies the search for a profound connectedness.

The secularist reads all religious expression in reductionist terms, through Freud, Darwin or Marx, or their many intellectual inheritors. But, likewise, the religionist reads all of secular life through the prism of an absent spirituality. Instead, one can read many of the events of a so-called secular life in terms of the spectrum of connectedness and alienation. For no religious reason at all, a Belgian father forgives the murderer of his child in the film *The Son*. Yet the drama of it can provoke the most intense of spiritual reflection and even joy, because the father is recognizing the kinship with the youth who took that life so precious to him, a kinship impossible for a narrowed constricted vision of self. Similarly the moral dilemmas explored in *21 Grams* do bump up against the ubiquitous presence of organized religion in America, but the resolution of the film is framed non-religiously and becomes a celebration of all the connections of life itself.

The spiritual or religious life as considered here, and waiting to be illuminated by film, is understood as any kind of life in which some expansiveness occurs, not through self-aggrandizement, aggression or merely an intellectual or aesthetic "high," but through love, or realization of profundity, or something as apparently simple as the turning back from anger.

The context for this glimpse of profound connectedness or expansivity might be some thing dramatic, an ethical crisis, or the simple human mutual experience of hurt or compassion.

Clearly the spiritual life includes everyday experience and also rare moments of heightened spirituality, spiritual crisis and peak experience. But any extensive consideration of it across different periods and cultures shows that it is enormously *varied*. What suits one person in the spiritual life may not suit another. To give just one example: some people have a strong devotional impulse, even if they appear outwardly rather intellectual. Such people include luminaries like St. Augustine, Blaise Pascal, Soren Kierkegaard, and the scholar of religion, John D. Caputo. Others appear to have not a shred of devotionality in their relig ious thinking, or even describe it as a lower form of spirituality. Spiritual temperaments are different everywhere, and this is made dramatically clear in the films to be examined. Some forms of spirituality clearly belong to the ancient past, including animism and sha manism, various forms of polytheism, and what could be called a "goddess" religious sensibility, even if these forms are subject to contemporary revivals. In the Western tradition, such older forms were largely sidelined during the rise of Christianity, though it is also clear that they all shaped it to some extent. The most important counter-religion of the West derives from the Greek tradition, and for the sake of simplicity will be termed "Neoplatonism" here, though other authors prefer "Gnostic" to cover some of the same history, or other terms. A number of films will be looked at here that convey either this Neoplaton ist religious form, or show the tensions—sometimes creative, though often not—between Christianity and Neoplatonism, or, to put it another way, between the Hebraic and the Hellenic.

In looking at the world's spiritual traditions through history one is struck by a common dynamic: a movement from a life-affirming engaged religiosity to a more inward renunciative religiosity and back again. This cycle seems necessary as the extremes of one orientation require the correction of the extremes of the other. Humans, it seems, rarely seek balance, though in some religious forms, for example in some variants of the Native American religion and in Taoism, "balance" or "harmony" are central spiritual goals. The West is not so inclined to the middle ground, so, for example, after the extremes of outward explorations in science, the arts and military conquests of the Greek and Roman periods, the Middle Ages became a period of intense religious inwardness. As a shorthand for describing a religious path which is world-curious and engaged the term "*via positiva*" can be useful, while for the inward more renunciative kind of religion the term "*via negativa*" is useful.[8] From the time of Thomas Aquinas in the thirteenth century, the West began to turn again towards an outward engagement with the world, from a *via negativa* spirituality to a *via positiva* spirituality: this revolution is still ongoing, and affects old and new religions alike.

The origins of the "death of religion" are Western. There was nothing in the inner dynamic of the Eastern religions that led them to the civil war of cultures that took place in the West where religion and mainstream culture parted company in the Enlightenment. "East" and "West" in spiritual terms needs a little definition, so it may be useful to suggest that the East-West religious pivot of the world for our purposes is Iran: west of it saw the genesis of the three great monotheistic religions, and east of it all the rest. Iran is also home to the world's two great syncretic religions, Manichaeism and the Baha'i. For other purposes India might be the pivot, partly because for centuries monotheism has been absorbed into its spiritual pluralism, and partly because it was subject to Aryan invasions that brought a warrior-based patriarchal religiosity. In the lands to the east of India profoundly different spiritual sensibilities rule, with roots in shamanism, Buddhism, Taoism and Shinto.

Russian filmmaker Andrei Tarkovsky wrote a wonderful book called *Sculpting in Time*, in which he says, on the subject of East and West:

> The East was closer to the truth than the West; but Western civilization devoured the East with its materialist demands on life.
>
> Compare Eastern and Western music. The West is forever shouting, "This is me! Look at me! Listen to me suffering, loving! How unhappy I am! How happy! I! Mine! Me!" In the Eastern tradition they never utter a word about themselves. The person is totally absorbed into God, Nature, Time; finding himself in everything; discovering everything in himself.[9]

Tarkovsky, as a Russian, more easily turned his head first to the East and then to the West. In this characterizing of the West he has hit upon something which Westerners traditionally discovered in reverse: that the Eastern temperament appears inscrutable. At some level it has to be admitted that the Western mind is more individualistic or even egoistic than the Eastern mind, because its root religion, Judaism, is infinitely more concerned with the individual and his or her fate than the root religions of the East, Hinduism and Taoism. To push the point further: The Western mind *is the mind of the drama queen*, while, as Tarkovsky says, "In the Eastern tradition they never utter a word about themselves." This point is not raised as an uncomfortable comparison to prepare the reader for a journey of self-criticism; rather it is raised to show how both Western religion and Western filmmaking share an essential passion for drama.

Two films that illustrate the archetypal Westerner as a drama queen are Jonathan Caouette's *Tarnation* and Julien Temple's docu-drama *Pandaemonium*. *Tarnation* is a self-portrait of the artist in recovery from his schizophrenic mother, perhaps rescued from total narcissism only by its critical commentary on mental health care and the use of the *Desiderata* of Max Ehrman to anchor its meanderings, while *Pandaemonium* dramatizes the relationship between Coleridge and Wordsworth. The entire Romantic movement, so epitomized in *Pandaemonium*, is a product of the Western preoccupation with self, and now an enormous influence on Eastern filmmaking, for example in the work of Wong Kar Wai, director of *In the Mood for Love*.

What this means for film and religion is that a key linking characteristic of each, when film is understood in the first instance as a Western production, is *drama*. When we extend the scope of religion to the East, and filmmaking to include non–Western filmmakers, we can be on the lookout for a film sensibility that is significantly less dramatic in its structure and more in keeping with Tarkovsky's assessment of the Eastern mind. The films of the Japanese director Ozu are one example. Or, if we look at the films of Mongolian-born Byambasuren Davaa, working in Germany, we find good examples of docu-drama that portray that quintessentially Eastern characteristic in a Buddhist-shamanic context.

In the astonishing documentary *Into Great Silence*, the camera follows the life of Carthusian monks in France. The spiritual beauty of this film lies in what many would call a Zen quality of stillness, coupled with a poetic cinematography. But the inner drama of the spiritual life, as experienced by the monks, is not easily recoverable from the outward portrayal of even this most intense of religious practices. Hence Eastern concepts are resorted to in the film's description.

Since the time of Voltaire, Western writers were able to ridicule Christianity, and in the twentieth century writers, artists and filmmakers were able to create cultural masterpieces that were high art and at the same time a vehicle to convey their authors' distaste for religion. Much of secular culture simply ignored religion, but works like *The Life of Brian* and *Monty Python and the Holy Grail* were able to satirize it with only ineffectual protest from religious apologists such as Malcolm Muggeridge and the Bishop of Southwark—this in an infamous televised debate that left the Python team the clear moral victors. (The debate itself became the subject of the 2011 film *Holy Flying Circus*.) *The Life of Brian* was re-issued in its twenty-fifth anniversary year to place it again in the top sixty supermarket video releases, a feat that only a minuscule proportion of the industry outpourings can match. Its casual dismissal of religion is all the more powerful because of its nonchalance—it's not angry enough to suggest that its opponent is worth taking seriously. Its casual atheism can be understood as an entirely Western phenomenon.

The Spiritual Life and Film

While music, painting, architecture and theatre all have religious origins, the media emerging out of technological innovations during the Victorian period, such as photography and cinematography, were invented during the period of great religious retreat. The electronic media in the late twentieth century were even more clearly products of a secular-oriented culture. But there was, right from the start, also a stream of religious filmmaking—as the great French film theorist André Bazin comments on.[10] The very fact that film can address the everyday, in a way that arguably theatre cannot, makes it a surprisingly useful medium for spirituality and religion. However, the real strength of Western filmmaking (and its adoption in the East when unconstrained by religious tradition) is that it is at heart an *artform* serving its own criteria. An artist operates as a vehicle for social commentary, in a way that, for example, a social scientist or philosopher never can. An artist uses intuition as a kind of antenna to pick up what is in the air, in the water, in the Zeitgeist, often anticipating rather than playing catch-up (as the more rational philosophers or social scientists do). Of course, given their location in an intensely secular context, they mostly don't deal with religious or spiritual issues, but, as film production is so vast, we are still left with enough important films that do. The artist, however, unlike the scientist, has no tested "method"—and so they can often fail spectacularly, not just in their art, but in life: one thinks of the shambles that was Pier Paolo Pasolini's life and art, in which his brilliance failed his target as often as it hit.

A question that baffles some conservative film critics in America is why, when such a large proportion of the American population are religious, or at least nominally religious, Hollywood should so often produce films that either reject its beliefs or set out to offend its values. This is usefully explained by a British academic at the London School of Economics, David Martin, who proposes what he calls a "centre-periphery" theory in which the wider population, including those in areas remote from urban centers, tend to retain traditional faith, while those in the urban centers and particularly those who enter the media industry tend to be highly educated and attracted to atheism.[11] Martin's theory of secularization is just one of a number of attempts to explain how Western culture became so universally secular, even though significant areas of the population retain their faith tradition or are experimenting with new religions.

Whatever the reason for the secularization of mainstream Western culture and the relative ghettoisation of the world of religion, it remains true that most mainstream film critics and scholars of religion belong to Martin's secular "centre." It usually falls to the more culturally conservative group of critics and writers to survey cultural production as a whole, and film in particular, for the relevance to religion. But they are generally writing for a religious audience who are offended by the sex and violence in much of secular production or are simply looking for a guide to safe uplifting family viewing that does not challenge their beliefs. A typical American critic of this nature is Michael Medved. His book *Hollywood vs. America* presents a detailed case that "the entertainment industry has broken faith with its audience."[12] Medved is a radio talk show host, film critic and author who represents the views of religious Americans who object to the mass media, and his opinions will be cited on some films later on. Between the world of the cultural conservative on the one hand and the secular critic on the other, we do find a range of sympathetic scholars working in the interdiscipline of religion and film, though they are not usually mainstream critics. They will, however, be drawn on extensively here.

For example, Peter Francis says of the theologian's role: "It is not to dole out an imprimatur to films that are morally uplifting, nor is it to utter condemnation of particular movies that are deemed morally dubious."[13] But something "morally dubious" may be untrue at an emotional or existential level, so any careful search for truth is bound to question such films. Or one could say perhaps that the moral structure of a film is its emotional structure seen from a spiritual point of view. The term "emotional intelligence" and variations on this theme have been around for some time, and so it is natural that some thinkers have explored the idea of "spiritual intelligence."[14] When emotional intelligence or emotional literacy is debated its opposite is sometimes referred to as an "autism." In 2009 the French president Nicolas Sarkozy was criticized for flinging the term "autistic" at an opponent, and it turned out that it is quite a habit of the French to do this. Critics of this popular usage say that the term describes a medical condition and the popular usage is demeaning to its sufferers, but the fact remains that "autistic" is—in the absence of a better term—a useful way of criticizing cultural productions that lack emotional or spiritual intelligence. Here the term "cultural autism" will be used here to flag up a film that embodies a rather brittle intelligence, or perhaps a reductionist point of view, or gratuitous violence, in which not only the emotional but also the spiritual is clumsily dealt with.[15] If spirituality is understood as a profound connectedness, then ordinary human empathy, the ability to connect to others, must have something spiritual about it. Hence an impairment of this ordinary connectedness—which is the essence of the autistic condition—is also a spiritual question, and also often a moral question. For a film to demonstrate cultural autism, as defined here, it is not enough, however, to have a character or characters who lack ordinary human warmth or empathy. For example, films about autistic people, such as *Rain Man* or *Snow Cake*, are not in themselves products of cultural autism, because the prevailing context within these films is of ordinary warmth and empathy. It is in films where *nobody* exhibits these characteristics that one suspects cultural autism: they don't reflect real life where populations are mixed, even within the same family. There are certain directors whose work consistently appears to demonstrate this, such as Andrei Tarkovsky and Jane Campion. This is not to belittle their achievements, but to make clear that this quality in their work is likely to make their films less pertinent to the spiritual life, even if, on the surface, they may have spiritual or religious themes. Another type of director, typified by Steven Spielberg, consistently makes films where emotion is overplayed, formulaic, and ultimately always ersatz: emotion-by-numbers. The cultural autism here comprises a missing sense of empathy overlaid with obligatory elements of New Age or psycho therapeutic "touchy-feely" correctness.

Religion often suffers from an unsympathetic examination from disciplines such as psychology, sociology and brain science. This is not to say that such approaches yield nothing of interest, but to suggest that these disciplines have a history of being intrinsically "unmusical" to spirituality and religion. The idea of being musical or unmusical to religion is a useful one, because it is not hard to imagine someone with no feel for music at all being baffled by a concert, particularly as the audience is obviously moved in some mysterious way. Rousseau may have been the first to draw this analogy,[16] but the term "unmusical" appears to derive from the writings of the sociologist Max Weber. The Monty Python team were clearly unmusical to religion when they satirized it in their films, but most of the films looked at here have writers or directors who are not.

In the first instance, however, the maker of a film is pursuing their own craft, and not the discipline of the religious life. Martin and Oswalt, in their introduction to *Screening the Sacred*, say:

> Religion, like literature, or history or art, warrants its own academic discipline and specialized modes of study. Some scholars of religion express this claim by saying that religion is *sui generis*— that is, religion constitutes a domain of human activity "of its own sort." Religion orients communities towards something or someone or some place sacred or inviolate.[17]

This contains both a useful short definition of religion as what orients communities to the sacred, and the use of the term *sui generis*, meaning "self-originating," or as defined above, "of its own sort." Treating religion as if it were a branch of psychology or sociology, for example, generally does it some violence, as do scientific attempts to "explain" music.[18] By the same token, film must also be regarded as *sui generis*, and not a cultural epiphenomenon to be exploited or censored according to a political ideology like Marxism. The approach to film criticism of the Frankfurt School, for example, subordinates film to a largely Marxist and Freudian agenda, to the point where film can no more speak from its nature than religion can when examined by the same tradition. Neither should film be subsumed within cognate artforms such as photography, theatre, opera, the novel and so on.

Tarkovsky also uses the term *sui generis*: "The artist expresses these things by creating the image, *sui generis* detector of the absolute. Through the image is sustained an awareness of the infinite: the eternal within the finite, the spiritual within matter, the limitless given form."[19] Here he is saying that the artistic image is a thing "of its own sort," a detector of the "absolute." Having said this about art in general, he later makes clear his feelings about film in particular:

> Turning now to the film image as such, I immediately want to dispel the widely held idea that it is essentially "composite." This notion seems to me wrong because it implies that cinema is founded on the attributes of kindred art forms and has none specifically its own; and that is to deny that cinema is an art.[20]

In the first instance, Tarkovsky is sensitive to the habit of early film criticism to regard cinema as a kind of reduced theatre. It took time in fact for cinema to develop its own unique language, and to be understood as a medium in its own right, *sui generis*. Clearly, then, on each side of the film-religion debate there is a necessity to avoid casting one field in terms of another.

John R. May comes at this issue from a slightly different angle when he suggests that the interdiscipline of religion and film throws up three kinds of scholarship, which he calls heteronomy, theonomy and autonomy: "Heteronomy considers literature the hand-maiden of faith, whereas autonomy insists that literature can only be judged by its own norms, with theological implications sought in terms of their literary analogues. Theonomy, following theologian Paul Tillich, sees both literature and religion grounded in ultimate reality, that is to say God."[21] May's "autonomy" is close to the *sui generis* principle pursued here.

With these points in mind, it is easier to tackle one of the most difficult subjects for the inter-discipline of religion and film: how to identify significant films for study, and, more difficult still, how to construct a canon, a set of must-see films. The sheer size of the world's filmic back-catalogue—growing almost daily—means that a complete acquaintance with all spiritual-religious films is impossible. However, there are various means whereby one can carry out a reasonably systematic sampling, following natural leads such as existing listings compiled by enthusiasts, academics and religious organizations, including online listings provided for example by the *Catholic Film Reviews* or the online *Journal of Religion and Film*. Once in possession of the totality of these listings—with perhaps thousands of films thus included—it becomes obvious that many films are included for rather trivial reasons. One then needs to develop criteria for narrowing down the field.

Melanie J. Wright, in her book on film and religion, says that "despite many connections between the worlds of religion and film, relatively few extended studies try to tackle the topic systematically."[22] She adds:

> In numerous religion (or theology) and film books, the choice of subject matter appears to be fairly random. In simple terms, this diffuse approach seems to be underpinned by the assumptions that:
> (a) films are about "life" and its meaning; (b) religion is about "life" and its meaning; ergo
> (c) all films are "religious," or are amenable to some kind of religious reading. [23]

Wright warns us off an approach which would blandly assert that all film is religious. Putting it another way, perhaps we should be alert to scholarship which reads religious or spiritual elements into film when they are not there. Some writers even argue that setting a boundary between the secular and religious in film is unnecessary, as film conveys powerful emotions that are necessarily religious in some sense. David John Graham says, "In the words of Paul Tillich: 'everything that expresses ultimate reality expresses God whether it intends to do so or not.'"[24] But the simplistic idea that "all films are religious" makes a systematic survey impossible. Gerard Loughlin, in his book *Alien Sex: The Body and Desire in Cinema and Theology*, tells us up front that "the choice of films was the result of accident rather than method ... most are not obviously religious."[25] On the one hand, then, the net can be cast too wide for lack of selection criteria, or for the same reason the net can be reduced to a few films that present themselves just by accident.

Here we begin the selection process by starting with the expanded list, derived as described above, and then eliminating whole categories of film. The first category of films to be avoided in this book is escapist fantasy such as in the *Star Wars* films or *The Da Vinci Code*. The main reason for rejecting them is that real religiousness or spirituality begins where escapism is firmly rejected. A related reason is that while fantasy may be an entertaining way to explore certain ideas, it always operates by giving quite unrealistic levels of agency to its protagonists. Putting it another way, escapist fantasy is ersatz, a fake, as much in fact of the secular life as the religious life. Opposing this view is C. S. Lewis who famously observed that the only person who opposes escape is, by definition, a jailer. As a writer of religious escapist fiction he would be a natural defender of the genre, and there is not doubt that "fantasy" at some level is necessary to any fictional art form. At a more serious level, however, the kind of inner liberation that the spiritual or religious life promises as its goal ultimately requires a keen distrust of make-believe.

Feel-good movies—usefully termed "Capraesque" because such Capra films as *It's a Wonderful Life* set a benchmark for the form—will also not be given any extensive airing. This is not because of the assumption that religion must be dour, but because feel-good movies tend to be a close relative of the escapist fantasy film, and because the spiritual life— while promising a certain kind of happiness perhaps—has to encompass the whole gamut of human emotion. This is where this book is in sharp contrast to works by the cultural conservatives such as Medved, who are looking only for "uplifting" fare. Yes, "uplift" is also sought here, but it will often be in the context of a struggle with the darker sides of life.

Films that proselytize or document religious history or ideas, for example *Luther*, the biopic of Martin Luther made by Eric Till in 2003, though a fine example of the genre, will also be mostly excluded from fuller discussion. The religious costume drama in general is also excluded because these are historical and have little relevance to the religious life of today. Most useful for us here is this longer comment from Bazin:

> The history of religious themes on the screen sufficiently reveals the temptations one must resist in order to meet simultaneously the requirements of cinematic art and of truly religious experience. Everything that is exterior, liturgical, sacramental, hagiographic, and miraculous in the everyday observance, doctrine, and practice of Catholicism does indeed show specific affinities with the cinema considered as a formidable iconography, but these affinities, which have made for the success of countless films, are also the source of the religious insignificance of most of them. Almost everything that is good in this domain was created not by the exploitation of these patent affinities, but rather by working against them: by the psychological and moral deepening of the religious factor as well as by the renunciation of the physical representation of the supernatural and of grace.[26]

Even though Bazin is writing about Catholicism, his point can be generalized to the whole of the spiritual life across all religious traditions. To parade the outward symbols of religion, particularly if they are visually compelling, is to usually guarantee the "religious insignificance" of the film.

Joseph Cunneen, in his book on Robert Bresson, cites film critic Michel Estève speaking on Bresson's *The Trial of Joan of Arc*:

> Michel Estève says, "Historical reconstruction ... would have dispersed attention, turning the spectator away from the essential. Hence neither decors nor costumes have autonomous existence, and the medieval crowd is heard but not shown. The past becomes hazy through concentration on the picturesque; only the present can produce genuine involvement, inciting the spectator to participate in the tragedy."[27]

Paul Schrader—screenwriter, director and author of *Transcendental Style in Film*—is likewise adamant that the "spectacle" is not the right way to present the sacred on film. He writes, "Throughout this essay there has been one persistent, overriding assumption: that the transcendental style is the proper method for conveying the Holy on film. This has been assumed, but is it necessarily so? Why do austerity and asceticism stand at the gates of the Transcendent; cannot the Transcendent also be expressed through exuberance and expressionism?" He then goes on to answer his question:

> The abundant means are indeed tempting to a film-maker, especially if he is bent on proselytizing. With comparative ease he can make an ardent atheist sympathize with the trials and agonies of Christ. He has not lifted the viewer to Christ's level, he has brought Christ down to the viewer's.[28]

Removing most escapist fantasy, most biopics of foundational religious figures or saints, and most costume dramas of "abundant means," helps to narrow down the focus considerably, and at the same time makes clear the serious intent of this study. But what about the question of popular cinema versus arthouse film? Writers such as Martin and Ostwalt tend to favor popular cinema, while others such as Jasper and Plate favor arthouse. This question is not so easily settled in advance however, as it is not so easy to find a general guide from spiritual or religious considerations. However, this does suggest a useful question to ask along the way: are the serious masters of cinema, the auteurs such as Martin Scorsese, Ingmar Bergman, Andrei

Tarkovsky and Akira Kurosawa, along with modern social realists, all of whose work comprises a less-accessible canon, more likely to create a spiritual masterpiece than populist directors? We will see.

Paul Schrader has written a highly regarded book on religion and film, so this makes him and his work of particular interest—plus the fact that he was often Scorsese's screenwriter. David John Graham suggests of Schrader that "arguably, he himself later became the leading exponent of what he describes, especially in his long association with Martin Scorsese."[29] Schrader's book has a Zen perspective, Chapter 5 discusses where a Zen concept is used as a way to explore the film genre of "rubber reality." As Scorsese's and Schrader's films are examined across this and other chapters we can eventually discover whether Graham's question is answered: do their films meet the aspirations of Schrader's book?

So, certain categories of film are out, and certain directors and screenwriters are in, at least in the first instance. What will guide the selection for consideration and indeed the value placed on a film will be its importance for the spiritual life: films that hint at the sacred or at a profound connectedness. But religion or spirituality can also be *read into* film. David Jasper makes this objection to a specific instance:

> I would hesitate a little before I give assent to the claim that the issues raised by the *Terminator* movies are the issues explored by Isaiah, Jeremiah and Ezekiel. ... Of course the images, particularly of a futuristic Los Angeles torn by war and destruction, relate to biblical passages like Jeremiah 4:23–6. But I do not think that for this reason they necessarily prompt theological reflection, for in the end they are just good entertainment within both myth and an environment (the cinema) that is ultimately reassuring and safe.[30]

Jasper's point is interesting because his objection revolves around the fact that the "environment" of the film—its broader character as an action adventure or as escapist fantasy—is ultimately *safe*, meaning that it does not challenge the viewer in any religious, spiritual, or moral sense. As Schrader says, it does not confront the viewer. The fantasy film invites suspension of disbelief for the duration of the film, but requires no transformation of one's being. Jasper's position is respected, but challenged by Gerard Loughlin, saying that he is "too quick in making this assessment."[31] However, here we go with Jasper in looking for films that are not "ultimately reassuring and safe." For a film to be relevant to the spiritual life it must at some level confront the viewer with real possibilities, choices that they may face as ordinary human beings in ordinary circumstances.

As Jasper points out, theologians can be too quick to read religion into film because they see parallels with specific Christian themes or symbols, for example the Last Supper or "biblical" levels of violence or catastrophe. Scholars of film and religion can also be too quick to subsume all kinds of other spiritualities under a single umbrella term, as mentioned earlier. Mike Tucker, as a British academic, has plotted an unusual course by focusing on the term "shamanism" in his cultural studies approach to art, cinema and music. Laboring under what is an almost universal obligation in British cultural studies to accept the broad tenets of left-wing postmodernism, Tucker has carved out a sacred space within a terrain that is mostly hostile to the spiritual. Admirable as this effort is, by using the term "shamanism" to delineate all that is sacred, Tucker has blunted its precision, and sidelined other possible sacred traditions. In one book he usefully begins by describing cave-paintings at Lascaux which depict the essential shamanic image: a half-human, half-animal hybrid figure. He goes on to say: "The stick-like figure at Lascaux and the hybrid of Les Trois Frères are two of the earliest images know to us of the shaman, or seer, of ancient cultures."[32] So far, so good. But he continues: "Charged with the responsibility of maintaining the health of the tribe, the prehistoric shaman retains the archetype of all artists." Effectively this is his thesis, that the artist is a kind of shaman, because the shaman is a kind of artist. But this inverts the priorities of the shaman: if and when he or she used artistic images, it was in the service of shamanism as the ur-religion of mankind. The artist, particularly in modern times, may or may not create imagery of a shamanic kind, but almost never in the *service* of religion. Similarly, the filmmakers that Tucker examines include elements of the shamanic mostly by accident, while many of them, although dealing with cosmic, religious, or spiritual themes, are mostly calling on a religious sensibility that is far removed from the shamanic.

When Paul Schrader sees film through the lens of the transcendent—as he defines it—and Mike Tucker sees film through the lens of the shamanic, they are providing just two examples of attempts to work within a single religious category. This is a style of analysis that depends on using a catch-all concept to mark out spiritual or religious films from the secular sea around them. There are more. For Eric Wilson it is Gnosticism and the Golem, which he uses in his book *Secret Cinema: Gnostic Vision in Film*. Most of the films he studies are excluded here for being escapist fantasy, but his thesis has some interest, particularly when the "Gnostic" label is understood more widely as Neoplatonist or Hellenic, i.e., as describing a Greek spirituality. For Stephen Simon it is the New Age idea of the "mystic message" that is the common factor for his selection of films in his book *The Force Is with You: Mystical Movie Messages That Inspire Our Lives*. Another strategy is to pursue the idea of the religious "hero," perhaps as explored in Joseph Campbell's famous book *The Hero's Journey*. The Buddha and Jesus are seen by Campbell as heroes who undergo a typical journey of transformation, and which others can follow. Gaye Ortiz and Maggie Roux analyze Sarah Connor, the female protagonist of the *Terminator* series, in this way.[33] They go on to say:

> Through the course of the *Terminator* films, then, the circumstances which awaken a prophetic response in Sarah are resolved in a salvific act by a machine. Christians can read the Terminator's totally selfless act as a heroic scene, resonating with the Christian belief that humanity can become, through the sacrifice of Jesus on the cross, a new creation.[34]

While it has an interesting lineage of thought from C. G. Jung through Campbell to the writer of a book on screenwriting, Christopher Vogler, and then to George Lucas, the creator of *Star Wars*, the idea of the "hero" as a religious archetype is avoided here. It has Western origins in Greek mythology, and emerges as a deeply American mode of thought, but one which is so intimately entwined with the justification of violence as to oppose all deeper sense of spirituality. Even Vogler admits that there can be resistance to the universal myth of the hero: "Here and there in my travels I learned that some cultures are not entirely comfortable with the term 'hero' to begin with. Australia and Germany are two cultures that seem slightly 'herophobic.'"[35]

It is simply inappropriate to apply the term "hero" in Campbell's sense to great religious figures, though many do. For example, Peter Malone counts Jesus as "hero" in his adoption of Campbell's so-called monomyth; he then applies this to the character in *Edward Scissorhands*. He says:

> Joseph Campbell, following Carl Jung in his exploration of the meanings of these stories, uses the phrase, "the hero with a thousand faces." Jesus is one of these heroes. He has become a universal figure and his life, death and resurrection have become symbols of human experience.[36]

While this is certainly an interesting approach it has a profound contradiction in it: the "heroes" of all conventional action films become so through *violence*. No such hero negotiated life's challenges by acting out the dictum: "turn the other cheek." What makes the Buddha and Jesus completely different from a "hero" in the normal sense is firstly that they oppose no obstacles with violence, secondly that they renounce all personal agency in their jour-ney—it is the "will of God" or equivalent eastern concept—and finally violence is done unto them.

Another quite different catch-all approach to religion and film is to assume that religion is essentially a form of political liberation. Ian Maher writes:

> True knowledge of God thus comes through commitment to the cause of those cast out to the margins and rejected by society. In *Awakenings*, whilst Dr. Sayer does not convey any overt theological stance it is arguable that an implicit theology of liberation is at work in him.[37]

Awakenings is a Robin Williams vehicle in which the actor is type-cast as the compassionate doctor who helps patients suffering from post-narcolepsy. Maher's assumption about working with the "rejected of society" is a deeply Christian idea, but, as he says, there is no overtly Christian element in the film. To read a theology of liberation into the film is to suggest that its compassion is Christian. More specifically, "Liberation Theology" is a movement originating in Catholic South America where Marxist ideas were adopted by some activist priests, not always with church approval. But to understand religion *solely* as liberation from oppression is to make it solely political.

Cinema involves watching images created with moving light in a darkened room, usually with others. Light itself has been used as a metaphor in the spiritual life in all religious traditions, though interestingly darkness is occasionally the term of choice, for example in the "divine darkness" of Dionysius the pseudo–Areopagite. Mostly it is metaphors of light or illumination, however, that the mystic reaches for to convey the moment of insight, self-realization, and divine grace or however these experiences are described in their tradition. In looking for films of importance to the spiritual life it is therefore natural to consider the term "luminous" as one that is both physically true of the medium of film and an appropriate metaphorical image for the spiritual life. Hence "luminous" will be used to describe moments in a film that convey something of the profound connectedness of the religious experience, or something of the sacred, or a breakthrough or transformative moment, perhaps one that is even challenging or uncomfortable for an audience to face, but which has the potential to change the viewer, even perhaps at some profound level. Luminous moments on film may be conveyed through a heightened filmic aesthetic or cinematography, in which case they are perhaps doubly luminous, though such special treatment is not strictly necessary. But luminous moments in the sense used here are often found in the context of quite negative emotions, or grief, or violence abandoned or set aside, or of human conflict in general, whether an inner struggle or outward strife. Hence "dark" becomes a companion metaphor, though it is in no way intended to suggest a genre such as film noir. Because the filmic image is a contrast between dark and light, the terms "luminous" and "dark" are appropriate to the inter-discipline. In the religious literature "dark" does not simply have a negative connotation, but can imply a preparatory period, a purgation, a purification, or a crisis which anticipates the light. St. John of the Cross's famous "dark night of the soul" is in no way a negative condition, but a preparation or stripping away of what obstructs the entry of the sacred.

The "dark night of the soul" may be too archaic a term to be relevant to some contemporary filmmaking so "darkness" can also be couched in the more modern language of alienation from self. This darkness of alienation should be pregnant and is clearly distinguishable from a darkness that is merely a secular reductionist contraction of spirit, a continuum of despair or meaninglessness or nihilism. Such moments, or films, that don't touch on the issues of religious darkness and light can be usefully referred to as "dull." Hence, while much of Tarkovsky has a cinematography of the utmost aesthetic luminosity, we will explore whether it is perhaps mostly dull in this sense, rather than luminous. When Woody Allen took on Bergman's cinematographer Sven Nykvist, the result was far from the aesthetic luminosity of Bergman's films, but whether either filmmaker has left us "luminous" moments as defined here will be explored under several of the chapter headings to come. Conversely, a poorly lit film may have many moments of luminosity, because of the spiritual and religious nature of that moment, told through the filmic medium.

In the spiritual literature there is no doubt that the "dark" can also merge with negative emotions such as doubt, fear, terror, and even horror. Otto used the term *mysterium tremendum et fascinans* to convey something of the darker sides of religious awe—and which becomes perverted in the horror film as we apparently enjoy encountering our darkest fears. These include fears not just of physical butchery, dismemberment, torture and agony, but also the anticipation of fear and dread, and more deeply still of supernatural forces that can bring a kind of living death: a contamination of self, soul or spirit that saps all health-giving pleasure in life itself and turns us instead into morbid, listless, and malevolent shadows: the "zombie." In this state we contemplate only that which is vile, and ultimately turn to murder or suicide. But the question that surrounds the horror film is: to what extent is it genuinely cathartic and hence transformative, and to what extent is it the most dubious of titillations? We shall see that *The Exorcist* in this sense is perhaps more dubious than *The Omen* or *Carrie*, because the parading of the horror elements of possession by the devil is mostly ungrounded in either religious tradition or psychological dynamics. While *The Omen* and *Carrie* on the other hand have more religious and psychological credibility neither of them are perversions of the luminous sufficiently acute to be instructive, however. They are mostly dull rather than dark.

The special meaning of the terms "luminous," "dark" and "dull" can reinforce a point made earlier. We can understand the costume drama mostly as "dull"—e.g., *Jesus of Nazareth*, *Luther*, *Becket*, and *A Man for All Seasons*, though they are possibly fine films and convey important religious ideas. What makes them dull in the sense used here is not that they are unexciting or lacking in drama—they are dull because they do not much illuminate the *lived* spiritual life. By making a spectacle out of them, complete with heavy period costume, they are made remote to the ordinary viewer, who can then easily suspend disbelief—until the end of the film when disbelief is put back on like one's coat when leaving the cinema. These points were put earlier in the quotes from Bazin, Estève and Schrader. This remoteness is avoided in filmmakers like Bresson and Dreyer through the "transcendent style," as Paul Schrader would have it, though this may not guarantee luminous moments either. What Bresson and Dreyer do is remove an alienating layer, the "faux-historic," and replace it with the under-dramatized, a sparseness foreign to the usual thrust of the costume drama. Hence their films will be included for consideration.

To be truly luminous in the sense defined here, a filmic moment must have the potential for transforming the viewer. In her discussion of the film *Babette's Feast*, Maria Consuelo Maisto insists on the transformative potential of the film. She draws on and reinforces Schrader's ideas of the encounter that leaves the viewer confronted with something raw and transformative, as opposed to the temporary identification with the costume-drama protagonist. Maisto appeals to both religious studies scholars and film scholars to step outside of the limitations of their discipline, because it "is not only to close the door on the possibility of a transformative interdisciplinarity, but also, ironically, to ignore the film as *film*."[38] Hence for a film to succeed at all it has to engage the audience; for a film to be memorable it has to move the audience; and for a film to be luminous it has to have the potential for spiritual transformation.

Twelve Categories

In seeking a rationale for narrowing down the films for inclusion we have so far been warned off approaches that declare all film as religious; approaches that read spirituality or religion into film where the pretext for doing so is slight; and approaches involving a single criterion like the transcendent, the shamanic, or the Gnostic. Along the way we also have eliminated the escapist fantasy, which rather precludes much of science fiction and the Western genre, not to mention other popular genres such as the costume drama, crime and romance.

Once these various kinds of film are eliminated there remains the job of taking what is still a vast field and letting some kind of taxonomy emerge from it, a taxonomy not based on division by religion. As in any taxonomical venture it is a question of starting with kinship, in this case looking for films dealing with common issues. It is a question of making heaps of similar size, so that an issue in the spiritual life dealt with in only one film would suggest that the issue is not important enough, or that, with a bit of flexibility, the film could be included in another category. It is a surprise, for example, that films dealing with reincarnation are so plentiful as to require a category separate from death and dying. In contrast, when seeking out films that might explore the devotional, almost nothing is found. Such a discovery in itself is telling about contemporary spiritual life—perhaps the devotional is too alien to modernity—or about what kinds of filmic narrative are possible in the first place; perhaps the devotional life is too inward a drama to be conveyed in film. Unless it involves gurus, in which case such a film will find a home in that context.

Hence the twelve categories used here, although at first glance perhaps a rather arbitrary mix, have logically evolved out of a systematic survey. As each category suggested itself, further films of that type were sought, and, if enough were found, the category proved itself; other divisions got lost as more films were added to the total pool.

The categories pan out like this. As the book is intended as much for a curious secular audience as for the committed religionist or New Ager, it seems appropriate to start with a category of the aesthetic. Can the heights of aesthetic experience segue into the spiritual? Can Nature as a setting provide a spiritual aesthetics? Hence our first chapter: "Spiritual Aesthetics, Nature and the Romantic." This then takes us naturally to a Western tradition of spirituality that often includes the aesthetic which is broadly labeled as "Neoplatonist" here. This also involves esoteric spiritual practices, and so our second chapter becomes "The Esoteric, the New Age and Neoplatonism." We then take a leap to the issues of death and bereavement; these are issues provoking some of the deepest questions about meaning, often framed as religious questions, making our third chapter, "Dying, Suicide and Bereavement." From dying we move in the fourth category to the question of the afterlife and the possibility of a discarnate state, "Ghosts, Angels and the Afterlife." In the fifth category we then look at two versions of persistence of self beyond death, "Reincarnation and Resurrection."

The sixth category to present itself does so directly out of a film genre labeled "rubber reality"; here we relate it to the experience of the spiritual crisis, hence "Spiritual Chaos and Rubber Reality." In the seventh category we then turn to the question of the spiritual teacher—one who is needed in a crisis—in a chapter called "Wisdom, Teachers, and Disciples." This leads naturally to the eighth category, the more familiar world of "Priests, Monks, Nuns and Spiritual Community." From here the progression is to questions of spiritual discipline and practice, thus making the ninth category, "Spiritual Practice, Discipline and the Martial Arts." In the tenth category we explore issues relating to violence, hence a chapter on "Violence, Compassion, Forgiveness and Atonement."

The last two categories then round up issues that crop up many times in the first ten chapters. In the eleventh chapter we look at how East and West square up in religious terms on film, and in the twelfth and final chapter we encounter an issue that runs through the whole book: films that deal with the debate across the spiritual-secular divide.

1

Spiritual Aesthetics, Nature and the Romantic

For the committed secularist—perhaps mildly allergic to all talk of the spiritual or the religious—art and music can be a sufficient locus of heightened consciousness. To be transported by a great exhibition or architecture, perhaps explicitly drawing on sacred geometries, or by great music, perhaps explicitly sold in a boxed set marked "sacred music," is perfectly legitimate, and makes no immediate demands to hold beliefs in the supernatural or the tenets of any religion. All can participate in this experience, and, as the aesthetic pleasure has something of the ecstatic in it and hence something that takes one out of one's narrower psychic confines, it has some family resemblance to the spiritual, or may segue into it. Hence we start with films that are widely acknowledged to be aesthetic triumphs, though recognizing that for some religionists aesthetic pleasure is regarded as unreligious, or even to be actively avoided.

The visual aesthetics of painting, sculpture and architecture served religious purposes until very recently in history, undergoing a secularization in the twentieth century that gave these art forms a different kind of status. The "aesthetic" is now a category of its own, instead of integrated within a culture of religious purpose, though quite often the aesthetic is coupled in contemporary culture to a political purpose. Kierkegaard placed the aesthetics of the Romantic tradition as beneath the moral beauty of the Christian tradition; for him the love that the poets celebrate is merely self-love.[1] He believed that there was a hierarchy in which the aesthetic was the lowest order, outstripped by the ethical which enfolded it, while superior still was the religious which enfolded both lower orders. Not for Kierkegaard was Nietzsche's dictum "it is only as *an aesthetic phenomenon* that existence and the world are eternally *justified*."[2] Film, as a visual medium, has an aesthetics of its own, born in the era of the machine, a technologically mediated and fluid medium of moving light. In the service of the merely romantic it has all the flaws that Kierkegaard takes his scalpel to, but it is not so confined: it can also serve the ethical and the religious. Hence we are looking for films where the ethical and religious enfold the aesthetic.

For the definition of luminous employed here, the lighting could be poor, the palette dull, and the photography uninspired, but the filmic moment could still be "luminous" in the spiritual sense. A heightened filmic aesthetic, a conscious artistic intent, may however make such a luminous moment more intense, more unforgettable. It is even possible for a heightened aesthetic to come close to the luminous in only artistic terms, and so it is important to pay attention to directors whose works are universally acknowledged as aesthetic triumphs.

Perhaps the most stunningly lyrical aesthetic film ever produced—the one that comes closest to painting—is Tarkovsky's *Nostalgia*. It also has deeply mystical and religious themes, so it becomes an important case study when we pursue it further and ask if it can stand as being luminous in the sense used here. Using Kierkegaard's distinction between the religious and the Romantic, we will be asking: Is *Nostalgia* only ultimately a Romantic affirmation of beauty?

We will look far afield for the true meeting of aesthetics and spirituality, in films as different as *American Beauty* and *Anchoress*. The former may appear an unlikely candidate because it is a film located in the very specific American cultural space defined by TV series such as *Sex and the City* and *Desperate Housewives*. *Anchoress* is unlikely because it appears at first to be a combination of costume drama and indictment of the Christian oppression of women. Where the cinematography of *American Beauty* is perhaps not especially exceptional, even in the key scene of a plastic bag blowing in the wind, the cinematography of *Anchoress* is as lyrical as anything by Tarkovsky.

Marjeet Verbeek points out that theologians and artists "obviously have not enjoyed harmonious relationships during the ages," but goes on to add: "Once human beings are able to have a loving openness towards creation, they are able to 'experience' its beauty. Theologically, this means that the experience of beauty in creation is, first of all, the result of a loving praxis that comes to rest in aesthetic experience."[3] This suggests that a "loving openness towards creation" can be understood as a spiritual stance, from which aesthetic experience can flow, but is there a necessary flow in the other direction, starting from the aesthetic, and towards the spiritual?

Urban Aesthetics

We start with *American Beauty*, a film that offers us all that is morally ugly in suburban middle America and holds up a white plastic bag blowing in the wind as beautiful. Its protagonist, Lester, is serene in the face of his impending death. We don't know this at the beginning of the film, but his disembodied voice floats down to us from an eagle-eye view of his suburb, reinforced at the end in a similar aerial shot. This is after his brains are blown out by his disgruntled neighbor Colonel Fitts, whose misfit son Ricky is the one whose habit of capturing the world on video leads to the scene with the plastic bag. Ricky describes the moment to Lester's daughter, Jane:

> It was one of those days when it's a minute away from snowing. And there's this electricity in the air, you can almost hear it, right? And this bag was just ... dancing with me. Like a little kid begging me to play with it. For fifteen minutes. That's the day I realized that there was this entire life behind things, and this incredibly benevolent force that wanted me to know there was no reason to be afraid. Ever.

Of course, the denizens of affluent suburbia have no *real* reason to be afraid; all their fears are so much affectation as the film shows, but the point somehow is reinforced between Lester and Ricky, that even if one knows how banal the middle-class life is, *it is still beautiful*. This is the surprising conclusion of a film that appears in the first instance to be about a mid-life crisis. Lester gives up his middle-class profession to work flipping burgers, the job that in America quintessentially marks one as a "loser." He wants to make love with his wife on their expensive sofa, an idea that outrages her because everything must have its proper— bourgeois—place. In other words his rebellion appears to merely recapitulate that of a teenager, emphasized by the fact that teenagers become central to the film and his love interest. So how does this lead to a "loving openness towards creation?" It is the slow realization that the rebellion is as predictable as what is rebelled against, brought home finally in a moment of pathos where Lester discovers that his proper emotion towards the teenage girl of his sexual fantasies is *fatherly*. The story of this revelation is really a story of redemption, so will be returned to later, but what matters here is the unusual theme of this film: that there is actually nothing banal anywhere. Not if some crisis provokes the crucial spiritual quality of openness to creation.

The "beauty" in *American Beauty* has called forth some interesting analysis. Dean and Ean Sluyter, for example, write from a Buddhist perspective: "In the enlightened state you come to see that that beauty is in the world, not just sometimes but always."[4] David L. Smith points out that commentators have struggled to pin down the success of the film: "In the same spirit of puzzled wonder, the terms 'mystical' and 'spiritual' frequently crop up in connection with the rapt aesthetic of beauty that inspires some of the film's characters."[5] Smith goes on to cite the "Beautiful Necessity" of Emerson, meaning "that there is no gap between the conditions that seem to constrain us and the values we hope to realize."[6] Lester's serenity in the face of death shows that he finds freedom in that ultimate constraint bearing down on him. In this case, at least, we can grant that the aesthetic leads to the spiritual.

Nature and Contemplation

The film *Anchoress* is ostensibly about a Christian form of religious commitment known as anchorage, but in the opposition to and ultimate symbolic overthrow of all that is Christian its protagonist Christine Carpenter asserts an entirely pagan sensibility. At least, this is one possible interpretation of a film that is highly poetic, and verges at times on magical realism. It opens with Christine, surrounded by a lyric nature of wheat fields and open skies, reverently unwrapping a statue of the Virgin Mary. A distant bird, perhaps a skylark, sings; otherwise, the only sound is of wind in the grasses. Christine and a female companion are next seen arranging an extraordinary offering to Mary: snaking lines of apples emanate from the statue, lit by devotional candles. Christine becomes rapt in contemplation of the statue, a crude medieval carving of Mary, apparently suffering. Her companion cannot rouse her and goes for help, but in the meantime the camera cuts close-up between the eyes of the statue and its worshipper, stillness and mystery ebbing and flowing between them.

Christine is found asleep among the apples, a chaffinch singing outside, and, framed by the barn door of the simple church, stand the various officials, temporal and spiritual, who will direct Christine's future. The priest argues that the apples can only be released by the church as alms, and points to a fresco of Adam and Eve at the Tree of Knowledge. This sets the scene between the instinctive religion of Christine—which can legitimately be termed a goddess sensibility—and the patriarchal Christian world in which she nominally lives. "Nominally" because rural areas across the Christian world were notorious for their lapses into "paganism" and "heathenism," two terms that both derive from words meaning countryside.

The film is quite astonishing in how it uses sounds and images to build up the overwhelming sense of a religious sensibility predicated on Nature, the breath, and the body. Lighting is overlaid on Christine's face at night, and the close-up fluttering of wings—perhaps a shamanic trace—repeatedly segues into scenes of harvest or of death. Masculine and feminine are starkly present, as when the Reeve mounted high on his horse gives Christine an apple, and she gives it to the horse: a sexual advance rebutted, but perhaps not. All this is framed by sky and field, the rank masculine and the rank feminine juxtaposed as if in a poem by Walt Whitman.

Next, the women pour a libation on the earth, holding a corn dolly, and dance and sing. The corn dolly is one of the great symbols of pagan religion, but can be argued more specifically to belong to the goddess era. Its use was widespread across pre–Christian lands and is described by the anthropologist Sir James Frazer, either as the "Corn-Mother" or the "Corn-Maiden,"[7] and is intimately associated by him with human sacrifice, though this is probably a relic of male prejudice. They scratch a hole in the earth, and one of them holds the jar aloft. "Right into her belly!" one cries, "She likes to drink!" says the other. But Christine's mother, Pauline, looks on aghast and runs away. The irony is that Pauline, critical of the pagan leaning of the other women, is the one who is eventually denounced as a witch and killed. This is not before she suffers the loss of Christine in a way perhaps more profound than that of death: the priest wins her, as it were, for the church, against the competing sexual advances of the Reeve. In the meantime, the camera lingers on Christine's woven straw hat, and fades into an image of the wheat, freshly cut, the blade of the scythe alternating its stroke across the wheat and braided locks of women's hair.

It is extraordinary that the telling of a historical woman's journey to anchorage, a uniquely Christian practice of the Middle Ages, and set in the village of Shere in Surrey, should have suggested to the screenwriter and director such a rich set of pagan or goddess-related imagery. It is in a sense a depiction of what is lost, by the placing of it in the context of what deposed it. Both of the men in the story, the priest and the Reeve, are in effect enemies of Christine, representing the ecclesiastical and secular arms of patriarchy that had historically crushed all traces of the goddess. But it is the priest who sets in motion Christine's application to be an anchoress, a role open to her after her claims to have seen the Virgin Mary. Even as he explains the implications to her, an owl hoots outside the church, and Christine holds a marble in her hand, a strange symbolic gesture. But, once ceremoniously incarcerated, her love of the Virgin takes the most unchristian forms of expression.

Alone in her anchorage, she again rolls the marble in her hand reflectively: is it a reference to Julian of Norwich, the great anchoress of that period who saw the whole world as a walnut in the palm of her hand and asked, how could such a fragile thing be sustained? (Answer: by God's love.) Christine's friend, or lover, calls from over the water, she answers bird-cry with bird-cry, and he flaps his sleeves like wings. Sounds of ducks, the laughter of children: the camera follows candlelight on her face, or the walk of a beetle. Her mother brings food; the villagers come, as is the custom, to talk with the anchoress. In the bread she has been brought she can hear the swish of the scythe on the corn: all of Nature is present in her consciousness. She advises one woman about her lover "to embrace him with burning love, till he gives you all he will." A barren woman touches Christine's lips with her fingers, in the hope of a child; a skylark sings.

But the confinement, however close it brings Christine in her love of solitude to the Virgin Mary, is at last so obviously antithetical to her vision that she simply burrows out from her entombment, emerging out of the sandy earth like a mole to a startled visitor. At that moment her mother is drowned as a witch. Christine is alive in a sea of feathers, while her mother floats dead in a well. She claims the sky and the earth; the priest discovers his missing anchoress; her world expands to the infinite; his collapses.

The Reeve wants to hang her, the priest cautions charity, but Christine beats them both to an audience with the bishop. She wants to be released from her vows. "You lied!" she tells the bishop. "The church is not our house, our house is in the ground." The bishop, no longer able to hide behind his Latin, tells her that she is dead, he can no longer see her, while she repeats that her house is in the ground. It is a bizarre finale, as priest and Reeve fight each other. But as the men struggle over her she finds a ladder down, and through a trap-door in the cathedral she enters her natural domain: a cave of the earth with water running through it. A wing beats, and her breathing is labored, but the men merely recite their empty scriptures above. To the sound of dripping water, she caresses the rounded rocks, her breathing slows down, and she walks through the womb of the cavern, alone but filled with all that is of the earth.

The film contains many religious themes in it, but has none of the failings that it could potentially have as a costume drama, primarily because it is subversive not evangelical. But it could never be a period costume drama—despite the period costumes—precisely because its aesthetics are so fiercely wrought. Here must be an example of a heightened film aesthetic in the service of the spiritual life, whether one empathizes with the religious ideas contained within it or not.

Hail Mary by Jean-Luc Godard is a quite different film, part social realism in the mould of the Dardennes brothers, part religiously lyrical in the mold of Pasolini's *The Gospel According to St. Matthew*, and part aesthetically lyrical in the mold of *Anchoress*. But the heightened aesthetics in this film are all Godard's own: color instead of black-and-white, and on an intimate, human scale. It tells the story of a virgin birth in modern society, immediately creating a set of interesting problems, most important of which is the question of dealing with the outer symbols of a world religion and the issue of the supernatural. On both these counts one might expect the film to fail our proposed criteria for relevance to the spiritual life. Can it be rescued, as in *Anchoress*, by the subversive nature of its polemic, in which case its heightened aesthetics might augment and make luminous its themes? The religious subversion of *Hail Mary* is that of *American Beauty*, however, not that of *Anchoress*. *Hail Mary* tells the story of the virgin birth without proposing a revolution against Christianity, but it sets it instead among the banalities of modern life. Marie has a boyfriend called Joseph, and her Gabriel is an uncle who arrives not on wings of feathers but those of a passenger jet. Marie's father runs a petrol station—and nothing in modernity can be more banal than working in a petrol station.

"I have a pain in my belly," she tells her doctor. He tells her to get undressed for an examination. "Does the soul have a body?" she asks him, but he tells her the body has a soul. "I thought it was the other way round," she insists. He confirms that she is pregnant, while philosophizing what men have already known, that woman is a mystery. We understand that she has not even kissed Joseph. Later, she is naked, smoking a cigarette, and muses to the jazz strains of Coltrane: "I think the spirit acts on the body, breathes through it, veils it to make it fairer than it is." She reads from a book which suggests that the flesh is as common as the candles in the grocer before winter. Not until one takes one home and lights it can it give comfort. Here is the clue to the subversion that Godard attempts in this film: in a materialistic society the flesh of Marie, filmed by him as potentially merely the object of the male gaze, is made untouchable. What is first to the materialist has become last. As she writes down the numbers on the petrol pumps for her father in the evening she has become a soul with a body, not a body with a soul, and particularly not a body whose soul is denied as a relic of superstitious dualism. Godard subverts atheism to arrive at Christianity, where *Anchoress* subverts Christianity to arrive at the paganism of the goddess religion. Yet oddly, both films have a similar polemic.

Godard had a devout Protestant upbringing as a child (Swiss Calvinist–French Hugue - not), but adopted Maoism as his adult "religion" and looked to Mao as a prophet, as did many French intellectuals of the 1960s. He says: "I was raised a Protestant, but I don't practice. I am, however, very interested in Catholicism." His interest in it stems from his awareness that it is fundamentally more visual than Protestantism, a religion whose origins were associated with the Word.[8] Hence *Hail Mary* can be seen as an embodiment of Bazin's two insights: that Catholicism has a natural affinity with film, but that the affinity must be pursued by eschewing its traditional iconography.

Into Great Silence and *Silent Light* are potentially two more films where the camera's lingering eye is essential to fulfilling the contemplative essence of the spiritual context in question. *Into Great Silence* is wholly structured around what is in effect a photo-essay of a Carthusian monastery and its mountainous surroundings. It draws on the natural beauty of the monastery and mountain to paint a portrait of silence. *Silent Light* is set in an American Mennonite community, and portrays a religious life confronted by the adulterous yearnings of a family man. The "silence" in question here is the silence of uncertainty, in which the answer to a difficult problem is sought. What is God's will? As both films will be further discussed later it only remains here to say that the cinematography in both cases is outstanding and central to their impact.

Kurosawa's *Dersu Uzula*—also discussed later—is a poetic essay of wilderness and steppe, which can profitably be seen alongside the other films in this section. Particularly notable is the scene in which the protagonists are lost on the frozen tundra and have to make a grass hide to survive the night: the big empty spaces are no Romantic vision, but a teacher of aesthetics in the deadly serious business of survival.

Korean cinema has produced a number of Buddhist films, the best known being *Why Did Bodhidharma Leave for the East?* and *Spring, Summer, Autumn, Winter, ... and Spring*, both of which will be considered from a number of perspectives. Bae, a teacher of painting, has a doctorate in fine arts and made *Bodhidharma* outside of any commercial system, while *Spring...*, which appears to be a loose remake of *Bodhidharma*, was made by the commercial director, Ki-duk Kim. Korea has a Chan Buddhist tradition drawn from neighboring China, but many of its people are just as likely to be Catholic, as is the case of Kim, who was therefore exploring Buddhist themes as more of an outsider than Bae, who spent time as a follower of Buddhism. Both films deal with an orphan growing up in a Chan temple, and present to us some rather harsh aspects of Buddhism: extreme renunciativeness and the unforgiving workings of karmic retribution. Early in both films the child harms an animal, and the ramifications of this spell out the Buddhist doctrine of karma, though more explicitly in the second film.

In *Spring...*, Kim Ki-duk brings both an external dramatization of the inner struggle and a stunning natural landscape together in a way that makes the aesthetic quite integral to the spiritual. This is natural to Zen, anyhow: it is almost as if the gesture to enlightenment must be made beautifully, or not at all. And this is not to denigrate the film that must have been its inspiration: *Bodhidharma* is every bit as beautiful. As Francisca Cho points out, "Bae's painterly attentiveness to imagery—for indeed, *Bodhi* is primarily a visual rather than a narrative film—draws self-consciously from traditional Chan icons and landscapes."[9] Another commentator on the film, Michael L. Gillespie, adds: "Visually as well as narratively slow-paced, scenic sequences are so seamlessly connected with the narrative that there is a blending of the story itself with long and careful inquiries of skies, panoramas, forests, waters, fires, and faces."[10]

Some contemporary academics have sought to describe animism without reference to spirits and the spirit world.[11] This strategy involves the recognition that all natural things are "alive" in some sense, but hesitates over the apparent dualism that allows objects, whether rocks, trees, animals or humans to be "animated" by a discarnate counterpart, the spirit. But there is another form of spiritual or religious response to Nature that leaves aside the difficult issues of supernatural entities, and this can be broadly termed a "transcendent" Nature, approached in the first instance aesthetically. The writings of the American Transcendentalists are typical of this kind of nature mysticism, as mentioned above, in which the unity of all things is understood in the contemplation of Nature. In England, the writer Richard Jefferies quite independently paralleled these spiritual discoveries, and one could say that the American nature writer Annie Dillard is the more recent inheritor of the tradition.

Can this "transcendent" Nature appear in nature films such as the *Qatsi* trilogy, *Baraka*, and *Microcosmos*? Documentaries or docu-dramas such as *Into the Wild* and *Grizzly Man* can be included here, as well as, perhaps, the rather odd film *Gerry*. Herzog's *Encounters at the End of the World*, seen alongside his *Grizzly Man* and the more fictional *Where the Green Ants Dream* are also of a similar kind. Given the working definition of spirituality in this book as a "profound connectedness," the American Transcendentalists found in Nature not only the embodiment of this, but also a spiritual practice. However, in this set of films we don't find individuals explicitly pursuing this practice, or a culture of such a practice, but simply the spectacle of nature as a meditative moment. So, is there something of relevance to the spiritual life here?

The *Qatsi* trilogy deliberately sets out to juxtapose the unspoiled landscape of the Hopi—and then many other terrains—with urban industrialization. These are three films by Godfrey Reggio in which recognition of Native American ideas appear in their titles: *Koyaanisqatsi*, meaning "life out of balance," *Powaqqatsi*, meaning "life in transformation," and *Naqoyqatsi* meaning "life as war." *Baraka*, directed by Reggio's cameraman, is that rare example of a derivative work that is equal to or surpasses its inspiration. It also contains more direct references to spiritual paths and practices, including a strange ritual in which many men seated at the base of a mountain participate in synchronized movements and guttural utterances. "Baraka" means blessing in Arabic, and its high-definition scan from the original 70mm film format is considered to be one of the highest quality DVD productions ever made. Terence Malick's *The Tree of Life*, a meditation on bereavement, pursues a similar aesthetic at times.

The films *Into the Wild*, *Grizzly Man*, *Gerry*, *Encounters at the End of the World*, and *Where the Green Ants Dream* are all curious blends of nature cinematography with varying meditations or narratives on the place of man in apparently "indifferent" Nature. This is of course also a spiritual question, but ultimately perhaps all of these films of extended natural beauty are of relevance to the spiritual life only if one is already spiritually "converted" to Nature—as it were.

Tarkovsky and Metaphysics

It is natural to turn now to the films of Andrei Tarkovsky. They need special consideration in any analysis of film and religion, partly because of his cinematographic mastery, and partly, as with Paul Schrader, because of the way he writes about film. The question is: do the aesthetics and metaphysics of his films combine to make them spiritual in the way we are defining it? Are they luminous? If we consider the metaphysics first, then a Tarkovsky film like *The Sacrifice*, *Andrei Rublev*, or *The Mirror* all have metaphysical speculations which border on the religious or theological. In fact these films give us the clue for our assessment of *Nostalgia* when we realize that Russian modes of thought, particularly when hemmed in during the Communist era, are not that familiar to the West. Put simply, we can read too much into his metaphysics. Perhaps it is a metaphysics of political freedom—much hedged about to avoid censorship—that really concerns Tarkovsky, rather than a metaphysics of the spiritual life. Both *Stalker* and *Solaris*—his two science-fiction outings—can be seen in that light, but what about *Nostalgia* and the material that explicitly relates to the "mystic" in the film, the mad Italian Domenico? He climbs a public statue and sets light to himself at the end of the film; onlookers fail to intervene. Is his final act of self-immolation a religiously redemptive gesture, or a futile political one?

Tarkovsky says, "Devoid of spirituality, art carries its own tragedy within it. For even to recognize the spiritual vacuum of the times in which he lives, the artist must have specific qualities of wisdom and understanding. The true artist serves immortality, striving to immortalize the world and man within the world. An artist who doesn't try to seek out absolute truth, who ignores universal goals for the sake of accidentals, can only be a time-server."[12] In this and many other passages in his writings Tarkovsky indicates his interest in the spiritual. But do his films really satisfy our criteria? Do they satisfy Kierkegaard's requirements?

In *Nostalgia* we have the peak of aesthetic perfection in film. Tarkovsky uses glass, water, mirrors, and the crumbling beauty of Italian domestic architecture to create an aesthetic world that is also palpably brooding and dangerous. Nothing in words can capture the interplay of light in these man-made grottos, particularly the derelict, rain-sodden dwelling of the disturbed mystic who penetrates the world of visiting Russian academic Andrei Gorèakov. As the film unfolds the lives of the two men are revealed in flashbacks, both exiles of a sort: the Russian from the homeland of his dreams and the mystic from his imagined utopian state on earth. But for all the sublime visuals, and intimations of a sublime metaphysics, we notice early on that there is something clumsy in the film's handling of human relations, a clumsiness that one finds everywhere in Tarkovsky once alerted to it, as suggested in the introduction. Andrei is accompanied by Eugenia, an attractive translator assigned to him, who herself is beguiled early on in the film by a religious ceremony. As they form a relationship it seems more and more that Andrei merely regards the love offered to him as an inconvenience, as a distraction from his manly pursuit of memory and metaphysics. He accepts her attentions as a homage to his masculinity, just as any male chauvinist would: it is not the kindly rebuttal that a truly religious person would make. But his common ground with Domenico is just as illusory; where after all does one go with "$1 + 1 = 1$," scrawled by the mystic on the walls? It ought to trigger an "aha" moment—haven't I heard something like that in Blake or the Upanishads? But no, it turns out that the metaphysics here is, after all, sociopolitical. Rather than a common transcendence the men share a common alienation, with roots not in the mysticism of transcendence, but more in the politics of Marx. In other words the exalted aesthetics, of word and image in the film, are not about a "loving openness towards creation," but an aesthetics that is merely virtuoso and in the service, ultimately, of the political utopia. This aesthetic has no theological resonance; instead it is simply pasted onto a series of dramatic cameos that singularly lack in love. The sensibility looked for here, the intimation of a profound connectivity, is lacking. One has to conclude from this film at least that whatever Tarkovsky might write in his book, the film is the product of a *secular* mind.

But what, then, about Tarkovsky's *Andrei Rublev*, which is about a priest in an era steeped in faith? *Rublev* is a magnificent record of a man in turbulent religious times, and the epic casting of the bell towards the end is fine cinema. But again, the obvious link is via the icon and hence to aesthetics, as Nigel Savio D'Sa points out in his thoughtful assessment of the film:

> The composition of many of the shots in Andrei Rublev has unsurprising similarities to icon painting. The numerous figures and faces lost in thought are quite often centrally and frontally positioned. Centrality, frontality and the "inward gaze" are a typical element of the icon.[13]

We will see later that the film usefully contrasts Christian and "pagan" sensibilities, with a sensitivity to the latter that suggest Tarkovsky's sympathies are not necessarily with the church. It is the bell scene towards the end which invokes "a redemption through art" as D'Sa calls it.[14] The physical beauty of the bell-form, the sonorities of its peal, and the unity of a people in their endeavor to cast it have a religious quality that cannot be denied. Yet it still remains true that such a feeling is called forth more through the icons of a tradition—which point at many removes to a source—rather than a direct manifestation of the source. The socialist background for Tarkovsky's thought also demands that the *collective* is the locus of meaning, and so we learn little of the interiority of the characters. Rublev the man is as much a cipher as Domenico the mystic, so the film's spirituality cannot be sought in his inner world.

Tarkovsky's films are perhaps best understood under the rubric of cultural autism, as discussed in the introduction. If the emotional remoteness of one character were contrasted with the emotional warmth of another that would be one thing, but in his films he consistently paints a community of persons alienated from each other. Hence in Tarkovsky, the coupling of aesthetic genius with cultural autism alerts us to this possibility: that sometimes the higher the art, the *less* the human. We have then a simple clue in our search here for films of beauty that might be relevant to the lived spiritual life: if they lack human warmth then even the most intensely beautiful aesthetics do not necessarily indicate a spiritual profundity. They may be aesthetically exalted—and little comes close to Tarkovsky anywhere else in cinema—but they are spiritually "dull" as defined here. And if the truly luminous in our sense is missing, then so is the truly dark: the struggles of the protagonists are not a dark night of the soul in any spiritual sense.

The Romantic

Tarkovsky's problem is that of all Romanticism: making an outer and beautiful representation of what is inner and spiritual, but becoming lost in the representation. *Pandaemonium*, a made-for-TV film dramatizing the relationship between Coleridge and Wordsworth, demonstrates this. It presents an engaging account of the two poets and their entourage, with considerable human warmth, and so not a product of cultural autism. Instead this portrait is of an amateur but excitable engagement with the truths of mysticism, philosophy and politics, which is brought down at every turn by a middle–England thespian indulgence. It is an acting out of the stereotype of the creative genius, which *appears* to have a mystic dimension because of the mysterious and unknown character of creativity. But the "highs" in the film are down to the use of drugs: in this case the very Victorian thorn-apple and laudanum. Kierkegaard's worst fears are illustrated in the film: the religious impulse is cut from its roots and wanders into fantasy, indulgence and aesthetic recreation.

In *Dead Poet's Society* such a fascination with the Romantic brings about its proper harvest, death. The height of the Romantic ethic is suicide, epitomized in Goethe's eponymous hero in his novel *The Sorrows of Young Werther*. In *Dead Poet's Society* such a death also comes too soon, too young. This film is a Robin Williams vehicle in which he plays Keating, a schoolteacher determined that his boys shall "carpe diem"—seize the day—rather than be confined by convention. He reads Thoreau to them:

> I went to the woods because I wanted to live deliberately, I wanted to live deep and suck out all the marrow of life. ... To put to rout all that was not life, and not when I had come to die discover that I had not lived.

But we know that Thoreau, though located in a Romantic tradition, was rigorous in his pursuit of Nature as a transforming agent: he *walked all day* as a spiritual practice and only knew at the end of the day whether his offering, his meditation, his sacrifice, had been received, and he was to undergo that precious transformation that comes from living the spiritual life deliberately.[15] His Nature was not the ancient shamanic Nature, but was a sacred site for transformation, as had been discovered by other Nature mystics of that period: Walt Whitman, Ralph Waldo Emerson, John Muir, and Richard Jefferies.[16] What marks these writers out from the populist Romanticism of *Pandaemonium* is their adherence to raw Nature as the teacher. Whitman is referenced a number of times in *Dead Poet's Society*, but his *Leaves of Grass* implies a man more reminiscent of the Zen Master. For example, Whitman says:

> No dainty dolce affettuoso I,
> Bearded, sun-burnt, gray-neck'd, forbidding, I have arrived,
> To be wrestled with as I pass for the solid prizes of the universe,
> For such I afford whoever can persevere to win them.[17]

Keating means well in the film, but in the scenes where the boys go off to the caves to read poetry at night the context is more *Blair Witch Project* than the real tough-minded Nature mysticism of Whitman, Muir or Jefferies. Thoreau did not go to Walden to *read*, but to make himself continuously available to the elements and their transformative erosions of the ego; Whitman's "barbaric yawp" did not arise from thorn-apple, laudanum, or schoolboy japes. To read poetry in a cave is to insult all of Nature. Neil, one of Keating's most promising charges, is held out as a Romantic vision of thespian daring, but commits suicide when his father forbids him the stage as a career. In all honesty, the film leaves it open as to Keating's culpability—for he certainly meant well—but the indictment is hinted at: the merely Romantic has as its only natural course suicide. Keating's story has prompted some interesting critical assessment of his role: at one extreme he might be responsible for the boy's suicide,[18] while at the other he is a redemptive figure comparable to Christ.[19] Deacy writes that "rather than an agent or model of redemptive activity, Keating is unable to be perceived as a redemptive figure since he has not himself come face to face with his limitations and fallibilities as a human being."[20] This is probably right.

Orphée, the central film in Jean Cocteau's Orphic Trilogy, is also worth a mention as a typically Romantic exposition. It is a loose reworking of the classic Greek myth, in which the mirror becomes the gateway to the underworld, the world of death, but for its beautiful principal character it also becomes the device for his narcissism. In the film the modern Orpheus happens to be a poet who has lost his avant-garde readership, which we can take to be a "death" far worse for him than that of his wife. This is arthouse cinema in love with its virtuoso aesthetics but incapable of conveying any fundamentals of the spiritual life. Art, literature and aesthetics become self-absorbed ends in themselves, and it is no surprise that the themes of death and suicide come to dominate.

If *American Beauty* avoids the usual traps of Romantic aestheticization—because of how it dwells on the banal—then *What Dreams May Come* (another Robin Williams vehicle) falls off the rails again. But it does so in a different context, the New Age. While this topic is taken up in more detail soon, what is interesting in *What Dreams May Come*, and what makes it an interesting comparison to the film *Akira Kurosawa's Dreams*, is the possibility of film as painting. Literally. *What Dreams* is mostly set in the afterlife—as opposed to Kurosawa's dream life—and its producers (including Stephen Simon, the New Age filmmaker) needed to visualize this in a new way. Williams plays a doctor, Chris, who dies in a car crash, and who leaves behind a wife, Annie, who is an art consultant and for whom painting is a passion. Their children have already died in another road accident, so Annie is now alone, and cannot bear it. In the afterlife Chris is escorted by an angel and they contemplate together a painting commissioned by Chris as a present to his wife, a celebration of the lake in Switzerland where they met. He then meets his dog in a nether-world painterly paradise, slipping on wet oils as they transform themselves into flowers and sky. He is *in* the painting, a kitsch version of the American Sublime at one moment, then Van Gogh heavy oils the next. But in real life painting is not sufficient solace for Annie in her despair, and before long she takes her own life. Her afterlife is of course no oil painting because suicide is a spiritually sin, and Chris is forced into a quest to rescue her. The parallel with the Orphic legend is pointed out by Susan L. Schwartz in her analysis of the film.[21]

Akira Kurosawa's Dreams is a series of unrelated cameos with sometimes supernatural themes. In one of them a Japanese painter walks into a Van Gogh scene and tracks down the painter, played, bizarrely, by Martin Scorsese. Vincent-Martin (his ear suitably bandaged) tells the Japanese man that "all of Nature has its own beauty," but that he is driven, as an artist, with the intensity of a locomotive. It is hard to fathom quite what Kurosawa was doing in his *Dreams*. The Van Gogh scene could almost be a way of saying that the Western approach to Nature is too forced, too driven—like a locomotive. Kurosawa does not have the high-budget special effects of *What Dreams*, so he makes do with a few painted props in a rural setting, until the Japanese man walks through, more or less convincingly, a series of Van Gogh paintings. Perhaps the key to this is the intensity of Van Gogh's life, one not just bordering on spirituality, but a pursuit of painting in a few short years that can be regarded as the growing thunder of a spiritual crisis. In Colin Wilson's *The Outsider*, Wilson regards Van Gogh's predicament as entirely spiritual.[22] What this tells us is that it is not the art itself, but the intensity behind it where the common ground lies.

Art as Salvation

In *Babette's Feast* a French woman redeems herself and her dour Calvinist community through a specific work of art: a banquet. The film will be examined in more detail later, but is introduced here as "an important catalyst for some of the resurgent interest in religion and film in the last decade" as Maria Consuelo Maisto puts it.[23] Returning to the Kierkegaard of *Works of Love*, we could understand Babette's act as an expression of love for her neighbor. In fact, the film is rich ground for detecting Kierkegaardian themes, given the Danish setting of both, and the parallels between the philosopher and the General in the story. Jean Schuler cites a passage from Kierkegaard's *Fear and Trembling* in which Kierkegaard describes his "knight of faith," i.e., the person standing at the highest of his three categories, and in continual intimacy with the infinite, as relevant to the film. But the knight seems so solid, says Kierkegaard; this person could be a butcher relaxing in the gloaming, or one with "a gait as steady as a postman's."[24] Could Babette be this "knight," asks Schuler; did it inspire the short story upon which the film is based?[25]

Kierkegaard is said to stand at the head of the Existentialist tradition, and so we might equally draw on Sartre, in which case Babette's act is an act of self-definition, as a culinary artist, and therefore making an entirely secular bid for immortality as the "Jew" and the "Negress" do at the end of Sartre's *Nausea*. In Sartre's novel his anti-hero Roquentin emerges from a period of existential depression to find himself in a bar listening to a jazz record composed by a Jew and sung by a Negress, and has a Nietzschean epiphany in which he realizes that art makes life worthwhile. At the end of *Babette's Feast* her hosts question her why she spent her entire winnings on the meal; now she is left in poverty. "An artist is never poor," Babette replies. And how can we know that Babette, though genuinely moved out of gratitude to her community, is conceiving of her act in religious terms? In her gentle undermining of asceticism, is she making an argument within religion (Catholic versus Protestant), or is it against religion? Is she firstly an artist, in Kierkegaard's lowest category, or firstly a "knight of faith" in his highest category? After all so much secular dismissal of religion in the twentieth century has been to characterize it exclusively as life-denying. But no one film can settle something as subtle as this: what matters is that film can open up such possibilities.

These questions go to the heart of the Romantic conundrum. At one level the tradition is epitomized by Blake, whose anti-science anti-establishment artistic practice has the most profound of religious underpinnings, and which is recognized in the ironic fact that the hymn "Jerusalem" is one of his poems set to church music. The revolutionary is co-opted for the establishment. Blake was an esotericist as gifted as his rival Swedenborg, and his legacy to the English language are legion. Yet the Romantic tradition as a whole is so often a sliding away from his authenticity into an aesthetic froth, as one can see illustrated so well in *Pandaemonium*.

Summary

From the films discussed here we could conclude that the aesthetic is an important border-world between the secular and the religious, a meeting place where broadminded secularists and religionists have some common ground. Beauty may be a plastic bag dancing in the wind, a floating temple in a forest-girded lake, or French cuisine served as a gift and celebration of community. Historically, those that lived most vividly in the inter-world of art and religion were the Romantics, who rejected on the one hand traditional religion and on the other materialist industrialization. Their vision permeates filmmaking of a certain type, and can create an artform approaching the sacred. However, the Romantic contains within it the delicacy of a forced flower and tendencies to the maudlin and the narcissistic, and this can prevent the aesthetics of a film—such as *Nostalgia* or *What Dreams May Come*—from carrying the gravitas necessary for the deepening of the spiritual life. But when the Romantic impulse is reined in by the harder edge of raw Nature, or when it is underpinned by a moral edge, then the sacred—the sense of profound connectedness—is approached.

Hence there is something of the luminous—as defined here—in some of the films just discussed, but the reasons may also lie beyond the aesthetic.

What though might constitute essential viewing among the films just examined, films which have something of the truly luminous in them? If the criticisms leveled here against the Romantic impulse are valid, then we can say that films like *Dead Poet's Society* or *Orphée* operate somewhere below a threshold of spirituality, while *American Beauty* can arguably be placed above that threshold. That also leaves some of these films as further real contenders: *Baraka, Dersu Uzula, Anchoress, Hail Mary, Into Great Silence, Spring, Summer, Autumn, Winter ... and Spring* and *Why Did Bodhidharma Leave for the East?* But of all these films it has to be *Anchoress* that stands out as truly luminous in the sense used here, not only for its provocative exploration of a pre–Christian spiritual sensibility, but for a heightened cinematography of nature that is inseparable from its dramatic flair.

2
The Esoteric, the New Age and Neoplatonism

The secularist is sharply divided from the religionist and the New Ager over the issue of the "supernatural." It might be less obvious, however, that the modern religionist, whether Christian or Buddhist for example, may also have reframed their faith in entirely non-supernatural terms. This is largely because many educated religious Westerners find the narrative of science so compelling as to force such a reframing. Signs of this are everywhere as sophisticated Christians abandon the idea of resurrection and westernized Buddhists abandon reincarnation. But modern science grew out of an intellectual tradition that is best described as "esoteric," and many Enlightenment scientists and philosophers were perfectly comfortable with alchemy, astrology, the Kabbalah, and other esoteric traditions. These in turn appear, in the mists of time, to have had their origins in shamanic practices and animist beliefs.

The lived spiritual life may often be punctuated by what is termed a spiritual or religious experience of various kinds, which often, perhaps because of their intensity and unexpectedness, suggest a supernatural source. At the very least a person trying to make sense of the experience may find that secular explanations are little help, and that of mainstream religion no better. "Suffer not a witch to live," says the Old Testament, a sentiment that acts as marker for all the extremes of violence promised to those that pursue what we broadly call the esoteric. This includes spiritual healing, trance flight, clairvoyance, mediumship and so on, skills often exhibited by women, or, in older times by men or women shamans. The Christian tradition continued the Old Testament prejudice against such practices into its witch-hunts of the fifteenth to seventeenth centuries; Judaism likewise had fits of public denunciation of so-called "witches." But the Greek tradition was not so condemnatory, maintaining the tradition of oracles, shamans, and, in Pythagoras and Plato, the belief in reincarnation and astrology. Hence in the Renaissance there was a flowering of interest in the literature of esoteric practices such as astrology and alchemy, the Greek writings of Plato and Plotinus, the Egyptian Hermetica, and the Jewish Kabbalah, all equally criticized in the twentieth century by Bertrand Russell as a revival of "antique nonsense."[1] The Renaissance not only revived these traditions but also gave them a specific aesthetic, drawing on classical Greek sculpture, painting and architecture. For want of a better term we can call an esotericism that has a Greek feeling to it—and is associated with a Renaissance aesthetic—"Neoplatonist," and can identify it in a number of films.

The Neoplatonist sensibility is above all a worldview that was opposed by the Christian tradition, and in *The Name of the Rose* we find this antipathy well illustrated. In turn, the deep rejection of Christianity by many modern philosophers is also partly a "revenge of the Greek," and in Philip Pullman's *Dark Materials* series of novels and the film *The Golden Compass* it is starkly obvious: a deep esotericism that viscerally opposes the church. Neoplatonism as defined so broadly here can be considered the "counter-religion" of the West. It contains within it many different streams of religious thought, all of which the great religious philosopher Pico della Mirandola wanted to bring together under one intellectual-spiritual system in the Renaissance, but was condemned for by the church. Another term for all these spiritual paths is "the Western esoteric tradition," which may be more technically correct, but "Neoplatonism" is more concise.

Despite its reference to Plato one can say that Neoplatonism in the broader sense originates with Pythagoras, who in turn probably learned much of his esotericism from the Egyptian tradition. However, the real origins of all esotericism must lie in shamanism. One could even say that European esotericism is shamanism refracted through the Greek scientific mind, or that shamanism is Neoplatonism without the geometry. After its flowering and subsequent suppression in the Renaissance, Neoplatonism was revived in the late Victorian period in movements like Theosophy and Anthroposophy, went underground after the devastation of World War I, and resurfaced in New Age movements after World War II.

When searching for films that provide thoughtful explorations of themes of the shamanic, the esoteric, the New Age and Neoplatonism, we find a surprising number of interesting examples. In the first set of films to be examined, the theme is animism or shamanism, moving then to a consideration of Neoplatonism in film, including versions for children and the theme of the "familiar." From here the question arises whether populist representations in mystery and horror films retain anything that is firstly true to genuine esotericism, and secondly of any relevance to the lived spiritual life. This chapter then concludes with a look at the New Age in film.

Animism and Shamanism

Perhaps the most influential modern work on shamanism is Mircea Eliade's *Shamanism: Archaic Techniques of Ecstasy*, published in 1951. As a first approximation Eliade defines shamanism as a technique of ecstasy, elaborating this by saying that "the shaman specializes in a trance during which his soul is believed to leave his body and ascend to the sky or descend to the underworld."[2] However, Eliade makes it clear that shamanism should be properly considered the religion of shamans, not the wider community: Eliade believes that the ideology, mythology and rites of the religions of the areas he refers to are older than shamanism, and not initially shaped by them. This older religion, for want of a better term, could be called "animism" but the fact remains that much of shamanism *does* permeate such religions. The most obvious symbol of this is the bird, itself a symbol of the trance-flight of the shaman, and the almost universal use of the feather in animist religions as a signifier of the sacred.

Central to animism-shamanism is the idea of the spirit world, not a remote realm but rather one that completely interpenetrates the natural and human worlds. These spiritual or religious traditions belong to hunter-gatherer societies, many of which survived in remote regions into modern times, and so have been studied since the European first encountered them in the Americas and elsewhere. However, modern scholarship is uncomfortable with the supernatural elements of these traditions, and so either mythologizes them or reframes them in secular terms. Filmmaking is not so fastidious, thankfully, so there are actually a large number of films that present elements of the animist-shamanic sensibility and the practices of such peoples.

The largest cluster of films that touch on these topics are those with Native American themes, but there are scatterings of such films set in the Arctic, Scandinavia, Europe, Russia, Africa and Japan. Japanese animism lives within or alongside its two major religions, Buddhism and Shintoism, and it seems in many ways that the Japanese—having been largely spared both Christianity and Marxist materialism—are the most at ease with animist concepts, as we will see in the films of the Japanese animator Hayao Miyazaki.

We start the shamanic theme with the action-thriller *Thunderheart*, which tells the story of a young FBI agent with Sioux background (Ray Levoi, played by Val Kilmer) sent to a reservation to investigate a murder, during the course of which investigation he has to grapple with the idea that he is in some way the incarnation of a Native American medicine man or shaman. The film is set in 1970s America and deals inevitably with the poor physical and cultural conditions in which Native Americans find themselves. Shamanism itself is only a background to the film, but actors in it, notably Chief Ted Thin Elk (who plays Grandpa Sam Reaches) and Graham Greene (who plays Walter Crow Horse), could be said to carry the shamanic sensibility in face, voice, and gesture, at least to some degree.

Levoi is a white man who makes a journey into the spiritual heart of the Native American world, often against his will and better judgment, and through the tutelage, however indirect, of a full Native American. Ray starts the film as a half–Sioux who belongs completely to the Western culture and militarism of the FBI, taking pains to point out to his boss, with reference to the Indians on the reservation, "They are *not* my people." He also says sarcastically to Crow Horse, the reservation policeman, "I flew in here from a place called the twentieth century. I don't need to listen to the trees or talk to the sand to get answers."

The film opens with a montage of natives dancing the Ghost Dance against time-lapse dawn of the mountains, and the obligatory cry of a bird, perhaps an eagle. This alone has already become a herald of the shamanic in such films, probably adopted rather unconsciously by most filmmakers in the context of Native American themes. The Ghost Dance was among the native sacred ceremonies proscribed by the U.S. administration in the late nineteenth century, and is a regular feature in such films. We see a young man silhouetted against the orange dawn shot dead, a reference to the Wounded Knee massacre of 1890. Ray arrives at the reservation to arrest a murder suspect, Jimmy Looks Twice (played by Native American actor and musician John Trudell). They bust up a sweat lodge ceremony to find their man, in whose eyes we read the lingering resentment of all dominated peoples. He complains, "It was an *Inipi* ceremony." This is a Lakota purification ceremony held under a frame of saplings covered with hides or blankets in which heated stones raise steam—the so-called sweat lodge. Jimmy says sarcastically, "You drag people from churches during prayer?" We also catch the first sight of Grandpa Sam Reaches—proper name Wica'sa Wakan—who then summons Ray via Crow Horse. Ray meets Grandpa in his run-down caravan. Crow Horse, who is translating, says to Ray, "You stopped the *Inipi* a few days ago. He says he's not unhappy because he knows you." "He knows me?" "He saw you in a vision some time back." Later, at nighttime, Grandpa has a vision about a place called Red Deer Table, where Ray and Crow Horse are present, but he is not sure if Ray is killed or not. He probably is, but it is a good day to die.

"A good day to die" has become a cinematic cliché representing the resignation of the Native Americans to their fate, but of course originally it represented the animist or shamanic conviction that the spirit simply leaves the body at death and there is nothing to fear in this. Like everything else there is a good time for it and a bad time for it, a bafflingly subjective distinction to white men it seems. Ray has an unwelcome flashback to childhood, as he begins to recover the buried memories of his Native American father. In his emotional state, he almost shoots Crow Horse. But his denial of his father and his origins slowly crumble. Grandpa, in one of many crucial encounters with Ray, tells him early on that the spirits had told him of Ray's coming. Grandpa has a vision in front of Ray in which he sees a boy coming out of school and pretending not to see the "dirty Indian" waiting for him, attracting laughter from his classmates—the boy walks past him, his father. "The Indian man stands alone, sad," Grandpa tells him. Ray is shaken by this. So far, so Freudian.

But Ray's boss Frank can tell that Ray is becoming less than objective as the reservation and its history works on him. Frank has studied the Indians. He tells Ray, "They're a proud people, but they're also a conquered people. That means their future is dictated by the nation that conquered them." Spiritually speaking we might say that just one religion, Christianity, replaced all the religions of the Native Americans, and leave it at that. But the reality is more interesting, as we might understand from Jung's dictum that a colonizing people "inherit" the racial memory of the natives they displace.[3] Is it possible that the progression from the early Native American stereotype in film to the revisionist and sympathetic portraits of more recent times, is a further illustration of this dictum? Does that "racial memory"—living in what Jung later termed the "collective unconscious"—dwell in the white American mind as guilt and paranoia? Does it also drive a hunger to re-learn and embrace the animist and shamanic practices of the past? Certainly in many urban centers in the U.S. and the world shamanism has become a popular new religion to sign up to.[4]

Ray encounters school teacher Maggie Eagle Bear who gives him lecture on "power": it is a river, a rainstorm, not a force dictated from the barrel of a gun. Earlier in the film, she had been sarcastic with Ray when he asked for the whereabouts of Jimmy Looks Twice. "He crossed the road in front of me about two miles back. And then he flew away." "He flew away?" asked Ray. "Yeah. Well, he can shapeshift." "Shapeshift?" "Into different animals. You know. Deer, elk, porcupine." Now she is more sympathetic, so Ray begins to talks about father, who drank himself to death: "I was ashamed of him, so I buried him. Until my own people dug him up. My own people." He has changed his stance on this, it seems.

Ray then "sees" Ghost Dancing in a kind of trance. He is in his car when suddenly he finds himself by the Wounded Knee memorial; he sees soldiers on horseback, runs, panics, runs faster past women and children, and is shot. He wakes up in his car, drenched in sweat and panting. Has Ray as a white man inherited the "racial memory" of the conquered Indians? Or has Ray as an Indian recovered his own cultural heritage, that he had buried up to now along with the memories of his father? Or both? He goes to Grandpa to seek some explanation of what is happening to him but is confronted by Jimmy Looks Twice, who is resigned to his fate as a man wanted for a murder he did not commit. He won't run from his natural home. "There's a way to live with earth and a way not to. We choose the way of earth," he says. He is then violently arrested, a process that Ray has to pretend collusion with. They search Grandpa roughly. An officer says, "You been teaching these criminals about the Great Red Spirit, Sam?" Another says, "Check him for peyote. He's got a knife." Both Ghost Dancing and peyote—Native

American religious practices which emerged during the period of encounter with the whites—are symbols of resistance to white culture even after all this time.

Perhaps the most intense exchange then takes place between Grandpa and Ray in his car where the old man tells Ray that he is the returning spirit of Wakiyan Cante, a holy man shot dead in the massacre, whose English name is "Thunderheart." Ray starts by saying, "Listen I'm not who you think I am." But he is buckling under the impact of the two conflicting worlds that he straddles. Grandpa insists:

> Back that way is a place called Wounded Knee. I was one year old there when they came and shot our people down, because they were Ghost Dancing. They believed that this dance would stop the white man from coming, and bring back the buffalo. They shot three hundred of us. One of those killed was a holy man called Wakiyan Cante. Thunderheart. He was killed, while running for the stronghold. It is his blood, the same blood that was spilled on the grass and snow at Wounded Knee, that runs through your heart like a buffalo. Thunderheart has come, sent here to a troubled place to help his people. That's what I am told. Run. Run for the Stronghold, Thunderheart, run. The soldiers are coming.

Towards the finale of the story, Ray is driving with Crow Horse, who tells Ray that Grandpa's visions are strong, which prompts Ray to ask about visions. Crow Horse tells him that they can come in dreams, or during sickness, in the sweat lodge, or in the vision quest. Ray hesitantly tells him that he had a dream of being run down with other Indians and being shot in the back by white soldiers, and that he had driven past the place where it had happened. He had seen it.

> CROW HORSE: Saw what?
> RAY: The Wounded Knee memorial.
> CROW HORSE: (turns in disbelief) You were running with the Old Ones at The Knee?
> RAY: It was just a dream
> CROW HORSE: Who the hell are you man?
> RAY: What do you mean?
> CROW HORSE: You had yourself a vision. A man waits a long time to have a vision. Might go his whole lifetime and never get one. And along comes some instant Indian with a fucking Rolex and a brand-new pair of shoes, goddam FBI to top it all up, has himself a vision.
> RAY: Sorry.
> CROW HORSE: Ah, maybe it was just one of them, what do ya call 'em, fitful dreams?
> RAY: Yeah. Fitful dreams.
> CROW HORSE: (pause) Fitful dreams, horseshit. You had yourself a vision.
> RAY: What the hell do you want me to do?

"Instant Indians": in this phrase there is the accusation towards all whites who want to appropriate Native American culture. Yet, if the gift for "visions" or the more specialist gift that the shaman has for trance flight is rare among Native Americans, the converse is perhaps also true: that the gift can be found among other races.

The ending of the film is perhaps the most strained of the fictional elements in the film, though to Michael Apted's credit his documentary *Incident at Oglala* provides the much-needed factual counterweight, dealing with the violent events at the Pine Ridge reservation in the 1970s that are the real background to the fictional story. But scattered throughout *Thunderheart* there are so many references to Native American spiritual practices as to almost make the film a primer in shamanism—in its externals at least. Grandpa Sam Reaches, though referred to throughout as a "medicine man" can be properly termed a shaman, and performs this role explicitly on many occasions. In addition, the key outward elements of shamanism are present in the references to "shape-shifting" and the appearance of an owl as the messenger of death both in words and visually. The owl manifests as the messenger of death in other cultures too: Jordan Paper tells us, "In current Chinese folklore, the cry of the owl is feared as a harbinger of death, as it is elsewhere—for example, in West Coast native North American cultures."[5] He goes on to explain that in the Anishinabe cultures (which include the Odawa, Ojibwe, and Algonkin Native Americans) the owl is related to death "but not in a fearful manner."

In *Thunderheart* the practices of an animist-shamanic culture are also visible in the powwow—in modern times a social gathering with a dancing competition—and other portrayals of ritual dancing and singing, while Grandfather is always making observances to the moon, offerings to the spirits, or consulting the spirit world. But more subtly than the outward signs of a shamanic religious practice and culture, is the way in which Ray's journey from the world of the white man to that of the Native American takes place. Even if it is in part a Freudian journey, its parameters are shamanic: he discovers that he is more than just an "instant Indian," as Crow Horse mocks him for. He has a vision that the average Indian might wait a lifetime for.

One can argue that Chief Ted Thin Elk who plays Grandpa Sam Reaches in *Thunderheart* conveys the spirit of an animist or shamanic culture in his face and manner, in a way that an actor of another ethnic grouping could never achieve, for example, a white European or American. Chief Dan George is another Native American actor who conveys this sensibility in two well-known films, *Little Big Man* and *The Outlaw Josey Wales*. In the latter he is Lone Watie, and is captivating as a counterpoint to the antinomian and displaced Josey Wales. Clint Eastwood directed the film, and appears in the title role as a Missouri farmer who is on the run from the Union soldiers who murdered his family. At one point in the film Wales sneaks up on Lone Watie, a Cherokee, who is mortified that a white man should do that.

A little later Lone Watie does manage to sneak up on Wales, cocking his gun and causing Wales to start. Lone Watie is proud of himself: "Only an Indian can do something like this." As Wales agrees with him another gun is cocked: this time by an Indian woman, and she is aiming at Lone Watie. She had been rescued by Wales, and causes the old Indian even more mortification than Wales did. "I used to have power," he mourns, indignant that a "mere" woman should sneak up on him. "Power" is an important concept in Native American culture. Early anthropologists struggled with various Indian terms that they initially hoped might have some correlation with the white man's God but mean broadly "supernatural power." These terms include the *manitou* of the Algonkin, the *orenda* of the Iroquois, and the *wakan* of the Sioux.[6] But at a personal level one acquires "power" through the practice of sacred rites and rituals, for example vision quest, the sweat-lodge, or the extreme example of the Sun Dance ceremony (as in the much-criticized film *A Man Called Horse*). What the films do here is to contrast the "power" of the Native Americans, understood as a spiritual quality with the "power" of the white men understood as a legal entity and backed up with arms.

In *The Outlaw Josey Wales* the friendship grows between Lone Watie and Wales as the renegade white man accumulates misfits traveling with him in search of a new home. Early in their companionship is a scene with shamanic significance: Wales wakes up slowly to find that Lone Watie has placed a horned toad in front of his face. Eastwood grimaces, his eyes narrowed, but it is not the average white man's revulsion; there is something of the wild man in his face that echoes that of Chief Dan George's, whose wildness is softer and more deeply tuned to Nature. Lone Watie explains that the horned toad will tell them which direction to travel, and goes on to lament that he used to be good at reading the animals. Again, the significance of the scene is not so much in the explicitly shamanic use of a creature, but in the manner-of-being of Chief Dan George, his facial expression and voice, and also in the subtle acceptance in Eastwood's features of this way of life, despite his character's refusal to have a lizard show him his path. As the film progresses we understand that Wales has in effect gone beyond the world of the white man, embracing to some degree the more ancient way of the Native American. When Lone Watie is injured by Comanches, Wales rides off to parley with their chief Ten Bears. Wales delivers a typical piece of Eastwood antinomian philosophy about the treachery of governments. He promises to live by Nature's laws as do the Comanche, and to exchange beef for security. He will place the sign of the Comanche on his "lodge." Ten Bears agrees and they become blood brothers.

Of course, these Native American films so far described are not much more than confections written by white men, and the scene with Ten Bears is more a vehicle for Eastwood's white polemic of rugged individualism than any real exploration of the Native American sensibility. Native Americans themselves are often the fiercest critics of such filmmaking, including the activist Russell Means, though he makes it clear that he regards the work of Chief Dan George as an exception,[7] and he plays Native Americans in a number of films himself.

The two films so far described carry the shamanic within a broadly realistic action genre, leaving the viewer to decide whether spirit healing, precognition, divination through animals and other shamanic practices are for real or not. The Polish brothers' film *Northfork*, on the other hand, uses the device of magical realism to convey, perhaps even by accident, something of the shamanic spirit. The film deals with a very sick child, Irwin, cared for only by an aging priest, Father Harlan, in the town of Northfork, shortly to be inundated as part of a hydroelectric scheme. The film is about loss at many levels, carried forward by the activities of the "evacuation team" that enforce the removal of the town's last citizens through bribes and low-level violence. Punctuating this is the parallel, dream-like encounter between the dying orphan and a group of angels who are searching for a lost one—perhaps him.

The Polish brothers have chosen a highly desaturated palette for the film, and its stunning cinematography of the remote Montana plains and mountains conspire to make Nature an intense backdrop to the dam and its impending destructive impact. This loss, and the location on the Plains, already permits of the parallel with the Native Americans' losses, but very quickly other signifiers reinforce the possibility that the film, at some level, is dealing with the destruction of the Plains Indians and their animist way of life. The first of these is the feather, which one of the angels, called Flower Hercules, plucks from behind Irwin's ear. He is walking in a dream state in a cemetery, and when he awakes, his hand lolls out of bed towards Father Harlan, who takes the feather from the boy's hand in wonderment and places it between the leaves of his Bible.

But it is whole wings, not feathers in isolation, which dominate *Northfork*, both visually and in their continuous use in spoken metaphor. For example, in an early sermon by Harlan he says, "We are all angels. It is what we do with our wings that separate us." Later, at the sick boy's bedside he tells him, "In the early 1800s European settlers named Northfork after the river that embraces their town. Word travelled throughout the world that angels roamed these plains like bison." This statement, and numerous others, leads one to wonder whether the angels that roamed the plains like bison were in fact the Native Americans. Does the film as a whole want to make the analogy between a broadly Western Christian concept of discarnate beings with wings, and the indigenous peoples of the plains, whose most significant animal was the bison (buffalo)?

The next clue to resolving this question is in the first encounter with the angel family—a surreal creation comprising Flower Hercules, Cup of Tea, Cod and Happy. They are considering the merits of a painting in which a cowboy is hurling a net over a "birdman"—a boy with wings. Happy suggests that the Celts had used the swan as a sacred symbol, and it is the wings of the swan that appear in the painting. But leaving the Celts aside, is the painting a representation of the white man hunting down, not bison, but the Plains Indians which had depended on it?

Naturally, young Irwin is led in his delirium-rovings to the home of the strange family, but by no natural creation. Instead the film lays on us one of its most surreal images: a semi-mechanical dog on stilts. It appears to Irwin as he dreams of playing on a swing, and walks off, framed by the exquisite Montana mountains. There is no telling quite what prompted the Polish brothers to dream up this creature, but it veritably screams "shamanic." As distant explosions remind us of the progress of dam-building, Irwin is introduced to the angels. He bargains with them to take him with them when they go, and then later returns to them, on the run, clutching a long case, with buffalo in the foreground. The case is significant, because the evacuation team use this as a bribe to those reluctant to leave: it contains within it a pair of white wings. But—against expectations—the boy's does not: instead it contains a rifle and tranquilizer darts which he insists were used on him: "Yes, I was running with my flock, and they shot me." Whoever heard of a flock of angels being hunted with rifles and tranquilizer darts so powerful that they could "make an elephant fly?" (This was Happy's analysis.) But what if angels were Native Americans and tranquilizer darts were all the trappings of modern civilization, such as is brought by a hydroelectric project? Or if Ray Levoy's "fitful dream" of being shot at Wounded Knee is a racial memory that also inspired the Polish brothers?

One cannot be certain of interpretation here; the film is too surreal. But there is one more clue that lends weight to the shamanic hypothesis: that of gender fluidity. It lies firstly in the name of Flower Hercules, and the juxtaposition of her person and a boy's comic version of the Hercules story at Irwin's bedside. She comments, "Hercules, the strongest man ever to wear a skirt." Irwin then asks her, "Are you going to be my mother or my father?" She replies, "I am both. Consider it the perfect soul. I search for no-one and no-one looks for me. Whatever I need, I look within myself to find. I am complete. I am not king nor queen, yet I am both. A mother and a father." Also significant is the role that Father Harlan takes, played by the gruff Nick Nolte with his trademark in-turning diction. He is the tenderest of carers to Irwin. A feature of many Native American cultures is the *berdache*, a person of indistinct sexuality. The writer on Native American religions, Ake Hultkrantz, tells us, "Transvestitism is extremely prevalent in North America; the transvestite, the 'berdache,' here represents both male and female potency, therefore possessing special supernatural power."[8] Many writers on shamanism have commented on this issue. For example Holger Kalweit writes that homosexuals and transvestites or hermaphrodites often become shamans, and that "as a rule, the psychically conspicuous, the most sensitive, the loners, are the ones chosen for shamanic training."[9] In fact, gender fluidity is an important aspect of the spiritual life because it points to the transcendent aspect of it: a going-beyond the normal categories of living.

Returning to *Northfork*, one can observe that when put together gender fluidity, feathers, wings, bison, a dog-on-stilts, the plains of Montana, and the all pervading sense of an older, more natural way of life about to be erased by one of the great symbols of progress—electricity—then the case for a shamanic reading of the film becomes substantial.

On the other hand, Kurosawa's *Dersu Uzala*, introduced earlier, explores the way of life of a hunter whose context would have been *explicitly* shamanic. Dersu Uzala (played by Maksim Munzuk) is a hunter from the Nanai tribe of the Tungusic people of Eastern Russia and Northern China, where the Tungus link is significant because the very word "shaman" is believed to come from the Tungus language, and hence the Tungus peoples are an archetype for all shamanic hunter-gatherers. Dersu Uzala himself was a real-life hunter discovered in the forest by Russian explorer Vladimir Arsenyev, and with whom a friendship developed during the period 1902–1907. Kurosawa's film follows Arsenyev's account in his book of the same name.

When Dersu meets Vladimir, he introduces himself as a "Goldi," which is another name for the Nanai tribe, and adds that he lives where he is, and that the soldiers have shot all the animals, which he depends upon for food. The first glimpse we get of the animistic world he lives in is when he scolds the fire for chattering. He also chides the soldiers that they could not survive alone in the mountains, because they were like children—when it came to tracking at least. In anticipation of the discussion in a later section on Kurosawa's ever-present sense of generosity in his films, it is worth pointing out the scene where Dersu makes good a shack, and leaves rice, salt, and matches along with dry firewood for other travelers, so that they would not die.

In Mike Tucker's book on shamanism in twentieth-century culture, he writes, "The wilderness supplies Dersu with an animistic, essentially shamanic wisdom. He talks to fire and wind and water as if they were people: when a soldier laughs and asks him why, he replies it is because they are alive."[10] At this point in the film Dersu actually says that *everything* is alive, human; he conceives of all the forces of Nature as "men." In all his conversation, as in other films conveying the shamanic sensibility, it is the actor Munzuk's voice that holds a softness and resonance with the natural world he inhabits. He has become an archetype for ancient wisdom—the small, gnarled old man whose utterances, though gnomic, purvey insights from a lost way of life. George Lucas modeled his *Star Wars* concept on the Kurosawa film *The Hidden Fortress*, and there is speculation that his Jedi Master, Yoda, was modeled on Dersu Uzala.

We turn now to a very different film style: animation. The animated films of Hayao Miyazaki can be taken as a pinnacle of Japanese anime, and also their most deeply animist. The stature of Miyazaki can be judged by this media comment: "The Japanese anime scene is like an artsy tourist village at the base of an active volcano. Everyone goes about their business for years, steadily building their brands or trying out new products until a volcano named Hayao Miyazaki goes off and buries them all at the box office."[11] "Bury" is right: his *Spirited Away* was the highest grossing movie in Japanese history.[12]

Miyazaki's anime is noted for its pacifist, environmentalist and feminist themes, and here is important for a strand of animism that runs through most of his works. Many of his films feature young girls or women in a variety of roles, placing his work in the category of what is known as *shōjo* or young girl anime. Anime specialist Susan Napier tells us: "It should be stressed at the outset however that Miyazaki's *shōjo* are of a very distinctive type."[13] Jolyon Baraka Thomas is convinced that Miyazaki's films are not only intended as religious but are received in that way as well: "Miyazaki's films serve as religious texts that inspire and exhort people to alterations in behavior; they are sometimes used ritually (repetitively, as liturgical texts, as scripture) for edification as well as entertainment."[14]

Shinto as the native religion of Japan is clearly to some extent an animist religion, and in its co-existence with Zen Buddhism is fortunate to have a partner that had been substantially transmuted from its Indian form by Taoism, the indigenous Chinese Nature religion. "Shinto comes into existence as soon as people are convinced of the existence of other worlds," says Motohisa Yamakage, the 79th Grand Master of Yamakage Shinto.[15] This is certainly true of Hayao Miyazaki, who says, "Of course I believe that other worlds exist ... It's like love: you can't see it but it exists—simply because you believe it. It's just a matter of believing."[16] Master Yamakage would probably say that it is more than just "believing," but the films of Miyazaki, as we shall see, convey much of an animist sensibility whatever the depths of his beliefs. He is one of only a handful of directors of whom we must ask the question: is his oeuvre as a whole relevant to the spiritual life? Here we look at just two of his films.

In *My Neighbor Totoro* two young sisters move into a rural setting with their father, and quickly discover spirits of various kinds but mostly all benign. In their new house, for example, they have to deal with "soot sprites" before they can be really at home; these are similar to the sprites that feed the boiler with coal in the bathhouse in Miyazaki's *Spirited Away*. As the younger girl Mei wanders into the nearby woods, they encounter spirits known as "kodami" who are miniature versions of the central spirit of the film: the troll Totoro. The father is unphased by the girl's discovery; he says such spirits are benign, and that she is lucky because most people can't see them. He suggests that they give the forest spirits a proper greeting. They come across a big camphor tree—Totoro's tree—but the elder sister and father cannot see the troll. "The forest spirits don't want to be seen," he suggests. He looks up. "Magnificent tree. It comes from back in time when trees and people used to be friends." The tree itself is engirdled with little flags suggestive of a Shinto or shamanic offering. When Mei gets lost towards the end of the film, she is shown sitting by a group of six statues of a Buddhist deity who takes care of children.[17] The rural landscape of the film is Miyazaki's response to his readings on early Japanese agriculture, and is a land criss-crossed by Buddhist and Shinto shrines and deities.

Princess Mononoke draws comparison perhaps with the DreamWorks film *Spirit, Stallion of the Cimarron* in the quality and ambition of its screen presence, but the ambivalence over the moral status of its characters make it a far more challenging film in respect of their shared themes of the wilderness and the status of animals. Susan J. Napier says:

> It is Miyazaki's notion that he and presumably other Japanese are the spiritual descendents of the "glossy leafed forests" that ... once covered Japan ... and that these vanished forests still exert a spiritual pull on the on the average urban dweller, and it was this that he attempted to dramatize in his creation of the forest of the *shishigami*.[18]

Although the conventional shaman as a character is missing from the film, the idea of the "glossy leafed forests" as the site of spirit-beings, including those of animals such as wolf and boar, and the major forest spirit itself and its millions of kodami (small tree spirits), is still a shamanic one. So is the absence of absolute good or evil: all the protagonists, on whichever side they fight, are necessarily adversarial of each other in some way or other. This adversarialism, because inevitable, also means that no side can have the monopoly on good or evil. Napier also points out that while "mononoke" traditionally means possessed by a human spirit, in this film it refers to possession by "the fearsome spirits of nature."[19]

The film starts as the protagonist, a young prince called Ashitaka, tells us that the "wise woman" Hii-sama has called them to the village, but encounters a monster—a giant boar possessed by writhing tentacles. He attempts to speak with it, but in its fury it drives headlong to the village, presumably the source of the human destruction visited on its world of the forest. Ashitaka kills it, but his arm is infected with whatever plagued the boar. The "wise woman," who is perhaps a shamaness or a Shinto priestess, understands that Ashitaka's wound is not merely physical. She prepares to give a proper burial for the boar, and the villagers kneel behind her. "Oh nameless god of rage and hate, I bow before you," she says. "A mound will be raised and funeral rites performed on this ground where you have fallen. Pass on in peace and bear us no hatred." Its departing spirit speaks only words of hatred however and its body putrefies in front of them.

Later she casts divining stones on a mat strewn with natural objects: sprigs, leaves, bones, horns and pebbles. She learns that the boar-god had come from the west and something had turned him into a demon monster. The concern in her voice for their predicament, and particularly Ashitaka's, is matched by the sorrow felt for the calamity that the boar-god had undergone. This is not his death at Ashitaka's hands but whatever had driven him to rage and hatred. She asks Ashitaka, "My prince, are you prepared to learn the fate that will befall you?" "Yes, I was prepared the moment I let the arrow fly."

This is the animist world, in Japanese flavor, where neither "salvation nor sin" is at the center of their religious tradition, as Shinto teaches according to Yamakage.[20] Instead each act is carried out with full acknowledgment of the karmic consequences it might bring. And Ashitaka's fate is perhaps to be overcome by the wound and die. "You cannot alter your fate, but you can rise to your fate," Hii-sama tells him. He is to travel to the West, with "eyes unclouded by hate" and see what he can do to lift the curse, the one initiated by the iron ball she found in the boar, and now infecting his arm. "Iron" is the key: the force turning the boar-god and other animal spirits mad is the iron workings he will find in the West.

It is by a river that he first encounters the Princess, San, who in turn is tending to the wounded wolf-god. She tells him to go away, and he turns to find wounded men in terror of a small wood-spirit or kodama. Soon a myriad of the little semi-transparent creatures are visible in the trees. Miyazaki's visualization of this ancient presence is haunting. Some of them imitate Ashitaka: they carry another spirit on their backs, as he carries the wounded man. "Empathy" is what is memorably visualized here. The men don't trust the spirits, but Ashitaka does, and they do in fact lead them to home: the semi-industrial village of Iron Town whose leader is Lady Eboshi. (Its historical archetype would in fact be Coalbrookdale in Shropshire, England, the ironworks of which heralded the Industrial Revolution.)

Later San is injured in battle and Ashitaka is shot rescuing her. They travel into the forest, where San now tends to him in scenes packed with spirits: they stream through forest tracks and up the limbs of trees, and under the moon and stars they stare up to evoke the primal forest god, or *shishigami*, towering over the mountains. A thousand tiny chatterings greet the gigantic figure, part deer, part humanoid, filled with the light of amoebic plasma-flow. Ashitaka, drawn in typical anime style as somewhat feminine, is cured of his wounds by the *shishigami*.

Lady Eboshi is out to kill the *shishigami*, but her gun's wooden barrel sprouts shoots and saplings. But it is too late: she fires and decapitates the god. The head is promised to the Emperor who believes that it will give immortal life. But the *shishigami* transmutes amoeba-like as kodami fall from the sky. Huge protoplasmic arms seek the bounty hunters. At the very last moment before sunrise, San and Ashitaka give back the forest spirit its head. Whole again, it collapses, and in so doing it destroys Iron Town. In the space of minutes the hills are reforested, and nature is restored. San will return to the forest and Ashitaka will help rebuild Iron Town, though this time, we presume, on a cooperative basis with Nature. A kodama has the last word: a little rattle as its head rotates.

These two films by Miyazaki are not the last we shall consider, but they feature some essential features of his animism. While his achievements as an animator make him a towering figure not just in Japan, but throughout the world, there is no doubt that it is his Japanese heritage that makes his animism possible. In America the Christian heritage has long consigned women such as Hii-sama to the status of "witch," while the spirits that populate the forest in *Princess Mononoke* and the local woods in *My Neighbor Totoro* are no more than a relic of the "savage" world-view of the Native American. Hence Miyazaki is essential viewing for the spiritual life, because the spiritual relationship between humans and Nature ultimately demands that all natural beings and phenomena be regarded at some level as "men"—as Dersu Uzula puts it.

Now for two more films that touch on shamanism, one set in Japan and one in Australia. Akira Kurosawa's *Rashomon* is a murder mystery set in the twelfth century. Although poorly received in Japan at the time of its release, it made Kurosawa's reputation in the West, and even gave the name to the "Rashomon effect" in psychology (the subjectivity of recollection). It tells the story of a Samurai waylaid by a bandit who kills him and rapes his wife but the film is inconclusive because the story is told from at least four contradictory points of view. At one point a female shaman is employed to contact the spirit of the murdered man, who may also be telling lies. Although closest to an actual shaman, she is placed in a post hunter-gatherer culture and could equally be called a medium, a psychic, or an oracle. What makes her performance more shamanic than that of a contemporary medium is her dancing, the use of a rattle, the natural elements around her (bamboo leaves) and her shaking. It is not clear what Kurosawa could have drawn on to construct her performance, but parallels are clear with the so-called "oracle" in *Kundun* and *Seven Years in Tibet*, discussed later, who are more clearly shamanic. She is just about the only female shaman in film to date.

Kurosawa's rendition of the shamaness fits well with Eliade's account of their principle functions: "They summon a dead person's soul from the beyond. In popular parlance this is called shinikuchi, i.e., 'dead man's mouth.'"[21] The staring eyes of the shamaness as she speaks with the dead man's eyes, could have been just indicative of a trance state, but could also be an acknowledgment that in some northern regions of Japan there is a tradition of the blind shamaness.[22]

The Last Wave is perhaps the best illustration of Jung's dictum that the white man inherits the collective unconscious of the peoples he conquers, in this case aboriginal Australians. The white man here is David Burton (Richard Chamberlain), whose interest in the Aboriginal people grows as a freak storm hits Australia. As in *Poltergeist*, nature and its spirits seem to be forcing their way into the white man's cocooned world: towards the end of both films a tree scratches and claws its way into the family home. Early in *The Last Wave* frogs appear on the steps of Burton's house during the incessant rain, and he finds it hard to sleep. In a dream or trance state he sees Aboriginal Chris Lee (David Gulpilil) holding out a talisman to him. This anticipates his encounter with Chris as a defendant in a murder enquiry, in which Burton becomes involved as their legal counsel. The legal case revolves around the issue of whether the men, accused of killing another Aboriginal, are "tribal" or not: this definition hangs on their upbringing and education, and if agreed to would allow them to be tried under their own laws instead of the white man's. But Chris and his presence in Burton's mind show that this distinction is meaningless, as the ancient shamanic connection to the land cannot be wiped out so quickly by so-called civilization. In his first real meeting with Chris, Burton is shocked at the recognition that this is the man from his dream: this works both at the level of a physical recognition, and perhaps at the level of the unconscious. From that point he is drawn deeper and deeper into Chris's Aboriginal world and its premonition of the coming of the White Man and the destruction of their way of life.

To describe the religious sensibility of the Aboriginal as "shamanic" is to label it with a term originally applied to Siberian tribal people, as much a possible source of error as it is to apply the term to the Native Americans. This is because the Americas and Australasia were the home to indigenous peoples whose developments were very different, and also because within these continents there is great variation. Nevertheless, and without another term at hand, "shamanic" is a perhaps a good starting point from which to consider the possible greater interest in dreams in Aboriginal cultures. This shows up early in *The Last Wave*, not just because Burton keeps dreaming of Aboriginals, but because Chris tells him at one point that Burton is in trouble because he doesn't know what dreams are any more. He also tells him that Charlie, the oldest of the accused men, "is an owl: he can fly through the air ... lots of magic, he got the power." Burton is courting danger because he is dreaming tribal secrets that are so sacred that it is death to reveal them (and was for this reason that their fellow Aboriginal was killed). He then finds the talisman of his dream in the property of one of the arrested men, and discovers from a museum curator that the crude face carved on it is "a spirit from the dreamtime."

Later in the film, after losing the case, and in ever-increasing climatic unrest, Burton sends his wife and child away. This is after a telling moment where his child sees Charlie and tells her mother that she doesn't like the black man standing outside in the road because she thinks he is a "witch." Burton's father, a priest, asks him if he is in trouble.

BURTON: Yes, but I don't know what sort of trouble.
FATHER: Do try and get it into perspective. You lost the case. But you haven't lost the world.
BURTON: Haven't I? I've lost the world I thought I had. The world where what you just said meant anything. ... Why didn't you tell me there were mysteries?
FATHER: David, my whole life has been about a mystery.
BURTON: (angrily) No! You stood in that church and explained them away! (pause) Dad, I'm being taken away into some sort of otherness. And I don't know what to do.

His father attempts to comfort him by saying that he had dreamt the death of his wife before it happened. But Burton's journey becomes a descent, in two forms: he appears to be encountering the "otherness" of the white Australian collective unconscious in which the Aboriginal trauma resides, and, more literally, he goes into a deep cavern containing their sacred symbols and prophecies. *The Last Wave* needs to be seen alongside films of Native American spirituality in order to see the parallels, particularly that of an older spiritual life confronting the white usurpers of the land. Again, it can be suggested that the older spiritual form is present not just in the filmic fiction—constructed largely by white men for a white audience—but in the face of the native actor. In this case it is that of David Gulpilil, a well-known Australian aboriginal actor, who also starred in Nicolas Roeg's *Walkabout*, *Rabbit-Proof Fence*, and other Australian films. His activism for the Aboriginal cause makes him perhaps the Australian equivalent of Russell Means.

African films, like many African novels, pursue a form of magical realism that makes it sometimes hard to discover something truly shamanic. In *Yeelen*, a young man with magical powers draws on his uncle to counter his father's powers: are these really that of a shaman? In

Exiles, set in France and Africa, a couple make a strange pilgrimage away from Parisian modernity to a possession-release ceremony in Algeria that appears to be located in the Ethiopian Zār tradition. This tradition apparently gives women and less-than-macho men in some Muslim countries something of a release through dance, music and trance in a supportive environment. From the film it appears to have pre–Islamic roots in what may well have been a shamanic past, though, strangely, it also lives on in the present among Ethiopian Jews in Israel.

Black Magic

Where Japan appears to be deeply at ease with its animist past, the West is not, and so it has played the corruption of it as "demonic," "black magic," "satanist" and so on. Films that deal with these themes are not wholly irrelevant to the spiritual life however, as they may indicate the true of which the corruption has become a popular dramatic form.

In *The Missing*, Maggie Gilkeson is a Christian healer whose father Samuel Jones "went Indian"—riding with the Chiricahua—when she was young. He turns up unexpectedly and to no warm welcome. The next day Maggie's daughters go missing. Riding off to search for them, she finds a scene of carnage: her man Brake has been ritualistically killed by Apaches who kidnap and trade young women into sexual slavery, and who now have her eldest daughter. Reluctantly she draws on Samuel's help to track the Apache. At one point they reach the camp where the captives have been held and in which a photographer-showman has been killed by the evil medicine man, Pesh-Chidin. In the film he is referred to as a *brujo* which derives from the Spanish word for witchcraft, *brujería*, and belongs to the South American tradition. However all early cultures were aware of the shaman, medicine man or witch-doctor who practiced their arts for evil ends instead of for good. In Central America the term *brujo* can be used for good shamans as well as bad, but Pesh-Chidin—played by Native American actor Eric Schweig—is wholly evil. Although there is no good shaman to directly contrast with Pesh-Chidin, Samuel is well played by Tommy Lee Jones, who is convincing as a white man who adopts the Native American way of life, including its spirituality.

While mainstream religions eschew what we are calling the esoteric—even to the point of persecuting it—there are many so-called cults and minority religions that explore it explicitly. Such religions may arise when the mainstream, such as Christianity and Buddhism, intermingle with local, more ancient traditions, and produce hybrids. One example where Christianity has mixed with what is normally anathema to it is in Santería, a religion arising in the context of Caribbean slavery, and which finds adherents in South American countries. This syncretic religion, originating in the Yoruba religion of Nigeria, is widespread in Cuba, as is hinted at in the film *The Last Supper*, and is also gaining ground in America, as three films indicate: *The Devil's Advocate*, *The Believers* and *Angel Heart*. The issue of animal sacrifice—a central practice in Santería—emerges in these films.

In *The Devil's Advocate*, Delroy Lindo plays Philippe Moyez, a practitioner of animal sacrifice—and therefore possibly of Santería—who is defended by the protagonist Kevin Lomax (Keanu Reeves). His defense draws on the First Amendment which prevents discrimination on grounds of religion, and might have been a reference to an actual case against the Santería/Yoruba religion heard in the U.S. Supreme Court in 1993 (*Church of the Lukumi Babalu Aye, Inc. v. Hialeah*). It is in *The Believers* that the most explicit reference to Santería appears in these films, although adherents of the faith regard the film as a travesty (actually it turns out that the killings in the film are carried out by the Brujería, a different group). This is a horror film dwelling on human sacrifice and murder, starring Martin Sheen as Cal Jamison, a police psychiatrist who has to deal with the aftermath of a freaked-out officer,

Lopez, who is a Santería practitioner. Cal discusses this with his superior who first of all says "A citizen's got a right to his own religious preference. That's the First Amendment." He then appears to backtrack when he says: "I don't call cutting up chickens a religion." In fact, the entire film can be seen as a betrayal of the First Amendment, in that it parades all the historical Christian prejudices against the ancient animistic religions. This is a way in which one can see the dramatic energy at the heart of many horror films: as an attack on religious practices rejected by Christianity.

Angel Heart is perhaps the most exploitative of these films, possibly referencing Voodoo, Brujería, or Santería. It doesn't matter, as the film parades the usual mishmash of chicken-slitting, orgiastic ritual-killing, carried out mostly by non–WASP characters, and for good measure chucks in Louis Cyphre—Lucifer, the devil—played by Robert De Niro. It is stylish, well-made nonsense, but only helps perpetuate prejudice against the older forms of religion.

The Neoplatonist Sensibility

In Europe and India, and in many other parts of the world, it is clear that esoteric traditions have existed for thousands of years. When the common features of them are laid alongside the common features of animist-shamanic traditions it seems obvious that the former grew historically out of the latter. In both sets of systems there are spirits, consultation with which confers knowledge, and which may intervene in human affairs. As both sets of systems predate modern science they are innocent of materialist notions of causality, or of the intellectual embarrassment now experienced in the face of "dualism" of mind or spirit and body. As a first approximation, what divides the two sets of religious systems appears to be the *city*. Animism-shamanism is located in a pre-agricultural culture unable to produce the surpluses of food and other goods necessary for urban life, and largely free of hierarchical structures that urban life inevitably appears to create. It is in the cities of the ancient world, it seems, that esoteric study prospered and in which shamanic ideas grew into disciplines like astrology, alchemy, and mathematics, though the transition itself is largely unexplored. The city was also the intellectual and spiritual world of Isaac Newton in the seventeenth century, and the risk of exposure as an alchemist was a constant danger to him. It is ironic that his discoveries, more than those of any other scientist in history, heralded the demise of the esotericisms that dominated his life. In the West, however, the character that seems to stand at that transition between shamanism and the esoteric is Pythagoras, and he can be considered the originator of the tradition now usually referred to as Neoplatonism, as mentioned earlier. In fact, "Neopythagoreanism" would be a better term for what is discussed here, but has little currency.

If we leave aside for the moment what kinds of spirituality the general term "esoteric" refers to, and ask instead what kind of aesthetics it generates, and how we would identify it on film, then perhaps its starting point is "sacred geometry," particularly as it developed in the Renaissance. In the Hebraic tradition knowledge of the sciences "puffeth up" a man, as St. Paul and St. Augustine insisted upon. But the great Gothic cathedrals needed the sciences, particularly geometry, for their construction and hence the origin of secret societies—Freemasons—and the popular suspicion of them. Christianity was always at odds with science, but the meeting of science with the arts in the great Renaissance practitioners was to deeply influence the course of Western aesthetics. A secularized history of the Renaissance pushes away the uncomfortable fact that the laws of proportion and perspective, and the very nature of architecture, had a Greek spiritual aspect to them, if not explicitly esoteric origins. Hence, in films of the esoteric, from the worst titillatory pap to the most thoughtful treatments, aesthetic elements from the Greek-Renaissance-Neoplatonist traditions abound. The pentagram for example appears in Fritz Lang's *Metropolis*, and in the film version of *The Da Vinci Code*. More generally, such symbols may be astrological, and part of an aesthetic tradition of drawing the Heavens in symbolic form.

J. A. Stewart sums up the Platonism—equivalent to Neoplatonism for our purposes—that infused the Romantic poets:

> Platonism I would describe, in the most general terms, as the mood of one who has a curious eye for the endless variety of this visible and temporal world and a fine sense of its beauties, yet is haunted by the presence of an invisible and eternal world behind, or, when the mood is most pressing, within the visible and temporal world, and sustaining both it and himself—a world not perceived as external to himself, but inwardly lived by him, as that which, at moments of ecstasy, or even habitually, he is become one.[23]

The key idea relating to Neoplatonism conveyed in this extract is that beauty hints at a transcendent world which is at the same time not external, which is within rather than beyond the material.

Perhaps the only film with direct reference to Neoplatonism is *Agora*, based on the life and martyrdom of Hypatia, the "Neoplatonist philosopher," as she is usually referred to. In *Agora* the presentation of Neoplatonist thought is entirely secular. At a crucial moment in the film Arestes, her would-be lover, ponders that their "pagan" gods have not helped them, and perhaps they should seek others. "The Christian God?" asks another. Hypatia is inspired by the night sky to ponder in turn, not a religious question, but a scientific one: could the heliocentric theory explain the mystery of the "wanderers" (the planets)? The Christians in turn destroy the great "pagan" library, though there is no historical basis for this, while later on Jewish dancers are stoned by black-clad Christians, for which there is historical record: the Jews were then expelled from Alexandria, provoking the public anger that eventually led to Hypatia's death at the hands of the Christian mob. But the film merely conforms to the long-standing notion of Neoplatonism as early *science* rather than as a religion. In the modern lexicon, Hypatia, just like Giordano Bruno, is a martyr to science, not religion. Yet "Platonism," as St. Augustine referred to it, was a genuine choice of religion for him after he abandoned Manichaeism and before he chose Christianity.[24]

It is the work of Peter Greenaway which may best represent the Neoplatonist aesthetic in film: in *Prospero's Books* above all, but also in *The Cook, the Thief, His Wife, and Her Lover*. *Prospero's Books* is an adaptation of Shakespeare's *The Tempest*, and was a personal project of John Gielgud, who plays the lead role of Prospero. The film starts with a recitation of the admirable qualities of *A Book of Water*, a semi-magical volume with pages that come to life. The aesthetic of water in the film is anything to match that in Tarkovsky (for example, *Nostalgia* or *Stalker*), but the palette is yellow-ochre rather than blue-green, and is profoundly Renaissance in character, rather than naturalistic. Greenaway used advanced film techniques and a graphic illustrative style that made the film ground-breaking. Prospero is possibly based on Thomas Harriot (1560–1621), who was an English Kabbalist, astronomer, mathematician, ethnographer, and translator, though an earlier theory suggested he was based on John Dee, astrologer to Elizabeth I. Either way, the Elizabethan era was the period in which science and esotericism were still mostly indistinguishable from each other, and *Prospero's Books* beautifully captures that world. Like other directors who started as artists, the intensely painterly nature of Greenaway's films make them essential viewing for the study of film aesthetics. This is Greenaway's only film that also explicitly draws on a spiritual tradition, in this case that of Neoplatonism (as we broadly define it). To watch this film is to be immersed in the ambience of that tradition, even if Greenaway has no direct wish to proselytize for it. Perhaps, rather, he unwittingly captures the possible madness of this world, tethered neither to Christian love, nor to empirical science. It is no anodyne English thespianism however, but a serious work of art.

In *The Cook, the Thief, His Wife, and Her Lover*, Greenaway employs nearly as lush a Neoplatonist aesthetic, all the more odd, as the film is about gangster-land in London. But its subject matter, the juxtaposition of cultural refinement with the brutal East End indulgences of the criminal nouveau riche, is more typically Greenaway: heartless. Putting it another way, Greenaway's oeuvre represents, as does Tarkovsky's, the meeting of high art and cultural autism. By contrast, *Eyes Wide Shut*, Stanley Kubrick's last film, also contains vaguely Neoplatonist imagery in the sumptuous setting of a masked ritual orgy of an exclusive club. The film explores the threat to marriage through external liaisons, but it does so with great warmth and understanding of everyday marital stresses.

Pi is a gem of an independent film directed by Darren Aronofsky, who cowrote it with the lead actor, Sean Gullette. It tells the story of Max, a brilliant mathematician, whose obsessive behavior leads him to the edge of insanity. It is all fiction, as opposed to *A Beautiful Mind*, which dramatizes the real-life story of the mathematician John Nash. Both films deal with similar mathematical problems: the discovery of mathematical regularities in natural phenomena, including the stock market. At the start of *Pi*, Max is walking past Tai Chi practitioners in the park and tells us, "Restate my assumptions. One: mathematics is the language of nature. Two: everything around us can be represented and understood through numbers. Three: if you graph the numbers of any system, patterns emerge. Therefore, there are patterns everywhere in nature." It is no surprise, then, that later in the film Max should add, "Remember Pythagoras. Mathematician, cult leader, Athens, c. 500 BC Major belief: the Universe is made of numbers." (In fact, Croton was Pythagoras's city for the major period of his life, where he established his religious community.) *Pi* references Neoplatonism, not just in the emphasis on numbers and the reference to Pythagoras, but also in the appearance of a Hasidic group of Jewish scholars who hope that Max will solve a 2,000-year-old problem for them. Ordinarily one would assume that the Hebraic and Hellenic traditions remain religiously antithetical to each other, but in fact the Kabbalah shows a kind of synthesis. What the Kabbalah has in common with Pythagoras—and may have drawn on him historically—is the emphasis on numbers.

Just as the esoteric discipline of astrology gave way to the scientific discipline of astronomy, just as the esoteric discipline of alchemy gave way to the scientific discipline of chemistry, so the esoteric discipline of numbers—called numerology in its broad sense and gematria in the Hebrew context—gave way to mathematics. Gematria, when applied to the Hebrew Bible, involves taking the Hebrew alphabet and assigning numerical values to each letter; words are then summed and esoteric meanings deduced from them. Max first learns of this in a local café where he meets Hasidic scholar Lenny Myer, who tells him that "Hebrew is all math. Aleph, a, is one, Bet, b, is two, ... The Torah is a long string of numbers, a code, sent to us from God."

Myer and his group of kabbalistic scholars are seeking a numerical pattern in the Torah (the first five books of the Old Testament) while Max is seeking a numerical pattern in the numbers of Pi. The stories converge as it appears that both are seeking a number with 216 digits: to the Rabbis it represents the name of God and to Max it is the key to stock-market fluctuations.

Max's mentor, an old man called Sol, warns him that his obsession is costing him his health: "The world can't be summed up by math, there is no simple pattern." Sol tells Max that once he is obsessed with the number 216 he will find it everywhere, that he will effectively read it into nature, and that by discarding scientific rigor Max is no longer a mathematician, but a mere numerologist. It doesn't stop Max or the corporate interests who offer him an advanced microprocessor to pursue his work. In the climax of the film, the same corporate interests want payback and attempt to abduct him. Lenny Myer and his group of Jews rescue him, but appear no less ruthless in their quest to obtain what is in Max's head, the 216-digit number that is the lost name of God and the intonation of which will usher in the Messianic age.

Apart from the Neoplatonist-Kabbalist elements in the film, and the visual representations of many related themes, *Pi* also usefully portrays in Max a certain kind of autism, or rather a mild Asperger's syndrome, and a radical solution to it. As Eric Wilson says, the film "portrays the insanity that might issue from the kabbalistic attempt to grasp God's secret code."[25] The solution that Max is driven to—auto-trepanning with an electric drill—is not however a recommended treatment for high-functioning autism, rather it is merely a plot device and the natural dramatic conclusion of the film. It leaves Max on a park bench, smiling benignly and in the warmth of human relation with a little girl who at the start of the film would come up to Max and give him long multiplication or division to do in his head, checking his genius against her calculator. He barely had time for her earlier, but now, "cured" of his autism, is happy to listen to her prattlings. He can no longer do the sums though.

A Stranger Among Us and *Bee Season* are two more films dealing with the Kabbalah, though it is in *Bee Season* that Jewish numerology takes center stage, visualized in a unique filmic manner. The central character is a young Jewish girl, whose father is professor of religion and student of the Kabbalah. His daughter comes rather suddenly to his notice because of her success in spelling competitions. He realizes that her affinity for words resembles something in Hebrew gematria, that holding a word in one's mind can bring its reality and the meaning of what it refers to into full comprehension. Letters therefore dance on the page, and flutter like birds, or take the shape of the word in front of her eyes.

If these films illustrate exceptions to the antipathy between Jewish and Greek thought, then *The Name of the Rose* presents a rather a neat illustration of it. What is at stake in this film is not science and mathematics as abhorrent to the devotional Christian impulse, but arts and entertainment: the realm of the Muses. The Hebraic tradition in its anathematizing of images did not lend itself to the arts or amusement (a–Muse-ment), as did the Neoplatonist tradition starting with Pythagoras—indeed the Muses are central to Pythagorean teaching.[26] In *The Name of the Rose*, a monastery library becomes the key site of conflict for the very good reason that its books contain both the sciences and the arts of an essentially Hellenic tradition, and—in Umberto Eco's fable—a lost work by Aristotle on comedy. Comedy is firstly an art, and secondly a frivolity: it is hence a double affront to the Pauline tradition. The film therefore ends with the burning of the library, the symbol for all freethinkers and heretics within the Neoplatonist tradition of Catholic repression. However, although the background to the film is that of two competing religious sensibilities, in the end it is not much more than a secular story in which religion in general appears the fool against the forensic logic of the rational investigator.

The Da Vinci Code is another example that draws on Neoplatonist elements. Based on Dan Brown's best-selling novel (tellingly only outsold in 2004 by the Harry Potter series) the details of it are not worth dwelling on, other than to say that it is about the supposed bloodline of Christ. There has been endless imaginative speculation on the possibility of Christ as sexually active and hence the existence of descendents via Mary Magdalene. In *The Da Vinci Code*, the last living descendent is female, and gradually discovers the magnitude of her secret, having been witness as a child to the rituals of a secretive cult dedicated to preserving the bloodline of Christ. These rituals bear a resemblance to those in *Eyes Wide Shut* and involve many Neoplatonist symbols scattered through the film, as in *Harry Potter*. But, as pointed out earlier, the shuffling of religious symbols of any tradition, and their presentation—in this case for little more than titillation—in an action drama does not make for a film relevant to the spiritual life.

Neoplatonism for Kids

Does a children's fantasy film have crystals, an orrery, an observatory, or even a compass? Or the widespread use of astrological-type symbols? Chances are that Neoplatonist elements are at work. In *The Dark Crystal*, the Castle of the Crystal contains a ground plan featuring pseudo-astrological symbols, and has been taken over by the cruel Skeksis. The four elements of Greek cosmology are introduced, along with the notion that the Skeksis cheat death through the power of their great treasure, the Dark Crystal. The conjunctions of certain heavenly bodies on a specific day make this possible, all of which pseudo-astrological information relates to knowledge that was historically central to Neoplatonism, and vigorously anathematized by the early church Fathers, including Augustine. The gentle Mystics oppose the Skeksis, and speak rather like large puppet versions of the Star Wars Jedi Master, Yoda, though the specific role of Master is assigned to the wise woman Aughra. It is she who has access to one of the most elaborate and improbable orreries in film history, but then, as the planet they inhabit has three suns, that is perhaps no surprise. "Everything in the heavens is here. Moving as the heavens move. This is how to know when. That's what." All that is missing from Aughra's exposition is the key Neoplatonist dictum: "As above, so below." In Egyptian-style hieroglyphics the mystery of the Dark Crystal and its healing is discovered, reminding us that the Egyptian tradition, through Hermes Trismegistus, is an essential element within Neoplatonism.

In the *Harry Potter* series of films, similar Neoplatonist elements occur in what is rather a pastiche of "craft" lore. These include the notion of wizardry itself and its alleged accoutrements, such as the broomstick, the magic wand, spells, potions, and so on. Broader elements of the paranormal such as psychokinesis and clairvoyance (mind reading) are included, though sometimes with ironical overtones of skepticism, as for example towards the clairvoyance teacher in *The Prisoner of Azkeban*. Sometimes the potpourri of such elements is hackneyed. Sometimes it is inventive, as in the use of mandrake extract to counter the spell of petrification (there is nothing in existing folklore around the mandrake that would suggest this) in *The Chamber of Secrets*. The only more specifically Neoplatonist elements in the films include the spheres and orreries in *The Prisoner of Azkeban* in a long scene where Pot ter is taught to conjure a "Patronus." The many libraries, forbidden books, and pseudo-astronomical instruments that turn up throughout the series, and the general sense that wizardry is an elite counter-culture, all have resonance with the history of suppression of Neoplatonism.

The Golden Compass is a film adaptation of Philip Pullman's fantasy novel *Northern Lights* (the first of the *His Dark Materials* trilogy), and is a far tighter creation of a magical parallel world than in *Harry Potter*. *Northern Lights* is a perfect example of "Neoplatonism for kids" on two fronts: firstly the inclusion of signature Neoplatonist elements such as orreries, astrolabes, and the signs of the zodiac; and secondly the obvious anger directed at the machinery of repression that forced Neoplatonism and related traditions underground. Because the novels so obviously target the Roman Catholic Church as persecuting that tradition, the film version deliberately avoided direct references to it, and so the "Magisterium" in the film becomes a generic oppressive body. The production company feared a Christian boycott of the film in America, and even after the watered-down version of its release, it still attracted calls for boycotts of the film and novels. It is thought that filming of the sequels may simply not be possible because of these problems—a contemporary relic of ancient antagonisms between Abrahamic and Greek faiths.[27]

What remains in *The Golden Compass* of the Neoplatonist sensibility is still highly visible however, and even the criticism of traditional Christianity is not hard to read into certain features. The golden compass of the novel is in fact a magical device called an "alethiometer" which reveals the truth if questioned properly, and which is clearly based on a variety of Renaissance-style instruments, and features zodiacal-type signs on its facing. The semi–Renaissance setting of medieval Oxford and the Royal Naval College in Greenwich which are proliferated in the computer-generated cities of the film all add to the general Neoplatonist sensibility, as do the various brass and glass instruments present within the grand meeting rooms of the Scholars. It is the emphasis on knowledge of a vaguely scientific kind and the mission of the Magisterium to control it and to suppress free thought as heresy that are the first indicators of a possible parallel with the fate of Neoplatonism under Catholic hegemony. More specifically, the wicked Mrs. Coulter (Nicole Kidman) tells the young protagonist at one stage in the story that in the ancient past people had made the terrible mistake of disobeying the authority of the Magisterium, which now existed to make people do the right thing. The details are close enough to the Eden story to be unmistakable, and the resulting harm—to do with a metaphysical "dust"—is unmistakably the suffering humans experience arising from original sin.

Giordano Bruno, a man who epitomized the Neoplatonist tradition, was burned by the Catholic Church in 1600. It is tempting to speculate that Pullman, perhaps unconsciously, wants to settle that old score in his novels and in his promotion of atheism. But in rejecting one religion, is he not actually promoting another? One which is now mostly lost to New Age indulgence on the one hand, or escapist fantasy on the other?

The Familiar

We turn now to an element of animism-shamanism that appears to resurface in a Neoplatonist setting, in children's films at least. This is the issue of the "familiar" or guardian spirit. What if the imaginary friend of childhood turns out to be real, and what's more is embodied as an animal? In the medieval European tradition the familiar spirit, imp, or just familiar is an animal-shaped spirit considered to be the companion and servant of witches. It may have divinatory or other powers. A visualization of such creatures occurs several times in the films of Miyazaki, in

Disney's *Pocahontas* as a raccoon and hummingbird that accompany Pocahontas, and most obviously in *The Golden Compass*. Arguably the small creatures in the Japanese film, game and toy franchise Pokémon have the same origin. In the *Pokémon* films the creatures are acquired by children and then do battle with them against all kinds of monsters. Indeed, the word "Pokémon" is a contraction of "pocket monster."

It may well be in Miyazaki's film *Nausicaä of the Valley of the Wind* where this version of the familiar was born in the Japanese context. The female protagonist, a young princess called Nausicaä, is given a small animal near the beginning of the film. Initially, making squirrel-style chatterings, it runs onto her shoulder and then bites her finger, but she doesn't react, and it calms down, licking the small puncture-wounds. A bond is created and she turns around, the animal now trusting her fully. From this point on the creature—which she names Teto—is always with her, either safe in the hood of her dress, or standing proud on her shoulder. So, when examining the design and characteristics of a key Pokémon character called Pikachu, one cannot help speculating that Teto was its progenitor, or in fact that Teto was the entire inspiration for Pokémon. Miyazaki's *Nausicaä* was a huge box-office success in Japan and a whole generation of animators grew up under its influence. In turn, Pokémon has spawned many similar franchises, all of which are highly popular in the United States. One could say that American Christianity is being subtly undermined by this import, one which promotes a favorite idea of medieval witchcraft: the familiar.

In *The Golden Compass*, computer-animated animals become the familiars for the children of the story. They sit on the child's shoulder, just as Teto does on Nausicaä's, and represent a threat to the religious authorities, the Magisterium. Let Michael Harner have the last say on the familiar:

> Outside of North America, the guardian spirit is similarly important, but is often called by other names in the anthropological literature, such as "tutelary spirit" in works on Siberian shamanism, and as "nagual" in Mexico and Guatemala. In the Australian literature it may be referred to as an "assistant totem," and in the European literature as the "familiar." Sometimes the guardian spirit is just called the "friend" or "companion." Whatever it is called, it is the fundamental source of power for the shaman's functioning.[28]

Gifts and Possessions

That there might be a genuine esotericism is mostly lost to the secular mind because of the borrowing of its symbols in various kinds of titillatory horror, sci-fi, and adventure movies. It is also lost to the religions of monotheism, which brand it as the work of the devil. But millions of people join esoteric societies, such as the Freemasons, Theosophy, Anthroposophy and so on, and make the esoteric an essential part of their spiritual lives. We saw that in North Africa and in the Ethiopian immigrant community in Israel the spirit possession religion of Zār lives on to this day, while spiritualist churches are found in most major towns and cities in the developed world. Many people are regarded within such groups as genuine mediums, clairvoyants or sensitives. In such circles a person with these inclinations and skills is considered to have the "gift," and their development in the spiritual life is to use them to help others. Indeed, the film *The Gift* is about a woman with a capacity for clairvoyance and precognition who becomes involved in solving a murder. But we saw in the concept of the *brujo* that such gifts can be used for evil intent. In the following set of films the corruption of such gifts are looked at, including the social anxieties around the idea, and how they are also a burden. Supernatural powers are frightening for those who fear their misuse, but even more frightening is the idea of being possessed by a spirit of evil intent.

To accept that there is a genuine esotericism, one has to accept the reality of the spirit world in some form or other. The implications of this are far-reaching, and the materialist is determinedly against it. However, even if the prevailing culture in which Western-style films are made is materialistic, there seems an endless appetite for pseudo-esotericisms, and which can be satisfied in a number of genres including the horror film. What is "horrible" in the horror film is often a malignant supernatural power, one that cannot be overcome by conventional means.

The Exorcist and *Carrie* are two highly praised examples of the horror genre, and they happen to both deal with a teenage girl. In *The Exorcist*, twelve-year-old Regan McNeil is possessed by the devil and is ultimately rescued by the combined efforts of a priest and an exorcist (the latter played by Max von Sydow). While the film was groundbreaking in its time, and very successful, it has precious little internal logic, being content to present a mishmash of esoteric themes and symbols. In *Carrie*, the girl of that name is also a teenager, but a bit older, shy, and awkward. As she becomes the butt of both her mother's frustrated cruelty and her peers' taunting, she discovers telekinetic abilities that are unleashed on her persecutors. What makes this film more plausible is our psychological familiarity with the problems of puberty, including awkwardness and apparently groundless rage, and the feasible extension of that adolescent rage into paranormal activity. Carrie's telekinetic powers are only aroused when she is frightened, and this is again plausible, in contrast to Regan's possession by a supposedly all-powerful malignant Devil, who cannot even undo her straps.

What then is the appeal of *The Exorcist*? The British film critic Mark Kermode has a Ph.D. in horror fiction and confesses in his autobiography to having watched *The Exorcist* some two hundred times. He writes, "I don't *think* there is a spiritual element to human life. I *know* it because I have horror movies to thank for that blessing."[29] At first sight we might return to Hegel's dictum, mentioned in the Introduction: "By the little which now satisfies Spirit, we can measure the extent of its loss." If *The Exorcist* is enough to bring the blessing of spirituality, then it is a spirituality which has indeed suffered a great loss. Yet it does point to something perhaps missing in the initial definition of spirituality given here, of a profound connectedness, and that is a quality of otherness, of mystery, of the *mysterium tremendum et fascinans* of Otto. The unconnected, alienated self, atomized in its belief of separation, can be shocked by a glimpse of something bigger, a door into the infinite as it were, by a sense of *power*. But while all of this is true, it will be obvious for anyone seriously engaged with the spiritual life that horror films present the false coin of such power. Hence the horror genre, whether plausible at some level or not at all, tells us little about the genuine spiritual or religious life; it merely alerts us to what many spiritual teachers have always asserted: that the willing courtship of esoteric gifts is no necessary advancement in the spiritual life.

The Omen continues this kind of theme, though this time technically the child is not so much possessed by the Devil, or gifted with powers, as he is a living embodiment of the Antichrist—whatever that means. As in the other two films, the powers of the church are invoked to end the child's powers, this time unsuccessfully. *The Exorcism of Emily Rose* is a quite different possession film: it is not played for horror but to explore the actual possibility of possession. Emily Rose is initially treated by conventional medicine for hallucinations and other worrying symptoms, but her family comes to the conclusion that an exorcism is the only real way to help her. The film thus thoughtfully pits the secular world of psychiatry with the Christian tradition of exorcism. As it is an example of a dialogue across the secular-religious divide it will be looked at in more detail later.

Poltergeist and *Poltergeist II: The Other Side* are an instructive pair of films, in terms of how the elements of traditional supernaturalism are assembled into mainstream fare, and how the "acceptable" face of esotericism is epitomized. In the first film Zelda Rubinstein plays Tangina Barrons, the medium whose comforting presence is called on and whose esoteric gifts are acceptable because she is a dwarf. In the second film Will Sampson plays Taylor, the medium whose comforting presence is called on and whose esoteric gifts are acceptable because he is a Native American. This role in film is a long-standing stereotype, examples of which include Madame Arcati in Noel Coward's *Blithe Spirit*, Oda Mae Brown in *Ghost* (played by Whoopi Goldberg) and the "Oracle" in *The Matrix*. Later on we look in more detail at the question of disembodied entities such as ghosts, but it can be mentioned here that in the *Poltergeist* films the spirits are those of the departed and they are not happy.

Traditionally esoteric gifts include telekinesis, as shown by Carrie, and also clairvoyance, clairaudience, bilocation, prophecy, materialization, and others including past life recall. No officially sanctioned Western religious text deals with these issues, the subject being relegated to an underground and often persecuted esoteric press, right up to the end of religion as a mainstream cultural force in the twentieth century, and the re-emergence of these themes in New Age writing. In India, however, a non-canonical but widely revered sacred text, the *Yoga Sutras of Patanjali*, deals with esoteric powers, or *siddhis* as they are known in Sanskrit. In the West any exhibition of such powers, or the interest in or pretense at, or the accusation of such powers, would label the person as a "witch." Carrie's mother as a fundamentalist Christian at one point shrieks at her daughter the well-known line from Exodus 22:18: "Suffer not a witch to live!"

In *Don't Look Now* a blind woman has the power of clairvoyance, but the film is ambivalent throughout as to whether she, and her sister who aids her, are evil and sinister, or kindly and wishing to help. The film is unfortunately more *Exorcist* than *Carrie*, in that the internal logic is weak, and in the end the apparently supernatural events are played just for kicks.

In *Powder* the protagonist Jeremy has gifts of telekinesis and clairvoyance, but the film portrays him sympathetically as he uses his gifts mostly to help people. Like Carrie, however, when he is really frightened, his powers can cause alarming phenomena or even harm, and like Carrie he is doomed (within the prevailing literary framework of the West) because we cannot suffer his presence among us. Where the film *Powder* scores over countless films of the supernatural, and moves beyond the largely titillatory function that they serve, is in a scene where the ability to read other people's minds has firstly persuaded the young man that all are connected, and has secondly moved him to compassion as he perceives their loneliness and isolation.

The protagonist Jeremy Reed is orphaned by a lightning strike which apparently is the cause of his albino appearance—hence his nickname "Powder"—and telekinetic gifts. These make him friendless in a state school where all he wants is to fit in. The combination of makeup and actor Sean Patrick Flanery's screen intensity make Jeremy a striking but believable oddball whose inner sorrow is partly that of the outcast and partly that of the spiritual teacher who sees the source of suffering in others. At one point in the film he witnesses a clandestine hunting party in which the local deputy shoots a deer. Outraged at the assertion that its dying convulsions are just "reflexes," he takes the deputy's arm in a vice-like grip while also holding the deer's head, and transmits its death-agonies to the man. The deputy suffers what looks like an attack or seizure, over which Jeremy is vigorously questioned by the Sheriff. "I let him see," says Jeremy. "I opened him up and I let him see. He just couldn't see what he was doing, so I helped him." When the deputy was recovered sufficiently for the sheriff to quiz him on the events, he was able to confirm the account, and added that he didn't want to hunt or carry a gun again. Jeremy also intervenes constructively in the sheriff's life, though only after much resistance from him.

Later in the film Jeremy is sitting with his putative girlfriend, who is attracted to his visionary qualities and inner strength, despite his bizarre appearance and her father's disapproval. She has a question for him:

> LINDSEY: What are people like on the inside?
> JEREMY: Inside most people there is a feeling of being separate. Separate from everything.
> LINDSEY: And?
> JEREMY: And they're not. They are part of absolutely everyone and everything.
> LINDSEY: Everything? I'm part of the tree? You're telling me that I'm part of some fisherman in Italy, some ocean I've never even heard of? There's some guy sitting on death row: I'm part of him too?
> JEREMY: You don't believe me?
> LINDSEY: It's hard to believe all of that.
> JEREMY: (Presses the spot between her eyebrows) That's because you have this spot you can't see past. My grams and gramps had it. The spot they were taught where they were disconnected from everything.
> LINDSEY: So that's what they would see if they could? That they're connected?
> JEREMY: And how beautiful they really are. And that there's no need to hide or lie. And then it's possible to talk to someone without any lies. With no sarcasms, no deceptions, no exaggerations, or any of the things that people use to confuse the truth.

Powder is a film that locates itself to some extent in the New Age, and the inclusion of Jeff Goldblum as the wide-eyed science teacher who befriends Jeremy also frames it as science-fiction. But when the above scenes are placed in the context of Jeremy's story as outcast savant they are neither trite nor implausible; the film becomes a vehicle for exploring unitive-transcendent ideas close to the heart, for example, of Buddhism, but without its historical superstructure.

The New Age

Many esoteric traditions which had been long suppressed or simply regarded with suspicion in mainstream culture found a home in what is broadly known as the "New Age." The term originated perhaps with Blake, and was the title of a journal started in 1894 that underwent various transformations as its publisher Alfred Richard Orage became a follower of the spiritual teachers G. I. Gurdjieff and P. D. Ouspensky, leading to greater esoteric content. The full flowering of the New Age is reckoned to have taken place from the 1960s on. Key popular texts of the movement include the 1980 non-fiction work *The Aquarian Conspiracy* and the 1993 novel *The Celestine Prophecy*, while its best-known philosopher is perhaps Ken Wilber. There are many films with New Age themes, which introduce elements of the spiritual life that are important to perhaps millions of people.

The Doors is an Oliver Stone docu-drama covering the story of the American rock band of the same name. The film opens with two Native Americans injured by the roadside, witnessed by the young Morrison; as so often in film, the image of their culture looms in the American imagination. A nameless Native American—played by Wes Studi—then appears at intervals in the film, at times of stress or hallucinatory experience. There is also a shamanic drug trip in which the shaman is played by the Dakota Sioux actor Floyd "Red Crow" Westerman. Other spiritual themes run through the film, most of them involving non–Western or counterculture spirituality typical of the New Age. Morrison is a poet: we see that he reads Artaud, Rimbaud and Marshall McLuhan. "The first time I did acid I saw God," says Pamela Courson, Morrison's girlfriend. Before long Morrison has found a name for the band which will be the vehicle for his poetry: "The Doors," taken from Huxley's *Doors of Perception*, the phrase itself originating again in Blake. The presence of the East in hippie culture—such as Transcendental Meditation and the belief in reincarnation—is adumbrated through drugs and the Romantic tradition. At one point on a plane Morrison tells a journalist, "You think all they want is two cars and a house. But you're wrong. You know what they want?... Something sacred." Similar sentiments are found in Scorsese's documentary *George Harrison: Living in the Material World*. The film contains much archival footage, including excerpts from the 1967 Beatles interview where David Frost, then a rising star of BBC television journalism, asks in all seriousness for meditation to be explained to the audience and the British viewing public.

If meditation was a new concept to the mainstream in 1967 then the film *Indigo* ought to be a flagship film for the New Age, preaching as it did to the converted in 2003. Its director and producer, Stephen Simon (also known as Stephen Deutsch) is the author of *The Force Is with You: Mystical Movie Messages That Inspire Our Lives*, a New Age take on films (as mentioned earlier).[30] He is also the director of the film *Conversations with God*, and the producer of other films with a New Age slant such as *What Dreams May Come* (introduced earlier) and *Somewhere in Time* (where time travel permits the protagonist to recapture lost love). The release of *Indigo* was sponsored by the Spiritual Cinema Circle, a nonprofit organization dedicated to bringing spirituality to cinema, founded by Simon and psychologists Kathlyn and Gay Hendricks. *Indigo* stars a key New Age writer, Neale Donald Walsch, author of the *Conversations with God* book series (on which the film of the same name is based). These nine volumes are immensely popular, the first staying on the *New York Times* Best-Seller List for 137 weeks. Simon's philosophy towards film is perhaps summed up in this quote from his book:

> *I am personally sick and tired of all the doomsday scenarios that seem so prevalent in our modern world, and I think that the spiritual messages in movies are actually leading us to a bright and beautiful future* [Simon's italics].[31]

Certainly *What Dreams May Come* attempts to paint a "bright and beautiful" version of this life and the afterlife in the face of the tragedy of bereavement, but *Indigo* is rather a vehicle for much ugliness. The story is about an "Indigo" child, which means a child that has esoteric gifts, as we have defined them. The term "Indigo" for such children appears to be a New Age invention, but whatever its origins, the topic is clearly an important one. The issue of children's spirituality is not confined to the esoteric, but cuts across all the spiritual and religious categories. Grace is the Indigo child in the film, who travels with her grandfather Ray (played by Walsch) and eventually reunites the estranged members of the family through her esoteric gifts. It is this estrangement which is particularly grim, a white trailer-trash world of petty crime, portrayed as unrelentingly unfeeling. Here is the paradox of *Indigo*: for a film that attempts to portray the delicacy of the spiritual, in a person of a delicate age, it is crass and alienated beyond belief. No one in the film rises even to the warmth of the average level of human intercourse, let alone the heights of love and compassion that religion and spirituality stand for. It is best described again as a product of cultural autism.

But perhaps this is the source of much New Age excess: the despair caused by such an alienated existence cannot imagine a solution in terms of ordinary human warmth, but must posit a supernatural plane of being which will make the necessary intervention. And because children and animals seem to be capable of the unconditional love that the New Age soul longs for, they become the focus for these supernatural imaginings. Children appear to embody this miracle, at least until they grow up themselves and succumb to adult alienation: "Shades of the prison house descending" as Wordsworth put it. The Indigo doctrine has to place on children not just the ancient and normal innocence that have always made them so important to adults, but esoteric and supernatural gifts. Hence *Indigo*, rather than becoming a flagship New Age film, reveals its darkest anxieties.

What the #$*! Do We (K)now!?, or *What the Bleep Do We Know!?* in its informal title, is a New Age film directed by William Arntz, Betsy Chasse and Mark Vicente, all of whom are devotees of "Ramtha's School of Enlightenment" led by a mystic called JZ Knight. The film pursues a key New Age obsession: that physics proves mysticism. The film revolves around a deaf photographer Amanda (Marlee Matlin) who appears to live in a world as emotionally dysfunctional as that of the *Indigo* child. Into this world of alienated modern American city life steps (a) quantum theory and (b) "molecules of emotion"—the science of neuropeptides—which result in her jettisoning her antidepressants and finding happiness.

While the New Age may have *some* cause to cling to quantum theory as a break with a claustrophobic scientific determinism, it is clutching at straws with the other theme in *What the Bleep*: the new science of peptides. This is popularized in the book *Molecules of Emotion*, by Candace Pert (who is interviewed in the film), and is a genuine breakthrough in the science of brain chemistry. It tells us that the brain can no longer be thought of as a biological computer, the electronic functioning of which controls the body.[32] Rather, it operates in an environment of bodily generated chemical messengers, called peptides, and hence is not its grand controller. The chemistry of emotions augments the electronics of neurons. But, is the biological determinism of brain-plus-peptides really any better than the biological determinism of brain alone?

Four more films with New Age subtones that are worth considering are *Altered States*, *Phenomenon*, *Signs*, and *The Fifth Element*. These mainstream offerings are not intended exclusively for a New Age audience, but *Altered States* deals with isolation tanks and hallucinogenics, *Phenomenon* deals with telekinesis and super-intelligence, *Signs* with aliens and crop circles, and *The Fifth Element* with aliens, all of which are New Age preoccupations.

Altered States in effect dramatizes the hippie trail of the 1970s in which any means at hand was used to explore and alter states of consciousness, including spiritual practice, sex, drugs, and isolation techniques. The film starts with its protagonist, Edward Jessup (William Hurt), emerging from an isolation tank, a tool for exploring states of consciousness pioneered by American psychoanalyst John Lilley. Jessup recalls, "I hallucinated like a son of a bitch. A variety of dream states, mystical states, a lot of religious allegory, mostly out of Revelation." He pursues his research single-mindedly, determined to reach some permanent insight or higher consciousness. His obsession elicits this response from his girlfriend at one point:

> Even sex is a mystical experience for you. You carry on like a flagellant, which can be very nice, but I sometimes wonder if it's me that's being made love to. I feel like I'm being harpooned by some raging monk in the act of receiving God.

He takes this as a compliment. But the strange thing about this film is that his mystical journey seems to be downwards rather than upwards: what is revealed to him is his unconscious, animal self, in which he revels, like in *An American Werewolf in London*, rather than in his Godhead. *American Werewolf* was made only a year after *Altered States*, so it is unlikely that one derived from the other; instead it seems that both films document an obsession in the American mind with reaching a primeval state (Ang Lee's *Hulk* can also be seen from this perspective).[33] In both films the protagonists undergo a Jekyll and Hyde kind of conversion, running naked through the city, breaking into a zoo and devouring prey, and waking up returned to normal consciousness the next day. But did Jessup also kill a man? He says after the experience: "I was utterly primal. I consisted of nothing more than the will to survive, to live through the night. ... It was the most supremely satisfying time of my life. ... I may have killed a man tonight." Hardly the stuff of spiritual development. Prior to this Jessup seeks his answers among the Hinchi Indians of Central Mexico and the Toltec ritual of sacred mushrooms, which leads to mystical experiences. But effectively the film is implying, like so many others, that ancient shamanic cultures, which sought consciousness-expanding experiences in drugs, fasting and ritual, were pursuing a *primitive* spirituality.

Phenomenon is quite different in that its protagonist does not seek out altered states of consciousness, but has them thrust upon him. George Malley (John Travolta) is forever changed by a strange flash of lightning that gives him increased intelligence and telekinetic powers. The film uses a plot device common to films of the supernatural: in the end a rational explanation is presented, this time that of a brain tumor. But in a culture increasingly in thrall to brain science the film is contrarian enough to have Malley resist science. His doctor cannot cure him but wants to autopsy his brain after death and find the mechanism for his changed state. "I can be your biographer. I can present you to the world." It is a brave screenwriter who then gives Travolta this response: "But that's not me, it's just my brain." Indeed, the film's message is that Malley is not made a better or worse man by the gift of esoteric powers: his basic good nature remains unchanged. This is effectively a rebuke to those who believe that pursuit of psychic powers is significant to the spiritual life. It is also a rebuke to science which increasingly claims brain-mind identity.

Signs introduces crop circles as a device to flag up imminent invasion by aliens, but is also a film about bereavement and its impact. The crop circles element is a reminder that the New Age takes alien presence seriously, as epitomized in the *Chariots of the Gods* thesis that religion was created by an earlier alien presence on Earth.[34] Mario DeGiglio-Bellemare, writing in the online *Journal of Religion and Film*, confesses that he tried very hard to like *Signs* because he believes that the horror film is a serious genre. Although he does find the film an interesting account of the loss and regaining of faith, his objection to it is a good one: the violence inflicted on the alien in the end is nothing more than brute American vigilantism.[35] Here we locate the film more in the New Age than in the horror genre, so DeGiglioBellemare's objection to the violence becomes a reminder that the New Age for all its apparent "niceness" hides rather dark impulses.

The Fifth Element isn't much more than amiable escapism, but does point to an ancient religious concept: the quintessence. More usually understood in Greek philosophy as the medium in which the four substantial elements combine and recombine to form the play of the natural world, the quintessence is a religious idea because of its kinship with Eastern ideas of the unmanifest. In this vaguely New Age outing it gets lost in a mishmash of alien invasion,

Neoplatonist symbols and sexual mythology, but nonetheless it is useful to have the fifth element raised as an issue. As might be expected, Eric Wilson includes it as a Gnostic film, saying that it "comically depicts the risk of alchemical experimentation, the possibility that the practice might unleash evil."[36]

Donna Yarri says of *I Heart Huckabees*, a quite different kind of film with New Age overtones, "What is the ultimate nature of reality? Are we all alone in the universe? What is the significance of coincidences, if any? What are we doing here? What is the role of God and organized religion? These are some of the intriguing questions raised, but not definitively answered, by this film."[37] The reasons why the film can raise such questions but not answer them are to do with the general New Age context of the film, or to be more precise New Age psychotherapy. Its protagonists are in therapy with the "Existential Detectives" to resolve their anxieties and aggressions. While the existential questions raised are interesting enough, they crowd in so fast, and are dispatched with such aggression and speed, that little more emerges than the usual platitudes of New Age psychobabble.[38]

Waking Life is a film which also attempts to pursue a range of philosophical and religious questions, this time in the more unconventional form of rotoscoped animation. While the attempt is interesting, it reveals again a number of problems: firstly that philosophy is not suited to the fast lane of conventional drama, even if it is psychodrama; that the New Age framing of such questions is a further hindrance to exploring them in depth; and that beneath the anodyne search for New Age truisms there seems to always lurk a very American violence.

Summary

Does the esoteric as portrayed in these films come closer to the sacred than the aesthetic? Or give a different route into the spiritual life? Does the spiritual life have any necessary dependence on the supernatural? These are not easy questions to answer, but in the films just considered it is obvious that the esoteric has a fascination for the human mind that can lead to different extremes in the spiritual life. In the historically earliest esotericisms of the shamanic life, it is Nature that provides the forces of simplicity and connectedness that make shamanism a lived spiritual life of a deeply sacred kind, as the writings of Native American holy men show us, and are refracted into many films. *Thunderheart* is such a film, while *Northfork* gives a tangential glimpse into that reality, or perhaps the loss of that reality.

The Native American holy man often gives an overwhelming impression of *sobriety* in the spiritual life. But the dark side of this tradition is manifest in the *brujo*, and sometimes lives devoted to these paths may simply slide into darkness, or get lost in intellectual abstractions, or a kind of intoxication with power, as the films show. The subject matter lends itself to many films which are mere titillation, such as *The Da Vinci Code* or *The Exorcist*, which provide apparently good reasons for avoiding the subject altogether. Other films like *Altered States*, *Pi*, and *The Name of the Rose* just suggest an unhealthy obsession with arcane matters best left to real scientists.

But there are characters who stand out from this collection of films that should provoke thought about the lived spiritual life and its relationship to the esoteric. Grandpa Sam Reaches and Dersu Uzula live an animist relationship with Nature and people, and the Aboriginal Chris Lee in *The Last Wave* is memorable for the same reason. The Miyazaki films introduced here are a reminder that non–Western cultures were often deeply at ease with the spirit world. Max in *Pi* eventually abandons esoteric research as leading only to power struggles and madness, while George Malley in *Phenomenon* has an integrity unchanged by his newfound esoteric powers, though these story elements don't make the films essential viewing. It is perhaps Jeremy in *Powder*—also the recipient of esoteric gifts after a lightningstrike—who is most luminously transformed by them: he sees the profound connectedness between all things. He stands as a rebuke to all those who seek knowledge for the wrong reasons, and to a secular world in which the self becomes armored against the sacred—even if only through sarcasms, deceptions and exaggerations, "or any of the things that people use to confuse the truth."

Whatever relationship the Neoplatonist and other esotericisms that flourished in city cultures had with the earlier spiritual paths of shamanic and animist times, it is clear that films of animism-shamanism are essential to a rounded view of the spiritual life. Hence *My Neighbor Totoro*, *Princess Mononoke*, *Nausicaä of the Valley of the Wind* and *The Last Wave* are important viewing alongside *Powder*.

3
Dying, Suicide and Bereavement

In daily life, the issue most likely to provoke spiritual or religious questions is, ironically, death. The secular mainstream is now so reluctant to engage with dying that it denies any possibility of the "beautiful death,"[1] but in other settings such an idea had a long history and considerable currency. A beautiful death is not about the absence of pain or biological horrors but about the frame of mind of the dying, and in Socrates we have the West's exemplar: he showed a serenity in facing his execution that brought even his jailer to tears.

The important tasks of a priest in any culture are to officiate in births, marriages and deaths. While secular or humanist equivalents to these religious ceremonies are available, the idea remains that these major events in life should be marked by a collective ritual, preferably with the sanctity of religious tradition. Of these it is death that provokes questions that are the most profound, and most likely to involve religious or philosophical thinking. The purpose of the functionary in the religious rites for death is partly to reflect religiously or philosophically on death for the benefit of the bereaved, and the secularist is often willing, it seems, to tolerate such orations. For many hard-line secularists and atheists death however is meaningless. The culturally received and unexamined atheist assumption is that death is the end and nothing more can be said about it. In later chapters we will look at films that explore possible theories of the afterlife, reincarnation and resurrection, but in this section we focus on films where dying provokes meaningful reflection on life, relationships and death, whether explicitly framed in religious terms or not.

Suicide is a form of dying that raises yet more difficult questions. The human being is the one animal prone to it, the one creature with the capacity to decide that death would be better than life, and to act on it. Whether suicide has religious, cultural or legal sanction varies greatly through history and nation. Outside of a rather extreme Romantic position, Western culture is mostly against suicide, and mostly provides legal sanction against those who assist in it.

Bereavement is one of life's sufferings, and perhaps the worst is the death of one's children. If a child dies through natural causes that is one thing, if it is murder another, and it is perhaps the worst when it is suicide. Whatever the nature of bereavement, surviving friends and family are faced with questions that are naturally the domain of religion, and these questions are the more acute the greater the grief. As these issues are universal, it is no surprise to find that film has dealt with them from a wide range of perspectives. In the film *Snowcake* we even find the issue explored of how friends and family—and strangers—might deal with a bereavement *not* mourned over by a highly intelligent but autistic mother. This is the exception: grief is the usual response, and the turning to or away from religion in this moment is a situation of considerable dramatic interest.

Dying

First we look at films in which dying itself, rather than its aftermath, are dealt with. To rage against death is normal, but perhaps not that interesting; more compelling are filmic accounts in which dying is portrayed as a journey in which all of life is re-evaluated, or where the inevitability of death brings a profound peace. Mystics, whose work it is to transcend death while still alive, give a sanguine picture of dying far removed from the mainstream horror of it. For example, John Burroughs, a Victorian naturalist associated with Walt Whitman, wrote, "This I know, too: that the grave is not dark or cold to the dead, but only to the living. The light of the eye, the warmth of the body, still exist undiminished in the universe, but in other relations, under other forms."[2] Whitman himself wrote:

> And as to you Death, and you bitter hug of mortality, it is idle to try and alarm me.
> To his work without flinching the accoucheur comes,
> I see the elder-hand pressing receiving supporting,
> I recline by the sills of the exquisite flexible doors,
> And mark the outlet, and mark the relief and escape.
>
> And as to you Corpse I think you are good manure, but that does not offend me,
> I smell the white roses sweet-scented and growing,
> I reach to the leafy lips, I reach to the polish'd breasts of melons.
> And as to you Life I reckon you are the leavings of many deaths,
> (No doubt I have died myself ten thousand times before)
> [Song of Myself, v. 49].[3]

Whitman as a mystic is much more than a mere Romantic, and what marks him as more is precisely his sanguine view of death conveyed in these verses, including the lack of any discomfort at the thought of his corpse as manure. So where in film might we discover not just the sentiment of serenity in the face of death, but the dramatization of it in life?

Touching the Void tells the true story of Joe Simpson, who was injured after a fall when climbing high in the Peruvian Andes. His climbing companion returned to base camp without him, and Simpson, dragging a broken leg, nearly gave up. Believing himself close to death, he became delirious, but continued crawling in pain because he wanted to be with somebody when he died. "It was just a slow steady reduction," he says, "not just physically ... but you, everything, yourself. I felt left with nothing." He felt that he became nothing, but in this there was no anger or regret. In the end he made it to base camp just before his companions left, and so survived. In his account of facing death there is a calmness, nothing religious, yet something transcendent, summed up in the phrase "touching the void." The film is entirely secular in its framing, but there is no rage against diminishment or death that is often the corollary of the secular certainty that death is the end. Instead there the film conveys a sense of peace, perhaps partly the impact of the mountain itself on Simpson's psyche.

In a similar vein, the fiction film *Henry Poole Is Here* portrays a terminally ill man facing his death, though throughout the film it has not yet robbed him of his strength or mental faculties. Like Simpson, Henry Poole faces a "reduction" of self, which he makes concrete by buying a tract house, the anonymity of which echoes his lack of personal effects. Wanting to meet his death without the distraction of relationships he is forced against his will to relate to a religious neighbor, Esperanza, on one side and a single mother and silent daughter on the other. One review of the film suggests that its director "asks the question, 'at what point does religious hope become a religious belief?'"[4] This is because of the inexorable movement of the film to a remission, mediated—perhaps—by the "miracle" of the face of Christ which appears in a stain on his wall. At least that is what Esperanza sees, and in her enthusiasm conveys to believers who come to be cured by it. Poole himself is at every turn courteous, but increasingly impatient with the Lourdes-style attraction that his home becomes, and eventually smashes the wall with a sledgehammer. He has no truck with either hope or belief, whether derived from the Christian tradition or otherwise. His is a secular but serious attempt to grapple with death by exploring his own identity, derailed in the end by events. Although he does console himself to some extent with drink, his facing up to death is largely sober, serious, and in some inexplicable way, again transcendent.

The film *Illusion* pursues the idea that nothing is lost in dying, and that all of life's events are recorded in the "Akashic Record." It starts with a voice-over proclaiming: "The story doesn't end here like you think it might. All the mortal pieces have scattered, but impressions remain—every last one of them." This rather Eastern way of putting it is nonetheless consistent with Burrough's sentiment earlier. Director Donald Baines is bedridden and dying, in the last performance of actor Kirk Douglas. The film moves at first to a conventional premise: that in dying we see all our life pass before us. Unconventionally this will be realized as a cinema performance overseen by the dead soul of Baines's editor, who has selected the appropriate "reels" from Baines's life. But breaking further with convention, the reels aren't directly about Baines, but about his son, abandoned when young in favor of Baines's film career. The boy has internalized his absent father's voice as perpetually critical, which comes as a shock and realization to his father that this is the cost of abandonment. The boy is to be a "loser," condemned as such by the absence of a father's encouragement. However, Baines can redeem himself in a final twist: he can directly intervene in his son's life to show him that the woman he loves returns that love, and he should not throw his life away. This done, the old man dies peacefully. The quality of the film that places it with the other two selected here is the equanimity before death, disturbed and then re-attained firstly by regret and then the miraculous chance to make good. However, rather than a man stripped bare by dying, we have a man reassured that nothing is in fact lost.

We can also mention here a series of films that will be dealt with again later on: *Jacob's Ladder*, *Northfork*, and *Donnie Darko*. The dying in these films is not a bald reality to come as in the films so far, but a nightmare journey akin to traversing the "bardo" realm of Tibetan Buddhism. The term "bardo" refers to an in-between state, in this case a series of states between dying and being reborn, many of which have a surreal or nightmarish quality to them. They are the subject of the *Tibetan Book of the Dead*, partly written, it is supposed, by the founder of Tibetan Buddhism, Padmasambhava. The book is an important text for Tibetan culture, where it is required of the family to recite from it to the corpse of the dead relative during the period after death in order to help the spirit of the departed properly detach itself from its former life.[5] (A pair of documentary films on the *Tibetan Book of the Dead* has been narrated by the singer Leonard Cohen, who is famous for spending years in Zen retreats.) *Jacob's Ladder*, *Northfork*, and *Donnie Darko* are worth grouping with the films in this section because of the sense of blessedness and liberation in them that accompanies the more conventional emotions of bewilderment and anger at dying. *Northfork*, and *Donnie Darko* are noteworthy in this respect because of the young age of the dying persons: perhaps joyous serenity fits more naturally the younger one is, despite the conventional outrage at life cut so drastically short. The older one is, after all, the longer one has had to unlearn heaven.

Bereavement

It is not that easy to explain why, but to encounter a person facing death with serenity or even joy—whatever else may be mixed in—is an uplifting experience for which there can be no secular rationalization. It's spiritual. The religious questions for the bereaved are of course somewhat different than for those of the departed, and are thoughtfully explored in a wide variety of films. In *Fearless*, bereavement is through a plane crash, whereas in *21 Grams*, *Signs* and *Three Colors: Blue* death is caused by an automobile accident and therefore also unexpected, though the bereaved respond in very different ways. In *Shadowlands*, death is due to cancer, and is therefore long awaited, and in *About Schmidt* illness is again the cause of death.

In *Fearless*, a young woman called Carla loses her baby in a plane crash and turns in vain to her Catholic faith for consolation. Max Klein (Jeff Bridges) survives the crash and helps many victims to flee the burning plane, and is the real focus of the story as his values are turned upside down. He becomes obsessed with Carla to the anger of his wife who fails to empathize with his post-traumatic shock. At one point he tells Carla, "We're safe because we died already," indicative of a kind of elevated mood which is close to being religious though denying the outward form of religion. It is not Carla's Catholic faith that helps her in the end, but Max's secular compassion for her, and so the film is discussed further later on. Here we just mention that Max makes the journey from this fearless state of encountering death so closely—one akin to the equanimity of the protagonists in the films of the previous section—to normality through his care for Carla. His return to earth—as it were—is symbolized by the fact that a dangerous allergy returns to him and he is saved by his wife. It is Carla's bereavement however which illustrates the loss of meaning that so often accompanies such tragedies.

Although religion is present in *21 Grams*, as it is universally so in daily American life, the film is ultimately a superb *secular* meditation on death, loss, and bereavement. Its characters are all deeply human, flawed, and suffering, but the film is far removed from the maudlin *What Dreams May Come*. There is no reunion in heaven with lost ones; they are lost for good. Yet what is lost, asks the film at the end, when it is clear that the deeply interconnected nature of human living together always brings new life and new love. It is indeed the strength of this film that it uses a non-linear intercut form of narrative to weave together the initially disparate lives of its not-that-appealing protagonists, to show that human lives are interrelated and deeply bound together; every action impacts on another, but in unexpected ways. The postmodern structure of the narrative—along with all the best skills of the art as it has evolved, including cinematography, screen acting, and sound design—all add up to an extraordinary vehicle for the contemplation of loss. The bereavement at the heart of its story is Cristina's: she loses her husband and two little daughters in a hit-and-run accident, the perpetrator of which is Jack, a newly religious man desperately trying to leave behind petty crime and drink. Initially too stunned to press charges against him, Cristina finally succumbs to the rage that any parent must go through when confronted with their loss in such circumstances. Paul, who has received the heart of her dead husband in a transplant operation, is trying to calm her down, telling her to take it easy. She shrieks at him:

Take it easy? My husband and my little girls are dead, and I'm supposed to take it fucking easy? I can't just go on with my life! I am paralyzed, I'm a fucking amputee, do you see that?

"*Amputee*": this word is evocative and full of anger; it accurately describes the nature of the loss. Jack's religion has not helped him at all, and Cristina appears to have none: she argues that she and Paul must kill Jack, and he reluctantly agrees (this is America after all). He cannot go through with it however, and when he confronts Jack with the appalling irresponsibility of leaving the little girls to die, it is clear that Jack is already suffering under the terrible anguish of his guilt. Nobody in this film comes out as morally complete, yet does any moralizing in the world help when faced with such circumstances? This film purveys a humanism with a small "h"—deeply compassionate, but unblinking in the face of human weakness. Its writer, Guillermo Arriaga, tells us in interview that he is an atheist who thinks that "life has more power than death," and that "life is our only chance." He goes on: "I am always obsessed with people who know that this is the only chance, and they use their decisions to correct the directions in their life."[6]

The film has drawn some interesting responses from the critics, particularly those with a Christian background. We saw earlier that hope was central to the Christian interpretation of *Henry Poole is Here* and so it is with *21 Grams*. Clive Marsh is intrigued that the film critic of the *Observer* newspaper, Philip French, considers that the film "might offer a better presentation of a Christian understanding of redemption" than *The Passion of the Christ* which was released at the same time. Marsh appears thrown by "the shabbiness of the context," and adds that "if this is indeed a film about redemption, then it is clear that redemption is not easy. Any hope present in the film is certainly underplayed."[7] One might respond: who thinks redemption is easy? It is precisely the alleged "shabbiness" of urban America and its ordinary citizens that gives the film weight.

In *Three Colors: Blue* Julie loses her husband and child in a car crash caused by mechanical failure. This time there is no one to blame. Julie lives a world away from Christine, not just because of the French setting of the film, but because of the literary conventions of the film's story-telling. Julie is *refined*, her anguish is *refined*, her world is not "shabby." This and the passion she shares with her dead husband for music makes the film closer to *Truly Madly Deeply*, to be discussed below. Kieslowski, the Polish director of the *Three Colors* trilogy, pursues a very continental European aesthetic in his films, and clearly holds the typical conviction of the French that culture is central to the well-lived life. Julie's recovery from the anguish of her grief is made possible by art (or music to be more precise). She resists the lure of music to start with, numbed through grief, but its draw on her is too powerful. Julie's healing takes place through the performance of an orchestral piece composed by her dead husband, a move she had initially denied by destroying what she thought was the only copy. Religion appears to have had no place in her attempts to deal with her bitterness over her bereavement, but in an operatic movement in the final concerto the well-known passage from St. Paul in 1 Corinthians 13 is sung: "Without love, I am nothing." But Julie's journey is a secular one, and the love—very genuine and generous—which she comes into at the end of the film is not the religious love, *caritas*, of St. Paul. Instead, the film rests in the same message as *21 Grams*: that life goes on through new life, and in this case it is through the pregnancy of Julie's dead husband's mistress. Her generosity is to the mistress, and her healing takes place as much through that as her music.

And yet ... who can really say where the aesthetic segues into the spiritual? Roy Anker puts Julie's experience well: "Ultimately, what the stricken protagonist has confronted within these aural-visual epiphanies is no less than the Spirit of God wresting her back from despair and numbness into hope and love. In short the music affords her a glimpse of divine love."[8] Perhaps Anker is right. The very French concern with art is also present in the film *Jesus of Montreal* where a young actor plays Jesus in an avant garde version of the Biblical story. When audiences queue up to see the open-air play, the interest lies palpably in the excitement accompanying the discovery of "great"—and preferably a little shocking—art. Here it is not a spiritual enquiry at all. (More on this film later.)

Returning to bereavement, we saw earlier that *Signs* was about a priest who loses faith in the aftermath of a car accident. This is quite a different film, however, lacking any of the gritty realism of *21 Grams* or the French sophistication of *Three Colors: Blue*. Mel Gibson plays a father of two whose wife is run over by a neighbor; the story then runs aground in New Age crop circle alien conspiracy concerns. Nevertheless, there is a return to faith at the end of the film, suggesting one interpretation that his crisis itself may have produced these bizarre manifestations, much as in the bardo imagery of dying. Faith is also central to *Shadowlands,* the story of C. S. Lewis and his romance with American author Joy Gresham. Lewis—famous for his *Narnia* children's stories and his theological works—had apparently stayed single to avoid the pain of loss he felt inevitable in marriage. Against his better judgment he fell in love with Gresham, but their brief marriage ended in her early death from cancer. Lewis's deep religiosity, and the time he had to prepare for her death, makes this film very different from the preceding three. His grief is complete and natural, but totally framed by his long preparation for suffering as a deeply Christian practitioner, and by the preparation for his loss that Gresham initiates. She asks him to think about her death, to which he replies that he will "manage." She insists that more is possible, that "the pain then is part of the happiness now" which they are sharing in a holiday in the country. "That's the deal," she insists. The reluctance to face the issue of death that is so widespread in Western culture could not, for her, be allowed as a very British "I'll manage." But Lewis tells us early in the film that "prayer flows out of me night and day. It doesn't change God, it changes me." This is prayer that has moved beyond mere supplication, and he is now put to the test as to whether it has really changed him or not. He has earlier told his audience in a lecture that pain was God's gift to us, to wake us up.

As Gresham dies, the camera pulls out of the room, and then out of the cottage scene, as if suggesting the departure of her spirit, as in *American Beauty*. "Experience is a brutal teacher," Lewis reflects to his brother in the aftermath, "but you learn, my God, you learn." He had attempted to shield himself from experience, and rest in his theological speculations, but he is angry after all. "Only God knows why these things have to happen," says the vicar, but Lewis is bitter: "God knows, but does God care? ... We're the rats in the cosmic laboratory. No doubt the experiment is for our own good, but that still makes God the vivisectionist, doesn't it?" Mary Dodson believes that the film is an accurate presentation of Lewis and that it "portrays Lewis as a brilliant debater, as a beloved public figure, and as an emotionally isolated man." Of Lewis's journey from a theorizer of faith—and a teacher of philosophy as a "way"—to having it challenged by events she says: "Attenborough's film illustrates that Lewis's way was less easily traveled than the scholar had—for twenty-five years—proclaimed."[9] In other words this film should sober anyone wishing to lecture on the value of suffering. In the end, it is the need to help Gresham's son, Douglas, deal with his loss that helps Lewis through his own process. As in *21 Grams*, the message is clear: life goes on, this time through an adopted son, and the young pupils at college. "We read to know we are not alone," he starts a tutorial. "Do you think that is so?" He continues: "We love, to know that we are not alone." The film concludes, as he walks with Douglas in the countryside: "The pain now is part of the happiness then. That's the deal."

In *City of Angels* the bereaved is a man who was formerly an angel, and is persuaded to give up his angelic status out of love for a woman, killed this time in a road accident. An angel, we assume, must have faith, but the twist now is that, having given up the remote station in which loss is unknown in the bliss of eternity, he has to face the real agony of loss in the knowledge that he has given up his former bulwark against such pain. Faith now consists not in a belief in the supernatural, but in a belief in the purification that will come from submission to earthly suffering. His first experience as a human is what Lewis comes to late in life.

It appears to be the privilege of the dying to find serenity, at least for some of them. For the bereaved there is a long journey of pain. So far we have looked at bereavement films where there is a new life at the end of that journey, in whatever form that takes: a literal new life—a baby—or a renewal of love and faith. But what happens when bereavement fails to take that course? When it becomes a purely secular nightmare? Or when grief itself is absent? Time to turn to the work of Ingmar Bergman, a key auteur director.

Bergman's *Cries and Whispers* is about the loss of a sister, but whether it is secular or spiritual depends on one's point of view. Certainly there is an abundance of outward religion in the film, notably in the form of the family priest who speaks at the death of Agnes, whose protracted dying from cancer has aroused only horror and not love in her sisters. Once Agnes is dead it is guilt that racks them, not grief. If religion is defined by its outward form, then this is a religious film. If religion on the other hand is defined as the awareness of profound connectedness, then this is a film empty of religion because the characters barely connect with others or even with life itself.

At Agnes's deathbed the pastor's speech begins conventionally enough:

> God, our Father, in His infinite wisdom and mercy has decided to call you home in the flower of your youth. Prior to that He considered you worthy to bear a heavy and protracted suffering. You submitted to it patiently and without complaint, knowing your sins would be forgiven through Our Lord Christ's death on the Cross. May your Father in Heaven have mercy upon your soul when you stand in his presence. May He let His angels divest you of the memory of earthly pain.

It is an undoubtedly religious idea that God might decide someone worthy enough to "bear heavy and protracted suffering," but one is tempted to think that in Bergman's hands this is irony. Had Agnes pronounced such a sentiment herself, it might be more convincing. But who can say? The words themselves, if they fall on receptive minds, would be engendering enough of a genuine religious impulse. Unfortunately, apart from the maid, one senses that there is little receptivity to such ideas among the bereaved. After delivering the first part of his speech the pastor then goes to the head of the bed and kneels. He continues:

> If it be that you gathered our suffering in your poor body and have born it with you through death. ... If it be that you meet God, there, in that other land. ... If it be that He turns His face towards you. ... If it be that you will know the language of Our Lord. ... If it be that you can speak to the Lord. ... If it be so: pray for us. Agnes, dear child, listen to what I tell you now. Pray for us who are left on this dark and dirty earth beneath an empty and cruel sky. Lay your burden of suffering at the Lord's feet and ask Him to pardon us. Ask Him to set us free at last from our anxiety, our weariness and our profound doubt. Ask him for a meaning to our lives. Agnes, you who have suffered so inconceivably and for so long, you must surely be worthy to plead our case.

Again, in other circumstances, parts at least of this speech could be understood as inspirational Christianity. But externally the film portrays an upper middle-class Freudian world of suppressed and festering emotions, and so the image of a "dark and dirty earth" and an "empty and cruel sky" are perhaps the real message, rather than that of redemption. They appear not to be the negative of a known positive, a dark crayon used to make the light colors brilliant: they appear *just* negative. The dark here is not the opposite of the "luminous," not the herald of the light: it is just empty, so, in our terminology, dull. The pastor stands again and faces the family, saying, "I confirmed her. We often had long and exhaustive conversations. Her faith was stronger than mine." We are of course used to priests who find their faith to be less than that of an apparently unreligious person in some dramatic trial, but such a person is not forthcoming in this film.

Better than an indictment of Christianity, this film should be understood as an indictment of the middle classes. Only the maid loved Agnes, and as the film progresses we see that the pastor's dutiful petition to God that Agnes might plead their cause, containing within it the despairing desire to be free of anxiety and doubt, is unheard. As a symbol of the surviving sisters' distance from redemption of any kind Karin subsequently mutilates her vagina with a shard of broken wine glass, and then smears the blood over her face while staring at her husband. "I can't breathe for all the guilt," she says later.

Sara Anson Vaux suggests that we should view the film from the perspective of missing authenticity, and that the power of the film is to challenge our own sense of authenticity.[10] By identifying with each of the characters in turn, we find our own lack of faith to match the pastor's. This is a good argument in favor of the Bergman canon, but one is left with the nagging caveat: certainly we can learn from what is missing, but where are we going to discover the shape of what is absent if we are invited, for example, to doubt the sincerity of the priest's speech? The route offered by Clive Marsh is not convincing either. He suggests that "the film is clearly to be interpreted in part through the visually striking imitation of the 'pieta,'"[11] i.e., in the scene where the maid Anna cradles Agnes. He has no choice but to add this: "There is less hope than Christian theology would want to see represented." Quite.

There is a certain kind of confident Western atheist who has been culturally liberated from religion to such an extent that its questions and that of religion in general simply don't arise. A great deal of Western filmmaking is produced within this context. For example, the filmmaker David Cronenberg was asked in an interview for *Rolling Stone* whether his parents were atheists, to which he responded:

> Yeah, they both were. The word "atheist" almost suggests you buy the religious system. Beyond atheism, they were simply non-believers. To me to say you're an atheist almost suggests *theism*. You can't have the atheism without theism, and I'd go beyond that. Non-belief. Period. And therefore all the structures that go with it.[12]

Cronenberg has described the position of most secularists: they are so removed from religion that to deny any of its structures is as meaningless as to affirm them. But there are many who can neither constructively engage with the life of the spirit, nor be rid of it, and, as filmmakers, they explore this compromised position in their art. In the West we can label such films as chronicles of an exhausted Christianity, its lingering power still holding the mind in its grip, but providing so little real sustenance as to create only anguish. Bergman might be the undisputed master of this field, his so-called "Winter" trilogy of *Through a Glass Darkly*, *Winter Light*, and *The Silence* exploring this theme from every angle. Yet he doesn't seem to understand this himself when he describes himself as similar to the anonymous re-builders of Chartres cathedral after it was mostly destroyed through lightning in the Middle Ages. He says:

"Thus if I am asked what I would like the general purpose of my films to be, I would reply that I want to be one of the artists in the cathedral on the great plain. I want to make a dragon's head, an angel, a devil—or perhaps a saint—out of stone. ... Regardless of whether I believe or not, whether I am a Christian or not, I would play my part in the collective building of the cathedral."[13] If we disregard this attempt to underplay his obvious status as auteur filmmaker, his metaphor is quite implausible. Bergman is quite obviously more like the laborer employed by the demolition company whose contract it is to *destroy* the cathedral. This is not to deny his prowess as a filmmaker, or even his auteur status; it is a comment on a secular world that he lost the categories of thought by which to understand religion.

Early in Bergman's *The Seventh Seal* he has his medieval knight say (quite implausibly for the period in which the film is set), "Why can't I kill God in me—why does He live in me in a humiliating way? A mocking reality I can't get rid of?" One could say that this theme is present in all Bergman's subsequent films, the inability to either recover the old innocence and meaning of religion or to move on and abandon it cheerfully. His characters are pinned down like bugs in the most horrible of laboratory experiments, still able to move their limbs, to feel pain, but not to either die or walk free. Through the agonies of Bergman's various protagonists religion is dismantled, stone by stone, leaving only a livid scar on the landscape where nothing can grow, far less a cathedral. Bergman himself says of these three films: "*Through a Glass Darkly* conquered certainty. *Winter Light* penetrated certainty. *The Silence*—God's silence—the negative imprint. Therefore, they constitute a trilogy."[14] However, this rather cryptic assessment does not provide any new way to assess his films positively. Our question must remain: Does a "negative imprint"—an absence—necessarily illuminate what is lost or missing?

In *Through a Glass Darkly* a mentally ill woman waits for God but only a spider appears. The setting is a bit like in Tarkovsky's *The Sacrifice*: a small, claustrophobically isolated group of people whose inner torments unfold. The title of the film refers to St. Paul's memorable phrase, which captures the difficulty that we have in seeing clearly. When Karin undergoes what might be some kind of psychotic episode, prior to being readmitted to an asylum, she tells them that God was a stony-faced spider but when God failed to seduce her he crawled onto the wall. By suggesting that God is merely the delusion of the mentally ill, Bergman has taken his wrecking ball to one end of the cathedral. He has no tools at all with which to rebuild the edifice of religion.

The experience of true, healing, and strengthening grief is not possible to the protagonists of *Cries and Whispers*, perhaps because they have not known true love, any love at all. In *Snow Cake* a mother cannot love or grieve properly for quite different reasons: she is profoundly autistic—in the clinical sense. *Snow Cake* stars Sigourney Weaver as Linda, the autistic mother with a quite normal daughter given a lift by a stranger, Alex (Alan Rickman). In a car crash that is no fault of his own, the girl dies, so Alex is drawn into the upside-down obsessive world of her mother. Alex himself is not long out of prison for manslaughter: he had intended to hurt but not kill a man responsible for the road accident which had killed his own long-lost son. In the unlikely meeting between Alex and Linda, a friendship develops, initially based on the request to provide Linda with the assistance she needs in the absence of her daughter. Alex lands up moving in, caring for her and arranging the funeral at which the grandparents and he grieve in the place of Linda. There is little explicit spirituality or religiosity in the film but it makes an interesting contrast with *Cries and Whispers*. It suggests that as a film, and despite its subject matter, *Snow Cake* is not at all an autistic cultural production, but that *Cries and Whispers* is. It also suggests that *Snow Cake* and *21 Grams*, located in similar lower social strata, shed light on the upper middle-class Freudianized world of *Cries and Whispers* as irredeemably false. Can the dramatization of such middle-class falsity really provoke a search for authenticity in us?

In *About Schmidt*, Jack Nicholson plays Warren Schmidt, a man whose life is largely meaningless. When his wife dies he is not much affected, but since he has also recently retired, he is at a double loss. Purchasing a Winnebago motor home he travels, presenting us with slice-of-life American cameos. The film sits somewhere between the working-class worlds of *Snow Cake* and *21 Grams* and the upper middle-class world of *Cries and Whispers*: Schmidt is trapped by the empty formalities of a professional life and suburban routine, yet has none of the high-culture trappings that should, by convention, make his plight interesting. Agnes and her sisters are numb to grief because of their misplaced emotional intensity; Schmidt, on the other hand, is numb to grief because of the lack of it. Still, there is more hope for him, because throughout the film a connection grows between him and an African boy that he sponsors.

As mentioned earlier *The Tree of Life* is an aesthetically profound meditation on bereavement. It obliquely unfolds the story of a boy's death and its impact on his brother and family. Its rather polarized reception points to its ambition perhaps: by eschewing most of the normal filmic structures it ventures into the abstract realm of *Koyaanisqatsi* and *Baraka* while attempting to tell a very human story. Because the father in this story (Brad Pitt) is something of a tyrant, it is the brother (Sean Penn) of the dead boy whose loss we identify with, and—if the film's transcendent lyricism works for us—with whom we are brought into a profound peace.

Suicide and Euthanasia, and their Aftermath

What separates us from the animals? Suicide. The human mind can project into the future in a way that we believe animals cannot, due to our ability to model our world. When that future looks sufficiently horrible we may make the choice of suicide, and like many of the issues around death, this has a religious dimension. Monotheistic religions mostly frown upon suicide, even declaring it a mortal sin. The Romans found it culturally acceptable, however, at some points merely requiring permission from a local official. Other so-called "honor" cultures may sanction suicide, or, in the horrible example of "sati" in India, long outlawed, a widow was expected to throw herself on the funeral pyre of her husband.

In this section we consider first the bereaved rather than the person committing the act. Suicide raises for those intimate with the deceased the natural and deeply unsettling concern: Was it something to do with me?

In *Maborosi* we follow a Japanese couple happy with each other and the birth of their first child. But one night the husband is killed on the railway track, in an apparent act of suicide. His widow, Yumiko, is devastated but eventually agrees to an arranged marriage with widower Tamio. His son and her daughter play well enough together in their new home in a remote fishing village and Yumiko seems to recover from her tragedy. Beautifully filmed—drawing comparisons with the work of Ozu, so highly praised by Schrader for his "transcendental style"—the story focuses mostly on minutiae until the final scene where Yumiko's pent-up grief is given vent. Her words are given force because of the long wait and the unemotionality expected by Japanese convention, and also the setting at dusk by the sea. She has clearly been turning the suicide over and over in her mind for years. She sobs:

I just ... I just don't understand. Why did he kill himself? Why was he walking along the tracks? It just goes round and round my head.

She weeps, and turns to her husband who has followed her out along the spit: "Why do you think he did it?"

The suffering brought to this woman is made vivid in a way that only good filmmaking can do: the combination of honed-down screenwriting and other factors such as good acting and cinematography. In this one scene is the indictment of all those Romantic images of suicide—going back to Goethe's *Sorrows of Young Werther*—as the ultimate in selfishness. It is the second husband, however, whose simple words complete her healing, and who stands out as the model of compassion. He says, framed by the sea and the low light:

> The sea has the power to beguile. Back when Dad was still fishing he once saw a *maborosi*, a strange light far out to sea. Something was beckoning to him, he said, it might happen to anyone.

We already know that Tamio, her new husband, while not prone to emotional displays, loves and cares for her deeply. Her healing began with their first meeting at a rail station, but his words now bring her to the completion of her grieving. By comparing the impulse that drove her husband to suicide with the *maborosi*—equivalent to the will-o'-the-wisp in Western folk traditions—he helps her see that her husband was not to blame, much less her. It could happen to anyone. It is perhaps too fatalistic an explanation for Western sensibilities, but for her circumstances, and because it comes from the man who really loves her, it hits home.

Love Liza, by contrast, presents the natural bewilderment of Wilson Joel, a man who has no faith to draw on, and who is led into erratic and addictive behavior patterns in the aftermath of his wife's suicide. Its American setting is not far from that of *About Schmidt*, and its protagonist is no more emotionally literate. In *Maborosi* Yumiko's emotion is held back for years; in *Love Liza* Joel's hangs out, American-style. Joel does receive an odd, rather impersonal support from those he meets in his rather Schmidt-like travels, and we know that time will gradually heal him. We are not party to any great revelation in the film, but it serves again to show what slow misery it is for those in the aftermath of suicide. While those who take their own life genuinely feel they have no choice, it is not a victimless act.

In *The Hours*, we find another dramatized Romantic justification for suicide, hinging around Virginia Woolf's novel *Mrs. Dalloway*, in which the protagonist comes to admire the suicide of a World War I veteran, and Woolf's own suicide. The aftermath of suicide is made generational in this film because of the link via Woolf's 1920s novel *Mrs. Dalloway* to a woman who contemplates suicide in the 1950s, and her son who actually does kill himself in the 1990s. Though the Bloomsbury group to which Woolf belonged did not subscribe to some of the more fanciful extremes of the English Romantics such as Wordsworth and Coleridge, their emphasis on romantic love over marriage and patriotism places them in that tradition. Above all the values of literature itself become the dominant theme in *The Hours* as is clear in the self-doubt of the 1990s character Clarissa Vaughan. Sharing the first name of Mrs. Dalloway, and, like her, preparing for a party, she only feels truly alive and authentic in the company of authors, and in particular Richard, a poet dying from AIDS. He is the son of the fifties woman reading *Mrs. Dalloway* who wanted to commit suicide but instead abandoned her husband and son as a small boy. Whether it is the despair over his illness, or the feeling of rejection suffered as a child, or both, Richard jumps to his death from his loft apartment window in full sight of Clarissa.

She then has to cope with an abandoned party and a visit from Richard's mother, now an old woman. Clarissa's torment is skillfully portrayed by Meryl Streep, but the fact remains that her loss as a bereavement is overshadowed by her sense of inauthenticity. Nominally, Woolf's suicide is due to her mental illness, but the film suggests that both hers and Richard's suicide are truly *authentic* acts, and admirable. In the Romantic tradition to be concerned about the suffering of the bereaved is to be inauthentic to oneself. It is never asked what it means to authentically *love*, conceived of as the non-sexual, non-romantic but profound connection to others. The Romantic love has preference in it. As Kierkegaard says: "The object of both erotic love and of friendship has preference's name, 'the beloved,' 'the friend,' who is loved in contrast to the world."[15] In the Romantic tradition the world cannot be loved, only the "special" person—the preferred one.

Returning again to *What Dreams May Come* we recall that it portrays a man searching the underworld for his wife, after her suicide has led to her self-incarceration in a dreamworld of negativity. Here, we find Romanticism in New Age garb, rather than in Bloomsbury mode. Schwartz, in her interesting essay on the film, proposes that the afterlife constructed in the film is South Asian in origin, i.e., that it represents the notion of projection in the Eastern concept of *maya*.[16] Chris's wife, Annie, is trapped in a Gothic nightmare because of the transgression of her suicide, while Chris, the virtuous doctor who died saving others, plays in painted bucolic meadows. Schwartz is much exercised that the Western God is not involved in judgment on the characters, and that instead "death has its own system that works independently of divine intervention, just as does life."[17] This is a telling indication of the difference between East and West, and the fact that the New Age owes more to Indian ideas than to the Bible.

Annie's suicide itself is provoked by bereavement, and so is not a completely narcissistic act. In the suicide in *Dead Poets Society*, which was the Romantic gesture of a person denied their artistic potential, we are conscious that it was the act of an immature mind, influenced by the high-flown phrases of a genuine but possibly misguided literary adult. As we saw, Keating's culpability is a worthwhile question, which can only be moderated by the question of the culpability of the entire Romantic tradition. The culpability of this tradition in *The Hours* has a different moral slant because the protagonists are mature adults, but highlights again the issue over aesthetics: can art really become, in the end, a route to what is essential? Does not the anguish of Clarissa's inauthenticity arise precisely because she has her eye on art instead of life? *The Hours* poses this question in a way that makes it a more rigorous investigation of the Romantic, and of the issue of suicide, than *Dead Poets Society*. While there is no explicit spirituality in the film it is beautifully shot and its lingering camera brings out the soulfulness of the actresses' faces (principally Nicole Kidman and Meryl Streep).

In the suicide films so far considered the fact remains that society as a whole, as opposed to the Romantic tradition, does not extend sanction, either moral or legal, to the suicides in each case. In the case of Clarissa in *The Hours*, there would in real life have been police questioning as to her role in the suicide of Richard. We know that she did not assist him, but the police don't (because Richard was alone in his flat with her), and would want to satisfy themselves of that. But some societies, under some circumstances, as pointed out earlier, do condone suicide.

The film *Masada* is the telling of the historical siege of the rock fortress of Masada in southern Israel where the whole Jewish community committed suicide rather than face capture by the Romans. The event of 73 CE is recorded by the historian Josephus, who tells us that some 960 inhabitants died in a collective act of suicide. His account apparently derives from that of two women survivors who hid along with their five children to evade the collective action. Little other historical evidence survives to support the story, but one can argue that the Masada legend has survived as a narrative trope appearing in a number of films, notably *The Matrix* trilogy.[18] Whether it is a nod to the Masada tradition or not, in *Schindler's List* there is a hospital scene in which the Jewish patients in the Polish Ghetto, about to be overrun by the Nazis, are given lethal poison by their doctors. These are extreme circumstances, but the Judaic tradition otherwise does not sanction suicide.

Buddhist cultures on the other hand appear more ready to sanction suicide, though it is not at all clear if this can be traced back to the Buddha's specific approval of the suicide of a monk called Channa, told in the story "Advice to Channa."[19] The monk was very ill, and found to have "genuine" reasons for ending his life by Buddhist elders. This story is found in the Pali Canon, and hence relates to the Therevada tradition in Buddhism. However, we can find two films set in a more Mahayana context in which suicide is clearly regarded as honorable. The first is *Mishima: A Life in Four Chapters*, in which the protagonist Mishima commits ritual suicide or *seppuku* after his failed attempt at a military coup. On this subject Joe Fisher speculates: "Torn between indigenous Shintoism's honorable death and the reincarnational pulse of imported Buddhism, Mishima would have refrained from taking his life if he had truly believed in rebirth."[20]

The Buddhist context of *Spring, Summer, Autumn, Winter ... and Spring* is Korean Zen, and hence Mahayana, but we pointed out earlier that the writer-director Kim Ki-duk is a Catholic. The scene in the film where the old monk commits ritual suicide in a burning boat may have little justification in any of the Buddhist traditions, though William R. LaFleur's account in his analysis of *Maborosi* of the Japanese tradition of "Fudaraku-tokai" — sea-suicide by holy men—may have a bearing on this. On the other hand Kim Ki-duk may have written in this scene to make a contrast with the Catholic proscription on suicide.

It may be that in countries with a belief in reincarnation, which would include most of the countries east of Iran and south of Russia, suicide is seen differently because it is not the end. In the reincarnation literature those who commit suicide for any but the most justifiable of motives are likely to come back with not only the physical marks of their self-harming, but also with additional psychological burdens.[21] Hence Joe Fisher, in his book on reincarnation, says, "In countries where the population at large believes in reincarnation, suicide, being regarded as a petty injunction against cosmic law, is rarely attempted. For it is felt that the problems that precipitate such an act of desperation cannot be avoided; they will only regroup to launch another, perhaps more serious, attack in another existence."[22] Writing in the 1980s Fisher may have had statistics then to support this idea, but in Japan of 2008 suicide was considered a runaway problem among professionals. Japan now has one of the highest suicide rates in the world, and it would be of interest if this correlated with the loss of belief in reincarnation.

The consideration of suicide would not be complete without the suicide bomber, and there are at least three films that deal with this subject. The first is *The Terrorist*, a pre–9/11 film that deals with the internal struggle of a would-be female Tamil suicide bomber. This is significant because it is generally recognized that the Tamils, who are Hindus, were among the first to use suicide bombers as a military tactic, before Muslims. The protagonist, Malli, is chosen for a mission, set in India, to assassinate a leader as he goes to garland her. The film is devoted to the short period leading up to the event, in which she is told by a kindly old man that she is pregnant. He has prefaced this insight with the observation: "What is the loneliest thing in life? A seed. Unless it is sown it belongs neither to the sky nor the earth." Perhaps it is this image that makes her choose life in the end. In *Paradise Now* a failed terrorist bombing by Palestinians leads the two would-be bombers to different conclusions. One gives up on the idea, while the other is seen in the closing shot of the film on a bus carrying Israeli civilians and soldiers. We don't know the outcome. In *Time of Favor* it is an Israeli Jew who plans a suicide bombing of the Temple Mount.

If the suicide of a family member can be as devastating as portrayed in *Maborosi* or *Love Liza*, then is it better when the family or friends collaborate in assisted suicide, euthanasia? The cultural sanction for this varies much more across the world than it does for the lone act. In *The Sea Inside* we are party to the long, drawn out decision of a quadriplegic Ramón Sampedro to take his life, in which all of his close family are involved. The film is based on real life events in which Ramón eventually loses a legal battle over his right to die and has to take recourse outside of the law. At one point a quadriplegic priest visits him in order to change his mind, but the religious basis of the priest's arguments doesn't wash with Ramón. This is perhaps the crucial issue in suicide from a religious point of view: What does submission to the will of God or to karma, or to fate mean at the deepest level? Those who believe in reincarnation might believe that submission is the only path and that to take one's life might make it worse in the next. The humanist, on the other hand, is certain that death is the end, and that the suffering of a man like Ramón, or those with other debilitating illnesses, justifies the right to medically-assisted suicide. While the plot involves assisted suicide, the *theme* of the film, argues Robert K. Johnston, is life. He writes, "That reviewer after reviewer points out this paradox—what on the surface seems to be a movie about death proves instead to be an exploration of life—is not surprising given the clear direction of the movie."[23]

Clint Eastwood's *Million Dollar Baby* presents a Ramón-like situation in which a female boxer Maggie is rendered quadriplegic in a boxing accident. With fewer remaining dignities left to her than for Ramón, her coach and manager Frankie Dunn yields to her demands and administers a fatal dose of adrenalin. What is clumsy and disturbing about this film, and could be considered an Eastwood trademark, is the way that Dunn acts as a lone agent isolated from the rest of society. While this trait is appealing elsewhere in the Eastwood canon—e.g., *The Outlaw Josey Wales*—here it is disturbing because of the heightened cultural autism in the film. No character has a meaningful relationship with any other, but instead we are presented with stereotyped gruff "buddy"-style interactions supposed typical in the world of boxing. Maggie herself appears utterly alone in the world, bar Dunn, and the inclusion of Morgan Freeman as an ex-boxer Dupris—who both narrates the story and hangs around the gym—only squanders the actor's legendary screen warmth in further ersatz "buddy" banter. Dunn, played by Eastwood himself, simply hasn't the depth of characterization to agonize convincingly over his role in Maggie's death. Hence it *feels* more like murder, the kind of murder undertaken to eliminate a problem. As if in some recognition of the compromised moral stature of the act, Dupris informs us lugubriously at the end of the film that Dunn subsequently "disappears." Okay, but where is the police manhunt?

In *A Taste of Cherry* the "assisted suicide" turns out to be an uncertain suicide, and by no means medically assisted. The Abbas Kiarostami film is set in Iran. Mr. Badii drives around in a rather barren landscape looking for someone who will help him in his suicide, and although we don't know whether he goes through with it in the end or not, what is interesting are the responses to his request from the strangers that he picks up. All that he asks is for the stranger to bury him after the deed: he has dug his grave, will lie down in it and die, and they are to shovel earth over it in a remote location, so no one will be bothered by his departing. However, the cash he offers is certainly not enough to persuade his first potential assistant, a young soldier who runs off before long. The impression is that the soldier is used to following orders, but has no guidelines here as to whether this is okay or not. The second occupant of the passenger seat is a Muslim seminarian who is subject to a much longer entreaty by Badii:

> I know that my decision goes against your beliefs. You believe God gives life and takes it when He sees fit. But there comes a time when a man can't go on. He's exhausted and can't wait for God to act, so he decides to act himself. There, that's what's called "suicide.".... I've decided to free myself from life.... You can't feel what I feel. You can sympathize, understand, show compassion. But feel my pain? No. You suffer and so do I. I understand you. You comprehend my pain but you can't feel it. That's why I ask you to be a true Muslim and help me.

The odd feature of the film is that we never learn why Badii wants to commit suicide, so we can't sympathize, understand or show compassion to him on that score. We can sympathize however that no one will help him. The seminarian refuses, saying it is against his religion. He adds, "God entrusts man's body to him. He must not torment that body." Badii responds, "I know that suicide is a great sin. But being unhappy is a great sin too."

But: third time lucky. A university professor agrees to help him, though not without first telling Badii that he, too, went to commit suicide once, but was saved by the taste of the mulberries that he found (these become the "cherries" of the film title). He extols the beauty of life to Badii, and this perhaps changes his mind. All we know is that he lies down in the grave that night and it begins to rain. What makes the film intriguing—and humor-ous—are the varying responses to Badii's request. Kiarostami himself made this comment on the film: "The person committing suicide might think that s/he is taking revenge on society, nature, life, powers to be, and so on. But s/he doesn't realize that after suicide life still goes on and things stay the way they are."[24] Clearly Badii's secular philosophy actually does understand this, and that is why he wants the traces of him erased at the end. But the other films here show different: nobody is an island, and then they sink the ripples have a moral impact on others.

In *They Shoot Horses, Don't They?* the request to assist a suicide is direct. The setting is the 1920s dance marathon craze in America, in which ambitious Gloria is partnered with unassuming Robert. Ostensibly the film re-enacts the coliseum-style brutality of the craze, where couples danced to exhaustion to win a desperately sought-after prize amidst Depression poverty. But the film has elements of a sixties or seventies psychological drama such as *Zabriskie Point*, *Westworld* and *Enter the Dragon*, where death is trivialized. Such films drew—though indirectly—from the Theatre of the Absurd, where inappropriate emotional responses are intended to critique or satirize social norms of the day, and to highlight their meaninglessness, or in the case of *Enter the Dragon* simply as the style of the day. Of course, despair might be a natural response to the hardships of the Depression, and no doubt many succumbed. But its specific flavor in *They Shoot Horses* is more sixties than twenties. As the competition progresses Gloria says to Robert, "Maybe the whole damned world is like Central Casting, they got it all rigged before you ever showed up.... I'm so sick of the whole stinking thing." "What thing?" "Life.'" When she pulls out her gun Robert doesn't react. She raises it to her temple but cannot pull the trigger. "Help me!" she says, "Please." He takes the gun. "Tell me when," he says. "Now." So he shoots her dead. In real life the police take a dim view of assisted suicide, particularly when the "assistance" in this case is indistinguishable from murder. "Why did you do it kid?" asks the cop. "She asked me to," says Robert laconically. "That the only reason you got, kid?" asks the incredulous cop. "They shoot horses don't they?" responds Robert.

Gods and Monsters is a fictionalized account of the last days of James Whale, director of such horror films as two Frankenstein movies. He forms a relationship with his gardener, Clayton, but because his mind is disintegrating, engineers a homosexual encounter in which he provokes Clayton into strangling him. He wants to die, but Clayton recovers his wits and refuses to kill him. Instead, the old man drowns himself in the pool the same night. Compared to *They Shoot Horses*, this is glossy, lightweight fare, but there is one good line, from Whale's loyal and distraught maid: "You could not wait for God to take you in His time?" This is the natural response from religion, which has no secular counterpart.

The "assisted" suicides in the films *The English Patient*, *Igby Goes Down*, and *One Flew Over the Cuckoo's Nest* are more incidental to their stories, but share some of the moral ambivalence of that in *Million Dollar Baby*. By contrast, Ramón is the only character in this group of films who administers his own means of death and then only after exhaustive discussion with an extended social grouping.

Summary

A graveyard is often the setting for horror films. At the very least, it is usually considered a sad kind of place. But really it is a place of love. To witness the little actions of friends and family as they bring flowers, tend to the grave, and talk quietly of the departed is to see expressions of love that in life are sometimes overlooked, or overshadowed by family strife. So, in films of dying and bereavement, love is often foregrounded in a way that films exclusively of the living cannot show. The response of love may take the outer form of conventional religion, or a turning back to religion as the comforter. Or if religion has departed leaving only an empty shell, we may find the meaninglessness of death, as in *Cries and Whispers*, but which, by the absence of meaning still might persuade some of the possibility of connectedness. At least, some commentators believe this.

We have looked at films covering almost every aspect of dying, often uncomfortable viewing, especially when the theme is suicide. Yet these films are valuable for showing the whole spectrum of responses: the Romantic impulse to suicide in *The Hours*, the bewilderment of the bereaved in *Love Liza*, and the various impulses of those asked to assist. At some level all the questions raised are spiritual. The aftermath of a death also touches people deeply: in *Fearless* a plane crash survivor is the only hope for recovery for a woman who lost her baby in the crash, while in *City of Angels* bereavement convinces a fallen angel that the life of the body is worth even loss of the loved one. We can say this: this is true even in the mostly secular drama of *21 Grams*, which turns out to be a luminous meditation on the value of life. And hauntingly beautiful is the scene in *Maborosi* in which the new husband—in a moment of deep compassion for his wife whose first husband committed suicide—gives her simple comfort and lifts her burden of repressed sorrow. This is luminous cinema. Death may provoke bewilderment, despair and numbness, but it also provokes situations of profound connectedness, either with others, or with existence itself in the serenity of a "beautiful death."

In the films of dying so far examined, the question of the supernatural has played no direct part in our discussion. But the question cannot be avoided, so the next section looks at different conceptions of the afterlife and the issues so raised for the spiritual life.

4
Ghosts, Angels and the Afterlife

We have so far looked at the question of dying in film from the point of view of the dying process or those left behind. But what happens to the deceased after death? This question must have occupied the thoughts of human beings from the dawn of rational thinking, and we know that it was central to the earliest religious rituals of shamanic times. Hence it is no surprise—despite all the secular insistence of death as the unqualified end—that there are many films exploring the question.

One may say: What has speculation about the afterlife got to do with an everyday lived spiritual life, or a secular one for that matter? The answer is that no one is immune to the question of the persistence of self. When materialists insist that selfhood is obliterated in death, it is rarely argued without a passion that suggests a great deal of interest in the question, and even perhaps an anger at impending annihilation. The passion also suggests that the question isn't *really* settled—whatever the bluster—hence the plethora of films that probe it. After death there must either be a disembodied life, in which conscious entities—including the just deceased—have experiences and relate to each other, or not. In Western fiction this question is mostly allowed to drift, allowing for the suspension of disbelief during a film, or the conceiving of the disembodied life as an artistic, mythic, or psychological framing of the question as a plot device with no obligation to take it too seriously. Clearly a materialist, reductionist, Marxist, or in any other terms truly modernist outlook cannot bear the idea, couched historically in the West more usually in terms of an afterlife, and in relation to such entities as ghosts and angels, and a host of more culturally specific "invisible people" such as goblins, pixies, fairies, elves, dryads, hamadryads, and so on. Apparently no committed modern can take the question seriously, but the spiritual life, however framed, must.

Let us put it this way: what is the ontological status of the "ghost?"

This chapter divides its films into three categories: those dealing with the afterlife, those dealing with ghosts, and those dealing with angels and demons. Ghosts here are assumed to be the spirits of ordinary departed human beings, often confused, while angels are distinguished from ghosts in that their origins are more obscure and—apparently—they know what they are doing. Demons, by convention, are "fallen" angels.

The Afterlife

The religions of the world, though the details may vary, offer perhaps three main accounts of life after death: an eternal afterlife, resurrection of the body, or reincarnation. At times these also get mixed up. Here we deal with films of the afterlife, as broadly conceived of in the Western monotheisms, while reincarnation and resurrection are dealt with in the next chapter.

Lubitsch's *Heaven Can Wait*, *A Matter of Life and Death*, Beatty's *Heaven Can Wait*, and *Afterlife* are four films which give varying accounts of the afterlife. The three Western films posit a surprisingly un–Christian vision of heaven and hell, though recognizable in broad outline, while the Japanese film *Afterlife*, is surprisingly Western (as it assumes an eternal afterlife instead of reincarnation). This suggests that by the middle of the twentieth century much cultural interpenetration between East and West has occurred. Where the three Western films depart from Christian doctrine is the extent to which the deceased person challenges their fate: there is no submission to the will of the Almighty, or to the traditional role of St. Peter as arbiter of destination at heaven's gate. In the 1943 film *Heaven Can Wait*, the protagonist argues that he should go to hell, but is finally sent to heaven instead—the point of the film being that an amiable privileged waster who leads a largely selfish life is nevertheless not really such a bad sort. In a *Matter of Life and Death* and the 1978 film *Heaven Can Wait*, those responsible for determining the fate of the individual after death have made a mistake, or are challenged to change their decision.

The visualizations of the afterlife are various and wonderful in these films. Lubitsch's antechamber to hell is rather like a dark red hotel lobby with immensely tall doors, while the vast stairway in *A Matter of Life and Death*—a realization of Jacob's ladder—gave rise to the American version of the film title: *Stairway to Heaven*. Beatty's *Heaven Can Wait* uses more conventional clouds but is just as convincing.

It is *Afterlife*—also known as *After Life* in the U.S.—that is the most puzzling: a non–Christian afterlife in which the deceased participate in something like a game-show. The dead are given three or four days to choose a key scene from their life, which will then be filmed. After the screening of the film, they disappear and will then have to live with the memory of that film for eternity. Interestingly, the deceased show no resistance to their fate, unlike the Westerners, who, even in the afterlife, are pursuing an individualistic path. When Warren Beatty finds out that his angel has made a mistake in taking up his soul after a car crash, he won't give up until the error is rectified: in life you fight a bad decision by the authorities, so why not in death? It's the American way.

Don't Look Now was introduced earlier as a film featuring clairvoyance but the film also involves bereavement. Laura and John Baxter lose their daughter Christine when she drowns in their garden pond. Laura's grief is mitigated when a blind clairvoyant tells her that Christine is happy in the afterlife. Laura (Julie Christie) is transformed at the possibility that her daughter survives in some form, and that she is somehow present with her and her husband. But John (Donald Sutherland) thinks the old ladies are manipulating his wife, and although he humors her for a while is eventually driven to rage: "Christine is dead, dead, dead!" It is he who dies, however, in completely mysterious and incoherent circumstances, the only narrative justification for which is the throwaway comment by his wife earlier that it was his decision to allow the children to play unsupervised by the water. So he deserved to die.

What is significant here for the afterlife is the idea that the recently departed have the capacity to reach across the divide and comfort the bereaved or in some other way communicate with them. The entire spiritualist movement—or Spiritualism, to give it its proper name as a Western monotheistic religion—is predicated on this. It is worth pointing out that Spiritualism in the U.S. and U.K. and its equivalent, Spiritism, in Latin countries, while Christian in origin, hold a view of the afterlife that differs from mainstream Christianity. Instead of a static heaven or hell for eternity, the soul ascends as it continues to make intellectual or moral progress on various planes. Perhaps it is this strand of Western religious thought, as well as influences from the East, which has resulted in such a variety of filmic representations of the afterlife.

Ghosts

Turning now to ghost films, we can say that the idea of the ghost seems to appear in all cultures as distinct from other forms of disembodied entity: ghosts are human, and have either not yet moved on after the death of the physical body, or have returned for some reason or other. There is a whole industry around the comic, the horror, and the comic-horror treatment of ghosts. However, both comedy and horror allow for the abandonment of any real engagement with the issue of a human disembodied life, and so films are chosen here that attempt to deal with the issue thoughtfully and generally lie outside of those genres.

In *Ghost* and *Truly Madly Deeply* we have quintessentially American and British ghost stories, respectively. In each case a woman loses her partner, and for a period is in contact with his spirit, during which the grieving process is completed. In *Ghost* the communication between Sam (Patrick Swayze) and Molly (Demi Moore) is only made possible by the extensive efforts of Sam and the intervention of a psychic, while in *Truly Madly Deeply* Nina (Juliet Stevenson) can see, hear and touch Jamie (Alan Rickman) from the start. Rickman's jaded Englishness in this muted performance perfectly conveys that of a talented cellist with a career before him finding himself dead through some dashed annoying inconvenience. As in *Three Colors: Blue*, music plays a considerable role in Nina's quirky resignation-cum-rage at her loss: at one point the dead Jamie accompanies her piano playing on the cello.

Clive Marsh writes about *Truly Madly Deeply* that "viewers with any experience of a close bereavement are unlikely to remain untouched."[1] What touches here is the knowledge of the bereaved that their loved one cannot return, and yet the yearning is so powerful that it appears to create the longed-for apparition. In commenting on both these films, the Jungian writer John Izod suggests a psychological explanation where the ghosts are projections: "Each ghost functions as a kind of fantasy mirror which, in the lineaments of the beloved man, actually reflects back at the woman a portrayal of her own feelings at a time when they are too painful to absorb."[2]

While the psychological interpretation of the two films detracts nothing from them, there still remains in each an interesting take on the question of the disembodied life as ontologically real. Put in Eastern terms, there is a karmic connection which requires the men in each case to fulfill some last obligation to the woman they love, and then fulfill their final obligation: to move on and allow their loved one to find new love. There are also questions of how a disembodied being can affect matter (in *Ghost*), a perennial question facing philosophers known as the body-mind problem and which has no better answers so far; and how disembodied beings relate with each other (in *Truly Madly Deeply*), which is answered by the amusing proposition that such ghostly friendships are cemented through watching old films on television.

But what if the spirits of the departed do not move on? Perhaps they have an obligation to fulfill, or perhaps the circumstances of their deaths and personalities are so confusing that they linger long past the decent interval. In *Heart and Souls* the spirits of four coach-crash victims hang around to fulfill ambitions or obligations, while in *The Sixth Sense* a child sees malevolent "dead people." *Heart and Souls* is largely comedy, but covers some interesting ground, including the phenomena of the childhood imaginary friend, multiple hauntings, and karmic or moral obligations of spirit entities in respect of their human lives. It even hints at reincarnation, though the conception of the afterlife follows more the pattern in films like *A Matter of Life and Death* and Beatty's *Heaven Can Wait* through the quirky character of the sometimes bungling angelic intermediaries whose job it is to guide the dead.

As a warm-hearted comedy *Heart and Souls* naturally lacks the element of fear and foreboding that so effectively pushes forward the story in *The Sixth Sense*, a film equally preoccupied with the unfinished business of the departed. This is perhaps the best of Shyamalan's offerings. His *Wide Awake*, *Unbreakable* and *Signs* all have his signature interests in the spiritual and the supernatural, but are less coherent. The central protagonists of *The Sixth Sense* are a prominent child psychologist Dr. Malcolm Crowe (Bruce Willis) and nine-year-old Cole, who becomes his patient. Cole has a model soldier who utters a Latin phrase that Dr. Crowe has to look up. He finds that it means: "Out of the depths I cry to you O Lord." Cole is troubled, and his mother is troubled; in the child's presence all the drawers and cabinets in the kitchen open themselves. She shrieks, recovers herself and asks, "Are you looking for something baby?" This might be *Poltergeist* territory, and indeed the actor Haley Joel Osment, who plays Cole, also plays the child robot in Spielberg's syrupy *AI: Artificial Intelligence*. But Shyamalan is a more subtle director: we glimpse the anxiety in Cole's mother obliquely as the sweat from her handprint evaporates off the kitchen table. Cole has gifts, rather like Jeremy in *Powder*, but he is much younger, and we are drawn into the gravity of his situation. As Dr. Crowe gains Cole's trust, he elicits from him a statement of what he *doesn't* want. "I don't want to be scared anymore," the boy tells him.

Shyamalan plays with us through the film because Dr. Crowe follows the standard pattern of conventional psychiatry in his attempts to diagnose the boy. It is highly effective because Crowe has to be convinced of the truth of the boy's fears. Cole finally confides to him: "I see dead people." The phrase is perhaps the lasting legacy of the film; it is often quoted and referenced, perhaps with irony as a way to flag up "here comes the supernatural again." Irony aside, Google tells us that there are over 182,000 results for the exact search "'I See Dead People' T-Shirt." You can even buy one for your dog. Cole elaborates: "They walk around like regular people. They only see what they want to see. They don't know they're dead." He sees them all the time, everywhere, and the burden of this shows in his face. But Crowe only understands this as hallucination, as the day-night terrors of a child suffering from school-age schizophrenia.

When Crowe accompanies him to school we see for the first time what Cole sees each day in a school with a history as a courthouse and site of the gibbet: the dead hanging from ropes. "When they get mad," he tells Crowe haltingly, "it gets cold." This is, of course, a standard horror device: the plunging thermostat on the radiators, the icy breath (in *The Exorcist* this need for cold-temperature acting caused multiple technical problems for the cast and crew). However, it is only after Crowe hears the voices of the dead on an old tape recording—almost drowned by static at the highest amplification—that he finally believes Cole. He then asks him,

"What do you think they want?" This is the crucial question. Cole pauses and then whispers: "Just help." But when Crowe puts it to him that he should help the dead by listening to them, Cole is not sure: "What if they don't want help? What if they're just angry and want to hurt somebody?"

The gamble is now on: Crowe can't be sure that listening to the ghosts will help them and allow them to move on, but Cole is the one who has to take it. His first "client" is a little girl. All that he confides in Crowe about her is: "She came a long way to visit me, didn't she?" But they are attending her funeral, and Cole is able to point out her sister, and ultimately the horrible injustice perpetrated against her. The "talking cure" works for the little girl, and also for Cole, who is now—implausibly quickly—ready to let go of his therapist and confide in his mother. "I see ghosts," he says. "They want me to do things for them." While his mother thinks this over, Cole has something else to impart: "Grandma says hi." He knows things that he could only have heard from his dead grandmother, and reduces his mother to tears—tears of confusion and sorrow, but also of recognition.

The twist in the end is one that some people see coming: that Crowe is himself one of Cole's "clients." He only becomes aware of this when he realizes that his wedding ring is no longer on his finger but held onto by his wife. His realization is triggered by this and the flashback to Cole saying, "I see people, they don't know they're dead." Crowe looks at the table in his wife's apartment, laid with a meal for one. "They only see what they want to see," intones Cole. Crowe now sees what he didn't want to see: that he too is dead. But as he absorbs the truth of it, he is able to say, "I think I can go now."

The Sixth Sense is one of only four supernatural/horror films that have been nominated for a Best Picture Academy Award, the others being *The Exorcist*, *Jaws* and *The Silence of the Lambs*. Its popularity is won by the over-simplification of its thesis and the shortcuts it takes, yet its moral strength and the value of its key insight is undeniable. In the world's esoteric literature we find the idea that the spirit of the departed may linger out of fear, confusion, or the simple human desire to see something finished. "Listening" to the ghost—acting as therapist—is an act of compassion that recognizes this fact, and which defuses the rage and hostility otherwise accompanying the desperate state of the ghost. This may well be the real basis of exorcism.

Blithe Spirit is one of several screenplays by Noel Coward that was directed by David Lean. It is a comedy in which an author, Charles Condomine—interested in debunking spiritualism—is haunted by his dead wife and then by his second wife, who is killed in a road accident. The first spirit is summoned up accidentally after a séance led by the local psychic Madame Arcati, who is later employed to rid Condomine of both of them. There is no intention to engage seriously with the issue of ghosts; the film is a sexual comedy of manners, and perhaps a comment on how men unconsciously fear women. What is interesting is the parading of Western assumptions of that period about ghosts, spiritualism and charlatanry. The belief in ghosts is also presented as a class issue: the educated middle-class characters are skeptical, except for the very English landmark of the eccentric Arcati (who properly inhabits that culturally acceptable category by being a caricature of the psychic), while the only working-class character in the film—the maid—turns out to be the person who summoned the spirits in the first place. Even so, there is one universal trait of the ghosts in this film that crosses all cultural boundaries: they can be mischievous.

The Others is also about a haunting set in roughly the same period as in *Blithe Spirit*, in a house representing a similar or higher social stratum. But the ghost film in the intervening fifty-odd years has evolved to allow for the well-crafted twist in *The Others*: that the ones experiencing the hauntings are actually the ghosts. Other than that, the account is psychologically more engaged than in *Blithe Spirit*: the ghosts linger for less trivial reasons, as they are the result of the mother's despair over her lost husband and subsequent smotherings of her children and her own suicide. Such a terrible family tragedy firstly binds the souls together—according to all conventional accounts—and also ties them to the place of the tragedy. The journey of discovery here is not for the living in the house but for the dead. Although there is no intervention as in *Sixth Sense* to help the dead move on, the realization by the family group that they are ghosts may be sufficient for them to attain a resolution. In other words, as in many of these films, *understanding* leads to exorcism.

Turning now to a very different film, Miyazaki's *Spirited Away*, we can hint at some radical cultural differences between East and West in respect to the ghost story. As in *The Others*, we are in a world of spirits into which intrudes the human, but the conception is otherwise very different. In this animated fantasy by Hayao Miyazaki, a little girl Chihiro and her parents accidentally wander into the spirit world, where the parents, overcome by greed for food, are turned into pigs, and the little girl has to struggle to survive and rescue them. Ghosts of the departed have to jostle with a myriad of spirit entities: those of water, forests, animals, and even radishes, all of which assemble each night to enjoy the luxuries of a bath-house run by an old witch. Particularly interesting is the River Spirit, originally assumed to be a "stink-spirit," who is tended by Chihiro. Her love and generosity of heart is crucial in her interactions with all the spirit entities, and makes a claim that the human being is potentially superior to spirit beings (it is an essential belief in Buddhism). She discovers what she thinks is a dart stuck in the side of the stink-spirit, and demands help in removing it. It turns out to be firstly the handlebars of a bicycle, which is followed by a complete scrap-heap of human trash, all of which have fouled up the body of the spirit. Once cleansed of this pollution the spirit is revealed as a River Spirit, who gratefully rewards the girl with a magic herb-cake. (This image of environmental damage restored has probably never been visualized in film so poignantly and so accessibly.) Another interesting spirit is No-Face, who appears to resemble what African traditions call the "hungry ghost." He latches onto Chihiro, in much the same way as the ghosts latch onto Cole in *The Sixth Sense*, and it is again her love and generosity that rescue him from his loneliness and confusion.

Angels

While disembodied beings are found in the lore of most cultures, we have pointed out that there are considerable differences in the way that they are portrayed in Eastern and Western traditions. The *angel* is a more Western category of spirit being, one who works solely for good, and in whom no evil is found. All evil is abstracted in Western thought into the entity known as the "demon." This absolutism of category is not much found in the East, and in *Spirited Away* and other Miyazaki films, for example, it is notable that none of the spirit entities are ever entirely good or entirely evil. Hence "demons" in the East may actually be helpful, though one can never be sure.

What is interesting about so many Western angel films in the secular era however is that very often there is a subtle inversion of the Christian tradition. Instead of seeing the category of angel as something elevated, as a higher moral achievement, we find what amounts to a reproach: they should get down here and experience bodily life. Alternatively, they goof up in their messenger role, and cause havoc for those who should not have died, or who should have died but land up in the wrong place.

First, we look at a few films where angels have conventional roles, even though these are still considerable deviations from Christian conceptions. In Frank Capra's film classic *It's a Wonderful Life*, an "Angel Second Class," Clarence Odbody, is assigned to George Bailey to dissuade him from suicide. Where the idea of first-and second-class angels (and the idea that they have to earn their wings) derives from is not clear, but already the film represents some departure from angels as conceived biblically. Clarence is presented as not-too-bright but sincere, and in saving Bailey he succeeds in his bid for promotion. His role here is to intervene in the lives of the living, which makes him a guardian angel. In *What Dreams May Come* it is the job of the angel Albert (played by black actor Cuba Gooding, Jr.) to guide the recently deceased Chris through the afterlife. His status as angel is not made clear however, as he has no wings or other usual trappings, so he could also be interpreted as a spirit guide, a category generally found outside of Christianity. In *Northfork* the angels are part of a highly allegorical fantasy in which the Native American peoples can be understood as angels-by-metaphor, as we saw.

It is, surprisingly, in *Jacob's Ladder* that we find an angel who best fits the conventional Christian notion of superior capacities and perfect morality, despite lacking wings or any other of the usual trappings. It is a surprise because of the gritty nature of it as a Vietnam trauma film, yet the chiropractor Louis, Jacob's healer and mentor, turns out to be his guide to dying and the afterlife. Louis could be the "good doctor" who as a mortal has the status of benign and ever-caring confidante and protector and is unambiguously good, but turns out here to be the benign supernatural agent, the firm guide in the chaos of death. His most incisive offering to Jacob is this: "So, if you're frightened of dying and ... and you're holding on, you'll see devils tearing your life away. But if you've made your peace, then the devils are really angels, freeing you from the earth."

In *Meet Joe Black* the "angel" is the devil, or the Grim Reaper, but we postpone consideration of his case because he rather fancies a bit of life himself. In *Illusion*, as we saw earlier, the messenger of death, the angel, is a dead friend who was the director's editor. Fittingly, he edits the life-story for replay just before the end, and is generally cast as compassionate and competent.

Angels are only human, or that it seems is the message of a slew of films where the comic potential of angelic screw-ups is exploited. In *A Matter of Life and Death* a bomber pilot killed in his plane crash should have been collected by an angel known as Conductor 71, but they miss each other in thick fog. While he wanders around not properly dead he falls in love, and protests when Conductor 71 comes for him shortly after. The matter is taken to a heavenly tribunal where human romantic love is pitched on a moral scale against cosmic bureaucracy—and wins. In *Heaven Can Wait* (the Warren Beatty version) the opposite occurs: the angel responsible for Joe Pendleton is over-zealous and takes his soul after a car crash which he should have survived. When Joe's body is cremated the mix-up is exposed and he demands another body so that he can fulfill his proper life-ambition. In both of these films the human soul, far from being overawed by the process of death, acts as a consumer whose rights have been violated and demands recompense for a faulty product. "Thy will be done" is an injunction of profound religious significance long-forgotten in this tradition of filmmaking.

In *Heart and Souls*, the angel responsible for the group of people killed in a coach crash just plain forgets to tell them what is going on, while in *A Life Less Ordinary* the two angels assigned to sort out the mess of a misfiring kidnap situation are on probation for having failed in a series of earlier tasks.

The issue of angels on film gets interesting when the very basis of their existence comes under attack from a thoughtful materialism in the idea that to be disembodied is not just to miss out on earthly pleasures, but that it is almost a dereliction of duty, the duty to *experience* life. Hence the criticism of angels is also the criticism of embodied humans who somehow seek sublimation of their desires in merely intellectual pursuits, or an indictment, such as Nietzsche's and Marx's, of the pursuit of the afterlife as a compensation for failure in this one. Nietzsche was famously scathing of what he called the "afterworldsmen." Part of Nietzsche's scorn for Socrates was for his "beautiful" death, regarding the old man's equanimity as a betrayal of the love of life.[3] Hence in a range of interesting films we see angels regret their floating existence despite its many apparent advantages. For example, in *The Last Temptation of Christ* an angel tells Jesus: "Maybe you'll find this hard to believe but sometimes we angels look down on men and envy you." This is consistent with the materialist message of the film, and is delivered by an angel—in the form of a child—whose job it is to show Jesus how beautiful the manifest world is.

It is perhaps Wim Wenders's *Wings of Desire* which most poignantly explores the "what-if" of an angel finally choosing embodiment over the disembodied life. Two angels, Damiel and Cassiel, have always existed in Berlin, even before it was a city, and before there were any humans. Their role is recast from the traditional ones of guidance and protection to that of "assembling, testifying, and preserving" reality, which they do by comparing notebooks in which they record the little acts of imagination, generosity, and spontaneous enjoyment of the small things of life. Significantly—as an emblem of a German culture less anti-intellectual than the English-speaking world—they hang around the city library, connoisseurs of those moments in the intellectual life of its readers where insight is born. What they can't do is intervene; they are strictly observers.

One element of the traditional angel role remains in the film: that of a benign or sacred presence, one often only perceived by children or the devout. As Damiel and Cassiel pursue their vocation around the city, a child may smile in recognition, or an adult—unable to perceive them directly—may sense something of the beyond. The angels however know every thought of those they observe. The film opens with various such scenes, and then a recapitulation in a BMW car showroom to each other of the day's "research." They record everything, including the precise times of dusk and dawn, and the levels of various rivers. Already, there is a sense of the sacred in the fact that nothing is lost to eternity, that each act of each anonymous person in the crammed city has significance—as in the Akashic Record posited in *Illusion*. The angels particularly like the quirky, the thoughtful, the unique; moments where a person ceases to act as an automaton and allows a spontaneous act to erupt from an unknown—and therefore sacred—source.

"Just before dashing his head against the wall, a prisoner said: 'Now.'"
"Instead of the underground station's name, the guard suddenly shouted 'Tierra del Fuego.'"

"A passer-by who, in the rain, folded her umbrella and was drenched."
"A blind woman, who groping for her watch, felt my presence."

As one angel reads out from his notes, the other nods in appreciation. "Nice." But Damiel is beginning to have doubts:

> It's great to live by the spirit, to testify for eternity only what is spiritual in people's minds. But sometimes I'm fed up with my spiritual existence, of forever hovering above. I'd like to feel a weight in me, to end the infinity and tie me to earth. I'd like at each step, at each gust of wind to be able to say: "Now, now, and now." No longer: "Forever" and "For eternity." ... To be excited not only by the mind but by a meal.

It helps in understanding this film to know that "spiritual" in German is "geistige," a term which has a broader connotation than the English equivalent: it encompasses more broadly the life of the mind, and aligns itself better to the Neoplatonist sensibility than to the world-denying Catholic piety of pre–Thomist Christianity. In a sense Damiel is completing the trajectory of the West since Aquinas, which is a retreat from the fiercely renunciative piety of early Christianity, and towards a world-curious and celebratory spirituality. For some this is understood only as a regression to paganism, and in the German context this move is tainted perhaps with the legacy of National Socialism. But Damiel's articulation of his yearning to experience the life of the body is better understood as a sacred impulse that appears in many religious contexts, for example in Blake, in Thomas Traherne's extraordinary seventeenth-century prose and poetry, in the *Upanishads*, in Taoism, and in all the traditions one can broadly call shamanic, animistic, and polytheistic.

Damiel does the obvious next thing: he falls in love. Wim Wenders then does something absolutely the opposite of obvious—he brings the delightful Peter Falk as himself, the actor famous for his Columbo role, in rehearsal for a historical documentary. Wenders' stroke of genius is to reveal that Falk is a one-time angel himself, who converses with Damiel and advises him to take the same course. It is a one-way journey, involving the selling of his "armour" and the acquiring of all the frailties of the human body along with its pleasures. The world is now in color; Damiel can bleed; he can take in a live performance from the British pop band Nick Cave and the Bad Seeds; and he can now meet his love, a circus trapeze artist who feels she has always been waiting for him. She speaks at length to him, finishing with: "There is no greater story than ours, that of man and woman. It will be a story of giants. Invisible. Transposable."

At one level *Wings of Desire* sets out the same stall as *The Last Temptation of Christ*. It turns on its head the conventional story of religion, raising as the ultimate value what is a deeply secular discovery: the sexual. But *Wings of Desire* is subtle where *Last Temptation* is crass. *Wings* suggests that in fact the celebration of life which is modern sexuality is not a new discovery which negates an exhausted and compromised conception of religion, but a particular re-affirmation of the sacred which was lost to the Christian world. Sadly, *Faraway, So Close!*, the sequel to *Wings of Desire*, falls far short of the original, despite cameos from Lou Reed, Mikhail Gorbachev and, again, Peter Falk. Its descent into a counterculture action movie is a great disappointment after the first film, and can only be put down to a different writing team.

Wings of Desire is a typical product of German culture. So what happens when the film crosses the Atlantic and is reworked for an American audience by director Brad Silberling in *City of Angels*? Berlin is replaced by Los Angeles, and Damiel is replaced by Seth, a Biblical name more familiar to Americans. Nicolas Cage was chosen to play Seth, his personality suggesting perhaps a more engaged compassion, though one element is largely removed from the

German original: its celebration of the intellect. After escorting the soul of a dead child to the afterlife, Seth compares notes with Cassiel, as in *Wings of Desire*. He asks Cassiel, "Do you ever wonder what that would be like? Touch?" Cassiel denies it, but Seth doesn't believe him. "Touch" then becomes the symbol of what is lacking in Seth's life as a disembodied being. In an echo of Angel Second Class Clarence Odbody, Seth tells Cassiel, "The little girl asked me if she could be an angel." "They all want wings," says Cassiel. "I never know what to say." "Tell them the truth. Angels aren't human. We were never human." But the little girl understood anyway, as Seth reports: "She said, 'What good would wings be if you couldn't feel the wind on your face?'"

Seth then stands in front of Dr. Maggie Rice, who is mourning the loss of a patient on the operating table. Dry-eyed, Seth stares with longing at her tears. He is pondering the possibility that Maggie has seen him in the operating room, something normally only given to the dying or delirious. Like Damiel, his journey to corporeality starts here, but the emotional intensity is ramped up in *City of Angels* as his passion for Maggie is only fulfilled for a day. He falls to earth, not to commence a "story of giants" but to be bereaved within twenty-four hours. As she lies dying, she can see the angel come to collect her, but he cannot. But he can communicate later with his former angel partner Cassiel, who asks him: "If you'd known this was going to happen, would you have done it?" Through his tears Seth tells him: "I would rather have had one breath of her hair, one kiss of her mouth, one touch of her hand, than an eternity without it. One."

It is interesting to compare *City of Angels* with *Shadowlands*. The real-life C. S. Lewis and the fictional Seth have in common that in some way both "fell to earth" in falling in love with a woman, and both were quickly bereaved. Both are angry with God, but in an odd way Seth is free of the theological baggage that made C. S. Lewis's pain more agonized and protracted, despite the fact that Seth is an angel. Of course, Seth's story is only fiction: Lewis in contrast was a flesh-and-blood man.

The angels in *Dogma* are this time fallen angels, who do not elect to stay on earth, but for whom their stay—in Wisconsin—is a punishment. The film is a comedy that is deeply engaged with religious issues, mostly specific to Catholicism, but is so crass and scatological as to mostly lose its usefulness. Although the fallen angels do not much relish the embodied life, another angel called the Metatron (Alan Rickman), is irritated that he has no genitals and cannot imbibe his favorite drink, tequila. In *Michael* John Travolta plays an angel who is effectively a slob, but is on his last permitted visit to earth, and who will greatly miss its delights, including wrestling with bulls, and eating sugar. "I'm doomed to live in one place and crave the pleasures of another," he says. For the angel in *Meet Joe Black* it is not sugar that appeals, but peanut butter. The angel here is the angel of death, come to escort Bill Parrish to the afterlife, but who takes on the body of another near-deceased in order to learn the delights of earthly life. It is up to Bill (Anthony Hopkins) to guide Death (Brad Pitt) in the niceties of life.

One theme dominates all of these angel films: that the embodied life is superior to the disembodied life. So are we to understand this as a kind of secular revenge on religion? A steady drip-drip of counter-propaganda? Merely the playing out in popular culture of Nietzsche's insight from a hundred years ago? Perhaps, yet there is more going on in these films than atheist skepticism: by all means it is a celebration of incarnation, but, in many and varied ways, the love of life portrayed in these films is framed as something *sacred*.

Summary

In the first instance the films examined in this chapter show great interest in the persistence of self beyond death, firstly from the point of view of the self that does not want life to end just yet, and secondly from the point of view of the bereaved. It is also obvious that the standard Western idea of heaven and hell is not that dramatically interesting for filmmakers—instead, all kinds of alternatives have been invented as plot devices. But the simple yearning for the departed loved one also gives rise to straightforward hauntings, as in *Ghost* and *Truly Madly Deeply*. The departed may have unfinished business as in *Heart and Souls*, or may be so frightened and confused as to lash out in anger at the living, as in *The Sixth Sense*. Alternatively, moving from ghosts to spirits—and who can say exactly what we mean by that difference—we find a truly luminous menagerie of them in *Spirited Away*.

Angels also receive a non-standard treatment in film. They are sometimes portrayed along traditional lines as capable messengers of the afterlife, but more often than not they mess things up. Most interesting are the films which effectively castigate angels for their detachment—films in which the joys of the body are argued as preferable to heavenly bliss, even when the body will inevitably suffer physical and emotional loss. *Wings of Desire* stands out as such a film: it is both a secularist hymn to the physical life and a remarkable meditation on what angels might actually do. The moments where Damiel and Cassiel compare notes on the moments of grace in the lives of the embodied are truly luminous. Perhaps other luminous inventions of the cinematic imagination here are the angels in *Northfork*, the chiropractor in *Jacob's Ladder* and the transformation of little Cole in *The Sixth Sense* as he realizes that the departed need love as much as the living.

The dead are known as "the departed," and this is taken merely as a euphemism in secular society. But what if the "departed" might somehow return, not as ghosts, but as physical persons?

5
Reincarnation and Resurrection

The idea of the afterlife implies a persistence of selfhood beyond the death of the body in some kind of discarnate form. But what about the long term? Is there a physical body to be had again in which our selfhood, our unique personality, can continue to express itself in the material world? Resurrection of the body and reincarnation are two possibilities for the self to persist in physical form, and each has very different implications for the lived spiritual life. If true, that is.

In *The Wicker Man* a Calvinist Scottish policeman called Neil Howie is sent to investigate a disappearance on a Hebridean island, which, he is horrified to discover, has reverted to "paganism." The local schoolteacher, Miss Rose, is trying to explain to him what has happened to the missing girl:

> ROSE: We believe that when human life is over it returns to trees, to air, to fire, to water, to animals. So Rowan Morrison has simply returned to the life forces in another form.
> HOWIE: They never learn anything of Christianity?
> ROSE: Only as a comparative religion. The children find it far easier to picture reincarnation than resurrection.

It *is* easier to picture reincarnation than resurrection, at least in the rural setting of the film, because of the cycles of Nature. And it turns out that there are far more films about reincarnation than about resurrection: in all more than thirty films are referenced here in which reincarnation plays either a major or minor role. But a Christian believes in the Resurrection rather than in reincarnation as an article of faith, and clearly these are incompatible doctrines. The Resurrection—to give it capital letters—is a one-off event that Christians believe to have been undergone by Jesus. To a lesser degree Christians believe in personal resurrection, depending on what weight they attach to the Revelation of John, and to a lesser degree they adapt their lives to doctrines found there, for example around the idea of the "Rapture." The film of this name, and related films, will be examined at the end of this chapter.

First, we look at the issue of reincarnation in film. In the radically challenging position where a father is told that his child is the reincarnation of a previously living person, the natural secular response is to reject the idea. This is what takes place in the films *Audrey Rose* and *The Little Buddha*. In the first of these films, the father of the little girl, told by a stranger that she was formerly the stranger's daughter, responds angrily with the secular assumption, almost a shibboleth: "When I die, it's going to be the end of me."

But is it? The East largely thinks otherwise—the Buddha for example gave clear accounts of his previous lives in the Pali Canon[1]—and so did the West in the past: Pythagoras and Plato were convinced of reincarnation, Pythagoras going so far as to state who he had been in an earlier life.[2] In the nineteenth century Papus, the founder of the Martinist Order, wrote an extensive treatise on reincarnation, carefully distinguishing it from metempsychosis which he defines as the retrograde movement of the soul across the animal-human boundary.[3] Likewise, Rudolf Steiner wrote extensively on reincarnation, making it an essential tenet of Anthroposophy.[4] In the early twenty-first century Roger Woolger has turned reincarnation workshops into a therapy and has written widely on it; his *Other Lives, Other Selves*[5] is recognized as a seminal and definitive work in the field. The Past Life Therapists Association of England lists at least a hundred "accredited" practitioners. Many well-known individuals in the West have claimed to know their past lives, for example the popular entertainer Liberace believed he was the reincarnation of the composer Liszt; General George Patton the reincarnation of many Roman warriors; and Salvador Dali said that he vividly remembered his previous existence as St. John of the Cross.[6] Of course, any one of these individuals might have reasons of their public constructed persona to make such a claim.

Reincarnation disappeared as a mainstream belief in the West since the Fifth Ecumenical Council of 553 CE—or rather went underground into Neoplatonist and other esoteric traditions—after Emperor Justinian issued an anathema on the subject.[7] After the Christian faith took hold of the West the notion of resurrection replaced reincarnation. Schopenhauer thought the issue most clearly divided East from West, and is cited in the novel *The Reincarnation of Peter Proud*:

> Were an Asiatic to ask me for a definition of Europe, I should be forced to answer him: it is that part of the world haunted by the incredible delusion that man was created out of nothing, and that his present birth is his first entrance to life.[8]

Peter Proud's girlfriend puts it bluntly in the film version: "Take it from me: when you're dead you're dead."[9] However, within Eastern traditions where reincarnation is a central doctrine there is widespread agreement on its basic features, which are that the soul leaves the body at its physical death, may spend a short or long period in a discarnate state, and then returns to a new body, at some point between conception and birth. Furthermore, the moral structure of the previous life intimately shapes the circumstances of the new life. This aspect of reincarnation is usually referred to as "karma" and points to another fundamental difference between these systems and monotheism: in the workings of karma there is no deity whose job it is to make judgments. The Eastern concept is bafflingly impersonal to a Westerner. Recall the complaint of Susan L. Schwartz about the East: "Death has its own system that works independently of divine intervention, just as does life." This is a very difficult idea for those brought up with the idea of a personal God that intervenes in life and makes judgments at death.

Shrink-wrapped Reincarnation

The Reincarnation of Peter Proud is based on the novel by Max Ehrlich. At times the book reads a little like the quintessentially New Age novel *The Celestine Prophecy*, in that the protagonist is a self-absorbed seeker of his own truth who finds signs everywhere of his own importance. But *Peter Proud* as a novel and film is more focused and morally complex. The protagonist is determined to discover the source of dream and semi-waking material that emerges from his unconscious, which is probably not like ordinary dreams or fantasy (this is tested in a sleep lab). He is challenged not only in his sense of physical and emotional identity, but in his sense of moral identity. When the flashbacks and memories become clear enough for him to consider that they derive from a previous incarnation, his first anxiety is: was he formerly an evil man?

The film cuts down the novel's longer development that explores just about every objection to reincarnation that the Western mind has come up with, and to some extent misses the dramatic potential of the slow realization that builds up in Proud's mind. In narrative terms this is an important issue; if an outlandish scenario is delivered suddenly to an audience then it is easier to dismiss it than if one is slowly prepared for the enormity of it. A protagonist who slowly and painfully, piece by piece, has to accept the new reality is one we much better identify with. At each turn we recognize the objections and evasions that we would also make. Hence, while Spielberg may often be a clumsy exploiter of human emotion, and his films often examples of cultural autism, his instinct for drama in *Close Encounters of the Third Kind* actually paints rather well a picture of a person obsessively attempting to decipher powerful but initially meaningless mental images.

Peter Proud as a film also suffers from some poor editing, but despite this conveys much of what one would encounter if one participated in past life regression workshops, or read the voluminous literature on the subject. Early on it references the work of the American "radio prophet" Edgar Cacey, who gave past life readings while in a self-induced hypnotic trance.[10] In the book, Proud pays for a reading by a clairvoyant who is a follower of Cacey. What is really oppressing him is the vivid memory of being murdered by his wife of the time, an image that grows in clarity rather like the mashed-potato and shaving-cream mountain in *Close Encounters*. When Proud finally tracks down the woman, Marcia, who is now about twenty-five years older than he is, there is not so much moral outrage, but moral anxiety: what had he done to provoke such a desperate act? The real twist to the story however is the mutual and powerful attraction between him and Marcia's daughter, who was only three months old at the time of his death. The attraction is something neither can resist in the end, but to what degree is it incest? And does it warrant Marcia killing him all over again?

An interesting subplot to the story involves a professor of paranormal studies who sets Proud up to be the "living proof" of reincarnation, a prophet. While Proud himself—more in the novel than in the film—also ruminates on the enormous impact that reincarnation is having upon himself, and therefore would on others, he doesn't want to be a prophet. Anyhow, "prophet" is the last thing that the freaked-out Marcia calls Proud, as she faces the ghastly fact that the husband she killed has returned from the dead, and has seduced their daughter. "You're some kind of monster!" she screams at him.

In *Chances Are*, Corinne Jeffries's marriage is shattered by the death of her husband in a car crash. We know from their wedding day that the husband's best friend Philip also loves Corinne, and it falls to Philip to support her over the next twenty-three years in bringing up her daughter Miranda. Corinne's therapist is concerned that she is not moving on and finding a new partner, but despite Philip's devotion she never sees him as anything more than a family friend. Into this scene steps twenty-three-year-old Alex, who has uncanny knowledge of Corinne's life and home. What this film shares with *Peter Proud* is the return of a man in his new life to the wife and daughter left behind, and the anxieties about an "incestuous'" relationship. Otherwise it is played quite differently, as a romantic comedy of errors which comes out good. However, it also has a serious side, because it is a meditation on the need to forget, and on the inauthenticity of a relationship based on privileged knowledge. In *Groundhog Day* the male protagonist attempts to woo the female protagonist through knowledge gained by his effective daily time-travel (as we shall see later on); in *Chances Are* Alex woos Corinne by knowledge that comes to him from his past life. In the end, the question of *identity* that is at the heart of the reincarnation issue is resolved: Alex is *not* her former husband, he is a much younger and quite unsuitable lover for her.

The question of forgetting is dramatized with humor and insight in this film. When the former husband Louie dies he enters a between-station visualized as a featureless white space with rolling ground-level fog, filled with the newly departed queuing to be "processed," as in so many films of the afterlife. He is so freaked out at his death, and so determined to be reunited with Corinne, that officials take him to the reincarnation booth, where he protests at this too, but gives in and chooses "boy" to be reborn as. In the general confusion and haste the angel Omar forgets to administer—via an alarmingly large syringe filled with an amber liquid—the vital "forgetting" serum. Hence, on encountering Corinne twenty-three years later, all his past-life memories return. In some ancient Greek traditions it was held that the souls of the dead drank from the river Lethe before being reincarnated, in order to forget their past. Clearly, for the skeptics, this is always the first objection to reincarnation: Why don't I remember? Whatever one's views on the issue, Lethe is visualized as an amber liquid in this film, and makes a return when Alex lies in hospital after a fall. Omar gets the chance to sneak in and administer the overdue inoculation, resulting in Alex quite forgetting about his love for Corinne, and making himself available to her daughter instead.

This is a well-made film that uses gentle comedy to ostensibly explore the theme of reincarnation, though its real subject matter is firstly how the bereaved cling on to the hope of being reunited with their loved one and secondly how privileged knowledge of the love object—however flattering—is an inauthentic basis for a relationship. In the end, through the filmic device of reincarnation which shows Corinne the futility of her hopes, she is liberated to marry the faithful Philip.

Switch is not strictly a reincarnation movie because its protagonist Steve does not die to be reborn in the normal sequence as a baby, but re-appears suddenly as a grown-up woman, Amanda. Also his dead body is still around which results in Amanda being framed for his murder, all of which is decidedly unconventional, if not to say logically inconsistent. But in the film the process is continuously referred to as reincarnation, and the ethical sub-context is familiar: Amanda is privy to facts that only Steve could have known. Amanda *is* Steve, which raises again the core existential problem of reincarnation: what does it mean to be somebody else? However this is a black sexual comedy where the "reincarnation" element is merely the ploy for the exercise of pop gender psychology. Steve is an unabashed male chauvinist pig, so irritating in fact that three of his girlfriends conspire to murder him, first by drowning, and then, as this does not suffice, by shooting. He arrives naked and dripping into Purgatory, and becomes the subject of male and female divine voices contemplating his fate. Yes, he wasn't really a bad chap, so why not heaven, says the male voice; hold on, what about his unrepentant womanizing says the female voice. In the end, they agree to send him back on a kind of wager: if Steve can find just one woman who truly likes him, he will go to heaven. The devil gets involved in the discussion however and points out that Steve will simply turn his charm onto an impressionable female and win the bet too easily. Why not make him a woman?

And so the story develops as Steve-Amanda has to learn to walk in high heels, cope with a man's world generally and come to terms with being date-raped by his/her best friend, while seeking a woman who might genuinely like him/her. It's not reincarnation as we know it, but the idea of a moral development brought on by awareness of a selfish previous existence is pertinent. To start with, Amanda is little better than Steve in her new body, but the moral epiphany—when it finally comes—is moving: while incarcerated in a psychiatric prison she gives birth to a little girl who becomes the first female to love her.

And why should she be confined as a madwoman? Because her defense in the murder trial was based on the idea of reincarnation, allowing for the film to present to us the arguments in its favor, including the testimony of an Indian swami. Of course, the jury is unpersuaded.

East-West Borrowings

Surprisingly perhaps, the American film *Witness* was remade as an Indian film *Paap*—which has reincarnation elements that *Witness* does not—and will be considered shortly. Such borrowings are common to Indian cinema, but it is all the more intriguing when it is a Western reincarnation film adapted for the Indian context. There are at least two more examples: *The Reincarnation of Peter Proud* was remade as *Karz* and *Switch* was remade as *Mr. Ya Miss*. In fact the storyline of *The Reincarnation of Peter Proud* extends beyond *Karz* into the Kannada film *Yuga Purusha*, the Tamil film *Enakkul Oruvan*, and the Bollywood film *Karzzzz*. And, although Farah Khan the director of *Om Shanti Om* insists that it is not another remake of *Karz*, there are some common story elements.

In the great Indian text the *Bhagavad Gita*, Arjuna has reincarnation as his cultural heritage, but is dubious of it as it applies to him. So how do Indians make reincarnation films? The transposition of *The Reincarnation of Peter Proud* into the Indian *Karz* some five years later involves a drastic shift of culture and many changed details, such as murder by being run over with a jeep, rather than drowning. But the psychic truths remain the same, principally the emergence into the conscious mind of a coherent and emotionally significant scenario that appears to have nothing to do with this life. It's the mountain in *Close Encounters* again. The protagonist of *Karz* is a pop singer, Monty Oberoi, whose wife in his previous life had killed him in order to inherit his estate. In this life Monty's trajectory so far has been the conventional stuff of Bollywood, but one of his best hits has an unfortunate effect on him when he plays it on his guitar: it triggers hallucinations, nightmares, and eventually a stage collapse. Babbling to his doctor about flashback images of a jeep and murder solicits only skepticism: "You might have seen such an incident in a film? Book? Novel?" He denies it, but modern Indian medicine has no time for reincarnation it seems: the doctor recommends a holiday. He needs a break, and of course he "accidentally" picks the Verma estate, the surroundings of which are spookily familiar, including the Kali statue on the rural roadside which had been the sole witness to his murder last time round. Is it déjà vu? Is anything in life an accident? These are the questions that reincarnation raises, though other less popular theories also exist, such as Nietzsche's revival of the Greek idea of eternal recurrence. Otherwise the film is about on par with its America original, neither of which have space within their narratives to do the original novel justice.

Mr. Ya Miss as a remake of *Switch* is again interesting in terms of East-West comparisons. Where *Switch* is a rather dark comedy of errors its denouement is intended as a serious resolution to the central dilemma of the film. On the other hand its Indian re-working, while reasonably faithful to the original, bar the ending, is mostly played as slapstick. It is simply aimed at a less sophisticated audience. Political correctness for a popular audience in India in 2005, it seems, is not quite the fixture that it is in the West. The *poignancy* of the story of just deserts survives well however.

Mahal and *Madhumati* are examples of where reincarnation serves mostly as a context for romantic love. In *Mahal* a young lawyer, Shankar, comes into the ownership of a mansion that is spookily familiar to him. Prior to this we see its former owner promise to his lover Kamini, who has drowned in the nearby river, that "I will come back again." So he does, but love has to be postponed again. In *Madhumati* an engineer, Devendra, whose car breaks down in a storm, is given shelter in a mansion that is spookily familiar to him. As he wanders through the house in the night, disturbed by what he thinks is a woman's scream, he discovers a portrait, every brush-stroke of which he seems to know. Anand then encounters a beautiful young woman, Madhumati. Her father comes from a line of kings, and each side is forbidden to see the other, but Anand meets her and falls in love. After her first encounter with the king, in which she has to run and hide, she takes Anand to a burial ground. She finds peace there though she does not believe that she is alone; the dead speak to her, she insists. He is doubtful. "Really sir," she says. "Nothing dies in this world."

Some Older Cultures

The films *The Cave of the Yellow Dog*, *Atanarjuat: The Fast Runner* and *The Secret of Roan Inish* all contain passing references to reincarnation which support the general contention that older societies, particularly hunter-gatherer cultures, believed in it. The herdsmen culture of Mongolia is partly shamanic and partly Buddhist, a syncretism that is widespread in the Far East, and to which the belief in reincarnation is central.

The film *The Cave of the Yellow Dog* suggests that children are more likely to have spontaneous past life recall than adults, and makes a very Buddhist idea vividly clear: that it is most fortunate to be born in the body of a human being. Nansal the young daughter of the herdsmen family asks her mother: "Mum, do you remember your previous lives?" Her mother responds: "I don't think so." "Why not?" "Only little children can do that. They tell colorful stories. People say they are talking about previous lives." The discussion then revolves about a yellow dog and whether it would be reborn as a person with a ponytail. This raises a question in the girl's mind which she then puts to her grandmother: "Will I be reborn as a person in my next life?" Rather than answer her directly, her grandmother places a needle in the upright position and proceeds to pour grains of rice over it. "Tell me when a grain of rice balances on the tip of the needle." "That's impossible!" exclaims the girl. "See my child? That's how hard it is to be born again as a person. That's why a human life is so valuable."

These and other passing references to reincarnation give the Western-educated person a glimpse into a world where it is taken for granted. Unlike Peter Proud and his professor of parapsychology, there is no sense that this doctrine is either revolutionary or to be anathematized; it is an idea intimately linked with the precarious life-and-death experiences of nomadic peoples whose livelihood involves the rearing and killing of animals, and which depends intimately on the vagaries of seasons and animal fertility. The director, Byambasuren Davaa, is herself of Mongolian herdsman tradition, but educated in Germany in film studies. She comments incisively on her experiences in the West and key East-West differences, saying: "death is omnipresent ... and I am not afraid of dying."[11]

Atanarjuat: The Fast Runner is an Inuit film in which there is a brief mention of reincarnation. Atuat, a young woman who is the object of love-rivalry, is rather bizarrely called "little mother" by her own mother, Panikpak. The old woman talks to her daughter about the past, concluding, "when I was a child in your arms." Atuat then asks, "When I was your mother was my namesake very beautiful? Did you love me very much?" To this her mother replies, "Yes. That's why I named you Atuat! I recognized you straight away." Atuat was the name of Panikpak's mother, now reborn as her daughter. The anthropologist and filmmaker Hugh Brody has this to say about reincarnation in the Inuit part of the world:

> I have never been able to believe in reincarnation. Many peoples do, of course, including the hunters of the Subarctic. Parents and grandparents look at every detail of a newborn to see who has returned: there will be a birthmark, some sign to tell them which loved one they are welcoming back. My difficulty with literal belief is not matched, however, by any doubts as to the *importance* of reincarnation.[12]

In *The Secret of Roan Inish*, set in rural Ireland, a young girl Fiona learns about her brother Jamie who was swept out to sea as a baby (and who makes some magical reappearances during the film). Her grandmother tells her, "I always remember his eyes. Dark they were. With a great soul behind them. Oh, he was here before." Although the film is set in recent modern times, the implication of much of the story is that the events are part of an unbroken tradition receding into a past that we might well call shamanic, as the shapeshifting *selkies*, or seal-humans, point to.

The Tulku System

Wherever Buddhism is absorbed into or by older shamanic traditions, the understanding of reincarnation and practices around it may diverge from the Buddha's original teachings (as far as we can ascertain them from the Pali Canon). One interesting variation is the "tulku" system of Tibetan Buddhism, where a lama or spiritual teacher once reborn is actively sought for as a baby, and then brought up as the reincarnated teacher. This is a variation because originally an enlightened person is unique in *not* being reborn. The Dalai Lama is the most famous example, and his story is told in a number of documentary films and also in the feature films *Seven Years in Tibet* and *Kundun*. These are two important films for the spiritual life, not least because the Dalai Lama has a world presence as a spiritual teacher.

Kundun opens with the search for the boy reincarnation of the thirteenth Dalai Lama, a succession that supposedly goes all the way back to 1391. Traditionally a shaman or clairvoyant—referred to rather oddly in the film as an "oracle"—would be employed to "see" where the soul of the departed lama had been reincarnated, and a delegation would be sent to the family. This is regarded as a mark of honor despite the possible trauma to the family of having a child removed, effectively for adoption. The issue of the trauma to the child him-self—now given the name "Kundun"—is not skirted by the film when later, in his new surroundings, he confides to his mentor how lonely he is. The case of the celebrated Tibetan teacher Chögyam Trungpa is revealing of how a young tulku might resent his circumstances. In his autobiographical work *Cutting Through Spiritual Materialism*, Trungpa shows however that his Buddhist training helped him overcome such negative thoughts and harness his anger to constructive ends.[13] His teachings have an edge over many of his contemporaries who appear to add little to the tradition they were taught, where Trungpa's voice has the unique color and authority of intense personal experience. Unfortunately Trungpa's colorful life was cut short by heavy drinking and other excesses, often a feature of Tibetan teachers transplanted into the American New Age-hippie context.

In *Seven Years in Tibet*, the story of the Dalai Lama only begins with his meeting with Heinrich Harrer, so we do not have an account of his early life. Reincarnation is mentioned however in a scene when Harrer is about to build the young Master a cinema, and work stops because of the worms that might be killed in digging the foundations. The Dalai Lama explains to Harrer: "We Tibetans believe that all living creatures may have been our mother in a past life ... so we never harm a living being." It is in *Little Buddha*, however, that the tulku system is brought alive into the Western context. The film interleaves a mythologized account of the Buddha's life with the search for a reincarnated lama in America. This plot device allows, as in *Peter Proud*, for the question of reincarnation to be contemplated by characters that a Western audience can identify with, and raises again the issue that the young tulku will be removed from his parents.

If reincarnation is true, and if the phenomenon of the Tibetan diaspora now means that souls are likely to be more widely dispersed than in the past, then why shouldn't a lama be reincarnated in America? Steven Seagal, the American film star, has been recognized by Tibetan lama Penor Rinpoche as a reincarnated tulku, Chungdrag Dorje. Of course, what drives *Little Buddha* is partly the fact that a typical American family lacks the cultural familiarity with the tulku system. Their initial rejection of the whole idea is only tempered by their fascination with the deeply engaging Lama Norbu (played by a real Tibetan Buddhist, Ruocheng Yi), and the tantalizing possibility that their young son Jesse really does have such an exotic past and possible future. In the end there are three potential candidates for the Lamaship. A shaman is required to pronounce on the matter, who comes to the startling conclusion that it is all three. Jesse asks: "But how can we all be Lama Dorje?" The answer apparently is that there are separate manifestations of the body, speech and mind respectively of the deceased lama. There is little in the literature of reincarnation, East or West, that supports such an idea, but as poetic license it made for a good end to the film. It is more democratic, after all.

Paap is the odd one out here, because, although the tulku system appears in the film, reincarnation is dealt with skeptically, as is in fact traditional religion as a whole. *Paap* transposes Peter Weir's *Witness* into a modern-day Indian setting, retelling the story almost scene by scene. In *Witness*, a mother and her little boy appear in a big city merely in transit to visiting another Amish community, while in *Paap*, a young woman appears in an Indian city to escort a child tulku back to a Buddhist community in the mountains, after the traditional method of testing involving artifacts of the deceased. It is notable that for Weir's story the religious foil to the hard-boiled city cop is the Amish community, while for the Indian version a Buddhist community takes its place. One can speculate that for the majority Hindu culture of India, Buddhism is genuinely exotic, and also perhaps that it represents a more extreme and renunciative lifestyle. This is the ultimate message of the film, that it is "paap"— a sin—to repress one's sexual feelings in the name of some religious ideal. Along the way there is an interesting discussion within the middle-class Indian family of the policeman and his sister over reincarnation, which they dismiss. "One life, you can barely lead," the sister quotes, "and you'll have to lead another." She rolls her eyes. "Oh God," she drawls, and they both laugh at the absurdity of it.

One is led to wonder if middle-class India is now so westernized that it systematically ridicules its entire spiritual heritage. Where *Witness* pre sents a genuine dialogue between a secularized city cop and an Amish woman, *Paap* is one-way traffic: the Buddhists get a lecture at the end about their repressive and regressive tradition. The hero tells the beautiful young Buddhist woman: "You think you are doing a pious deed by killing your love for the sake of your father. Wrong. You are committing a sin. A sin."

Passing References

As in *The Cave of the Yellow Dog*, *Himalaya* represents a world where Buddhism and shamanism interpenetrate. Set in Nepal where Padmasambhava—the founder of Tantric Buddhism in Tibet and Nepal and reputed author of the *Tibetan Book of the Dead*—is second only to the Buddha in the Buddhist pantheon, it is no surprise to hear a protagonist say to his grandson early in the film: "I told you: your father will be reborn in the realm of Padmasambhava." But this simple statement represents a mythologizing of reincarnation, which is a widespread feature of Eastern countries which believe—nominally at least—in the doctrine. In fact one can see much of the Mahayana Buddhist tradition as an allegorical elaboration on what was originally a very literal system, unsurprising as the actual experience of either enlightenment or past life recall is probably confined to the very few.

Turning now to the shamanic world of the Native American, we find a couple of films in which reincarnation is mentioned: *Thunderheart* and *The Education of Little Tree*. We saw earlier that the protagonist in *Thunderheart* is told that he "is" Wakiyan Cante, a holy man (shaman) shot dead in the massacre at Wounded Knee. But this identification of one man with a deceased other is not explicitly named as reincarnation, and we have instead another plausible route to the possession by one person of the memories of the previously deceased: ancestral or racial memories. In Jungian terms the collective unconscious is a more "scientific" or Westernized alternative to reincarnation. In shamanic cultures the spirits of the ancestors are powerful entities, and may hold a more dominant position in the psyche than actual past life recall. In *The Education of Little Tree*, as Little Tree's grandfather lies dying, his grandmother imparts to him some of the wisdom of the "Way":

> There's all kinds of dying, Little Tree. I've seen people at the settlement walking around like you or me, but they're just as good as dead, because they spent their lives in meanness and greed. The spirit inside of them has shrunk down to no more than the size of a pea. Because the only way to make your spirit big is to work on it. You've got to use it to understand. The more you try to understand, the bigger it gets, till it gets so big and powerful you come to understand everything. Then you remember all your past body lives.

We saw in *The Wicker Man* that the schoolteacher insisted that children found it easier to picture reincarnation than resurrection. This is an interesting point because resurrection—however framed—always contradicts science. Incontrovertible scientific knowledge of the brain indicates that after even a short period without oxygen, it is irreversibly damaged, as is of course the rest of the body after a longer period. Resurrection of a body which is clinically dead therefore contradicts science, and is a belief held in the "teeth of evidence" as the celebrated atheist Richard Dawkins likes to put it. But science, because of its methods of investigating matter, cannot have any opinion on the soul or spirit. To say that the spirit is "shrunk to the size of a pea" is poetic, because, by Descartes' useful definition, the soul, spirit, or mind, has no extension. This means that the doctrine of reincarnation is not necessarily against science as is the doctrine of resurrection, unless resurrection is understood as *allegory*.

In popular Western parlance reincarnation may also become an allegorical way of expressing certain convictions. In *The Fisher King* a young woman called Lydia confides in a friend who is doing her nails: "I think some people are meant to be alone. This is my idea, that I was born a man in a former life, and I used women for pleasure and now ... I'm paying for it." What this insight gives to Lydia is the stoicism to face what seemed to be the inevitable disappointment of relationship, and the film suggests—partly because its other protagonists are on a moral journey—that her penance is coming to an end because it was willingly endured. The same notion of course drives the entire film in *Switch* and *Mr. Ya Miss*. A literal belief in reincarnation was not necessarily needed for Lydia however.

Reincarnation as Western Bugbear

Reincarnation is an affront to the Western mind, at least to the extent that it is hemmed in by the monotheist traditions. "I'm not Callicrates, I'm ... Leo!" asserts Leo in the film *She*. He is faced with the same memory that Peter Proud struggled to come to terms with: that his wife had killed him in a previous life out of rage. In this case it is Ayesha—the mysterious sorceress queen—who stabbed Leo/Callicrates in ancient Egypt, and who has sought him ever since across the "sea of time." She asks him, "Do you remember your death my love?" "My death?" he naturally queries. She mysteriously facilitates the memory in him of his faithlessness and his murder at her hands. He is overwhelmed by the vision he endures of his earlier life and death. "Time, my love," she explains to him, "is but a sea eternal. We are drowned in it many times, and are washed ashore again and again. But I have never drowned in it. I was given the secret of eternal life." This is a mixing of afterlife accounts, reincarnation on the one hand, and immortality of the body on the other. Both serve nothing much more than an excuse for a gothic "lost world" plotline which makes eternal love something rather to be feared, or perhaps a vehicle for the fear men have of women: "she who must be obeyed." Still, Leo's initial reaction is instructive: I am me, not someone else. This is a key objection to reincarnation.

In David Lean's *A Passage to India* a local pundit called Godbole delivers a clichéd account of reincarnation which is nothing more than a means to reinforce the general exoticization of India. Godbole tells one of the central characters, Mrs. Moore, that she is an "old soul," and informs her that he has designed a dance to illustrate reincarnation. The lugubrious delivery—plus the fact that he is incongruously played by Alec Guinness—makes for what can be called pseudo-esotericism, the parading of interesting spiritual beliefs as shallow titillation.

In Hitchcock's *Vertigo* we find—as in much of his work—the borrowing of an esoteric idea which is demonstrated by the end of the film to have a psychological or Freudian, i.e., "scientific" explanation. Madeleine, the wife of a rich man who hires Scotty to trail her, is subject to either spirit possession or past life recall, in which she becomes obsessed with a woman called Carlotta Valdes who had killed herself a hundred years earlier. When Scotty (James Stewart) takes Madeleine (Kim Novak) to a forest of giant sequoias, she doesn't like the two thousand year old trees because they are called "ever living" in Latin, and she knows she has to die. They look at the cross-section of a cut tree, labeled with the historical events of its lifetime up to the point of its felling in 1930. In the classic trance-voice of Western cinema, she points in turn to two rings, saying, "Somewhere in here I was born, and there I died. It was only a moment for you. You took no notice." Is she referring to God's indifference here? Perhaps, but there is no other interpretation of her broader statement than a reference to her past life as Carlotta. Scotty interrogates her on those lines, apparently determined to discover her past-life identity.

Scotty then drives her to the sea, where she describes a scene that keeps appearing in her dreams. She sits alone in a room; then there is a grave into which she stares—it is her grave—with no name on the gravestone; there is a tower and bell and a garden below, perhaps in Spain. Scotty is entranced; he is sure that this is the key to the mystery he is pursuing. But it isn't Spain he discovers, rather the Mission San Juan Bautista in California, and the climax of the film takes place there. Scotty has been tricked by her. In reality she is the mistress of Gavin Elster, and has plotted with him to kill his wife Madeleine, who is thrown off the tower. Scotty's "vertigo" has prevented him from reaching the top, so he is fooled, as is the court hearing, into thinking that the real Madeleine has committed suicide. But after a nervous breakdown Scotty finds the fake Madeleine—real name Judy—and forces her up the tower to confess. Scotty's fury is that of a man who has not only lost the woman he thought he loved in a suicide he ought to have prevented, but who finds her again only to discover her as a fraud and accomplice to murder. The husband had "made her up" to look like the wife, he shouts at her, "the clothes and the hair, the looks, the manner, the words." He finishes, furiously: "And those beautiful phony trances."

So the reincarnation in the film is phony, just a device dreamt up to get Scotty hooked on the case. It is also a typical strategy of many films of the period, effectively allowing the audience to indulge in pseudo-esoteric shenanigans through the bulk of the film, while allowing them to leave the cinema with their rational world restored intact. Forensic science and modern psychology have debunked the charlatan.

Vertigo is also interesting as a morally compromised film, along with *Taxi Driver* and *Crimes and Misdemeanors*, though on a smaller scale. It lies in Scotty's fury being so self-absorbed: his moral outrage is entirely to do with being made a fool of, of a love betrayed, but he shows little revulsion at what Judy had done as willing accomplice to murder. Of course, she has to die in the end, in a rather hurried denouement, which perhaps makes up for it.

Birth is undoubtedly a personal project of director Jonathan Glazer, exploring again the subject of reincarnation. The protagonist is Anna (Nicole Kidman), who lost her husband ten years ago. She is about to remarry when she encounters a ten-year-old child called Sean who claims to be the reincarnation of her dead husband. Unlike *The Reincarnation of Peter Proud*, this film leaves the issue frustratingly open at the end, but like *Peter Proud* it engages with the issues rather than ducks them. In *Chances Are* Corinne confronts a man roughly half her age as her possible former husband, which is bad enough. But a ten-year-old? How would anyone respond in this situation? We saw in *Truly Madly Deeply*, and in *Ghost*, that in the immediate aftermath of bereavement, the ghost of the departed might linger to help in the transitionary period. But what if one still has feelings of love for the dead man, in a full, adult, sexual fashion, and he re-appears as a ten-year-old? And how is the new fiancé going to react? Or the mother of the child? The film is disturbing, creepy even, particularly over the sexual tension between Anna and the child, epitomized when she and the boy are naked in the bath together. (This may have been a direct reference to the equally unnerving bath scene in Bergman's *The Silence*.) Evidence is sought of course of his status as the reincarnated husband, something intimate that only he and Anna would know, as in the tulku system. "We did it on your sofa," he tells the deceased husband's brother. As the evidence mounts Anna's doubts crumble and she even hatches the far-fetched plan of living with Sean for another eleven years, and then marrying him so as to continue her former life. But at the same time the boy's convictions fade. Eventually, he tells her bluntly, "I'm not Sean." This is the course taken, though via a slightly different route, by the possible reincarnation of the former husband in *Heart and Souls*: I am not, after all, the former person. Anna is angry at first, but soon recovers.

We are left with an interesting take on reincarnation: that it is an *imposition* on all concerned. It is an imposition on the boy, because it prevents him being himself, a ten-year-old with an unformed potentiality, and it is an imposition on Anna because it interrupts her long-overdue remarriage. It also leaves us with the idea that Anna's psychic needs to interact again with her dead husband, and his own psychic trace, somehow combine to create the memories in the boy. As an explanation it comes closer to Jung's collective unconscious than conventional reincarnation, and is interesting to compare with the psychology of the bereavement films examined earlier.

Reincarnation as Horror-Thriller

Reincarnation films exist which belong to the horror genre, and in a small way both *She* and *Vertigo* fit this category. In contrast, the Japanese film *Reincarnation* by Takashi Shimizu is full-on reincarnation and full-on horror. This does not prevent it from being an intelligent investigation of the subject however. The film is about the making of a film about a massacre in which a college professor—in a bid to learn more about reincarnation—filmed himself killing eleven people in a hotel, including his own daughter. He then committed suicide. Thirty-five years on, an actress called Nagisa Sugiura is drawn to the role of the daughter because the story seems familiar. However, as shooting starts she is increasingly haunted by flashbacks. The twist in the end is that she is not the reincarnation of the murdered daughter, but of the professor.

The film usefully includes a scene where a psychology lecturer dismisses reincarnation as "cryptomnesia" or false memory syndrome. Hearing this one of the students is prompted to seek out another girl with past-life memories, who had been auditioned for the film. She reveals marks on her neck which she believed were due to death by strangling. Unlike *Vertigo*, reincarnation is not dangled in front of the viewers, only to be withdrawn at the end as it is exposed as charlatanry in the service of fraud. In the entirely different culture of Japanese religious history the film *Reincarnation* can juxtapose its debunking as cryptomnesia with full acceptance of both the fact and the ramifications of reincarnation, and allow the viewer to decide.

Dead Again tells the story of lovers reincarnated to experience again a murder at the hands of "Frankie" an art dealer who happens also to be a past-life regression therapist. The film is Hitchcockian both in its general approach and in the absence of characters with any elevated moral purpose. Unlike *Switch*, for example, reincarnation brings no insight or moral development to any of the characters. All we learn, as a psychological truism perhaps, is that we tend to fall into repetitive behavior.

Anthony Hopkins stars in *Audrey Rose* as Elliot Hoover, an initially sinister individual from the UK who appears to be stalking the daughter of a happily married couple. The girl, Ivy, has nightmares and is approaching her eleventh birthday when Hoover, challenged by the girl's father, arranges to meet the parents in a restaurant to explain himself. He tells them of his own daughter, killed in a car crash nearly eleven years ago, and gradually comes to the point: he believes that Ivy is the reincarnation of the dead child, Audrey Rose. Hoover reveals to us that after the crash he went to India to find himself and wisdom, as the protagonist of *Razor's Edge* does. While there he learned the truth of reincarnation, but things come to a head when the child exhibits more disturbed behavior one night and Hoover abducts her. Before long he is apprehended and charged with kidnapping. The subsequent trial, as in *Switch*, allows for the evidence for reincarnation to be examined, including evidence from an Indian holy man.

Light-Hearted Reincarnation

Many great spiritual teachers seem capable of moving in a flash from the most earnest and serious of expositions to joking good humor—one thinks of the Dalai Lama as an example, and many other Tibetan teachers for that matter, including the Tibetans in *Little Buddha*. So why not play reincarnation for laughs in a movie? *Fluke* does just this though it certainly has a serious turn here and there, which one might not expect from the opening where a man killed in a car crash comes back as a dog. Nor from the antics of his new doggy companion Rumbo, voiced by Samuel L. Jackson. But Fluke the puppy is on a journey of revenge, taking him to his former wife and son and into the presence of the man who caused the crash and now seems to be making out with his wife. This is a theme common to *Ghost*, *Chances Are* and a number of other films, but in the end Fluke realizes that his rival was not the cause of his death, and that he must leave the family alone and move on. In the final scene Fluke hears Rumbo's voice, but his old friend has now reincarnated as a squirrel.

Perhaps the funniest reincarnation film is *Dean Spanley*. It is based on a 1930s short novel *My Talks with Dean Spanley* and stars Peter O'Toole as a wheelchair-bound curmudgeon, Horatio Fisk, whose son feels perpetually put down by him. He dutifully visits the old man every Thursday, but, on some hunch Fisk Jr. takes him to something unusual: a lecture on reincarnation by Swami Nala Prash. On inquiring of the old man's housekeeper as to whether she believes in the transmigration of souls the son is bemused to hear from her: "I don't believe in letting foreigners in, if that's what you mean."

During the Swami's talk—in which it is made clear that a cat or dog can reincarnate as a human—Horatio briefly encounters Dean Spanley, and then bumps into him again at his club. Spanley's view on reincarnation is offered only obliquely in the first instance: "Only the closed mind is certain, sir." Spanley won't share his favored tipple: a '91 Hungarian Tokay, but does offer the first hint at what is to come in respect to its special properties when offering this further opinion on reincarnating as an animal: "One might wish to possess the olfactory powers of a canine." Fisk Jr. then becomes intrigued with the question of reincarnation and also with Dean Spanley, who appears to be a fount of curious statements. The Dean is however obstinately uninteresting, in the formal Edwardian manner of the period, until the obscure transformation triggered by his favorite wine.

Hence Fisk, Jr., is motivated to track down, at great expense, more Tokay in order to entertain Spanley. Slowly—and this is the strength of the film—what appears initially as slips of the tongue or odd figures of speech build up into a complete and bizarre picture of Spanley's inner life. The denouement takes place at dinner with Fisk Sr.—a complete upturning of his normal routine, but achieved by the insistence of Fisk Jr. At first the old man rests in his acute curmudgeonly wit, his natural defense against any real human exchange. Here is an example of what Jeremy in *Powder* was talking about when he cited sarcasms, deceptions, and exagerations as accepted modes of speech, but which bolster the sense of separation. Horatio is not intending to deceive of course, but merely to hide his emotions. However, despite himself, he gradually becomes intrigued as the Tokay-powered Jekyll-and-Hyde transformation takes place. The transition is as smooth as usual, and before long the dignified Dean is recounting in detail the last moments of his previous life as a Welsh spaniel. He turns out to have been Horatio's dog, shot by a farmer for harassing his livestock, and the death of which had been such a blow to the old man. The upshot is the breaking down of Horatio's emotional defenses and the realization that his inability to mourn the death of his other son—killed in the Great War—has shut him off from the living.

Resurrection and Apocalypse

Whether Jesus underwent the resurrection as described in the Christian tradition is not an issue that affects a person's daily life, apart from being an article of faith if one is a Christian. This is in fact explored in the film *The Body*, but otherwise the theme of Jesus' resurrection is not widely found in film (beyond the costume drama retelling of the bible story). However, the idea that I as an individual—with Jesus as the crucial exemplar—might be resurrected does impact on many believers through certain doctrines of salvation, particularly those found in Revelation. Where the four gospels leave open the exact nature of the "kingdom of heaven," Revelation rather reworks the Jesus story to fit Old Testament prophecies of messianic eschatology.

To take a slight digression: the film *Oh God!* presents a view of religion far removed from what we are examining here. It is a charming comedy albeit with the serious intent of re-imagining the Western God. In one exchange between God and his chosen prophet, a supermarket manager called Jerry, his prophet, is anxious about the future of mankind:

JERRY: Is it going to get any worse?
GOD: How should I know?
JERRY: What do you mean, what should you know? Why, you know everything!
GOD: I only know what is. Also I'm very big on what was. On what isn't yet, I haven't got a clue.

So, God in the film *Oh God!* is amiably confident that he knows nothing of the future. Not so for his religions, however: all three monotheisms incorporate a future-orientation known as millenarianism, the belief that "God's kingdom" will be established on earth after a global disaster or apocalypse. All three monotheisms believe in a Judgment Day, or an "end-time," when humanity is judged and divided into the righteous and the damned, and they will live respectively in an eternal heaven or eternal hell. As a metaphor this scenario might be psychologically instructive: to have committed murder for example is to experience a kind of living hell which, by virtue of the mechanisms of guilt and alienation, *seems* to go on forever (though Woody Allen for one does not subscribe to such a view). But when taken literally, the stories of the end-time—envisioned as a lurid Apocalypse—become not only a damaging construct in religious terms, but act out on the world stage in sometimes negative ways. It may well be for example that Christian Zionist support for the founding of Israel in Palestine, in complete disregard for the Arab peoples who lived there, derived from the support that Biblical prophecy gives to it.[14] Similarly, Islamic millenarianism is probably part of the doctrine that drives Osama bin Laden and his followers. In the film *Kadosh* one of its Jewish protagonists drives around Jerusalem proclaiming the Apocalypse through a loud-hailer just ahead of the year 2000.

The apocalypse, with its source in Judaism, is historically a foreign concept to cultures east of Iran, which have a more cyclical view of time. However, Susan Napier—writing on Japanese anime films—tells us: "Given the distance between Japanese religious tradition and Christianity, it is fascinating that present-day Japanese notions of the end of the world echo so much in Revelation."[15] It seems that modern Japan, for example, has absorbed Western cultural tropes so thoroughly that we see the imagery of Revelation reflected back to us in Japanese film, notably in anime. The horrors of the atomic strikes on Hiroshima and Nagasaki, so vividly present in the Japanese consciousness, may have also provided the ground from which apocalyptic themes are turned to.

Was Jesus literally resurrected? Some Christians regard it as a basic article of their faith, and may succeed in holding this belief alongside conventional acceptance of modern science. It is perhaps the central miracle of Christianity, and hence theologians are keen to find hints of it in film. *Jesus of Montreal* was introduced earlier as a product of French culture in which salvation can be had through art, and will be discussed later from the secular-spiritual perspective. Here it is just worth mentioning that the young actor in the film, Daniel, who appears in an avant-garde version of the Jesus story, dies in the end. His organs become available for transplant, prompting Clive Marsh to say: "*Jesus of Montreal* is one of the cleverest Jesus films ever made."[16] He says this partly because the transplant of his organs at the end is a modern kind of resurrection.

Given the centrality of the Resurrection, what if archaeological investigations in the Holy Land were to uncover a skeleton at just the right site, and which science could prove to be that of Christ? This is the theme of the film *The Body*. It is a more serious film than *The Da Vinci Code*, dealing with related issues. While it is true that the discovery of a Jesus bloodline would rewrite some of Christian history, notably the assumption of Jesus as celibate, the discovery of his bodily remains would call into question a more fundamental Christian assumption. In its bare outline the film is no more promising than *The Da Vinci Code*, but what makes *The Body* worthwhile is the lack of pseudo-esoteric trappings, and the genuine debate enacted between a believer and a non-believer over the issues raised.

We turn now to films of *personal* resurrection, of which there are quite a few, though this theme is subsumed into the larger question of the Apocalypse. Once reincarnation was ruled out in Christianity, the idea of personal resurrection took on more force. Essential to this cluster of beliefs is the idea that the body itself will be re-animated, an idea, as we saw earlier, that runs counter to scientific understanding.

The Rapture is a film intended as an indictment of American apocalyptic beliefs in which the end time will come and a select few will be taken up in the Rapture for a bodily resurrection in an earthly heaven. Its protagonist Sharon has a meaningless job and a swinging sex life to compensate. She encounters evangelists at work and at the doorstep who are trying to convince her of Jesus's imminent return. To start with, she makes the response natural to a secularist:

> There are five billion people on the planet. There's I-don't-know-how-many religions. Why does the God of some little country on the Mediterranean have to be the God for everyone? Isn't that a little arrogant? I mean, really? The Buddhists get along okay without Jesus Christ. The Hindus get along okay without Jesus Christ. The Moslems seem to be getting along okay without Jesus Christ.

However, before long she is converted, and so is her partner. Religion offers a genuine love that was missing in the arid playground of her secular life, but a crisis looms: her husband is shot dead. Left with her small daughter, she appears serene at first, but then begins to hallucinate her dead husband and understands in her visions that the end time Rapture is now approaching. She should prepare for this by taking her daughter to the desert. Without any provisions she despairs within the dry landscape as the promised event fails to materialize. Her little girl, convinced that they will go to heaven and meet daddy again, just wants to die. Her mother is finally driven to the desperate act in which she shoots her child, after which she is imprisoned on suspicion of murder. The film ends with the actual arrival of the Apocalypse, in which the policeman who arrested her is taken up, but she is left behind. Her faith is not strong enough.

The film is intended to make this point: if there is a strong enough belief in another life, then suicide, or murder—even of the ones one loves the most—is legitimate. This other life must of course be perfect—and if one's own real life appears either arid, or stricken with misfortune, then it is not hard to imagine the perfect life of the resurrected body in paradise. Reincarnation on the other hand is no solution at all: it means more of same.

Left Behind is a popular U.S. book series which has spawned three films. In the *Left Behind* trilogy the Rapture is envisaged on a grand scale, centered round cataclysmic battles over Israel and the fate of Jerusalem. It is a more direct imagining of the ideas central to Revelation. What becomes clear from its muddled proselytizing is how incoherent the resurrection doctrine really is when taken literally. As a metaphor of renewal it has perhaps a valid place in the spiritual life, and it has a long history predating Christianity.[17] But, in the first place, Revelation makes it clear that only 144,000 people are to be saved on the Day of Judgment (twelve thousand each from the twelve tribes of Israel, according to Revelation 7:4). This is hardly the basis for an egalitarian spirituality. Secondly, what happens to the body, exactly? In the *Left Behind* trilogy it physically disappears, so that if you happened to be driving a car or train, too bad for the passengers. Those left behind will see the destruction of all the "enemies of God," though not before the Antichrist—in the form of the Secretary General of the United Nations—attempts to create a world economy, a world currency, a world religion, and world peace.

The lesson of history *ought* to be that futurology is an exercise in failure. Whether they are Old Testament prophets, Sri Aurobindo, or Marx, their predictions come true only as often as random guesses do. No film better illustrates this in the context of apocalypticism than *The Late Great Planet Earth*, which predicted the Apocalypse to come about in the 1980s. It is based on the book by Hal Lindsey, who also appears in the film. Wheeler Winston Dixon, writing on Apocalypse cinema, says of the film version that it was "cobbled together from stock footage and some hastily recreated sequences and narrated by a transparently desperate Orson Welles."[18] But was Welles desperate or did he take the job because he, like Ronald Reagan, loved the book?[19] The early part of it presents what is at first sight a convincing account of how the prophets of the Old Testament were able, with remarkable accuracy, to predict the events of the New Testament. On a little reflection however an alternative explanation presents itself: not that the Old Testament validates the New, but that the New Testament was written to validate the Old. We have no historical knowledge about the authors of the Gospels, and so claims about their historical reliability are dubious, but what Lindsey does is rely on his audiences' acceptance of the New Testament to legitimize the prophets in the Old Testament, and in Revelation, and hence to accept his interpretation of their predictions regarding the "End Times."

Why is the American imagination so in the grip of Revelation? The short answer is that it is a Protestant country, born of the persecution of Protestants, whose historical moment was born in the Reformation, and which resulted—for complicated reasons—in a preference for the Old Testament over the New. Revelation can be understood as bookending the New Testament of Jesus and St. Paul, with a tract closer to Judges than Jesus. Just to give one example: the story of Jezebel is recycled from Kings 1 and 2 as a prophetess in the church of Thyatira. John's vision has Jesus address that church and demand that she repent other wise he will "kill her children with death" (Revelation 2:23). The old Jezebel's horrific "crime" was to teach the religion of Baal—a Nature god—instead of Yahweh, and her name became transliterated as "Whore of Baal" instead of "Virgin of Baal." Her name became synonymous with that of all evil women. The new Jezebel commits adultery and teaches idolatry, and Jesus in Revelation threatens to subject her and her lovers to "great tribulation" and to kill her children. But the Jesus of the Gospel of John is brought an adulteress, who according to Mosaic law should be stoned. Famously he responds, "He who is without sin among you, let him first cast a stone at her." He refuses to condemn her. The New Testament Jesus of John does not believe that an adulteress should receive "tribulation" or stoning; the Old Testament Jesus of Revelation does. (Whatever the shortcomings of the *Last Temptation of Christ*—to be explored later—the adulteress scene is dramatized as that of the New Testament Jesus.)

Apocalypse themes run through many more films including *Revelations*, *End of Days* and *The Omega Code* series. Heather Hendershot—another writer on apocalyptic films—discusses selected films in this genre, and evangelical Christians as a large market for such films, citing *The Omega Code* as an apocalyptical film, almost unknown outside such circles, which surpassed *Fight Club*'s per-screen box office average.[20] Their popularity in America can be understood as an important cultural indicator. In terms of a failed futurology it is worth mentioning that a whole slew of films predicting the end of the world on December 31, 2012—based on the Mayan calendar—were no more accurate than those, like *End of Days*, that put the date as December 31, 1999, or Hal Lindsay who dated it to the 1980s.

In considering these films from the perspective of the lived spiritual life, one might say that they represent an inversion of what is here considered as the core of the spiritual or religious life: a profound connectedness. Just as Revelation is often an inversion of the Gospels of peace and love, so the apocalypse on film is a retreat to vengeance and judgmentalism. If you resist our invincible Truth, then we, the "saved," condemn you, the "damned." More than this, these films appeal, it seems, to a deep desire for death and destruction on a massive scale. It is no surprise, then, that liberal commentators were aghast during the presidential campaign that elected Ronald Reagan, when he spoke of a coming Armageddon as one that certain theologians expected. If the man with his finger on the nuclear button is drawn into a belief system that anticipates nuclear destruction with joy, then he may not be the right man for the job. The American voter, however, thought he was.

Summary

While East and West seem to be sharply divided over the doctrine of reincarnation, Western filmmakers have found the subject worth exploring in many different ways. In the first instance there seems to be a resonance with Western therapeutic traditions which are based on the recovery of suppressed memories, and which have some debt to Freud. Hence, films like *The Reincarnation of Peter Proud* and *Chances Are* involve the slow revealing of hidden aspects of the personality, a suppressed past that just happens to be of a former life. There is also the "just deserts" angle in *Switch* and its Indian remake, along with other Indian reincarnation films such as *Mahal* and *Madhumati*. It turns out however that most Indian films on the subject of reincarnation also feature a healthy dose of skepticism towards it, or downright dismissal as in *Paap*. Instead, reincarnation can be played for its romantic angle: how else do you explain that sudden recognition in the eyes of a person across the room and the feeling of destiny as you fall in love, perhaps against the norms of convention, class and so on?

Reincarnation also provokes adverse reactions in film; perhaps the creepiest example of which is in *Birth*, whereas *Audrey Rose*, billed as a horror film, is actually quite comfortable with reincarnation. But at the same time reincarnation also provides a plot device for the rather unedifying *Dead Again* and the more morally complex Japanese horror film *Reincarnation*.

While reincarnation is what happens to ordinary people in these films, in contrast no serious filmmaker seems to have found the *literal* resurrection of an ordinary person a plot device worth exploiting. In other words, despite the suspension of disbelief that an audience is willing to make for a good yarn, physical resurrection is just too implausible—apart, that is, from zombie movies and the like, which are mostly by now a parody of themselves, and are certainly not the Christian vision of resurrection. Instead the only resurrection movies are those of the Christian Apocalypse, based on last book of the New Testament, Revelation.

So what is the relevance of reincarnation and resurrection for the lived spiritual life? The latter impacts on a certain kind of believer, like Sharon in *The Rapture*, who makes life—and death—decisions based on her belief. A belief in reincarnation—common in the East—has a specific manifestation in the *tulku* system, present in *Little Buddha, Kundun, Seven Years in Tibet* and *Paap*. Otherwise it becomes a matter of *identity*, not connectedness. It is simply a continuation of a story that would otherwise be bookended with birth and death, though this has moral implications in some of the films. What one might expect in a protagonist who discovers the truth of reincarnation is a complete loss of the fear of death, and by extension, a loss of all other endemic fears, but this angle has not been explored: perhaps such an insight would be the end of all dramatic potential.

Instead, perhaps the most valuable of all the meditations on reincarnation here is the humorous take in *Dean Spanley*, where an old curmudgeon meets the reincarnation of his former dog in the Tokay-swilling Dean. The film both gently subverts all the usual seriousness accompanying the topic, and suggests perhaps the kind of transformation that a real encounter with it might bring about.

But are any of the films here on reincarnation or resurrection luminous, and a "must-see" for the spiritual life? Not, it seems, because of these topics alone, as (for example) *Kundun* would illustrate. It is true that films that ask the question, "What is it like to be reincarnated," provide a range of thoughtful explorations, while the question, "What is it like to be resurrected," does not; even for the purposes of fiction resurrection simply has insufficient internal logic for a plot device. Ultimately reincarnation, however thoughtfully treated, belongs to the category of the esoteric: past life recall being a gift that has no necessary potential for elevating the spiritual life.

What was characteristic of the films in this section was a certain high drama. Birth, death and reincarnation have considerable dramatic potential. In the next section we look at films of high drama that portray a spiritual chaos born out of the breakdown of normal "reality"—much as reincarnation would challenge that same normality.

6
Spiritual Chaos and Rubber Reality

A crisis of any kind may also be a *spiritual* crisis for those involved. This means that either the crisis is prompted by a spiritual question, or that it raises a spiritual question, or at least existential questions, that is questions pertaining to the true nature of our existence. During a crisis the world may appear to descend from its once orderly nature into chaos. In extremity, reality appears distorted, but we could say that the real measure of a spiritual crisis is what kind of personal transformation it brings in its wake. In Zen the spiritual crisis is traditionally understood as a period in which the world is turned upside down and which may lead to enlightenment. Paul Schrader constructs his "transcendent style" in reference to a saying in the Zen tradition:

> The desire of Ozu, Bresson, and to lesser degrees, Dreyer and others to express the aware, ideal or ecstatic (not synonymous terms) is formalized in the triad of transcendental style, and it is perhaps not coincidental that these steps correspond to the classic Zen aphorism: "When I began to study Zen, mountains were mountains; when I thought I understood Zen, mountains were not mountains; but when I came to full knowledge of Zen, mountains were again mountains."[1]

The film scholar Irena Makarushka also cites this passage in Schrader, suggesting that it is a metaphor for the journey from "normalcy, into alienation, to transcendence,"[2] this being the triad or three-stage journey of spiritual crisis and resolution, which Schrader terms respectively quotidian, disparity, and stasis. The middle period of confusion or alienation is sometimes described as a period where "mountains are rivers and rivers are mountains." Film, with its proven ability to construct dislocated images, has been an ideal medium for portraying this crisis long before the advent of high-tech special effects. A range of genres encompass such ability to subvert normal reality, including film noir, surrealism, magical realism, and "rubber reality." The term "rubber reality" was coined for the title of an article about virtual reality (VR) films in the British Film Institute magazine *Sight and Sound*,[3] though here VR films will be regarded as a subset of the rubber reality genre. Before giving a full definition of the term some more thoughts on the spiritual crisis are in order.

Eric S. Christianson suggests that "film noir has become a concept of enormous proportions. My interest is in one of its core features: *ambiguity*. That is because *ambiguity* is more than a theme of noir. It is a lens through which characters struggle to make sense of the world, themselves and each other. It is an intellectual and spiritual *condition*, a stance of being in relation to others."[4] When such a struggle reaches a certain intensity, one might suggest, it tips over into something with an existential urgency, as either a full-blown psychological or spiritual crisis. But there are perhaps two different types of crisis, one with a secular resolution (most likely through psychotherapy, where drugs like Prozac can be successfully used in treatment) and the other with a spiritual resolution (perhaps through spiritual enlightenment or redemption). Tarkovsky, with an easy ear for the East, certainly believed in the "spiritual crisis" (and it is possible to make a reading of his films from that perspective):

> I believe that it is always through spiritual crisis that healing occurs. A spiritual crisis is an attempt to find oneself, to acquire new faith. It is the apportioned lot of everyone whose objectives are on the spiritual plane. And how could it be otherwise when the soul yearns for harmony, and life is full of discordance.[5]

Hence, Tarkovsky suggested that life itself will at some time or other provoke crisis. Additionally, the process of dying can be a time of stress, and, if one believes in any kind of afterlife or inter-life—such as the bardo—then these disembodied states may also be stress-filled. Hence we shall look with interest at films where the boundaries between death and life seem blurred.

Eric Wilson's "Gnostic Cinema" and "Religious Irony"

Eric Wilson's book *Secret Cinema: Gnostic Vision in Film* lays down a challenge that is appropriate to take up in this section. He would like to suggest that the middle stage of the spiritual life, where everything seems to turn upside down and inside out—as commented on by Schrader—could be described as "Gnostic." A fair criticism of his work, as leveled earlier, is that to subsume such a range of spiritual manifestations under a single term is to do violence to the variety of the spiritual life. Wilson's choice of category—Gnostic—is as good as Tucker's choice of Shamanic if one is forced to adopt a single category from a plethora of terms presumed foreign to a secular audience. If they are all equally exotic to a relentlessly secular world, then what does it matter? But for the purposes of this book it does matter a great deal, because it makes blunt the instrument through which we can consider the spiritual life on film.

Having said this, it is still instructive to consider Wilson's thesis, as there is something in the term Gnostic which can usefully be applied to at least some of the films he analyses. When he says that "films like *The Matrix* and *The Truman Show* have deployed Gnostic myths of the second and third centuries to explore the idea that the physical world is an illusion concocted by a tyrannical maker,"[6] he is making a useful point. Gnosticism—if we can really untangle all the misinformation handed down to us about it—appears to include something of this in its worldview. The tyrannical maker in this tradition is called the "demiurge," literally "worker in the service of the people," but in usage has become any oppressive power. In the Gnostic literature, however, the world is not just the embodiment of a generic oppression but also the place in which there are scattered clues for the upward or return journey to the Godhead. When Wilson goes on to say that *Vanilla Sky*, *The Thirteenth Floor*, *Existenz*, *Dark City* and *Pleasantville* are "overtly Gnostic films" he is overstating the case, but nonetheless there is a fluid quality to reality in these films that needs a handle. When he says that *Harry Potter and the Sorcerer's Stone*, *The Ninth Gate*, *Jacob's Ladder*, *Blue Velvet*, and *Excalibur* are "alchemical films with Gnostic undercurrents" he is again straining a comparison, but nonetheless usefully grouping some films for us. Instead of "alchemical" and "Gnostic" the categories of "Neoplatonist" and "rubber reality" are used here as more precise. But, as exercised throughout this book, a much tighter net is needed in casting for such films: for example *Harry Potter and the Sorcerer's Stone*, while deservedly regarded as good children's entertainment, is excluded from serious consideration for being escapism. Likewise, Polanski's *The Ninth Gate*, while a competent fantasy outing in terms of dramatic framing, sets, acting and cinematography, is also no more than escapism.

In another book by Wilson, *The Strange World of David Lynch: Ironic Religion from "Eraserhead" to "Mulholland Dr.,"* he applies further categories, variously "ironic religion" or "transcendental irony" to the films of David Lynch. He draws on the Socratic dialogue as an example of irony, and also uses the ideas of theologian Rudolf Otto, Romantic theorist Friedrich Schlegel and Romantic writer Friedrich Schiller to illuminate his thesis. "Irony" for Wilson seems to be a rubric for the paradoxical or ambiguous, but the existence of a valid category of "religious irony" is doubtful. Irony is a figure of speech intended at some level to mock its audience, or to mock its subject matter—at least as Wilson embellishes it—but in religion what appears as irony is unlikely to be intended as such. Certainly mysticism—if not the whole of religion—is paradoxical, and the statements of the mystics may appear contradictory, paradoxical, or gnomic, but this is more likely to do with the subject matter than a stylistic intention. At best irony is playful, but at worst it smacks of bad faith. When Jeremy in *Powder* indicts such modes of speech, he does not do so as if he were a pofaced Sunday school teacher, but as one who regrets the evasions and barriers irony places between people: in Buddhist traditions it would be regarded as "unskillful" communication, while in the Quaker tradition it would suggest a lack of simplicity.

To mistake the paradoxical statements of the mystics as irony suggests a secularist approach, one unmusical to religion. But we will see if Wilson's approach yields insights into the film that above all stands as the epitome of the "rubber reality" genre: *Mulholland Drive*. Does it embody "ironic religion," and does it lend support to Wilson's "attempt to cast Lynch as an original religious seer, an almost mystical presence who regardless of his immediate contexts creates artistic products that work to alter for the better our hearts and minds?"[7] First, some further thoughts on "rubber reality."

Rubber Reality as a Film Genre

"Rubber reality" may not be universally recognized as a term in film studies, but is useful for films that pose serious questions about our perceptions of reality. We can distinguish it from Surrealism, which has a historical basis in early twentieth century art movements (Cocteau's *Orphée* is an example), and magical realism, which has its origins in South American literature but is also present in French or African cinema (for example *Pan's Labyrinth*, *Amélie* and *Yeelen*). In surrealism, elements are in bizarre juxtaposition to each other, or are bizarrely exaggerated in one or more aspect, while magical realism requires the general context of realism into which a magical element is inserted. Films containing dream sequences are not necessarily either surreal or of the magical realism genre, because it is normal for dreams to be bizarre. Rubber reality, while it may also contain dream sequences, is not rubber reality because of them. Rather the key element is *the undermining of constancy within realism*: a person may become another person; a house or setting might become another house or setting; or a time might become another time: before might become afterwards, or vice versa. Like magical realism, it requires realism as the overall context. While magical realism may share some of the features of rubber reality, it is more likely to involve supernatural elements. Similarly, in a sub-genre we could call the virtual reality film, it is the technology of VR that provides for the shape-shifting character of such films: the *Matrix* trilogy being an oft quoted example.

Jacob's Ladder is an early exemplar of rubber reality, and is perhaps the film that most often prompts that description. While the identity of the protagonist is not under question, his setting is: Does he live with his wife and dream of his girlfriend, or vice versa? Is his doctor imaginary, or part of a network of references being erased by the army? And, above all, is he alive or dead? In fact, the films *Jacob's Ladder*, *Donnie Darko* and *Siesta* are all about a person already dead or in the final stages of dying, but we don't know it until the end of the film. *Siesta* is the least spiritually interesting of these three, but the protagonist's anxiety as to whether she had murdered someone or not makes for a good ethical dimension.

Jacob's Ladder was written by Bruce Joel Rubin (who also wrote the film *Ghost*) and is said to have been inspired by *The Tibetan Book of Dead*.[8] It could be argued that *Jacob's Ladder* is indeed about the mastery of the bardo realm, which is the nightmare domain of demons and ghosts that are part of the dying process. However, the film does not draw on Eastern understandings of death but on the teachings of the Christian mystic Meister Eckhart. The works of Eckhart play a minor role in the film, but his central teaching of detachment relates to the theme of letting go which protagonist Jacob Singer (Tim Robbins) is forced to understand in the end. The Buddha asserts in one of his discourses that "suffering is born from those we hold dear,"[9] not because we should not hold dear our loved ones, but because we become *attached* to them, or to the emotions we have for them.

The central device of *Jacob's Ladder* is of a man having flashbacks after serving in Vietnam. But Jacob's whole life is a shifting sand of identity and context: he oscillates between two women, and is also haunted by the loss of one of his sons. His one point of stability— oddly and wonderfully—is his chiropractor Louis, who keeps patching up his bad back. Louis is generally filmed from below, from the point of view of Jacob as client on the couch, and backlit to the effect of almost giving him a halo. "You know you look like an angel, Louis?" says Jacob, "Like an overgrown cherub? Did anyone ever tell you that?" "Yeah,' says Louis. "You. Every time I see you."

As Jacob stumbles from one bizarre experience to another, we gradually realize—and there are many clues—that he is in fact already dead, or at least dying. His journey involves the discovery that his bizarre mental states may be the result of a U.S. army experiment with an aggression-enhancing drug called "the ladder" which, according to its inventor, puts the soldiers through "a fast trip down the ladder to the primal fear, the base anger." Out of control, the soldiers' performance was not enhanced, but led to their slaughtering each other, a karmic burden that Jacob has to deal with. He may have physically died in Vietnam, on a typical MASH camp bed, but psychically, he is bound up with "those he held dear" including his wife and children, and a woman he worked with and with whom he either really had an affair, or did so only in his imagination. It makes no difference: these are all attachments that he has to relinquish. It is Louis who shows him how:

> JACOB: Am I dying, Louis?
> LOUIS: From a slipped disk? That would be a first. ... You ever read Meister Eckhart?
> JACOB: No.
> LOUIS: How did you get your doctorate without reading Meister Eckhart? Eckhart saw Hell too. He said: The only thing that burns in Hell is the part of you that won't let go of life, your memories, your attachments. They burn them all away. But they're not punishing you, he said. They're freeing your soul. So, if you're frightened of dying and ... and you're holding on, you'll see devils tearing your life away. But if you've made your peace, then the devils are really angels, freeing you from the earth. It's just a matter of how you look at it, that's all.

It is extraordinary how this saying of Eckhart's should match so well the teachings in the *Tibetan Book of the Dead*, but then perhaps the most obvious common ground between him and the Buddha was an emphasis on detachment. What also sets Jacob free is the truth—in this case about the experiment performed upon him—and he is now able to physically return to the empty flat where he had lived out his life, free from a continued imagined life with his wife or girlfriend, and able at last to meet his dead son who escorts him into the "light." In the MASH unit, the medic says: "He looks kinda peaceful, the guy. Put up a hell of a fight though." To the observer, a dying man looks a certain way from the outside, as Burroughs pointed out; from the inside we have to draw on the world's religious literature. *Jacob's Ladder* does everything we can ask of a film in this respect: to visualize the bardo of dying.

It is worth citing the Bible on the original conception of Jacob's ladder: "Jacob saw a ladder in a dream, and in it God was at the top, and angels could descend it to man, and man ascend it to God." (Genesis 28:11–19) At the end of the film, Jacob ascends the Biblical ladder, having been subject to the degradation of the U.S. army's chemical ladder; one, it turned out, only of descent. If Louis was an angel then perhaps he regularly ascended and descended in his mission to help the dying.

Jacob's Ladder is a rubber reality movie because "mountains become rivers and rivers become mountains," i.e., the identities of things and places become unstable. In the final resolution mountains become mountains again, because he can see clearly now as his projections fade out under the discipline of detachment.

The film *Donnie Darko* has similarities of structure, primarily in that we only understand that the protagonist is dead or dying at the end of the film, even though he has effectively been journeying in the bardo throughout. Donnie Darko (Jake Gyllenhaal) is a teenage boy whose world is similar to that of *American Beauty*: he comes from a middle-class background, but normally disturbed enough to warrant a therapist and medication. Early in the film he spends a night out, falling asleep on a golf course, drawn as usual into such pranks by his imaginary friend, Frank, a large rabbit. This supernatural creature also tells him that there are just over twenty-eight days before the end of the world, so Donnie is in a countdown situation in which his life becomes progressively more bizarre. But it turns out that the mysterious event of the golf-course night—the crashing of a jet engine through the roof of the family home—did actually kill him, and the entire twenty-eight days is a hallucination, or a time-alternate world. In terms of the bardo however, such a period makes sense: normal time is suspended at the moment of death, and the soul undergoes the kind of imaginative re-evaluation of its life that is familiar to us in dreams. In Jacob's case his bardo guide was Louis the chiropractor, while in Donnie's case it is Frank the giant rabbit.

But does *Donnie Darko* represent more than sweet serenity in the face of death, a lyrical acceptance, intermingled with confusion, terror, and humor? Without the Eckhart references, does it match *Jacob's Ladder* in terms of spirituality? Or might one really place it more with *American Beauty*, as a gentle mocking of the American dream, or perhaps *Blue Velvet* as a rite-of-passage teenage film? This would all depend on how the issue of death is acknowledged as a spiritual issue: in a society where death is all but banished, do not films such as these allow serious consideration of a difficult subject, especially, as in the case of Donnie, when it is such a young death? But in both cases, that of Jacob and that of Donnie, the serenity of the subjects is mesmerizing. After all, when Walt Whitman says, "No array of terms can say how much I am at peace about God and about death,"[10] he is staking out a spiritual claim.

Rubber Morality

To follow the actions of a saintly character who finds it impossible to utter a harsh word, or to act selfishly, would make a dull film. Both *Nazarín* and *Viridiana* have impossibly good protagonists, which is Buñuel's point: what have such people got to do with the rough house of actual living? Hence, a film which has initially unsympathetic characters and a lack of sermonizing can have a greater religious impact.

Two films which meet these requirements, and also have something "rubber" about them are *Groundhog Day* and *The Fisher King*. Interestingly, in both cases a woman provides the benchmark by which the moral development of a man can be plainly seen (for the reverse, see *A Passage to India*, in which Fielding is the moral benchmark for the agonizing choice facing Miss Quested in her court testimony). Neither *Groundhog Day* nor *The Fisher King* are explicitly religious, though Harold Ramis tells us that after the release of *Groundhog Day* he was contacted by Jesuits, Buddhists and Yogis, saying that his film perfectly encapsulated the teachings of their religion. Time is the issue at the heart of the film. The weatherman protagonist, Phil Connors, is woken by his alarm clock at 6:00 each morning, on the *same* morning, February 2. He is stuck in what Nietzsche and Ouspensky refer to as "eternal recurrence." Phil is the epitome of the secularized smart aleck who expends his wit and intelligence on the denigration of others and furthering his own supposed superiority. The weather item he is covering for his TV station is beneath his contempt, as it involves a rural ritual concerning the supposed ability of the groundhog to predict the coming of Spring, as is Punxatawney, the "hick" town he is confined to.

The impact of *Groundhog Day* and most of the films that are serious contenders for the canon of film and religion derive from stepping outside of traditional tropes and providing an unfamiliar challenge. Phil goes through a sequence of reactions to his predicament that we can both identify with, because the moral challenges are familiar, and are engaged by, because the setting isn't. To start with he is subdued by the disaster that has overcome him; then he becomes reckless in his driving; then he realizes he can get away with anything and robs a security van; then he becomes desperate. He kidnaps the groundhog and drives off a cliff, but to no avail: he wakes up at 6:00 as usual. A series of further suicide attempts are likewise futile. But running through all of this is his attempt to seduce the lovely Rita, his TV producer. Robert Jewett makes a Christian reading of their relationship:

> After Rita discovers that he has set her up for the romantic evening by studying her reactions, they begin to discuss what love is. In response to his statement that he loves her, Rita replies with a moral perception that seems rooted in the Pauline tradition: "You don't even know me. ... Is this what love is for you?" she asks, meaning knowing how to seduce someone. ... To use the ancient categories, it is the difference between *agape*, genuinely caring love, and *eros*, seductive love, driven by the desire to achieve pleasure by controlling others.[11]

Jewett is on to something in that Rita, who does not know that the day is being repeated endlessly, simply responds to Phil in his changing and increasingly desperate response to the situation. She responds to his *being* as it is slowly transformed, as he slowly grows in moral capacity. But is it really a journey from *eros* to *agape*? Or has modern scholarship managed to secularize even the term *agape*, which means religious love? Phil starts from the position—as seen from her perspective—of a cad. She knows this instinctively, whereas we know for example that when he suggests they drink to "world peace" he does this merely because he has learned that this is what would make him attractive to her. She lets this slip one day; he uses it the next. Rita only knows the day she is in, but that is no disadvantage to her: as a woman her antennae can pick up a caddish act a mile off. So, his attempts to kiss her are repeatedly met with a slap, day after day. But, slowly, in a world that has spun out of his control, and in which his smart aleck superiority has been blown apart, he matures. Early on he muses with bitterness that: "I'm a god. Not *the* God. A god. I think." His immortality and omniscience point in this direction, but it brings him no comfort until he begins to use his prescience of the day to perform acts of kindness, rather than caddishness or robbery. What was a curse slowly becomes a gift, and, when his transformation is nearly complete, Rita is able to understand the anguish of his eternal recurrence, as he shows her a trick he has learned in his endless spare time:

> RITA: Is this what you do with eternity?
> PHIL: Now you know. That's not the worst part.
> RITA: What's the worst part?
> PHIL: The worst part is that tomorrow you will have forgotten all about this, and you'll treat me like a jerk again.
> RITA: No.
> PHIL: It's all right. I am a jerk.
> RITA: No you're not.

In the following days he carries out a sequence of kindly acts, and this time he kisses her without a slap as a response. The next day it is finally February 3, and his ordeal is over. Jewett, like so many other religious thinkers, has responded to something transcendent or unitive in the film, as we can clearly see that Phil is now no longer alienated from the world by his presumed and cocooning superiority: he has been made vulnerable and, through the extremity of his anguish, has been healed of his separateness. It is a spiritual crisis redeemed. But it is hard to concede the claim of Jewett that Rita's "moral perception of him is rooted in the Pauline tradition," when most women—whether Christian or not, whether religious or secular—would rumble Phil instinctively. It is of course an interesting question as to why the moral person becomes attractive in a specific way that we could *call* religious, and perhaps to that extent Jewett is right that we can call such a love *agape*. But the operation of real *agape* is outside the realm of the sexual or romantic, as St. Paul himself was adamant.

Weatherman Phil was played by actor Bill Murray, and it is interesting to speculate whether his own spiritual interests helped him carry off the role so well. It is known that Murray was keen to star in the remake of *The Razor's Edge*—a film about a young man disillusioned by war and transformed by a spiritual awakening in India—and was only permitted by his studio if he agreed to make the sequel to *Ghost Busters*.

In *Donnie Darko*, what is "rubber" is time rather than identity. To that minimal extent we can also regard *Groundhog Day* as a rubber reality film, as its central device permits a warping of reality characteristic of the bardo state. We can understand *Groundhog Day* as a lesson in karma and the subsequent moral unfolding of the protagonist. In *Vanilla Sky* and the film it was based on, *Open Your Eyes*, the protagonist is subject to a reality-warping device, this time that of virtual reality technologies. Interestingly, it is not the VR itself that warps reality—it provides what should be a perfectly consistent universe—but the protagonist's unconscious that causes eruptions of the bizarre into that ordered construction, building up to a nightmare that both arises out of a moral quandary and poses a new deeply moral question. As *Vanilla Sky* follows *Open Your Eyes* so closely, it makes little difference which version we chose to consider, though the former is of interest because the protagonist, named David Aames in this version, is played by Tom Cruise. Given that he spends most of his time hideously disfigured in the film, one can count it as a tribute to the actor that he agreed to the role.

David is an unlikeable character, whose wealth buys him everything including the attention of beautiful women. But he has a moral choice between Sophia (Penélope Cruz) and Julie (Cameron Diaz) which provokes the forces of his unconscious: the constructed reality of his world is undermined by the continuous interchange of the two women (a little like Jacob's wife and girlfriend). Here is the rubber of this reality: Why should the transmogrification of one into the other cause such horror in him? And why, at other times, is he locked up and in conversation with psychiatrist McCabe (Kurt Russell) who is trying to get him off a murder rap? In the end all is revealed to us: Aames is taken to the top of a skyscraper and shown the world— perhaps he is Jesus tempted by the devil—and he has to make a choice between a repaired virtual world in which his facial disfigurement like the demons of his unconscious guilt are banished, or the gritty real world in which he cannot control either his face or his destiny. We understand that his wealth had made his Faustian pact with VR a possibility, but that his "Gretchen" would always haunt that world, a ghost in the machine: his carelessness of her had led her, not to kill her baby as in the Goethean story, but to kill herself and disfigure him in a deliberate car crash. The disfigurement was the record on his face of his carelessness for another human being: by choosing to wear it he is acting out a daily penance. When he makes that choice he is healed.

In *The Devil's Advocate*, the protagonist likewise steps back from the Faustian pact— literally with the Devil in this case—and pursues the course of honor. He too is shown the world from a rooftop and offered it, but in the end he refuses the stardom of a lawyer who never loses a case, by refusing to use a dirty tricks option. It almost qualifies as a rubber reality movie, though perhaps it is more of a daydream pursuing a "what if" scenario of temptation.

It is worth returning to the somber nature of David Aames's choice. He can retreat into a sanitized virtual world where not only his face is restored to its male-model perfection, but his conscience, it seems, can also be wiped clean. "Are guilty memories troubling you? It's just a glitch in the software. Give us the word and we'll fix it." This is the offer from the software company that has built his virtual world. But his spiritual development begins with the rejection of the false ersatz fantasy on offer, in favor of what is morally real.

For a certain sector of the New Age, the film illustrates a quite different preoccupation: it dramatizes the longed-for possibility of *control*. The producer-director Stephen Simon, involved with films examined earlier such as *What Dreams May Come* and *Indigo*, pinpoints a scene in *Vanilla Sky* where David Aames is approached in his virtual world by one of the engineers who constructed it. Aames is told that whatever he wants will come true. Simon comments on what happens next: "Aames flippantly says, 'Well, if that's true, I wish all these people would just shut up!' Whereupon, every person in the bar immediately falls silent and just stares at David. *Never in film has there been a better envisioned example of the notion of each individual creating his/her own reality!*"[12] These are Simon's italics, and with them he articulates a central New Age fantasy. There may well be a spiritual truth to be had that one's reality is at some level one's own projection, but this New Age version of it is just narcissism. Every person in that bar represents a real and inescapable moral question for Aames: their silence may be Aames' gratification, but the converse is also true: each person in the bar might well want from Aames what would least gratify him. Every person is embedded in this moral net of interrelatedness, and to impose one's own demands on others is never without comeback. Love is not control, as Robert Jewett pointed out regarding Phil in *Groundhog Day*.

In *Jacob's Ladder* and *Donnie Darko*, the bardo worlds of the dying give us a filmic exploration of the moral and spiritual dimensions of death, while in *Groundhog Day* and *Vanilla Sky* the protagonist is restored to linear time and the world of cause and effect after a prolonged and anguished moral development. These are some of the spiritual possibilities in the filmic form of "rubber reality"—a vehicle for the exploration of spiritual crisis. In Gnostic terms we have, arguably, an agent in each case that acts as the demiurge: in *Jacob's Ladder* it is the army experiment; in *Donnie Darko* it is the engine strike; in *Groundhog Day* it is the inexplicable onset of eternal recurrence; and in *Vanilla Sky* it is the software agency that constructs the virtual world. Each of these agencies are effectively oppressive, or at least ensnaring, but are at the same time accompanied by indicators of the way back to the Godhead or liberation. Wilson's thesis of Gnosticism or Gnostic undercurrents therefore holds for these films.

With these reflections on rubber reality films we are now prepared to return to *Mulholland Drive* to see whether Wilson's advocacy of this film as either Gnostic or religiously ironic is valid. We saw that Wilson is explicit that he wants to cast Lynch as a religious seer creating a mystical presence in his films. Can we draw this conclusion from *Mulholland Drive*? Put more simply: Does it deal with spiritual or moral issues? And if so, does the journey undertaken by the protagonist(s) engage the viewer in such as way as to offer the possibility of transformation? We can be clear that following Jacob, Donnie, Phil or David in the above films *does* engage the viewer this way.

In *Mullholland Drive* are we going on a comparable journey with Betty/Diane and Rita/Camilla, two women drawn into the Hollywood cesspit of schmoozing and ambition? Certainly, just in the ambiguity of identity in the two lead female characters we have plenty of "rubber": in fact, the film could be classed as *the* leading rubber reality movie. In both women we also have a journey of discovery: Rita has lost her memory after a car crash, and Betty is out to discover herself as an actress. And there is no shortage of moral dilemmas, not least the huge amount of cash in Rita's handbag, the source of which is initially unknown. But to summarize a plot of almost infinite complexity: they become lovers and then betray each other, leading to murder. To some extent their degradation and the base motivation of all the other characters around them is sobering. But there is no real journey, no development, no crisis provoking a breakthrough, and here is why: mountains remain rivers throughout.

Wilson's essential claim is that the ambiguity of interpretation in such a film—what he calls "religious irony"—is effectively a crucible in which the audience must form a "third term," a redemptive resolution to the relentless contradictions. Yet there is no "third term" that arises in *Mullholland Drive*: nothing in its internal logic can generate such a thing. The film is hermeneutically closed, and that is its greatness: its irony doesn't allow the kind of interpretations that we have pursued in *Jacob's Ladder*, *Donnie Darko*, *Groundhog Day* and *Vanilla Sky*. It is a work of art pure and simple.

But let us press the "Gnostic" claim further. Wilson states at one point that "Mr. Roque plays the Gnostic demiurge."[13] This character is the shadowy figure controlling the studio system in which the other characters' Hollywood careers are arbitrarily made or broken, but we have to ask: Why is he *necessarily* Gnostic? One can attribute demiurge-like characteristics to any tyrant, but what is there in such tyranny that makes a Gnostic interpretation necessary, when a Marxist or Foucauldian one would do? Mr. Roque is just an evil capitalist. Surely it is the film director who bears a closer resemblance to the demiurge, because of the creativity of that role, rather than a capitalist or mobster who exploits the creativity of others. Even then, for the demiurge to be Gnostic there must be something more subtle in the fallenness of his created world: there must be signs of the way up, a trace of the Godhead, from which the demiurge appeared and from which all phenomena emerge—the *pleroma* of the Gnostic tradition. Wilson states, "In the end the dream is a Gnostic contemplation on how self-knowledge relates to the generative abyss, on how sacred identity emerges from an apprehension of the sacred origin of all phenomena."[14] But this is not convincing, sounding instead too much like an analysis in thrall to art. As we saw earlier, there is no *necessary* path from art to the sacred. Lynch, for all his greatness as a director, does not forge such a path in this film; it nowhere suggests a Godhead which is the "sacred origin of all phenomena," or a route towards it. Its characters, however shifting in their identities, undergo no moral transformation, find no pointers to the Godhead, and their destiny is no different from their starting point.

Reality Problems

Films with VR themes have been numerous, the most successful of which is no doubt the *Matrix* trilogy. It has not only been successful at the box office and with mainstream critics, but has spawned a small industry of critical writing, some of which draws explicit philosophical, religious and spiritual insights from the film. Hence the proposition that it is mere fantasy—though admittedly of a high class—may not suffice: it is necessary to show why. Its claim to be taken as more than high class escapism hinges for many on the link with the French philosopher Baudrillard and for others on its religious symbolism, so both will be considered.

As the films are so well known, only a brief summary is needed here. The Matrix is a virtual reality world provided for humans trapped in pods for use as energy sources. The captors are sentient machines who appear in various guises within the virtual world, and who police the physical world in which some escapees are mounting a rebellion aiming to free the captives. As science fiction goes, this is one of the more far-fetched premises: that one can extract more energy from an organism than one has to provide it to stay alive. There is an argument that a central conceit like this—which violates one of the most fundamental laws of nature—is bound to produce a narrative of little relevance to the life we live. Be that as it may, the story unfolds with great visual flair and narrative inventiveness. Its hero is a computer programmer called Neo who becomes the messiah for the revolution, facing various trials along the road to salvation. If this sounds rather like the story arc of Western messianic monotheism that is no accident. Indeed, by the third film Neo clearly *is* the Messiah, and the setting for the final battle is reminiscent of Masada fighting off the Romans (though without the mass suicide).[15] The underground stronghold is even called "Zion."

The value of the rubber reality genre to the spiritual life is that it probes the question of what is real. Central to many Indian strands of religious thought is the idea that so-called everyday life or reality is an illusion or *maya*. Hence, the *Matrix* films can be claimed for Hinduism or Buddhism. On the other hand, the messianic elements can be claimed for Judaism, Christianity or Islam. But such claims can be disposed of fairly quickly when one recognizes the extent of the New Age narcissism at work in the character and story of Neo. He is geek-turned-caped-crusader, and indeed at the end one would find it hard to distinguish his actions from that of Batman, Spiderman or Superman. Like the original comic book heroes, no arduous physical training is needed: in this case one "downloads" relevant skills, including aerobatic martial arts. One doesn't even need a shower afterwards, because sweating is also abolished. In any case the idea that violence in a good cause makes one a "redeemer," let alone a messiah, is suspect, and will be examined closely later on.

But what of the claims for the film that it lets us examine the nature of reality, either in Western philosophical terms or in Eastern Hindu or Buddhist terms? Starting with the latter, we can take an essay by Michael Brannigan in the compilation *The Matrix and Philosophy: Welcome to the Desert of the Real* as typical of thoughtful responses to *The Matrix* (as is the whole volume). Brannigan uses the mirror as an image to draw comparisons with *The Matrix* and Buddhism, citing a spoon-bending episode in the first film. But he is forced to concede that "there are at least four ingredients in the film that appear incongruous with Buddhist teachings."[16] These are the typical elements of Western dualism (good versus evil); the scenes of violence that contradict Buddhist teachings on *ahimsa* (nonviolence); the scenes containing crass or aggressive language that contradict the teachings on "right speech"; and the proposition that the "programs" are lesser sentient beings than humans.

In *Exegesis of the Matrix*, Peter B. Lloyd suggests that the trilogy can be seen in terms of a Plotinian or Neoplatonist demiurge, as in Wilson's thesis. But this is stretching a point because the demiurge in this case turns out to be simply a manipulative human being with megalomaniac software engineering skills.[17] Behind him is nothing more than ambition: as in *Mullholland Drive* there is no sign of the necessary Godhead, and no route to that Godhead provided for within its structure or clues left as to how to set out on that journey. The sole purpose of the Matrix is to be the bread and circus that pacifies the restless consciousness of its captives, and the revolt against it is that of any revolutionary political cause. It is, of course, a journey to political freedom, if highly romanticized, but just as there is no *necessary* path from art to the sacred, we can observe that there is no *necessary* link between the struggle for political freedom and the struggle for spiritual liberation.

The connection with Baudrillard is also implausible, as is confirmed by the fact that Baudrillard himself disowned any resemblance between the message of the film and his writings.[18] His work specifically relates oppression to capitalism, whereas the oppression in the trilogy is merely that of any powerful group against the weak, and indeed the criticism of the Matrix as a world by the rebels seems to have nothing to do with its capitalist system; rather the whole film feels like product placement for the fashion and armaments industries. A critique of the film more consonant with the one pursued here is that of John Shelton Lawrence, who lambasts the films as fascist and an example of the political poverty of Joseph Campbell's monomyth.[19]

But what about the fact that Neo chooses to live in the real physical world, grim as it is, when he could stay in the virtual one, accept the pleasant tyranny of it, and enjoy himself? One of his fellow rebels succumbs, partly because he can't take the slop they eat in real life, compared to steak and wine in the virtual world. Isn't Neo's principled stand against the virtual on the same moral level as David Aames in *Vanilla Sky*? The answer is not really, because as Lawrence points out, *The Matrix*, however imaginative, embodies Campbell's hero myth. It was suggested in the Introduction that the problem in most escapist fiction is that the "hero" is given quite implausible *agency*. In this case the superpowers manifest in Neo are all virtual: they operate in a virtual world, are "downloaded" rather than acquired the hard way, and provide for such an exaggerated spectacle of violence that it almost becomes a kind of chic pornography.

He becomes an invincible god, a savior, with infinite sex appeal. In the real world he is strapped to a chair. He has chosen that instead of steak and wine, all very good; he faces real danger in a grim battle-craft, where the scope of his agency is that of the ordinary soldier. But it cannot challenge us: we play computer games like him but no robotic tentacles are going to smash through our living room window and tear at our bodies should we fail the level. But we *are* challenged by the predicament of David Aames whose virtual life is plagued by his subconscious guilt, a very real guilt for the harm he brought others. In *Vanilla Sky* Aames will carry his disfigurement for life as a penance for his cavalier treatment of a girlfriend. We suspect that Neo on the other hand will stay pretty in any world: that's his job. In *Vanilla Sky* Aames undergoes a violent struggle with his own conscience, deploying only his own inner moral resources. In the *Matrix* Neo undergoes a violent struggle with machines, deploying unfeasibly destructive weaponry and fantastical super-hero skills.

So, the *Matrix* films are high-class imaginative escapism. When C. S. Lewis said that only jailors object to escape, he has a point: religion shouldn't be dour and it shouldn't shut off all the light-hearted ways in which we enjoy life. But to take the *Matrix* seriously is a mistake. The point about escapism is that it is unchallenging, just as bland foods are for a baby's digestive system. The audience remains safe: no-one leaves the cinema morally touched by Neo's life.

The Lawnmower Man, *The Thirteenth Floor* and *Existenz* are further VR films where religious parallels can be extracted with dubious justification. At one level all the VR films like to play with the idea that if a perfect VR world can be constructed, then perhaps *this* world is also a simulation. When Chang Tzu dreamed he was a butterfly and then woke up to wonder whether he was now a butterfly dreaming that he was a man, he spoke of the ancient puzzlement we all have about how convincing some of our dreams are. The *Matrix* trilogy, *The Thirteenth Floor* and *Existenz* all pursue this question, though *Existenz* is more properly rubber reality than the other two because ultimately neither the protagonists nor the audience knows which world is real, nor what is true about the characters, or who they are. These three films, while pressing the question of "what is real?" here and there, in the end are only escapism, and hence we cannot really relate the choices faced by the protagonists to those in our non-fiction lives.

The Lawnmower Man, an earlier VR outing than *The Matrix*, reinforces the perception that VR might enhance our capacities and intelligence (though in real life it is more likely to turn us further into screen addicts). The protagonist Jobe, who starts as educationally subnormal, receives both drugs and VR sessions, so that his intelligence leaps forward exponentially. Strangely, "intelligence" is here conflated with aggression, so that Jobe's transformation becomes a military project. In the end he becomes a kind of cyber–Christ and dies, crucified on his machine. But why shouldn't an enhanced intelligence lead to a mind as acute and pacifist as the Buddha's?[20]

Summary

A feature of the spiritual or religious life when lived with any intensity is that it challenges many assumptions of reality and also the norms of society. It is also true that when religion ceases to be a journey of enquiry and becomes dogmatic it tends to align itself with social forces that resist any challenges to the norm. The films examined in this section show how the artistic mind revels in providing narratives which undermine conventional accounts of reality. But how do they relate to the lived spiritual life? Clearly, many of the films in this chapter are about spiritual crisis. As in an earlier chapter *Jacob's Ladder* and *Donnie Darko* stand out as films where the protagonists, suffering from the most extreme of distortions of normal daily life, face their fate in the end with a kind of joyous serenity. In addition *Groundhog Day* and *Vanilla Sky*, while illustrating different aspects of "rubber reality" are also stories of moral development, which, put in different terms, means the increasing awareness of self as connected to others.

This chapter also took the opportunity to examine a number of approaches to religion and film, particularly the idea of virtual reality films as Gnostic or Neoplatonist. The *Matrix* film series has received much critical attention from the religion and film community, but in this and similar films we have seen that the relevance to the spiritual life is rather slight. This is ultimately for the same reason as for most films of the esoteric: there is nothing inherently spiritual in gaining mastery over the world and others. Mostly this is just narcissism.

Instead, what stands out as luminous in these films are moments where the Faustian pact with supernormal powers is spurned in favor of the harder journey, or where the protagonist quietly says—in whatever formulation—"thy will be done."

7
Wisdom, Teachers and Disciples

If a spiritual crisis looms, then one may turn to a spiritual teacher. Tarkovsky was convinced that the spiritual crisis is part of the spiritual life, perhaps as the artistic crisis is part of the artistic life. If so, then there might be spiritual chaos for a while, as we have just explored. In the Zen understanding of this—and in many other traditions—this is just the time when a spiritual teacher is needed. Such a person has been known as the guru, sage, Master, or wise man or woman; in earliest times the shaman, later on the prophet. Such gurus, sages, shamans, teachers, or prophets, depending on personality or tradition, can be a point of stability through a personal crisis. Or—controversially—they can actually engender the spiritual crisis in the pupil, in which case they are known as "crazy wisdom" teachers.[1]

The idea that a certain kind of person has a depth of insight or wisdom such that they can teach other adults persists into democratic times. The idea is under attack; for example, the "genius" is a discredited idea among postmodernists, and even the master class in woodworking, cello playing or software design has a faintly disreputable air of elitism, unless rescued by the cult of celebrity. Nevertheless, there are icons of wisdom in the secular world such as Nelson Mandela and the Dalai Lama (despite his religious status), a vast array of self-help gurus, and in the explicitly spiritual worlds of the New Age and faith traditions the spiritual teacher and the religious guru may have considerable followings. The fact is that in the lived spiritual life it may well be contact with such a person that initiated the spiritual journey in the first place. The extraordinary story of how the Sufi poet Rumi met and was inspired by Shams-i-Tabrīzī is just one of countless such initiatory encounters in the world's spiritual literature.

There is a distinct East-West divide over the issue of the spiritual teacher, the preacher or the guru, partly because the monotheist West is more a tradition of texts, while the pluralist East is more a tradition of teachers. In the West the preacher teaches on the authority of the church or the Bible, while in the East the guru teaches more on the authority assumed to them as a result of personal spiritual status, the most significant term used in this being *enlightened*. The Western preacher has a tight and somewhat fixed canon of Scripture, while the Eastern guru, not without access to holy books it is true, is often regarded as the more authentic the less they rely on a text. In its extreme in Zen, the written word is regarded with suspicion, as in the Zen story of a Master who, late in life, hands his writings over to a sen ior disciple, saying that he had summed up all his insights in them. The disciple promptly threw the writings on the fire. Aghast, the Master said, "What are you doing?" The disciple responded immediately:

"What are you saying?"[2] No more is needed in the Zen tradition; it is understood that the reproach was properly delivered by the disciple, not the Master.

"What are you saying—that a written account can possibly convey the lived experience of Zen?"

This story not only illustrates how canonical Scripture in the East is greatly downplayed against the importance of the teacher, but also that the teacher, guru, or Master can be challenged by the pupil if their insight and personal development has reached a certain stage. No ill-feeling results. The guru has a high social status, but a pupil may reach a point where they leave, simply, and with no drama, because they have learned enough, or have found a better guru. Apparently, the Buddha had six gurus that he studied with in his own journey of spiritual seeking, and each one at a certain point told him that they had taught him everything they knew, and it was time to move on. In other words, no guru carries *absolute* authority, only the authority of personal insight and realization, *relative* to that of the pupil. In the West preachers carry no authority at all on account of their own insight, but do carry the absolute authority of the church, and, traditionally, this brooked no debate or question.

When teaching woodwork, the cello, or software design, it is clear enough what kinds of knowledge the master imparts to the pupil, even with the caveat that this knowledge is not like a liquid that can be poured from one vessel into another. Spiritual or religious knowledge is harder to pin down, even with the same caveat, though sometimes it is referred to as "wisdom," as in "the wisdom traditions of the East." When the guru principle traveled from the East to the West in the second half of the twentieth century it was uprooted from its historical context and placed in the context of a history of religious absolutism. Hence, the catalog of guru malpractice in the West, documented by writers such as Anthony Storr,[3] Georg Feuerstein and Maria Caplan.[4] But the relationship between preacher and disciple, or guru and follower, fascinates us and has had a number of filmic treatments, ranging from absolute skepticism in *The Life of Brian* to absolute sincerity in *Meetings with Remarkable Men*. We will see in a later chapter that in *The Quarrel*—in which two Jews argue over the Holocaust—the secular minded Chaim is moved by the conviction of Rabbi Hersh's plea to him, and tells him that if he were to return to God it would be for the sake of the Rabbi's passion. Why shouldn't one person in the spiritual life say to another, You know more than me, would you be my teacher? For now?

Gurus and Disciples

Of course, the question arises: who is to authorize the genuine Master, guru, or spiritual teacher? Where is the system for national accreditation as in the case of the teacher of woodwork, the cello, or software design? The secular person can simply dismiss the question, but the serious seeker has to make the choice. The life and work of the Greek-Armenian spiritual teacher G. I. Gurdjieff is something of a touchstone for Western attitudes to gurus. Many are content to dismiss him as a charlatan; others were devoted to him in his lifetime; and some others still count themselves as his disciples today. A considerable number of artists, writers and intellectuals have been influenced by Gurdjieff, including the film director Peter Brook, and the screenwriter for the film *The Wicker Man*, Anthony Shaffer. Hence, Brook's *Meetings with Remarkable Men*—a dramatization of Gurdjieff's autobiography of the same name—is something of a tribute to the master. For viewers on either side of the guru debate there is interesting material in the film. For the skeptic it might be obvious that the young Gurdjieff as a seeker himself is ludicrously naive and easily impressed by Oriental trickery, though this might just be Brook's stamp on the story: the book portrays a seeker just as determined, but somehow less picture-book earnest. For those that regard the term "seeker" itself as valid, and are open to both what Gurdjieff learned and then later taught, there is interesting material. Most important to the Gurdjieff tradition are the "sacred dances" at the end of the film. Although their exact origins are unknown, Gurdjieff claims to have learned them from Sufi or other esoteric teachers hidden away in mountain retreats in the Middle East. He developed them into his own system, and their rehearsal and performances to this day are held rather private to the teachers and organizations of his legacy.

As we saw earlier, in *Spring, Summer, Autumn, Winter, ... and Spring* a Zen Master has an errant disciple who originally arrived at the small floating monastery as an orphaned baby. As a child we see him exhibit a streak of cruelty, tying small rocks to a fish, a frog and a snake. His Master looks on, but does not intervene. Instead, he is harshly punished: in the night the Master ties a rock to his back, and in the morning tells the child that it will not be removed until he has untied the creatures. Struggling with the rock through the forest, the child returns to find both the fish and the snake dead, though he is able to free the frog. The Master tells him that he will carry the stone in his heart for evermore. The film has a staged quality about it, verging on magical realism at times, with the central theme of the cycles of Nature, and the cycles of discipleship and mastery. As such, it serves as a metaphor for the entire Eastern spiritual outlook, set squarely against Western linear time and its teleology of some future one-off apocalypse or salvation. As a young man the disciple, so far locked into a world containing only the Master as companion, is subject to the torments of sexual desire when a young woman is brought for a retreat by her mother. They have an affair leading to the young man leaving the monastery, though not before his Master tells him that "lust leads to desire for possession, and possession leads to murder." And so it does, as the man returns as a fugitive from justice: he has murdered his wife. The Master asks the pursuing detectives to wait until the young man is punished in religious style: he ties him up, and then is released to carve the *Heart Sutra*—a key Mahayana Buddhist text—into the decking of the monastery. Once finished he leaves to serve his time in prison. The Master grows old, and commits ritual suicide, after which the disciple returns, and continues various penances. In turn another woman leaves a baby at the monastery, and the disciple now becomes the new Master.

There is no doubt that the film is beautiful, at many levels, as mentioned earlier. The natural environment of the mountain lake fringed with forests, and the simplicity of the floating monastery made from traditional materials conveys in itself considerable spirituality. The Buddhist rituals and the carving of the *Heart Sutra* convey the gravitas of a venerable tradition. But there is little joy in it: the human being it seems is condemned to an endless round of sin and atonement. Given Ki-duk Kim's Catholic background, it is tempting to think of this as more a caricature of Catholicism than of Buddhism.

We later return to the issue of atonement in this film, while here we consider the question of the spiritual knowledge imparted by the Master. Perhaps here we find the real weakness of *Spring, Summer*: beyond the lesson of the iron law of rebirth and karma, and instruction in the outer rituals of Buddhism, there is little imparting or receiving of the spiritual wisdom that makes an inner reality of the tradition. We don't grapple with the *Heart Sutra* itself and its challenging denial of the distinction between emptiness and form, or what it means to become a Bodhisattva. But for our purposes here there is another problem: in the cycles illustrated in the film the disciple becomes one by chance. There is no sense, as with Gurdjieff, of a person purposefully turning away from conventional pursuits to the path of the seeker. It is in the film's precursor, *Why Did Bodhidharma Leave for the East?*, that there is a third character interposed between the Chan master of the temple and the orphan child: that of Kibong, a young man who deliberately turns away from the "World"— including family—to become a Zen monk. His spiritual journey involves the painful lesson that the abandonment of family ties has moral implications.

The Master-disciple relationship seems relatively unchallenged in the East. But the Western cultural downplaying or even complete rejection of the idea of apprenticeship in general and in the spiritual life in particular has considerable lineage by now. Marx is one source of this no doubt—with his negative view of the medieval guild system—but so, too, is the Romantic cult of the individual. Virtual reality films suggest that we can "download" learning and skill without all the bother of study, apprenticeship, or discipleship, as we saw. If other aspects of modern life can be accelerated, why not these? If knowledge can be stored electronically, why bother with a teacher? The Master-disciple relationship is, then, doubly remote: foreign because it appears to be an Eastern import, and foreign because all such ideas of long and arduous study appear old-fashioned.

But if we just go back to the 1930s, we see that Somerset Maugham's novel *The Razor's Edge* provides evidence that "reading the mystics" was a common cultural attainment then, whether or not it provoked any serious personal seeking. The mystics here are understood as spiritual Masters, their words as revered texts. The novel tracks the progress of Larry Darrell as he survives World War I to find that the pursuit of wealth is less to his taste than the pursuit of knowledge. His journey takes him to India where he studies with a Master or guru in the mountains, and then returns to the West. The details of his searching and the Indian experience are few, but Maugham uses the Flapper-era high society context to keep his readers on board while he muses on many of the great names and themes in mysticism. A filmic version of the book is bound to provide even less genuine insight into the arduous world of the seeker and the teachers he or she might encounter, and both Edmund Goulding's 1946 version and John Byrum's 1984 version starring Bill Murray are subject to this disappointment. Nevertheless, the films point to an era, not so long ago, where there was a greater credibility in mainstream society towards the concept of seeker and teacher than there is today.

The difficulties of translating the guru system into the West have led to cynicism about it. But cynicism towards the guru is not confined to the contemporary West: India with its enormous guru industry and its fair share of poor or downright fraudulent practitioners can now be just as hostile. V. S. Naipaul, of Indo-Trinidadian descent, mocks the idea of the guru in his 1957 novel *The Mystic Masseur*, which was made into a film by Ismail Merchant in 2001. The film tells the story of a Trinidadian writer of Indian descent who fakes a talent as a healer. In reality the film is more a satire of the politics of the time and region, into which can be conveniently inserted the assumption that gurus are as corrupt and venal as politicians. *The Guru* is a 2002 film following an Indian dance teacher who comes to America, starts on a porn career, but then stumbles into the role of guru. This piece of candyfloss has been lambasted as representing no advance in attitude to Orientals since Blake Edwards' 1968 film *The Party*, starring Peter Sellers. It is telling, however, that as a target of satire the guru has the full weight of cultural disapproval to ensure the easy success of anti-guru films. The 2008 film *The Love Guru*, written by and starring Mike Myers, pursues this route, and no doubt more will follow.

A more highbrow critique comes from Bergman in his 1958 film *The Magician*. Although its protagonist Albert Vogler, played by Max von Sydow, is not cast as a guru in the way we understand it today, Bergman probes the credulity offered to the archetypal "mystery man" (which category includes magicians, psychics and gurus), particularly from women. Vogler is a fraud but is riding high and seems to believe in himself, thus somehow representing a blank canvas for the hidden yearnings of his audience for the magical. Vogler leads a small troupe of performers who arrive in a Swedish town where they are challenged by local officials to prove that they are genuine. What is interesting is that a local woman is deeply stricken by the mute darkly clad magician, whispering to him that she had "known" he was coming. In the end when he is proved a fake she disowns him. The film is a study of charisma and illusion, with perhaps Bergman implicating the filmmaker as an illusionist. But here is another example where Mike Tucker overlays a film with too much meaning. He says of it: "Bergman offers a rich examination of both the sociology and phenomenology of shamanism."[5] There is only the most *remote* of parallels between Vogler, the knowing fraud, and that of the shaman, either in their stance to the world, their belief systems, or in their cultural setting. A better parallel is with Jonas Nightengale in *Leap of Faith*, considered below.

Preachers, Healers and Followers

As pointed out, the guru is an Eastern idea that has transposed badly into the Western context, so it is not surprising that filmic treatments are few and mostly unrevealing. The *preacher* however is a familiar Western category, and finds his way into many more films, some of which are sympathetic to the subject.

The Apostle is written and directed by Robert Duvall, who stars in the title role of Sonny, known later in the film as "The Apostle E. F." The film usefully portrays both the more unappealing aspects of southern American church life and its best. Sonny is a preacher with a temper who loses his church to his wife, provoking him into violence which leaves a man in the hospital. Fearing the worst, Sonny goes on the run, faking his death and emerging with his new moniker as a stranger in a small community. He is a talented and inspiring preacher and also a hard worker, so he rebuilds his life and takes on the parallel project of rebuilding a derelict church. It is in the church scenes where Duval gives us a fine filmic glimpse into the core of the Christian religion and in the role played by the preacher. That core is love, and the role of the preacher is to shepherd his congregation into the experience and expression of it. At least this is what is conveyed in the first service held in the newly opened church with a congregation of eight or so who attend that day. This is a religion of the ordinary person, drawn to collective worship through the warmth and sincerity of a preacher who evokes from them the classic response to Christ in the Paulian tradition. Worship and care for the needy go hand in hand, as it did in the early Christian communities established and nurtured by St. Paul. Peace is also the message, as Sonny demonstrates in the uneven course of his atonement, when a man hostile to the church pulls up in a bulldozer and threatens them with it. Sonny has first responded to the man's racism with his fist, but is now pressed to reach the man through his gift with words. His last sermon, to a much swollen congregation including the newly converted bulldozer man, is made in the knowledge that the police are waiting to arrest him for homicide.

A Man Called Peter is the film version of the biography of the Reverend Dr. Peter Marshall, a preacher who twice served as Chaplain of the United States Senate. The general respect in which he is held makes for an aura of sanctity around him, in contrast to the conflicted character of the fictional Sonny in Duvall's film. But there is no doubt that Marshall's sermons had a truthful integrity about them, and there are three fine sermons in the film, which raises it above the usual biopic of the saintly person. In the first of them he says:

> The great things by which we live are not proven by logic, but by life. And as that is true of love, and beauty, so it is true of finding God, and learning how close to us he stands.

The anti-Greek element in Christianity has been watered down since Aquinas and the rehabilitation of Aristotle in Catholicism, so it falls to a Presbyterian to point out, in simple terms, that religion has nothing to do with logic. It is not that logic cannot serve us, but that it is a tool unsuited to the pursuit of love, beauty or God. Marshall's skill and popularity as a preacher seems to lie with his ability to get behind the formulas of his religion and speak to the issues with fresh energy. In doing so he occasionally strayed from convention, but not so far as to alienate authority, as his career showed.

The editors of the *Journal of Religion and Film* interviewed Robert Duvall, and recorded this about him:

> He pointed out there have been other movies about Pentecostal religions, but they never gave the people and their religion their due. Movies such as *Leap of Faith* and *Elmer Gantry* were fakes. "They patronize," Duvall says. "They put quotation marks around the preacher. They don't give the minister or his congregation their due."[6]

We look at *Leap of Faith* a little later, but for now *Elmer Gantry* is considered as on the cusp of charlatanry (rather than a certain fake). What makes Gantry as a character more than a charlatan is his personal generosity and basic decency. The film charts his accidental rise from con man to preacher, occasioned by his infatuation with Sister Sharon Falconer, a revivalist preacher. Gantry, played by Burt Lancaster, is never a blameless preacher like Peter Marshall, or even a compromised one like Sonny. Ivan Butler comments that the film is unfailingly interesting and often exhilarating, indulging in neither easy moral indignation nor cheap satirical sneers. In fact, it continually throws out hints that beneath all Gantry's showmanship and money-grabbing there may—perhaps—exist a genuine belief in what he preaches.[7]

Duvall's point still holds however: films rarely give either the preacher or their congregation their due. There is a chemistry here in real life, as there is between guru and disciple in the Eastern context, which film has yet to paint with full conviction, Duvall's efforts perhaps coming closest. The secular world of course has plenty of cases to draw on when seeking to deny the validity of the whole exercise.

The image of the guru is serenity; the image of the preacher is passion. But that passion can tip over the edge into madness, as explored in *Wise Blood* by John Huston and *Ordet* by Carl Theodor Dreyer. The protagonist of *Wise Blood* is young American soldier Hazel Motes, honorably discharged, who believes in nothing and has nothing to go to. He has preaching in his blood however, and is impressed by salesmanship, whether for potato peelers or God. He decides to strike out on his own in a town square, delivering a rant that starts like this: "My church is the church without Christ, where the blind don't see, the lame don't walk and the dead stay dead. It's the church that the blood of Jesus don't foul with Redemption."

Huston, considered to be an atheist, has taken the novel of the same name and given it what the filmic medium is so good at: the intensity of good direction, and particularly the dramatically focused intensity of the lead actor. We have all seen the madness in a person's eyes that conveys both enormous energy and the perversion of reality they are pursuing with such intent: in this case it is the perversion of religion. Hazel's delusions are utterly believable, and by making his vision the direct inversion of Christian truth, the source of his energy is all the more convincing. If a truth stands out there—*but one doesn't get it*—then those who would stand to gain most from it are bound to rage most ferociously against it. Hazel's downward spiral through self-blinding to murder and apprehension is inevitable and bleakly nihilistic. There is not a scrap of human warmth or understanding between any of the characters, not a scrap of peace, forgiveness, atonement, or insight into the divine order in the film. But its portrait of human madness is masterful, and at the same time it curiously confirms religion's deepest truths by their inversion.

Ordet can be placed with Bergman's films among the chronicles of exhausted Christianity. Beautifully shot, it is reminiscent at times of the aesthetic pursued in the much later film *Anchoress*, though the latter is set in much earlier times when atheism was unknown. *Ordet* is set in remote rural Denmark in the 1930s, where two families pursue different forms of faith: one austere and one more earthy, in a context of growing atheist challenge from scientific materialism. Morten, of the earthy persuasion, has three sons: Mikkel, who has no faith, Johannes, who has lost his mind and believes he is Jesus, and Anders, who wants to marry across the divide. Mikkel's wife, Inger, undergoes a difficult labor ending in stillbirth, giving scope for the doctor's belief in science to be aired. His view on Johannes is Freudian: "He will get better, just give him time. One day a psychic shock will clear out the rubbish of his subconscious." Indeed, after Inger's sudden death Johannes disappears, only to return with his reason apparently restored. A young niece, who has faith in Johannes, tells him to hurry up and cure Inger, lying in her coffin. When pressed, the child tells him that she believes in him, and so he responds: "Thy faith is great, it shall be done according to thy will." He proceeds to bring Inger back to life, after which Mikkel's faith is restored. The madness of Johannes is less convincing than that of Hazel however, and the ending no more than *deus ex machina*. This is because, as with Bergman's films, Johannes's condition is a Freudianized hysteria: he is frozen, close to cataleptic. This tells us nothing about the pathology of religion, or the religious source of madness. Hazel's trajectory is the inverse of faith, but Johannes simply goes nowhere until his implausible restoration and ability to bring the dead to life. This act of resurrection is no more than the drawing forth of a symbol, as one might draw an ace from a hand of cards to trump a rival. The symbols of Christianity are shuffled, selected from, and presented to us, but the inner world of Johannes is closed to us. Hazel's world, on the other hand, in its progressive darkening, shows what a journey into light could be. The preaching of neither man, of course, yields direct light on how preacher and congregation pursue authentic religion. Duvall's dictum stands.

Preaching and healing are gifts sometimes associated with each other, a partnership strongly figuring in the Christian tradition. *Touch* is a Paul Schrader film about an ex–Franciscan monk called Juvenal who has the stigmata and can "heal" people. He is picked up by salesman Bill Hill with an eye to big profits. The problem with the film is that Juvenal, despite losing his "touch" at one point, genuinely heals people, even despite Hill's attempts at commercial exploitation of the gift. This means that the film evades the issue of miracles and healing by placing them in a commercialized context where they can be understood perhaps as a plot device, central conceit and so on. The believer is left as unsatisfied as the unbeliever.

Leap of Faith works better because its protagonist, Jonas Nightengale (played by Steve Martin), is a fraudulent Christian faith healer who knows he is a fraud. He works large crowds, but his own assessment of his fraudulence runs like this: "Maybe, maybe not. If I get the job done, what difference does it make?" The job, as that of any preacher in any tradition, is to hold an audience together in acts of worship and communion. The apostle E. F. may have preached to a dozen, Nightengale to thousands, but the job is to bring that group together and feel some higher force, some togetherness, some *connectedness*. Nightengale doesn't have to believe in anything to perform his role, because the audience brings their religiousness with them. But when a child *is* cured in one of his staged set pieces, Nightengale's world view is challenged. Returning again to the theme of the suspension of disbelief required in these two films we can see that this requirement of fiction is not a simple one. The very act of reading a novel or watching a film requires the suspension of disbelief, at the minimum level at least of engaging with something made up. The ancient human habit of story telling requires a willing audience—and there is a great moment in *The Life of Brian* where the audience for the opportunist preacher comically refuses to follow the normal rules of listening, by asking awkward questions. But the step from following the made-up story that is a film, whether based on real life or not, to accepting the supernatural is a huge one. In both *Touch* and *Leap of Faith*, there is potentially an interesting exploration of how one relates to the preacher-healer. Yes, they are fiction, but how would I react if I came across such a person in real life? This means that the film confronts the audience, as Schrader would say, or makes the context feel unsafe as Jasper would say. But if the healing that takes place is pushed firmly into the category of the "miraculous" and therefore of the supernatural, then one can just doze off. Oh, it's just a fairy-tale. The potential for confrontation is lost in the category of fantasy. *The Apostle*, by contrast, is deeply engaging, as Duval intended, because the supernatural is entirely eschewed. And for an American audience in particular, used to ordinary folk who solve their problems with a fist or gun, the apostle E. F. is the man next door. You can't so easily dismiss his embrace.

Idiots Savants and Nature Wisdom

We love the wisdom of the idiot. Indeed, this is a cultural stereotype that seems to transcend place and period, appearing in the Mullah Nasruddin Sufi stories, Dostoyevsky's *The Idiot*, and the secular world in the urban myth of the Asperger's genius. The anti-intellectual culture of Britain and America prefers the shambling intuitive Columbo to the suave erudite Poirot; it prefers Captain Kirk to Spock; and it prefers Forrest Gump to Foucault.

Being There is a fable of the idiot savant for the modern West; *The Enigma of Kaspar Hauser* a fable of the idiot savant for the early Victorians. *Being There* stars Peter Sellers as Chauncey Gardiner (Chance), a man with no past apparently brought up by a wealthy eccentric who provides him with food and a TV. The eponymous Kaspar Hauser is a man with no past brought up in a dungeon and suddenly released in early adulthood onto the streets of small German town. Hauser was a historical character; Gardiner the product of Jerzy Kosiński's imagination. Both films indicate the fascination that the modern world has with the person who lives outside of time and money—that is like a child—with no planning for the future or fear of what it might bring. "The child is father to the man," says Blake, perhaps echoing our appetite for the wisdom that comes from the person otherwise classed as an "idiot." The maid who provides Chance with his meals says he has "rice pudding between his ears," but his naïveté is his protection as he is forced onto gang-infested city streets after his patron dies. He is taken up by a rich woman, played by Shirley MacLaine, whose husband finds his simple homilies to be the epitome of wisdom. "You have the gift of being natural," he tells Chance, and later on: "There is something about him that I trust. Since he has been around, the thought of dying has been much easier for me." The end of the film sees Chance walk across a lake, Christ-like.

Kaspar Hauser, on emerging from his cell, knows only enough language to repeat that he wants to be a cavalryman as his father was, but does not know what the words mean. At first taken to be a conman or fraud, before long he becomes the object of scientific enquiry, and is eventually feted across Europe. He is schooled in German and music, attracting attention again because of the simple wisdom expressed in his responses to a world he cannot understand. For example, when outside the tower where he had his room, he exclaims that the room was bigger than the tower. This is because his view from the window was so expansive. He is the Noble Savage of Rousseau. The early Victorian world—obsessed with the distinction between the civilized and the uncivilized—reveled in the frisson of doubt that Hauser created over that very distinction. He even appeared in a circus.

Part of the attraction for Vladimir Arsenyev of Dersu Uzala is the same apparent naïveté, combined with skills of survival in the forest that he knows well enough that he and his soldiers lack. As shown in countless films of the encounter between the white man and indigenous hunter gatherers, the white man perceives the natives as unable to plan the future properly and to live so intensely in the present as to be like children. At the same time, their apparent wisdom in all matters of intuition astonishes and humbles.

A fascinating pair of films, one documentary and the other fictionalized, deal with the life of Ishi, the last of a Native American tribe called the Yahi. The documentary film *Ishi: The Last Yahi* describes how Ishi, after all his family and tribe were killed by whites, walks out of his remote Californian fastness into the white civilization of 1911. He is taken up by the renowned anthropologist Alfred Kroeber, and soon makes headlines naming him an "Aboriginal Indian" or the "Last Stone Age Man." He is that quite literally, as the film reveals that his way of life includes no metal tools. Kroeber described him as "the most uncivilized and uncontaminated man in the world today." Ishi became a fixture at Kroeber's museum, and appeared as an exhibit at the Panama-Pacific International Exposition in 1915, much as Hauser appeared in a circus. This was a normal feature of the day (for example, the Native Americans Black Elk and Sitting Bull both performed in Buffalo Bill Cody's Wild West circus). *The Last of His Tribe* dramatizes the life of Ishi, with Native American actor Graham Greene in the title role. It is clear, when cross-referencing the two films, that Ishi had a natural dignity and quick intelligence that made him an easy part of the Edwardian civilized world, yet at the same time presented such profound challenges to Edwardian assumptions that Kroeber in the end abandoned him. What exactly is this vaunted modern "civilization" if a so-called savage can learn it in a decade? We also learn much about the spiritual life of the Native American, little of which gives consolation to the assumed superiority of white man's religion.

At one point, Kroeber takes Ishi back to his tribal lands, and is delighted as Ishi shows his mastery of the ancient way of life. But Ishi is increasingly troubled by his loss, the loss of contact with the land. "Put your hands on the earth," he tells Kroeber, who kneels down slowly to do so, embarrassed. "Do you feel her breathing?" "Er, yes." "Do you hear her singing?" "I don't know ... I think so." "What's she singing? Sing it." "I can't." Ishi insists, but Kroeber simply can't do it. Ishi is overcome with grief, clutching handfuls of the sandy soil by the river, and attempts to sing it himself. Crouched on all fours on his native soil Ishi looks up at us, his face contorted with grief as he cannot utter the syllables of the song he barely knows, or has forgotten, or the meaning of which is slipping away from him. As he squeezes his eyes tight shut in wordless misery he turns his head down, quaking, away from Kroeber's gaze—and ours; only strangled sounds now escaping him. Ishi's wisdom is understood in some remote way by Kroeber, but he cannot receive it: his world is now too different. On his death, Ishi's brain was preserved after his autopsy, much as Hauser's was investigated and found to have an abnormality in it. Ishi's own religion forbade any such interference with the dead, but Kroeber was too late in his attempt to prevent it.

Summary

Woe to the person who sets themselves up as a spiritual teacher, preacher or healer! The cynicism of all secularists will descend upon you. At least that is what most of the films of spiritual teachers would like to tell you. The exception seems to be in the biopic of the Reverend Dr. Peter Marshall—*A Man Called Peter*—whose personal life seems impeccable while capable of delivering a sermon that was genuinely fresh and insightful. However, what these films do is to give us a glimpse of the genuine teacher now and again hedged around with various caveats. It seems in the first instance that the idiot savant is the teacher with the most kudos in the Western system, but this respect also extends to indigenous people whether or not they are considered "holy men," as some Native American teachers came to be described. This leaves us then with a small set of films that present the West with the uncomfortable and unfamiliar figure of the genuine spiritual teacher. In *Meetings with Remarkable Men*, however, there is just too much sycophancy and too many British actors to make the various Masters convincing. In *Spring, Summer, Autumn, Winter, ... and Spring*, the Master is controversial because of his harsh treatment of the disciple, though its precursor, *Why Did Bodhidharma Leave for the East?*, presents a more credible portrait of a similar figure. It is left, rather oddly, to the two film versions of *The Razor's Edge* to hint at what not only the nature of the Master, but also the disciple might be, and in both film versions this is mainly a dim refraction of what Somerset Maugham presented in the novel—which was itself rather short on detail.

The skepticism towards the spiritual teacher has understandable origins in Western religious history. What makes for a more comfortable fit with the democratic ethos of modernity is the idea that a group of seekers can learn from each other, or at least share in the spiritual life. Hence, in the next section we turn to priests, monks, nuns and spiritual community.

8
Priests, Monks, Nuns and Spiritual Community

In the previous chapter we looked at what might be called "transmission"—the direct passing of religious teachings or spiritual wisdom from person to person (rather than by reading or personal experience). This included even the possibility of a spiritual insight gained from an idiot savant or an indigenous person fully immersed in an ancient more sacred way of life, as well as the obvious routes via the preacher, guru, spiritual teacher or director, even though there is much skepticism towards this. In this section we shift emphasis to those who sign up to a religious order or who in some other way participate in a spiritual community. Those who formally enter the religious life may become simple participants such as monks and nuns, or may also become *officiates* of the tradition. The latter we call "priests" for simplicity. Priests—whether men or women—may also be gifted preachers and spiritual teachers, but in this chapter we look at those who show no such exceptional talents but are simply committed to their pastoral duties. The spiritual communities in which monks, nuns and priests find themselves will go through good times and bad, and film is a good medium to explore the inevitable tensions within such communities.

In pre-secular cultures, including those of the West, a significant proportion of the population would commit themselves formally to the religious life, usually as an alternative to the family life. In secular times such a commitment has largely lost its cultural sanction, and so film may choose to paint a skeptical portrait of those who enter the religious way of life. In Bazin's essay "Cinema and Theology" he discusses the nun's or priest's story as a third category of religious film, beyond the Jesus spectacle and lives of the saints.[1] Clearly, it is these ordinary men and women who commit themselves to the life of the spirit who are closer to us than the founder or saints of a religion, and hence their filmic treatment is often more engaging, even to a secular audience.

Some Sympathetic Portraits

The Nun's Story, starring Audrey Hepburn as Sister Luke, follows the challenge to a nun's faith presented by World War II, leading eventually to her leaving the order. It is a well-known film, and is mentioned by Juvenal at the start of *Touch* as portraying a woman in a religious order dedicated to healing. *The Nun's Story* is useful in conveying the realities of a typical Catholic order. Sister Luke is the daughter of a doctor, and her desire to practice medicine will come into conflict with her faith. At induction the Mother Superior tells the novices, "Dear children, it is not easy being a nun. It is not a life of refuge from the world. It is a life of sacrifice. In a way ... it is a life against Nature. It is a never-ending struggle for self-perfection. ... Poverty, chastity, obedience are extremely difficult."

Sister Luke's struggle is not in fact with the temptations of the world per se, but with her brilliance in medicine and the temptation to put her fulfillment in that role above her obedience to the church. At one point, she is directly ordered to fail her medical exams, but she cannot betray herself like that, with the result that she is denied her wish to serve in the Congo. However, she is eventually posted there and meets Dr. Fortunati, a secular foil to her religiosity, who understands better than she that her obedience is not deep enough for the convent. It is the killing of her father by the Nazis that provokes her final departure from orders: she confesses that she "wears the cross of Christ above a heart filled with hate." She cannot forgive the enemy. The last scene of the film, of her alone, departing the convent into the cobbled streets of the secular world, is memorable. For the atheist this is all that they may take from the film, but in fact, although religion is portrayed at times as rigid and unresponsive to the individual's spiritual journey, it is far from an atheist film: we glimpse instead the simple tests that authentic religion places on the aspirant. We neither feel that those tests were too harsh, nor that her failures were dishonorable. Ivan Butler rightly calls the film a "serious and fairly uncompromising study."[2]

La Religieuse is interesting because the play was originally written by Denis Diderot in 1780. Diderot was one of the leading thinkers of the Enlightenment, and seems to have made an early journey from theism to deism to atheism, though the last step is uncertain. At any rate he stands at the dawn of modern atheism, and so his play's commentary on the Catholic system was controversial then, and, more surprisingly, also at the time of the film's 1966 release. Given that France can be understood as the world's epicenter of secular atheism, it is shocking to learn that Rivette's film version of *La Religieuse* was banned for two years in that country.

The film tells the story of Suzanne Simonin (Anna Karina), a young woman forced by her family into a convent, where she suffers all kinds of abuse at the hands of authoritarian and ultimately depraved characters. Ivan Butler comments:

> *La Religieuse* is not only a protest against moral and physical oppression at any time, but also an illustration of the fact that—as Elliott Stein neatly puts it in his full account of the film's adventures (*Sight and Sound*, Summer 1966)—"when religious life is not the result of spontaneous engagement it can lead to depravity."[3]

For secular commentators at the time, the film was a powerful attack on the Roman Catholic Church, and also perhaps a metaphor for the authoritarianism of De Gaulle's France. But, as Butler is hinting at, Diderot's argument may not be *against* religion, but *within* it. At no point in the film is the concept of the religious life attacked per se, but only the corruption of its administration. Suzanne has no spontaneous engagement with the religious life, or to put it another way, she has no calling, and hence her experience is alienating to her. Hence, the real argument of the film is to draw attention to the fact that religion must be voluntary, not that religion is mistaken in itself. The same point is made in *The Nun's Story*.

At her induction Suzanne Simonin says "no" to chastity, poverty and obedience: she is a nun against her will. But the nuns are familiar with this situation and still optimistic for Suzanne:

> REVEREND MOTHER: How are you my child?
> SUZANNE: Resigned.
> REVEREND MOTHER: No more than that?
> SUZANNE: Frankly, no, Reverend Mother.
> REVEREND MOTHER: You love God, don't you?
> SUZANNE: With all my heart.
> REVEREND MOTHER: The rest will come to you unawares. God steals into us like a thief ... giving us no warning of his presence.
> SUZANNE: But what if I find no vocation?
> REVEREND MOTHER: Make yourself blind, let your instincts wither away. Accept that God will come to you when He will.

Diderot was writing at a time of universal belief in God and when such a conversation had universal meaning. But where today—even within communities that are nominally religious—can one person ask another if they love God, and expect the response: "with all my heart?"

What Diderot wanted to expose back then was the folly of forcing orders on those in whom no vocation had spontaneously arisen. The story follows a downward spiral leading to Suzanne leaving the convent (which was effectively a criminal act) and then committing suicide. Diderot's closing sentiment is a quote from Jacques-Bénigne Bossuet, a French bishop of the period:

> As a man's setting sail without pilot or navigation, such is the folly of accepting religious orders without the will of God as a guide.

Dead Man Walking is based on the true-life story of a nun who befriends a death-row prisoner, attempting to reduce his death-sentence to life imprisonment. Susan Sarandon plays Helen Prejean—a Catholic nun and leading American advocate for the abolition of the death penalty—and received the Academy Award for Best Actress for her role. In contrast to the first two nun films discussed here, Prejean firstly remained true to her vocation, and secondly found a path of activism or work in the world that appears to have no conflict with her church.

It is telling that Prejean's orders are Catholic in a country so deeply Protestant that in the mid–nineteenth-century Catholics were social pariahs on a level with Jews. The journey to religious and social acceptance is part of the growing tolerance in America to all minorities, but is regarded by author Susan Jacoby as more than that: Catholic activism, particularly on abortion, taught the American Protestant, or the religious right, how to organize politically.[4] The election of America's first Catholic president, John F. Kennedy, is symbolic of Catholicism's rehabilitation in that country. What *Dead Man Walking* illustrates—as incidental to its main theme of the wrongs of capital punishment—is that America is more Old Testament than New. We see this in an exchange between Prejean and the chaplain of the penitentiary:

> CHAPLAIN: Are you familiar with the Old Testament? Thou shalt not kill. If anyone sheds the blood of man, by man shall his blood be shed.
> PREJEAN: Yes father. Are you familiar with the New Testament, where Jesus talks about grace and reconciliation?

Later on Prejean argues with a warden who cites the Old Testament injunction: "An eye for an eye...." She responds by saying, "You know what else the Bible says? Death as punishment for adultery, prostitution, homosexuality, trespass on sacred ground...." She clearly agrees with none of this. There are of course Protestants more committed to the New Testament than the Old, and Catholics more committed to the Old Testament than the New, but as a broad generalization it holds that the effect of the Reformation was to make the various Protestant traditions—and hence the American religious heartland—inclined to the harsher judicial notions of the Old Testament. We saw in the section on the Apocalypse a good example of this is in the reworking of the Jezebel story: Prejean could as well have asked the chaplain which Jesus did he believe in: the one who would refuse to condemn the adulteress or the one who would kill her children and bring her "tribulation?"

The film is unsentimental about the murderer, played by Sean Penn, leaving viewers to make up their own mind on the issue of the death sentence. But if one is inclined to Prejean's interpretation of the Christian message, then the film is unsparing in its detailing of the consequences of capital punishment and is an encouragement to support organizations like National Coalition to Abolish the Death Penalty, of which Prejean was chair for a time. The victim's family initially has no such feelings and is hostile to Prejean's mission, though in the end the boy's father prays with her at the funeral of his killer.

The category of "nun" remains however an unfamiliar one to the largely secular culture of Westernized countries. The daily life of such a person and the secular daily life usually portrayed in the media are a world apart. Hence, the film *Agnes of God* provides us with a useful dramatic contrast between a Mother Superior with a cool clear vision of her vocation, and a thoughtful secularized lawyer on her first immersion in the unfamiliar—and hitherto seemingly ridiculous—religious life of a convent. Jane Fonda stars as the lawyer Dr. Martha Livingston and Anne Bancroft as the Mother Superior Miriam Ruth, whose exchanges make up the most interesting parts of the film. The story concerns a novice played by Meg Tilly in whose room is found a dead baby, and which provokes—unfortunately—a whole scenario of is-it-a-virgin-birth or was it some lecherous priest. Both the issue of the virgin birth and that of failed celibacy are tired accidents of the Christian tradition, but ultimately the freak-show implications of this are outweighed by the filmic chemistry between lawyer and Mother Superior. While the former presents us with a classic Freudianized secular skepticism of religion, the latter is portrayed as equally worldly but secure in her vocation, and is hence perhaps one of the best portrayals of a nun in film, along with that of Helen Prejean in *Dead Man Walking*. In both cases, however, the inner spiritual life of the ordained is mostly dramatized through their outer engagement with the specifics of the legal process surrounding the grave issue of murder.

The Diary of a Country Priest is a film that has prompted some of the highest critical responses and religious praise. For example Bazin says:

> It is unlikely that there exists anywhere in the whole of French cinema, perhaps even in all French literature, many moments of a more intense beauty than in the medallion scene between the curé and the countess.... The decisive clashes of their spiritual fencing-match escape us. Their words announce, or prepare the way for, the fiery touch of grace.[5]

Bazin is right, and one could even paraphrase him: there is hardly a more beautiful filmic moment of Christian grace in all the world's cinema. And the "decisive clashes" that take place between the priest and the countess should not escape one, if one has explored the idea of transmission, as in the previous chapter, the moment when one soul touches another, religiously. But in this film the curé does not set out to teach anything, for he is gripped by the deepest anguish over his faith; and, we discover, he is dying.

The sickly young priest arrives in a village parish which is broadly hostile to him and, it seems—in the grip of the secularist half of the French soul—equally hostile towards religion. The film traces his unequal struggle with his environment and with his illness. At all times he retains his simplicity however: there will be no rationalization or quick fix to his predicament. The film goes to the heart of Christian teachings because it effectively dramatizes the notion of "thy will be done"—surrender to God. Here this principle is dramatized under the rubric of grace, meaning the spontaneous irruption of what is good, liberating and of love, into an otherwise bleak existence. No human act can force such a moment into being : one could say that the life of the Christian is constituted by the waiting for that moment. As Bazin notes, the key scene in the film is when the curé visits the local countess, a woman made bitter by the loss of her son. The conversation opens with the curé telling her that he fears her death more than his own—which is already saying something. She is more worldly-wise than him, but in this statement he has already pushed past her defenses. It is typical of how a deeply religious person, through instinct, breaks down the barriers erected by those who have withdrawn from the hope of life itself. Their sparring now begins, as she flings at him her circumstances, her husband's infidelities, her bitterness. He wants to leave, under this onslaught, as she accuses him of naiveté. He is staring into her eyes at the door: "God will break you," he says.

"Break me?" she retorts, livid. "He has already broken me! He took my son. What more can He do to me?" He tells her that her hardness of heart will keep her eternally from her son. She is furious. At this point in the film her impassioned diatribe gradually fades out and his thoughts are narrated instead: "With my back against the wall before this imperious woman, I looked like a guilty man trying to justify himself." His abstracted look makes her realize that he is not well and she makes him sit down. She repeats to him her outrage, finishing with "love is stronger than death, your scriptures say so."

"We did not invent love," he responds, "it has its order, its law." He explains further, adding, "If you would love, don't place yourself beyond love's reach." "This is insane!" she cries. "You speak to me as you would to a criminal!" They argue further, and in the end she is provoked into saying: "What will you gain by making me admit that I hate God, you fool?"

He stares at her. "You don't hate Him now. Now at last you are face-to-face. He and you."

She retreats to her armchair by the fire, and brings out the locket with the picture of her dead son from her bosom (the "medallion"). He tells her that there isn't one kingdom for the living and one for the dead. "There is only the kingdom of God and we are all within it." But she tells him again of her struggle with God and her anger, to which he shows no surprise or condemnation: it is his struggle too. He reflects and then stands up to deliver a line that is deeply rooted in the French tradition, going back to Blaise Pascal: "Madame, if our God were the god of the pagans or the philosophers, though he might take refuge in the highest heavens, our misery would drag him down. But as you know, ours does not wait." This is not just his rebuke to her, but to all the religions of the intellect and of detachment: he rebukes the Buddha and Eckhart; he rebukes the French philosophers and the Deists who Pascal also rejected, and he rebukes the secular mind that knows no God at all.

At the end of this long scene, after further exchanges, she has been hit hard, and is reeling. She acknowledges her transformation: "You have left nothing standing." Her anger against existence and its apparent bleakness is transformed into love. But she is not made meek in a moment: in the grip of a returning fury she tears the locket off its chain and throws it in the fire. He rescues it: "What madness," he comments, and then adds a much-quoted line: "God is not a torturer. He wants us to be merciful to ourselves." Now she breaks down and sobs. He blesses her and leaves. Later the countess writes him a letter, which he receives late at night when arriving home. She tells him: The despairing memory of one young child locked me in a terrifying solitude and it seems as if another child delivered me from it. I hope I don't hurt your pride by calling you a child. You are one, and may God keep you so always. I ask myself how you did it, or rather, I have ceased to ask. All is well. I didn't believe resignation was possible, and in fact it's not resignation that's come over me. I'm not resigned—I'm happy.

"Resignation" is too secularized a term to properly convey the Christian idea of surrender to grace, so the countess corrects herself and casts about for the term that conveys instead what grace leaves behind—a simple religious happiness, or "felicity" as the great English chaplain-poet Thomas Traherne called it. Even if the entire parish is as malicious as he has been told—and we see it in many spiteful acts—his calling as a priest means that the curé has achieved in that one act what any spiritual teacher always hopes for. The countess dies that night, and when he stands by her bedside the following night, surrounded by flowers, candles and relatives, he thinks to the camera: "The memory of our struggle came back so vividly I thought I would faint…. What wonder, that one can give what one does not possess. Oh miracle of our empty hands!"

But he does possess grace, despite his doubts, because he has rejected the self-sufficiency of the secular mind. The countess had imprisoned herself in her grief over the loss of her child, and this had kept her protected in her secular solitude from all that is love; he had pushed past her defenses and given her, not what was his, but what is available to all if they but wish for it. That this priest is somebody unusual is confirmed by his superior when he says to him: "People don't hate your simplicity—they shield themselves from it. It's like a flame that burns them." The countess had already told him that he knew nothing of the ways of men, and so his fate is already written: not just to be crucified by his cancer, but by those around him who feared what was feared in Jesus and in Socrates: the truth. His actions are willfully misinterpreted, but he takes no step to defend himself.

For the spiritually inclined who are yet alienated by the God language of the Western religious heritage—and there are good reasons to be so alienated—the entire scene may simply be an embarrassment. To balk at it is understandable, but if one has sympathy for the tradition, or can somehow transpose its terms into another spiritual framework, then the wonder arises: How is it that one person can touch another like this? Here is no fire-and-brimstone preacher, but one who feels like a criminal in daring to confront another's inner sorrow; one whose own doubts ought to disqualify him, but which are perhaps the source of his compassion. It is fiction of course: originating in a novel, then reworked in the screenplay, and then spoken by actors. But it is hard to find anything in fiction that conveys so well the essence of the four Gospels and St. Paul's adumbration of Jesus into the world.

If Schrader's book on transcendent style in cinema is one of the most important books on the details of cinematic style appropriate to spiritual or religious themes, then Susan Sontag's essay "Spiritual Style in the Films of Robert Bresson" might be one of the most important essays. When considering this film she is moved to draw on the French mystic and philosopher Simone Weil. She cites a passage from Weil's greatest work *Gravity and Grace*, as the basis of Bresson's "anthropology."[6] Like Pascal, Weil is important to the specific French context for religion. *The Diary of a Country Priest* can be considered as capturing both something essentially religious and essentially Christian. But what of its portrayal of the curé himself, whose progress to grace the film traces? Bresson's trademark cultural autism is embodied in this solitary man, and externalized in the relentless secular hostility towards his ministry. There is an intense religiosity in the story but no *warmth* on either side of the religious-secular divide. Sontag has a different way of looking at it, however, suggesting that, while Bresson's work is undeniably "cold," this is only by contrast with art forms that are "hot." For her this is just a matter of artistic temperament.[7]

Despite the film's coldness the priest's vocation itself is not questioned: clearly the young man's calling is of the deepest kind and is clarified rather than swept away in the realization of his impending death. In a mere three words, "*all is grace*," this phrase sums up religiosity as a universal impulse and also its specific Christian instantiation. He is a true priest because firstly he is human and has doubts, secondly because he acts as a conduit for grace into an otherwise blighted life in his parish, and thirdly his faith overwhelms his doubt. Suzanne Simonin was told that "God steals into us like a thief." The country priest, despite all his misfortunes, is lucky enough to experience this where Suzanne does not. Who can account for the difference, beyond saying that he had the vocation she lacked?

Romero and *The Crime of Father Amaro* provide further sympathetic portraits of priests, but in a rather different setting: they both deal with South American religion and politics. *Romero* is essentially a biopic of the of assassinated Salvadoran Archbishop Óscar Romero, while *The Crime of Father Amaro* is a twenty-first-century retelling of a nineteenth-century novel about a young priest, Amaro. While Romero's only failing is perhaps stubbornness, Amaro's is lust, but both are appalled at corruption in the Roman Catholic Church. The portrait of Romero is more compelling however, simply because of his gravitas.

Perhaps the most compelling of recent portrayals of a group of monks led by a Catholic priest is found in *Of Gods and Men*. The *Guardian*'s critic Peter Bradshaw called it "severe, austere and deeply moving," and acknowledged that there was little concession to secularism in the film, which is based on the true story of Trappist monks kidnapped and murdered by fundamentalists in Algeria. Bradshaw continues: "The movie is in fact saturated with faith and belief, and part of its power is the absolute conviction of its cinematic language, an idiom of severity, austerity and high seriousness, imitating the spacious silences to which the monks have devoted themselves, and boldly supporting the validity and meaning of their dilemma." This could be an endorsement of Schrader's "transcendent style" but that would obscure this rather remarkable response from a British quality paper normally steeped in secular left-wing values. "Saturated with faith and belief " is stated by Bradshaw with no trace of anything but admiration, though perhaps the film as art, and the playing by the monks of a recording of *Swan Lake* ahead of their probable dreadful fate, swayed it for the secular mind. Perhaps this deeply religious film has come at a time more open to religion again, or perhaps the portrayal of each monk as he grappled with the coming dangers and the option of escape is simply very human. Given the possible escalation of violence around the monastery throughout which they were committed to serve God and the local impoverished population, should they return to their order in France? One by one they decide no, led at times by the impetuous Christian de Chergé, prior of the monastery. This is great spiritual cinema.

Some Skeptical Portraits

The Spanish filmmaker Luis Buñuel aired his skepticism of Catholicism in many of his films, notably *Viridiana* and *The Milky Way*. Tom Aitken has this to say:

> As *Nazarín* and *Viridiana* show, Buñuel thought Christianity impractical and naïve. But, although he proclaimed Jesus an idiot, it is not difficult to detect, in both films and in *The Milky Way*, an implication that there is, at least theoretically, a truer, more admirable version of Christianity than that practiced by the church. But, of course, like *Viridiana* herself, that truer Christianity is necessarily so vulnerable to attack and betrayal as to be useless.[8]

Viridiana is a deeply religious and charitable woman whose devotion to the poor of her parish backfires on her. Buñuel's mocking satire suggests that the person who makes any vulnerable gesture of sacrifice will be trampled upon. He believes, of course, that it is the church that does the trampling, and, historically, he has here and there some justification for that belief.

Interestingly the vulnerable woman as a vehicle for the argument against vulnerability is pursued in some other rather illuminating films: in the character Gelsomina in Federico Fellini's *La Strada*; in the character Bess in Lars von Trier's *Breaking the Waves*; and in the character Selma in *Dancer in the Dark*, also by Lars von Trier and starring the elfin singer Bjork. All these women are variously doomed: Viridiana for her high-minded naivety, Gelsomina as simple, Bess as a schizophrenic, and Selma as trapped by the love for her son.

The film *Nazarín* is taken to show how the director Buñuel thought Christianity impractical and naïve. The skepticism here is interesting: a nominally atheist director portrays priesthood as a failure, but a closer examination reveals other interpretations. The problem with so many films examining religious questions where a possible miracle is put forward in the story, as in *Touch*, *Leap of Faith* and *Agnes of God*, is that it leaves the status of the film in question: Is it partly magical realism? What are we as an audience supposed to believe? In *Nazarín* the prayers of the priest result in a miracle cure, but surely, Buñuel doesn't believe in that?

Like *Romero* and *The Crime of Father Amaro* the film *Nazarín* has a South American context—Mexico in this case—which implies perhaps to a North American and European audience the greater religious credulity of Catholicism. The film's protagonist, Padre Nazario, epitomizes the Christian life to the point of complete unworldliness. He is forced to flee his ministry after sheltering a suspected murderer, and, after his prayers for a sick girl appear to have cured her, becomes the object of devotion. Despite his continual Christian charity he is eventually imprisoned and suffers a crisis of faith at the end, unable to deal with a simple act of charity directed at him this time: the gift of a pineapple. He breaks down. On the surface, then, we have a religious figure who doubts his calling in the end, like Sister Luke in *The Nun's Story*. But the film so often portrays real generosity of heart and real compassion for others, that it is not hard to read it in terms of a *socialist* longing for a better world. The comparison of this fictional priest with that of Bresson's *Diary* is interesting. Both are portrayed as naïve, but Buñuel's priest wants the world to be other than it is, wants to find "God's kingdom" in socialist terms, whereas Bresson's priest understands "God's kingdom" as a quality of the heart, and is resigned to or perhaps simply expects the seeming callousness of everyday life. The former is imagined to perform a "miracle" in the one definition of the word as something against the laws of nature, while the latter is imagined to perform a "miracle" in a different definition of the term: a transformation of the heart.

The film *Priest* provides a very British context for examining the vocation of a Catholic priest. Father Greg Pilkington is starting a new parish in inner-city Liverpool in the 1990s. The link with the films of South American flavor just discussed is through liberation theology, a set of beliefs adhered to by Greg's superior, Matthew. Greg is conflicted over his vows of celibacy and his homosexuality, but effectively falls in with Matthew's social activism. While the sexual issues would be enough to create a challenge to Greg's vocation, the real difficulties begin over the issue of the confidentiality of confession: a young woman tells of her sexual abuse by her father, but both priests are bound by church codes not to go to the police. What *Priest* most usefully does is to place the typical contradictions of the Catholic vocation into a near-contemporary British setting with all the issues of class and social convention that imply. Where Latin settings for the same conflicts are played out in a necessarily more emotional way, *Priest* shows how repressed emotions simmer and boil in the British context. Britain's more intensely secular culture requires the religiosity of both men to be seen through two prisms: that of *loyalty* (in this case to the church, but it could be to any British institution) and of *social activism*. The actual nature of the calling or vocation as religious is not explored at all.

We turn now to Bergman's Sweden, the context for his films of "exhausted Christianity," and to a film featuring the pastor of a remote rural community: *Winter Light*. Needless to say, the pastor Tomas lives the despair of his departed faith, failing to wisely counsel a man on the edge of suicide or meet the needs of his unreligious but emotionally fuller girlfriend, Märta. As emblematic of his loss of faith the film revolves around the "silence" of God, that is in the negative sense of his failure to speak to them (we saw earlier Bergman's own comment on this). Märta simply responds to this by telling Tomas, "Sometimes I lose patience. 'God is silent; God doesn't speak.' He has not spoken because he doesn't exist. It's terribly simple." But, of course, it is not terribly simple, either for Tomas in the film or for anyone living under monotheism in the real world.

Butler has kind words for the film: "Ingmar Bergman's *Winter Light* has been criticized as sterile—but sterility of the spiritual kind is its subject, and every cinematic and scenic device is employed to examine, dissect and comment on this aspect of the pastor's situation."[9] So far, so true: Bergman is a master of this. But the question has to be asked again: Can we really learn from something by so relentless a portrait of its absence? We saw earlier that Bergman seemed to believe that his work could help rebuild religion in the same way that artists contributed to the rebuilding of the medieval Chartres cathedral. In the 1960s, when he made this film, his claim might have rung true, if only because he dared to make a film about religion when atheism had reached one of its high points in cultural production. But when set against other films we have looked at, even some made in the 1960s, his claim rings hollow. The despair of Tomas bears no resemblance to the despair of the curate in *Diary of a Country Priest*.

North and South America now provide a different backdrop for the skeptical portrayal of priesthood: contact with ethnic peoples and their beliefs. In *Black Robe* missionaries are dealing with Iroquois, Algonquin and Hurons in mid–seventeenth-century Canada, while in *The Mission* it is the indigenous Guaraní peoples of mid–eighteenth-century Paraguay. The portraits of the lower-ranking priests in these films are mostly sympathetic however, with skepticism being reserved for those higher up and for the religious system as a whole.

The black robe referred to in the film of that name is that of the Jesuits—an old nickname—and it is their missionary attempts to convert Native Americans in Quebec that provides the dramatic setting for the two priests who travel from "civilization" to the wilderness for that purpose. While the usefulness of missionary work for either the recipients or the priests involved is questioned, their vocation is not (though it is tested). If the church to which you belong commits you to labors with dubious justification, one might question the church hierarchy, but it doesn't necessarily bring the tenets of one's faith, or the wellspring of one's spirituality, into question. The portrayal of such spirituality is not *Black Robe*'s purpose however: it lies more in the balanced rendition of both sides of the story—Jesuit and Indian—and the detailed representation of their cultures and languages.

The Mission provides a similar setting for Jesuit missionary work, but unfolds a more interesting set of religious questions. It is a redemption film, so it is explored again later, but here we can consider the image of priesthood it conveys. Margaret Miles sums up the film like this:

> In the end, as Daniel Berrigan, a radical Jesuit priest who advises and acted in the film put it, *The Mission*'s intended message is quite simple: "How is [a religious] person to die? Either with gun in hand or with sacrament in hand. Both die with the people."[10]

The two priests in the film represent this choice, and "the people" here are the Guaraní natives protected in the Spanish Jesuit "reductions" or communities of that period. The external conflict of the film is provided by the Spanish-Portuguese agreement ending the Jesuit protection of the reductions and exposing the natives to lucrative slave trading. The two priests die in the battle that ensues, but the *internal* conflict of the film plays out in the life of Rodrigo Mendoza (Robert De Niro), initially a mercenary and slave trader. After he kills his brother in a duel he is consumed by remorse and takes vows under the guidance of Father Gabriel (Jeremy Irons). In their mission up river they are forced to take sides with the Guaraní against the colonists and join in the military defense of the reduction. Mendoza gives up his calling in order to revert to soldier, and hence dies with gun in hand.

The strengths of the film lie in Mendoza's journey of redemption and the interactions between him and Father Gabriel leading up to Mendoza's vows. Visiting Mendoza in prison, Gabriel confronts him with his "cowardice"—his unwillingness to face life, much as Bresson's priest does the Countess. Mendoza wants the priest to leave, and is provoked into physical threats, which are met with calmness by Gabriel. "There is a way out," he tells Mendoza. "You chose your crime. Do you have the courage to choose your penance? Do you dare do that?" The confrontation turns Mendoza around and he chooses his penance: to drag his heavy amour up the mountain with Gabriel, in appallingly difficult conditions. Once at the top one of the natives is affronted by the bizarre spectacle, or perhaps knows of Mendoza as a slaver. He holds a knife to his throat, but then decides to sever the rope that ties Menodoza to his heavy bundle, and the amour is kicked over the cliff into the river below. It is a moment of redemptive catharsis, and the priest hugs Menodoza.

Later, over supper, Gabriel gives him the New Testament, and Mendoza reads out the well-known lines from 1 Corinthians 13:

> ... and though I have all faith, so that I could remove mountains, and have not charity, I am nothing.
> And though I bestow all my goods to feed the poor, and though I give my body to be burned, and have not charity, it profiteth me nothing.
> Charity suffereth long, and is kind; charity envieth not; charity vaunteth not itself, is not puffed up.

In the film the word "charity" is replaced by the word "love," but otherwise it follows the King James version. The older term "charity" does not of course mean exactly what it does today, but is derived from "caritas" meaning something like unconditional love, perhaps close to the Greek "agape." This type of love is necessarily a religious love, and hence when it was used by Robert Jowett to describe Phil's later love for Rita in *Groundhog Day*, it was not quite right. There is a spectrum of love perhaps, and no doubt Phil makes a journey from a love that is little more than lust to a love that is "genuinely caring" as Jowett put it.

But *agape* and *caritas* go far beyond this: they become the love that Kierkegaard talks about which is no longer qualified by "preference's name."

Gabriel appears to embody St. Paul's sentiments here, and Mendoza, now a Jesuit under Gabriel's command, offers succor to the very natives he used to enslave. He has taken the vows of poverty, chastity and obedience. Roy Anker comments:

> ... there is hardly anything like it in cinema anywhere, this cogent, plausible, and full-blown religious conversion whose wrenching effect shows what it means to run head-on, unexpectedly, into the love of God, a love for all its compassion and ecstasy which is nonetheless relentless and not altogether tame.[11]

Anker's sentiment here is probably held by many Christians and this is why *The Mission* is a favorite, particularly with Catholics. But in filmic and psychological terms Mendoza's conversion is not really that convincing. It is too fast and too syrupy. The problem again is that of symbols. Gabriel pushes the New Testament over to Mendoza. The next instant he is reading out from St. Paul. If one has made the long journey of faith at the end of which one attains the understanding encapsulated in the words of 1 Corinthians 13, then the New Testament has become a symbol of something one knows experientially. Over the centuries, the New Testament has been pushed across the table to millions as a "holy book" to be taken on trust, as a symbol the reality of which lies unexperienced for most people. But the reality of the journey, of a "conversion" is nothing like its symbol. Mendoza's atonement is too quick, his remorse only hinted at, and Gabriel too sanctimonious for any of this to be real, at least in comparison to Bresson's country priest. It is not, of course, a skeptical portrait, but neither does it really illuminate the inner world of religion.

And where does priesthood lead? Mendoza has to renounce it in the end to take up arms in protection of the jungle community from the church-sanctioned slavers. The self-justifying myth of the Christian soldier now obliterates 1 Corinthians 13: even though Mendoza is now fighting for justice rather than against, he is still killing men. Where does Jesus recommend this? Mendoza's conversion is but skin deep.

The portrait of Gabriel and Mendoza as Jesuits is not at all skeptical; indeed it is too earnest. But the story is narrated by one who is legitimately accused: Cardinal Altamirano. He is the one sent to decide on the fate of the reductions and hence on the fate of the Guaraní peoples. He has to choose between their survival and the survival of the Jesuits as a political and religious force in the region: if the slavers do not get their way, then the Jesuits will be forced out. He writes in his report to the Pope: "Your Holiness, a surgeon to save the body must often hack off a limb. But in truth nothing could prepare me for the beauty and the power of the limb that I had come here to sever." But sever it he does: Father Gabriel's mission is to close, and the resulting carnage is the consequence of Altamirano's decision. Priesthood, it seems, leads to slaughter. Altamirano—once a Jesuit himself—is consoled by his subordinate: "You had no alternative, your Eminence. We must work in the world. The world is thus." "No, Seignor Hontar," replies a thoughtful Cardinal. "Thus have we made the world."

At Play in the Fields of the Lord is a film that is more interesting about South American natives than about white priests intent on their conversion. It paints a conventionally skeptical portrait of the missionaries whose certainty in the superiority of their religion is matched only with their implicit belief in the American doctrine of "manifest destiny" in which indigenous peoples are to be converted or swept away. Even though the natives are seen through much less skeptical eyes than the priests, one of the lead characters pronounces on religion in the end: "It's all hocus-pocus anyway isn't it?" This prompted the cultural conservative Michael Medved to write: "Though this line equates Christianity with the superstitions of the naked and painted jungle dwellers, the rest of the movie treats the native religions with far more respect than it accords any Western faith."[12]

In *True Confessions* a young and ambitious Roman Catholic monsignor, Des, is valued by his Cardinal for developing church projects, though this is achieved by overlooking the mob connections of their principal sponsor. Des's brother, Tom, is a detective, and his corruption investigation brings them into conflict. In the end Des is humbled and is given a remote and unglamorous parish, the same to which he had exiled a former troublemaker. Again, though the church hierarchy is seen as corrupt, and we learn perhaps the nature of those forces that make it so—"we must work in the world"—Des makes a journey away from corruption and towards sanctity which also finds a kind of support from the church.

The Magdalene Sisters is a film set in 1964 about the ill-treatment of young women in an Irish convent. This is documented in the film with little insight into the psychology of the nuns that inflicted continuous cruelty on the girls, though it was far ahead of its time: an eventual apology for the system by the Irish Taoiseach was only made in 2013. In *Doubt* Sister Aloysius (Meryl Streep) pursues an intolerant and disciplinarian vision of education for her young charges, bordering on cruelty. Streep's character gives us some insight into how St. Paul's exhortations to Christian charity can ultimately foster its opposite: through *suspicion*, nominally in the best interests of her pupils. The priest she works with, Father Flynn, appears to us as an exemplary man, but his slightly unconventional manner arouses the suspicion of Sister Aloysius: Is he abusing one of the boys? It is the portrait of this woman that is interesting here: her religious doubts transform into persecuting zeal, rather than into the profound compassion of Bresson's priest. In the contemporary context of continuing revelations of young person abuse within religious orders, and in particular in the Roman Catholic world, her suspicions have cultural sanction. In the end, despite his innocence, Father Flynn is forced from his post. However, it gives Sister Aloysius no comfort: her doubt in her faith extends to doubting her own actions. We could perhaps say that she, like Suzanne Simonin, doesn't belong to the cloistered life. But the point of the film is that doubt is part of that life, and the corollary of which is that faith is real.

Spiritual Community

In the Christian world we can speak of the Christian communion as the entire community (ecumen); similarly, in Islam there exists a comparable concept of the *umma*, and in Buddhism the *sangha*. In all manifestations of the spiritual or religious life apart from the most private, a sharing of common beliefs or practices gives rise to a religious community. To share in the religious or spiritual life is one of its deepest experiences, and probably the most inexplicable to the non-religious. From the outside this sharing appears merely as a collective cultural symbol, a means of binding a community together around arbitrary or irrational collective acts. But from the inside, whether experienced in the everyday pursuit of churchgoing, ritual, or festival, or whether experienced at its most intense in a conversion experience, through a charismatic teacher, or simply as a form of shared unconditional love, the collective experience of religion or spirituality has no equal. Even when at its most adumbrated, in a tired, or even corrupt, tradition, it is a powerful draw to the non-secular mind. But when lifted from dull routine it is luminous, and can appear so in film.

Spiritual friendship is a crucial part of spiritual community: it gives rise to a kind of love unknown elsewhere, and captured in the Greek term "agape" when it is used to mean brotherly love—and needs to be updated in its definition to include sisterly love. This spiritual friendship between two individuals in the religious life may be epitomized in a dramatic way in film.

Into Great Silence, mentioned earlier, is a poetic documentary on the life of a Carthusian monastery in France. It was shot by Philip Gröning, who waited sixteen years from his first request to being granted permission to enter the highly reclusive order. The film draws almost solely on the artistic device of beautiful nature photography to dramatize the religious journey undertaken by members of the community. In the absence of a conventional dramatic thread which could elicit responses from individuals and hence build up a picture of their religious character, we are left with the observation of daily life—and the discussions that take place on the one day in the week where talking is permitted—as the sole window into the Carthusian world. In a review of the film by the editors of the *Journal of Religion and Film* an interesting point is made about the West's tradition:

> Many people might associate Gröning's views and experiences of awareness, time, silence and presence with Zen Buddhism, but Gröning insists that Western cultures also have these values and practices. He believes that there is an enormous need, and potential, in the West to reflect on time and the meaning of life. And we can do this, Gröning says, "in our own culture, not on the back of Zen Buddhism."[13]

Silent Light has a promising basis: a film set in an American Mennonite community—a tradition not so far removed from the Amish. Its maker, Carlos Reygadas, spent some two years gaining the trust of the Mennonite community in which it was shot. As in *Into Great Silence*, the cinematography does much of the work in the film, though there is also a strong storyline: How does a respected member of this religious community deal honestly with his feelings for a woman not his wife? We glimpse something of a religiosity mostly unknown in popular culture: a religiosity of patience and understanding. This is manifest in the responses of the community members to the protagonist's difficulties and resembles the manner in which Quakers reach consensus, known as the "feeling of the Meeting." In the end, however, the film rather loses its way in a resolution that feels a little *deus ex machina*, but its strength lies in the exploration of tolerance within a religious community.

Babette's Feast was introduced earlier as a film partly about art as salvation. It is also about a religious community drawn together around a celebratory meal, and naturally, in the Christian tradition, this draws comparisons with the Eucharist. It tells the story of Babette Hersant, a refugee from counter-revolutionary violence in Paris, who is taken in as housekeeper in a remote and austere Jutland community. After fourteen years she receives notice of a substantial win in the Paris lottery, and decides to put on a celebratory dinner for the deeply religious community. Food is Babette's art, but the puritans of her small village are deeply suspicious of anything sensual. As the meal unfolds course by course the villagers, beguiled out of their hostility by the visiting officer of the Swedish cavalry who knows good food and wine when he sees it—and by the effects of the wine itself—relax and fall into an expansive and surprisingly religious mood. With her new-found wealth they expect her to return to Paris, but she explains that the meal has cost her the whole winnings, and she will be staying on in the life of simplicity.

One theme of the film is *gratitude*. Perhaps only an exile or refugee can know what it means to be taken in by a community with radically different customs and treated with friendship and acceptance. The fear born of forcible expatriation is deep, and when thus assuaged can give rise to a profound gratitude. At one level this is a religious feeling: in the Christian tradition it is the acknowledgment of Providence, of God's loving care, but more generally it is a reflection of the sense of belonging to existence, a sense of profound connectedness. If existence is fundamentally benign, despite temporary hardships, then gratitude, praise and then prayer well up spontaneously. Babette's astonishing gesture is all the more powerful a religious image as it takes place fourteen years after her initial receiving of sanctuary. She has not forgotten her debt.

The other side of the story, and the more visible one, is how the austere self-denying community responds to such a celebratory gift. Here we have a theme often pursued in film: that when religion is hostile to the beauties and pleasures of the world it has gone astray. The slow dissolving of suspicion, sternness and rigidity into the warmth of religious community is the set-piece of the film: a melting that is symbolic of the true workings of religion on cold hearts. The film *Chocolat* pursues similar themes but is a far lesser vehicle. This time the powers that resist the seduction of luxury happen to be Catholic, but the message is more uncompromising: religion is wrong. There is little to learn from *Chocolat* about religion or religious community.

Summary

Although skepticism towards the spiritual life in general is found among the films just considered, it is less than with the case of the spiritual teacher. This is because spiritual communities of laypersons, nuns, monks or priests are all seen as possessing the frailties and shortcomings of ordinary people. Even then the skepticism is usually reserved for officiates of religion or wherever ordained people exercise power over others. The most sympathetic portraits in this section have been of monks, nuns or priests struggling with their faith, or struggling with their hierarchies or against poverty and injustice in the world. Nuns such as Sister Luke in *The Nun's Story* and Suzanne Simonin in *La Religieuse* who were not suited in the end to convent life are treated sympathetically, while the Mother Superior in *Agnes of God* is also shown to be deeply humane. The monks in *Of Gods and Men* engage us in a way that is both deeply human and at times luminous. Dramatizations of real life figures such as Helen Prejean in *Dead Man Walking* and Óscar Romero in *Romero* also portray religious figures of genuine faith and integrity. Even in the more conflicted fictional constructs in *Nazarín* and *Priest*, the officiates are shown to be deeply caring towards their community. Priests who played a part in the European colonization of the Americas may or may not be shown as willing parts of a ruthless machine, while Sister Aloysius in *Doubt* is shown to be merely a brittle and suspicious woman. It falls to the nuns in *The Magdalene Sisters* to be portrayed as irredeemably cruel to the young women in their care. Otherwise there is much that is balanced and valuable in these films, dealing with those who make a total commitment to the spiritual life of a faith tradition.

This section also includes the film *Into Great Silence* as a poetic glimpse into the life of a reclusive monastery, and in its cinematography and sense of seclusion it has a luminous quality.

Other films also show aspects of religious community in positive ways, though there are also those that dramatize what can happen when things go wrong. But the single most luminous moment on film in this section is no doubt the extraordinary fireside scene in *The Diary of a Country Priest*. Bresson's trademark cinematographic sparseness and the vulnerable portrayals of both priest and the bitter countess combine to make what takes place between them one of the most elevated pieces of religious cinema to date. It is a moment when a religious person becomes the vehicle for the spiritual opening of another, but as the priest himself is in a state of confusion and doubt, he can in no way be called a spiritual teacher or guide. What happened came out of nowhere. He gives with empty hands.

This brings us to a related aspect of the spiritual life: the idea of spiritual practice. Here at least is the possibility of some kind of training or development of one's spiritual faculties, or a preparation for grace or spiritual knowledge. The Christians, as *The Diary of a Country Priest* shows in such luminous form, believe in grace, a movement from beyond which cannot be summoned at will. But one can practice to make oneself available, and, in other traditions, such as Buddhism, one can practice to be silent, which is perhaps the same thing.

9
Spiritual Practice, Discipline and the Martial Arts

In the *Desiderata* of Max Ehrman one of the verses begins: "Beyond a wholesome discipline, be gentle with yourself." This was also the call of Bresson's priest to the countess, when he said, "God is not a torturer. He wants us to be merciful to ourselves." The next verse of the *Desiderata* begins: "Therefore be at peace with God, whatever you conceive Him to be." These maxims are a useful starting point for considering the role of discipline and practice in the spiritual life. To the secular outsider much of what passed for "discipline" in old religion was either of an extreme form, such as lengthy fasting, mortifications of the flesh and abstinence, or it hid various depravities. When the Americans freed Iraq from Saddam Hussein, they were aghast at television images of the liberated Shias now able to pursue their long-suppressed religious practice of public self-flagellation. Since Freud the secular mind can only conceive of religious disciplines—whether mild such as abstinence, or extreme such as self-flagellation—as pathological, and, since Marx, as "internalized oppression." But if we take Ehrman's lead one can fruitfully ask: what is a wholesome religious discipline that is gentle with the self?

Of course one can object: does the religious or spiritual life need a disciplined practice at all? Andrew Rawlinson has proposed in his interesting *Book of Enlightened Masters* that one can make a distinction between "structured" and "unstructured" religious paths or teachings.[1] On the extreme structured end of this spectrum a disciplined practice is essential, and examples can be found in mainstream and mystical religions across the world: the penances of Teresa, the prayers of Carthusian monks, the meditations of Theravadan Buddhism— "the path of regular steps." On the extreme unstructured end of the spectrum all practice is regarded as futile; for example the spiritual teacher Krishnamurti thought that meditation as usually practiced actually dulled the intelligence needed for awakening. But even in the arguments between the Soto or "gradual school" and Rinzai or "sudden school" of Zen there is no doubt that practice of some kind is necessary: in the former quiet sitting, and in the latter the shock of the koan method.

One can make a first approximation—though of surprising usefulness—between the religious practice of the West as prayer and the religious practice of the East as meditation. Prayer is religious longing directed at a target such as God, saints, texts, relics or teachers. At its most elementary it is supplication for one's own benefit, at some intermediate stage it becomes supplication for others, and at its highest it merges with ecstatic thankfulness towards God or existence, a thankfulness we see quietly enacted by Babette, for example. It is largely a movement of the heart. Meditation on the other hand is the cultivation of mindfulness, to use a Buddhist formulation, or more generally the stilling of mental activities in favor of a limpid alertness. And within this, broadly speaking, there is a meditation of concentration—which Krishnamurti disapproved of—and a meditation of awareness: indeed Krishnamurti summed up his entire teachings in the two words: "choiceless awareness."

Spiritual practice may be a term unfamiliar to many adherents to faith tradition, because that tradition is often to a degree identical with culture. Hence, if one goes to church on Sunday, a synagogue on Friday, or participates in any Islamic, Buddhist or Hindu festival, one may do this simply as part of one's received and unexamined culture. But for the adherents who are more committed, the idea of spiritual practice will become more significant, and also becomes the common ground with others who pursue a spiritual practice in a different faith tradition. Moving away from a merely cultural acquisition, practice becomes a mark of inquiry and the recognition of the practice of others is possible through the acknowledgment of the fundamental common factor: discipline. In what specifics of practice is your spiritual discipline expressed? This is an interfaith question that goes much deeper than the comparison of exterior cultural elements.

Spiritual practice by its very nature is an inward and long-term affair not necessarily suitable to filmic treatment. But one can catch glimpses of the essential spiritual practices of faith traditions on film, though this is rather variable across the faiths. For Judaism there are a handful of interesting films, for Christianity there are many more, and for Buddhism there are both fiction, fictionalized and documentary films that are worth exploring. For Islam there is very little, and the Hindu spiritual paths are mostly drowned by Bollywood spectacle, or ignored by Indian secularist filmmakers.

Judaism

The Chosen is luminously religious: an intelligent film dealing with Jewish orthodoxy which both highlights its shortcomings and gives lyrical reign to its inner, austere beauty. It is based on the novel by Chaim Potok, set in 1940s New York City. Two Jewish boys, one of whose fathers is modern Orthodox and the other traditionalist Hasidic, get to know each other. Reuven is learning about Hasidism from his new friend Danny who explains about its founder:

> He lived with poor people in Poland during the 1700s. They called him the Ba'al Shem Tov, the master of the good word. He had studied cabala, the secret books of Jewish mysticism. He preached a popular idea that God is everywhere, that he should be worshipped in joy and singing and dancing, that to be a good Jew didn't depend on how much you know, but on how much you felt.

These may be specifically Hasidic ideas, but the disregard for "learning"—of a certain kind at least—is a key aspect of the whole Jewish tradition, and indeed of the Christian tradition outside of Catholic Thomism. The boys are on the way to the synagogue of Danny's father where the old man, Reb Saunders, is the rabbi. At the meal there is singing and clapping, the men sway, children are present. There is silence and the old man gives his lecture on the Torah (the Jewish Scripture). While learning of the kind practiced in Universities has no value for him, study of the Torah is everything. It is the rope handed to the drowning man by God—where the drowning, it seems, is immersion in the world. If a man interrupts his study to look at a field, and in that field he sees a tree: "Him does not the scriptures consider! As if he had forfeited his life! ... Only through the Torah can you lead a full life!"

This vision of the religious life is contrasted in the film with the worldly activism of Reuven's father, David Malter, who is involved in the campaign for the establishment of the state of Israel. This is Reuven's world too: modern, secular, educated. He has been to movies and heard the popular jazz of Benny Goodman, both foreign to Danny. So Danny learns of Reuven's world and begins to study in the library, encountering the works of another great Jew: Sigmund Freud. Danny is laboring under a harsh upbringing that goes beyond the strictness of Hasidism however: his father does not speak to him. What cruelty is this? A key moment in the film comes when the rabbi finally explains to his son why: he had discovered that his son was brilliant. "I cried inside my heart. I went away and cried to the Master of the Universe, 'What have you done to me? A mind like this I need for a son? A heart I need for a son, a soul I need for a son, compassion I want from my son, righteousness, mercy, strength to suffer and carry pain, that I want from my son, not a mind without a soul!'"

Whatever one's stance on the many issues raised by the film, which include Zionism, religion versus nature and the contempt for academic learning, there are many scenes of intense religiosity in which the essentials of Judaic spiritual practice are revealed. Hasidic Jews may find crucial details misrendered, but this film represents an outsider's chance to look into the religion. When Rabbi Saunders (Rod Steiger) gets up and dances at a Hasidic wedding—after exuberant displays from athletic Jews doing handstands—it may seem mannered to the insider, but to a student of the world's religions it seems that his somber ecstasy has a truth in it that is universal.

Kadosh juxtaposes glimpses of traditional religiosity with the theme of the patriarchal oppression of women. *Kadosh* (literally meaning "sacred") is considered by some to be a caricature of Israeli ultra–Orthodox Judaism. But glimpses of the sacred heart of Judaism are present in the film, and there can always be something to learn from a caricature. The film opens with Meir, a married Talmudic scholar, repeating a prayer: "Thank you for your compassion in rendering my soul to me. You are the source of all trust." He is wearing the traditional prayer-shawl or *tallit* as he rises from sleep. Once dressed he continues with his prayers which include thanks that he was not created a woman. He then straps on the tefillin or phylacteries, one on the head and one on the left arm so as to be near the heart. He kisses his wife Rivka goodbye, and, as he arrives in the *shul* (synagogue) or *yeshiva* (study room) prayers are being half-read half-sung: the religiosity of it is undeniable. But the women can only peer at them through a screen. Malka asserts that she won't get married. "Of course you will. We all do," says her sister. The prayers continue, and to the untrained ear they have a commonality with the sound of Arab Muslim prayer: very beautiful.

Malka loves Yaakov, a musician, but we discover that a husband has been chosen for her, Yossef. She has to choose between tradition and love. In the next scene, back at the *yeshiva*, Yossef prays volubly for God's love and for the ability to study Torah, while Meir sits through the racket immersed in his scripture. Chanting, bowing, improvisation, dancing. Then silence. Then they debate whether making tea is forbidden—as "cooking"—on the Sabbath. These details are serious to them. Once back at home, Meir is told by Rivka that she can see the suffering in his heart: she has not been able to give him children. "It's been ten years," he acknowledges. "But I will never leave you."

Meir is pulled between the force of love and loyalty to Rivka and the increasing pressure on him from his rabbi. In the *yeshiva* Meir is reminded: "The only task of a daughter of Israel is to bring children into the world. To give birth to Jews. And to let her husband study the Torah." With the production of children they will vanquish the "others," the Godless and the secular government—the one feared by Reb Saunders and his Hassidic followers.

Kadosh also introduces for us the particular nature of Jewish millenarianism in the run-up to the year 2000: the messiah is expected. Yossef drives through the streets proclaiming it over a megaphone. More singing in the yeshiva: it is exhilarating and masculine. Meir's rabbi continues his insistence that after ten years he must take another wife. "A woman's life is in him who makes use of her." The singing continues in the background, its beauty contrasted with the ugliness of the planned betrayal.

Later, the two sisters, their lives and feelings apparently of no significance to their religious menfolk, lie together in the rented room that Rivka has been forced to take up. "There's another world out there," says Malka. "It's so big. Our world isn't all there is, Rivka."

Kadosh then is a film of two worlds: the beauty of traditional religion lived by men of spiritual ardor, and the awkward sharing of it with women who are its casualties when the strictures of their religion cut across their needs. At every turn the Jewish religion is painted vividly in its religious *practices*, a reminder of Karen Armstrong's valuable insight: that it is a religion of orthopraxy, not orthodoxy.[2] And the "praxis" has a beauty quite of its own.

Trembling Before G-d is also a film of these worlds, where Jewish religiosity is presented lovingly and respectfully at the same time as critiquing that tradition: it exposes the agonies suffered by Jewish gays and lesbians because of the religiously-sanctioned prejudice they face. It is non-fiction, structured around a series of interviews, and is arguably a *poetic* documentary because of interconnecting scenes showing elements of Jewish life and ritual in choreographed silhouette. Once again, what comes over to an outsider to the religion is how intense the struggle is within the religion and with its God: this is conveyed, as in *The Quarrel*, by the capacity to engage in passionate and at times angry debate, quite foreign for example to the sensibilities of British secular society. One is left however with the longing for Judaism, as with all ancient religions, to change more quickly on gender issues. The potential loss of the men and women in this film to their community is so unnecessary. In *Kadosh* the women suffer mutely, but in *Trembling Before G-d* the gay men in particular, but also the lesbian women, engage vigorously with their tradition. The "other world," the big world of secular modernity, is no more an option to them than it is for Rivka and Malka: the religion of these gays and lesbians goes so deep that the only option is to struggle with it, to struggle with God. In doing so *Trembling Before G-d* gives us many glimpses into not just Judaism but the essence of religion itself.

My Father My Lord is potentially a film like *Kadosh* in which the beauty of traditional Judaism might be juxtaposed by modern criticism. The story concerns the fate of an Israeli boy whose father is a respected rabbi utterly bound up with the letter of the tradition. His wife is constrained by the same forces as in Kadosh: she lives for her husband and son, but cannot even share the same beach with them at the Dead Sea resort when they go on holiday. A theme that runs through the film is that of animals. "Do dogs have souls?" asks the child, to which his father replies: "Absolutely not. They have no will, no sins, no commandments, nothing." A collared dove and an Alsatian dog are filmed so beautifully as to immediately contradict the old man. Another bone of contention is a playing card that the son has collected, which has an image of natives with body paint and beads banging a drum. The rabbi forces the tearful child to tear it up as "idolatry." "I will have no idolatry in the house!" he shouts. He is even affronted by the mother's suggestion that the child should receive a new card to make up for his loss. "A reward for tearing up idolatry?" he asks.

While the critique of Judaism is clear and persistent through the film, it is not balanced, as in the other films here, with sufficient insight into the true power of the religion. Apart from the children singing and glimpses of the synagogue, there is nothing lyrically persuasive of religion in the film. The issues of animals and idolatry are also so important for the spiritual life that there is a missed opportunity here: where is the thoughtful modern Jew in the story who could debate the issues and help the old rabbi state more clearly the basis of his position? All we learn is that the Torah says so.

There are further films which give similar glimpses into the inner world and practices of Judaism. Such films set in Israel include *Ushpizin*, which revolves around the Sukkot religious holiday, *Time of Favor*, mentioned before and which involves a rabbi's daughter and a Jewish suicide bomber, and *Eyes Wide Open*, about a gay relationship between a rabbi and a Jewish interloper. Such films set in America include *A Stranger Among Us*, where a female cop enters a Hassidic gemstone community, *A Price Above Rubies*, where an Orthodox wife escapes such a community, and *The Pawnbroker*, which reflects the desperation and emptiness of the Jewish faith shattered by the Holocaust. Holland is the scene for both *The Diary of Anne Frank*, the Judaism in which is mostly diluted for a 1950s American audience, and *Left Luggage*, a glimpse again into a Hasidic community. The latter film also includes a fine performance from Chaim Topol, famous for his role in the 1971 film version of *Fiddler on the Roof*.

Christianity

It is unlikely that a Christian parish priest will address his or her Sunday congregation on the subject of spiritual practice. It is more the topic for a seminary. Indeed, if "practice" made perfect, as with carpentry, playing the cello, or software design, to some degree the spiritual life would progress on mechanical lines, which clearly it does not. But it is still true to say that prayer is the central practice of a Christian, and so when the priest in *Diary of a Country Priest* mentions that he finds it hard to pray, we know he is his grappling with his faith. But the real practice of Christianity is not bound up in the outward posture of prayer or even its inner ramifications: it is a whole stance to life. We saw that traditional Jewish spiritual practice covers all aspects of life from waking, to making tea, to all the rituals of family. In the sum total of all this "praxis" is the call to God, just as it is with the Christian or Muslim.

If Christianity starts with Jesus—leaving aside the proposition that perhaps it owes more to St. Paul—then what is it in the life and teachings of Jesus that creates the framework for a Christian praxis? And what films might demonstrate that? The answer to these questions is that perhaps only one Jesus film has ever been made well enough to convey Jesus as such a source of Christian praxis: Pasolini's *The Gospel According to St. Matthew*.

Jesuit scholar Lloyd Baugh asserts that "*The Gospel According to St. Matthew*, in the mind of most serious critics is still the greatest, the most authentic and 'the most religious film on Jesus ever made.'"[3] As many others have, he notes that Pasolini was already a controversial public figure in the arts, having run into trouble both with the Catholic Church for blasphemy in his earlier films and with the Communist Party, from which he was expelled over the scandal of his homosexuality. But his *St. Matthew*, heralded by a tripling of the police presence at its opening in the Venice film festival, won not only the Special Prize of its secular jury, but the prize of the International Catholic Film Office (later merged into SIGNIS, the World Catholic Association for Communication). Baugh quotes the following statement put out by this office:

> The author ... has faithfully translated, with simplicity and piety, and often movingly, the social message of the Gospel, in particular love for the poor and the oppressed, while sufficiently respecting the divine aspect of Christ ... this work is far superior to earlier commercial films on the life of Christ. It shows the real grandeur of his teaching stripped of any artificial and sentimental effect.[4]

Baugh continues, revealing that the archbishop of Venice didn't agree with this assessment, complaining: "Pasolini hasn't understood the Gospel. Jesus isn't like that." But after an assistant suggested he re-read the Gospel of Matthew, he changed his mind and said, "Pasolini had projected Matthew's very same Jesus on the screen, with great fidelity, word for word." This simply shows that "what Jesus is like" varies from person to person, and even Gospel to Gospel. It also shows that the artist, even if treated with suspicion by the church for being a communist atheist homosexual, has the power through the medium of film to convey something deeply religious, particularly if it avoids the costume drama.

In order to use Pasolini's film to examine the question of what is at the heart of Christian practice, we firstly need to pinpoint what it is about the film that consistently drew such praise from across the spectrum, including the Catholic Church and the film reviewer for the normally secularist *Guardian* newspaper. Part of its universal appeal is exactly what the International Catholic Film Office commented on: it is stripped of artificial and sentimental effect. Pasolini achieved this through a series of artistic intuitions: he used non-professional actors and wild and uncultivated landscapes in Southern Italy (he found the Holy Land unsuitable), and he chose a wide range of music from Bach's *St. Matthew Passion* to Negro blues and the Gloria from the Congolese *Missa Luba*. Otherwise the sound design includes only ambient street sounds and birdsong, and of course the voices of the actors (mostly dubbed, unfortunately). For Jesus, Pasolini chose a nineteen-year-old Spanish economics student who happened to speak against fascism at a party in Rome.

Pasolini was a man of the streets so he had no difficulty selecting locals and urchins from the small towns and villages in Italy he was shooting in, all of whom have immense personal character. The film simply follows the text of the Gospel, not shrinking from passages that are difficult for Christians, such as, "He is not worthy of me that loves his father or mother more." He speaks in paradox: "He who secures his own life will lose it." Miracles of healing are performed, and in the gap-toothed and gnarled faces of Italian peasants we glimpse what a spiritual teacher of an ancient era must have meant to those innocent of science and socialism.

Yet perhaps it is socialism that is the common bond between Jesus and Pasolini, and the parts of the film where Jesus speaks of not serving two masters, or when he speaks of giving alms, or when the rich man mournfully passes on after learning that he will no more enter the kingdom of heaven than a camel will pass through the eye of the needle—it is perhaps these scenes that best convey the message of Christian practice: simplicity. When he preaches no resistance, we are reminded not of Buñuel's bewildered Nazarín, but of Bresson's unresisting priest, yet ultimately of neither, because Pasolini's Jesus is full of fire, the landscape is wild, the people simple, and the music ecstatic. No scriptural committee could make a film as beautiful as this: only an artist can do it. The black-and-white cinematography, and the beauty of the young Enrique Irazoqui who plays Jesus, are the conceptions of an artist, not a theologian.

The film effectively declares the basis of Christian practice in the scene where Jesus is challenged by the religious authorities to declare which of the commandments are the most important. He doesn't hesitate in Pasolini's rendering of this Biblical passage:

> But the Pharisees, when they heard that he had put the Sadducees to silence, gathered themselves together. And one of them, a lawyer, asked him a question, trying him: Teacher, which is the great commandment in the law? And he said unto him, Thou shalt love the Lord thy God with all thy heart, and with all thy soul, and with all thy mind. This is the great and first commandment. And a second like unto it is this, Thou shalt love thy neighbor as thyself. On these two commandments the whole law hangeth, and the prophets [Matthew 22:34–40].

It is here that the Christian love of God becomes the center of Christian practice, along with care for the neighbor. Pasolini's film leads to this convincingly, and the audience of non-professional extras—the people of southern Italy that Pasolini found on the streets—listens receptively to the words of the "teacher" (rabbi). It is clear that they do not think them empty words, and neither does Pasolini, whatever his quarrels with the church.

Academics agree that this film is unique. For example, David Jasper says:

> The "Jesus" film (with the extraordinary exception of Pasolini's art-house *The Gospel According to St. Matthew*) struggles to be serious and, with profound irony, is subverted by the far more serious comedy of Monty Python's *Life of Brian* (1979) which leaves theology out of it and endlessly exposes what we do with theology and institutional religion as a means of self-justification. In the mainstream of Hollywood cinema perhaps only Martin Scorsese sustains a consistently "theological" possibility, by continually deflecting the aspirations and anticipations of the viewer in complex visions which both confuse and prompt attempt at systematization out of the threat of chaos.[5]

Jasper's points about *St. Matthew* and *The Life of Brian* are apposite, but we will see that his characterization of Scorsese, while widely accepted, is open to doubt. For Jasper it seems that a theological possibility is achieved by both prompting and preventing the viewer in their attempts to systematize what is shown. But is this anything more than a call for obscurity? More on this theme later.

The Apostle, starring Robert Duvall, was introduced earlier. Based on his own experience of the religious South in America, Duvall plays a preacher, Sonny, who goes off the rails, and then works to redeem himself. It is a good counter-example to poor religious films which are the personal projects of actors, usually having a reputation for being the hopeless meanderings of the recently converted, such as the John Travolta project *Battlefield Earth*—the outcome of his commitment to Scientology. Most pertinent to the portrayal of Christian practice in film is the first service Sonny performs in the newly opened church. He has a congregation of about a dozen, mostly poor, uneducated, some black, and some children. But his personal warmth and his embodiment of Christianity as *love*, makes this service more profound than one conducted in great modern temples and to thousands. He speaks simply, that the new church is the house of God, that they should give a tithe for the poor, explaining it in terms of potatoes and pigs. At the end he says, "Reach over and hug someone's neck and say: 'I love you and the Lord loves you today.'" A young man at the front is both shy and not that near to the others, so Sonny hugs him. There is no fancy theology here, simply a warmth that has its specific source in the religious impulse. It doesn't wait, because love is *today*: this is the crucial part of his message: it was the message of Bresson's priest too.

Into Great Silence is structured in sections prefaced by short religious quotations: perhaps the most poignant is this one from Jeremiah, repeated a number of times in the film:

You have seduced me, O Lord, and I let myself be seduced.

This has other translations, but "seduced" conveys something beautiful about the religious vocation: when genuine it is truly the response to something so deeply attractive that all one can do is to surrender to it. Prayer then becomes the natural response and spiritual practice in the Western monotheistic context. "Behold the silence," states another intertitle, "Allow the Lord to speak one word in us, that He is."

Buddhism

Buddhism makes a natural subject for thoughtful documentaries aimed at a Western audience, though proselytizing elements are not totally absent, and sometimes voiced with such hushed reverence as to be not much more than an exoticism. But the films chosen here do much more.

The Life of the Buddha starts with one of Ashoka's rock inscriptions indicating the birth place of the religion's founder. The inscriptions, scattered across India and the region are the only archaeological evidence for the existence of the Buddha and the details of his life, outside of the scriptures, so inevitably the whole story has become highly mythologized. The film offers glimpses of Buddhist practice, and has an additional section featuring the Vietnamese Buddhist teacher Thich Nhat Hanh, a short series of talks worth perhaps more than all the rest of these films put together, simply because he appears to *embody* the tradition.

Nevertheless, *Vajra Sky Over Tibet* offers wider glimpses into Tibetan Buddhist practice, though the film's main theme is how China's 1950 invasion led to the persecution of Buddhism as a religion and culture in Tibet, the major cities and temple sites of which are covered in turn. There is also a useful introduction to the legendary Padmasambhava. Scenes show the burning of thousands of ghee candles, pilgrimages, and the turning of prayer wheels, all of which give a sense of the outer rituals of Tibetan Buddhism, and resonate with the richness of Catholic imagery—perhaps that is why the Catholic Scorsese was drawn to the theme of *Kundun*. Something less familiar would be the "dharma talk": sessions where monks debate in traditional style with great vigor. Traditional dancing featured at one point is also a reminder that shamanic practice blended almost seamlessly into the incoming Buddhist rituals, as we also see in *Seven Years in Tibet* and *Kundun*.

Tibet: Cry of the Snow Lion is another documentary film that dwells on the Chinese occupation of Tibet, and is marked out by the most beautiful of contemporary cinematography. Within its largely historical theme, elements of Tibetan Buddhist practice are shown, including, again, costumes and dances that must have had a shamanic origin. Of the religious nature of the culture we are left in no doubt: "Prayer was part of daily life; even in the most humble tent you would find a shrine," explains the narrator. But a little later we have the assertion: "Buddha did not found a religion. Buddha founded an educational movement." This is true to a limited extent perhaps, depending on broader definitions of both terms, but one suspects that this sentiment is produced for a secular audience. School or college textbooks on comparative religion normally include Buddhism among the major world religions.

Some of the rural scenes in *Tibet: Cry of the Snow Lion* are reminiscent of the Mongolian nomadic way of life, while yet again the story of the Dalai Lama is told. Another common theme raised by the film is that the Tibetan diaspora are a spiritual gift to the world, a compensation for exile often ruminated upon by the Dalai Lama. What is clear, as shown by this selection of documentary films, is that the Western world probably knows more of Tibetan

Buddhism than any other branch as a result. One more example of spiritual practice from the film: the painstaking construction of elaborate spiritual paintings, known as mandalas, using colored sand. Scorsese chose this to open his film *Kundun*, and the blowing away of the sands as symbolic of the destruction of Tibet's religious heritage.

The Lost World of Tibet deals with Buddhist Tibet prior to the Chinese invasion. It starts with footage from the 1930s, when Tibet was still mostly cut off from the surrounding world including China and the British Empire. The Dalai Lama appears throughout the film, often delighted to see the rare archival footage of his lost world, including glimpses of his own father. It does not avoid the issue of feudalism in Tibet, cemented in place by the Buddhist religion, which kept the majority of the population in poverty, ruled by a small elite. But the real value of the film is to convey the breadth of religious practice, including countless religious festivals throughout the year, sixty-eight days in total, all of which are now banned by the Chinese. We learn that in the 1930s some 20 percent of Tibetan males lived in monasteries, and that *cham* dancing was very strenuous and taken up only by young men. This form of dance, using heavy costumes and masks, has obvious shamanic origins and is embedded in what Europeans of the Middle Ages would recognize as the form of the morality play. Another Tibetan custom dwelt upon in the film is the *lingkhor*, the practice of pilgrimage around a circular mountain path. In the past a more strenuous version was practiced where the entire five miles or so would be traversed while performing the traditional full-length prostrations. Incense offerings, mantras, and sacred stone carvings were all part of the pilgrimage.

Guge: Lost Kingdom of Tibet is a docu-drama telling of archaeological discoveries in the Eastern part of Tibet in a kingdom called Guge. It documents the spread of Buddhism to this part of the kingdom, and shows that no matter what the religion, power struggles may emerge: this one is a little reminiscent of that between Thomas Becket and Henry the Eighth.

The Tibetan Book of the Dead is a film distributed along with two documentaries, both narrated by Leonard Cohen, as mentioned earlier. The first film opens with the prostration pilgrimage, shown in other films included here. The two documentaries give a detailed picture of the Buddhist practices surrounding death, often through interviews.

Turning now to two major biopics of the Dalai Lama, *Seven Years in Tibet* and *Kundun*, it is clear that they have different intentions than the documentaries, but nevertheless convey both the historical plight of the Tibetans and useful reconstructions of Buddhist spiritual practice. As feature films, in one case directed by the well-known Martin Scorsese, and in the other case starring the well-known Brad Pitt, they will often be the first introduction to Tibetan Buddhism for a general audience. It is interesting in both cases that their directors are responsible for other films that are skeptical of religion. For Scorsese it is *The Last Temptation of Christ*, and for Jean-Jacques Annaud it is *The Name of the Rose*. The portrayal of Buddhism in *Seven Years in Tibet* and *Kundun* is uncynical, perhaps even uncritical, which suggests perhaps that the legacy of monotheism for Westerners is more contested than that of other religious forms.

Into Great Silence does not give us accounts of the monks' struggle with their practice of prayer: the ups and downs, the sudden breakthroughs, the periods of apparently hopeless dryness. They cannot speak to the camera. The brothers in *Enlightenment Guaranteed*— mentioned in the Introduction—enter a very different kind of monastery, Zen, and engage in a very different kind of practice, meditation, but they share their thoughts with us reality TV-style. The film gives limited insight into the inner lives of the Zen abbot and monks of the monastery, but does provide an excellent portrayal of the beginner, whose confused struggle to master the practice is offset by the advantage of "beginner's mind."

After a lengthy and mishap-prone journey, about halfway through the film, the brothers are finally on the way to the monastery by train. Gustav, with New Age inclinations, is explaining to Uwe, who has previously scorned Gustav's preoccupations: "Meditation is the way to enlightenment." "What's it supposed to do?" queries Uwe. "Help find yourself." "By just sitting there?" Gustav explains that one watches one's thoughts coming and going, to which Uwe objects that the more thoughts come, the more they bring new ones: a very pertinent observation if one has ever tried meditation. Later Uwe begins to read for himself, from a small book on Zen: "We must see through the illusion that there is a separate self. We practice to remove this divide." The brothers reflect on this, perhaps unaware that the Christian tradition of their own continent has sought the same goal, but using slightly different language. The Carthusian monk practices to remove the divide between self and God. Uwe reads further: "Enlightenment is not something one can achieve. It's the absence of something. You're after something your entire life, some goal. Enlightenment means giving that up." This is a telling extract from Buddhist thought, showing that the Buddha originated a set of metaphors that are in the negative: enlightenment is not an achievement but is there when something else ends. This is the etymological derivation of *nirvana*—to snuff out. It means the end of the separate sense of self, the end of "I-making" tendencies as the Buddha put it.⁶ Christ's metaphor of the kingdom of heaven is, by contrast, a metaphor in the positive. These may only be cultural differences, but seem to endow their religions with very different characters.

Once at the Zen monastery we find an environment as embedded in Nature as the Grande Chartreuse. The novice Westerners find much in their environment and the Zen practice physically demanding: their bows of courtesy take them down to the floor and up three times; they have to sleep on the ground; sitting—*zazen*—is an agony, and the chores of cleaning the floor is again a rude awakening to Western limbs always at one remove from the ground. The 4:30 awakening might not be so different to Chartreuse however. Gustav speaks to the camera later: "Meditation was hell this morning." He loves the atmosphere, but his knees are killing him. The scenes of meditation, chanting, and readings in the monastery, accompanied by deep-sounding gongs and bells make this portion of the film an intended contrast to the almost comic capers of the brothers' difficulties on the journey there. The struggle of Gustav and Uwe with meditation illustrates the early stages of encounter with the practice, but, as with prayer, we have not so much on film that takes us into the later stages, into the minds of the long-term practitioner.

Why Did Bodhidharma Leave for the East? and *Spring, Summer, Autumn, Winter, ... and Spring* present elements of deeper Buddhist practice, this time in the Chan tradition. Here we can take a scene from *Bodhidharma* to examine an important issue in spiritual practice. Early in the film the three principal characters discuss their situation. Haejin is the orphan child, Hyegok the Chan master of the temple, and Kibong a young disciple, whose earlier life in the city—the "World"—we see in flashbacks. The scene is lit by a burning wood fire.

HEIJIN: (staring downwards) At the bottom of the mountain, is there a big temple? And what is lower down?
KIBONG: The World.
HEIJIN: (looks up) The World? (pause) You ... came from the World?
KIBONG: Of course. You too, Haejin.
HEIJIN: And the Master?

KIBONG: Him too.
HEIJIN: Why have we all left the World?
KIBONG: It's because in the World, there is no peace or freedom of the heart.
HEIJIN: Why?
HYEGOK: (looms out of the darkness) Because people haven't enough heart to hold all the things of the world. In fact, they have enough heart, but it's full of the idea of Self.

What is remarkable about the Chinese version of Buddhism, Chan (and the later Japanese development of it called Zen), is that the extreme renunciativeness of Buddha's original teachings was greatly moderated by its confluence with Taoist thought. The Chinese never sought renunciative extremes like the Indians, instead expressing in Taoism a very Chinese preoccupation with *balance*. Hence, while the Master quite accepts young Kibong's assertion that "in the World, there is no peace or freedom of the heart" he immediately moderates his own statement to conclude that the human heart can "hold all the things of the World" if it is not full of the self. The essence of Chan—and also Zen—is renunciation of self, just as the Buddha taught, but, going beyond him, is the idea that in doing so the heart can then hold the whole world dear.

However, nowhere in the Pali Canon does the Buddha comment favorably on the natural world, let alone on the world of men and women. The story of the Buddha's abandonment of his wife and child, sneaking out like a thief in the night in order to seek enlightenment in the forest, is the emblem of Kibong's dilemma. The goal has become known, and spiritual practice appears to be the path, for which seclusion is needed. Kibong reflects to himself: "I was destined to take care of my family. Did I commit an immoral act by freeing myself of that destiny, going my own way?" He had the urge to seek enlightenment in a culture in which the Buddha legitimized that path, but Kibong is conflicted, not just over the abandonment of his duties, but also of the pleasures of the world. Most tellingly, he says, "I couldn't do two things at the same time." This is the challenge of the spiritual life: can one pursue spiritual practice in daily life, in "the World," or must one, at great cost to oneself and family, retreat to the mountain-top or forest?

Dance as Spiritual Practice

To say that the religious practice of the West is prayer and the religious practice of the East is meditation is of course a simplification: one can find prayer-traditions in the East and awareness-traditions in the West. Nonetheless, prayer as a Western practice is less inclined to lead to the insights into mind that are characteristic of Buddhism for example, and also less inclined to segue into martial arts practice as Eastern meditation systems can do. Prayer in the West does not inform the *technical* business of soldiering. But in China an ancient martial arts tradition was taken up by the incoming Buddhism, though at first sight this is a contradiction to the pacifism at its heart. The meditation practices of concentration naturally took on physical forms in the Indian system of hatha yoga, while in China concentration takes on the physical form of fighting.

Martial arts and spirituality are more usually associated with each other from Iran eastward. Iran has a tradition of religious martial arts using wooden clubs called *Varzesh-e Pahlavani*, meaning "Sport of the Heroes," which has a spiritual basis in Sufism. India's warrior caste had a strong religious basis as shown in the *Mahabharata*. In China, the link between Buddhism and martial arts is attributed to the fifth century monk Bodhidharma, originally from

India. In Japan, the Chan tradition of China transmuted into the Zen tradition and gave rise to the samurai *Bushidō*, meaning "Way of the Warrior," which developed from the ninth to the twelfth centuries.

We will see that films of the martial arts are effectively films of a contradiction, where the religious principle of peace is surrendered, with varying degrees of justification, for the principle of war. Sacred dance on the other hand represents a much less conflicted spiritual practice. It has been important in many cultures, though more extreme ascetic traditions shun or proscribe such activity: the Buddha for example discouraged devotional song or dance.

Meetings with Remarkable Men ends with Gurdjieff's experiences in a remote mountain monastery—its location secret to this day—in which he witness the "stop" exercises of Sufi tradition, movement exercises, and then their sacred dances. "Everyone in the monastery learns the alphabet of these movements," explains Gurdjieff's guide. He adds that the dances are exactly like books: "We can read the truths placed in them many thousands of years ago." Gurdjieff seeks an esoteric explanation of the meaning of the movements, and is told: "They tell us of two qualities of energy, moving without interruption through the body. As long as the dancer can keep in balance these two energies he has a force that nothing else can give."

The latter part of Brook's film, showing these dances, is a rare glimpse into sacred movement, and into key elements that were to become part of Gurdjieff's system. One memorable dance has a group of turbaned men performing stylized arm-movements of great accuracy, while facing them is the deliberate distraction of the single "fool" whose job it is to flop and flail about in the antithesis of order. More complex and highly choreographed dances follow in which it is clear that the slightest lapse of concentration would cause chaos or perhaps a blow to the head from a pivoting forearm. The sequence finishes with a dance similar to that of the whirling Dervishes. Brook was fortunate to have the assistance of Jeanne de Salzmann in staging the dance sequences, as she was Gurdjieff's heir in respect to his "movements."

Dance of a devotional nature appears of course in many Hindu films, including *Madhumati* and *Jai Santoshi Maa*. *Monsieur Ibrahim* is perhaps the only relatively mainstream film in which there is a sympathetic portrayal of Islam, albeit through its mystical branch, Sufism. Monsieur Ibrahim himself—played by Omar Sharif—is a corner-shop proprietor in Paris who befriends a Jewish boy living with his father. The mother has already disappeared, and before long the father gives up, and abandons the boy. Ibrahim looks after him, and takes him on a trip to Turkey in which they visit whirling dervishes, whose sacred dances in this film are worth comparing with the Gurdjieff dances. (There is also comparison to be drawn with *Spring, Summer*, in terms of the disciple becoming the master, but of a corner shop, not a temple.)

Devotional Song and Dance in World Religions

The worship dance in Judaism is known as messianic dance or Davidic dance (named after King David, who danced before the Ark of the Covenant), and it has dozens of forms, based around different songs. In Hinduism, *kirtan* is a form of devotional singing that may involve dancing, while Indian sacred dance itself has many forms. *Shiva Nataraja* is the name of the statue of the Indian god in dancing pose and his "dance of bliss" is linked to the Chola tradition of triumphant warrior dance.

There are a number of films of Judaic practice that demonstrate sacred song and dance: these include the wedding scene in *The Chosen*, the spontaneous hand movements in *The*

Quarrel, and the silhouetted family scenes in *Trembling Before G-d*. It is a moment of dance that marks the high point of the film *The Quarrel*, in which two survivors of the Holocaust meet up years later, representing the secularized Jew of the world of learning, in dispute with a religious traditionalist. They have shared the particular pain of the post–Holocaust Jews, and all that remains at the end of the film—given the secular-religious divide that remains between them—is to dance. They sing a little to start with, to find the mood and rhythm, and then sway in silence, their hands upraised. Anyone who has a feel for the sacred origins of such dance, as found in cultures as far apart as Judaism and Hinduism, will appreciate that the raised hands, moving in ascending spirals, and around each other, are both expressive of the relationship with God and with each other, two seekers of truth. Oblivious for a short while, they are broken from their trance by the applause of a small group that has gathered around them in the park.

A deeply religious portrayal of Indian song and dance on film prior to its trivialization in Bollywood is found in *Jai Santoshi Maa*, about a group of women following the goddess of that name. To this day in India, the Dravidian south and its cinema is more inclined to goddess worship than in the North, a point noted by feminist philosopher Luce Irigaray after her 1985 trip to India.[7] However, the appeal of *Jai Santoshi Maa* extended beyond the rural peoples of the South to urban groups also in the North. Philip Lugendorf, in an interesting essay on the film, tells us that it opens in what is called *dev-lok*—the world of the gods—centered on the elephant-god Ganesh, who also makes an appearance in *The Mahabharata*.[8] The Indian world of the gods is similar to that of ancient Greece and many other parts of the world where polytheism supplanted shamanism: it is conceived of as a parallel world populated by anthropomorphic entities with seemingly very human preoccupations. Ganesh is persuaded to provide his sons with a sister, who becomes Santoshi Ma. This has little precedent in other Hindu stories concerning Ganesh, so is an interesting example of the continued creativity of the polytheistic mind, and the receptivity of Hindus to new deities. No sooner is Santoshi Ma brought into existence on the heavenly plane than we cut to her earthly devotees singing and dancing in Her praises (interestingly, in 6/4 musical time). Lugendorf explains that this particular religious observance is called *vrat*, which takes place for a fixed period and involves fasting, ritual worship in song and dance, and the recitation of a relevant story. A story about *vrat* is called a *vratkatha* and is a popular Indian form. Mostly *vrat* are performed by women, and with the aim of receiving some blessing or fulfillment. The film follows a young woman called Satyavati, who leads the singing in the *vrat*, and who is hoping for a husband. Sure enough she meets her future husband, and is soon engaged to him, thanks to Santoshi Ma. But her sisters-in-law—who are analogues of the goddesses Lakshmi, Parvati, and Brahmani—are jealous and cause trouble for her. This narrative device, of human affairs mirroring that of the gods or vice versa, is familiar in Western polytheism, even if the devotional, expressive, and woman-oriented nature of the piety offered to them is not. Rachel Dwyer, in her book on Indian religious cinema, says:

> Although *Jai Santoshi Maa* was the biggest hit of its type it should be contextualized in a series of mother goddess films based on vratkhas which became popular from the 1960s onwards. Many of these were about localized village mother goddesses, "Maa," or, further south, "Amma" figures.[9]

Dwyer goes on to point out that this form of goddess is not destructive, as in female deities that represent power or *shakti*, such as the goddess Kali worshipped by Ramakrishna. But one only has to think of Satyajit Ray's *Apu* trilogy to understand that a sophisticated Indian middle class will more likely be drawn to his secularized version of India than to a new devotional cult.

More on his films soon. *Paap* and *Lagaan* also include typical Indian dance sequences, but they are secularized as erotic or romantic.

In the Hindu context it is easy to locate sacred song and dance as a devotional practice, flowering at times of new devotional movements. In Judaism, "devotion" is not quite the right word, as the relationship with the Judaic God is not, in the first instance, a love-relation ship. The ecstasy in it is undeniable, but it retains the sorrow of separation and the inevitable sense of struggle that characterizes Judaic spirituality. In the Sufi and Gurdjieff, dances considered above there is a different element again: the sacred dances embody spiritual *knowledge*.

Martial Arts as Spiritual Practice

Song and dance as spiritual practice probably go back into prehistory. Similarly, religion and warfare seem to have an intimate history going back to hunter-gatherer cultures dominated by animism or shamanism. To some degree the animist principles that guided the hunt in hunter-gatherer cultures also guided inter-tribal warfare, including the certainty that opponents killed in fighting lived on in the spirit-world, and serenity in the face of one's own death in battle. In this section we look at the relationship between religion and warfare in terms of the martial arts: a spiritual practice the ethics of which becomes problematic, particularly under Buddhism.

In *Whale Rider* a young Maori girl Pai saves her tribe by rescuing a whale stranded on the beach. She struggles to master the tribal rituals, opposed by her grandfather who wants a male heir. In fact, much of these rituals involve a form of martial arts, banned for women, which Pai has to learn clandestinely. The traditional practice is known as *Mau Rākau*, meaning "to bear a weapon," and the practice of which is solemnified by religious ritual and mythological history. Pai breaks into an intensely male warrior culture in a film with a largely positive tone, but in contrast *Once Were Warriors* portrays the negative legacy of a traditional Maori warrior culture hemmed in on all sides by Western-style living and belief systems. Urban Maori males, finding their lives adrift in Western materialism turn to gang warfare, alcohol and drugs—much as Native American men have done. As in *Whale Rider*, it is up to the women to resist the loss of traditional culture.

In the films *Asoka* and *The Mahabharata* we encounter the warrior cultures of India at a time when the religious context was only partially animist or shamanic. Instead, new religions had developed, creating rather different ethical systems. The story of the boy Asoka who grows up to be emperor of a region on the scale of the Roman Empire is one of a warrior tradition encountering the inherent pacifist moralism of a new religion: Buddhism. The film version draws on an ancient south Indian martial arts tradition called *Kalarippayattu*, meaning "school of fighting," which has a choreographed element in it, and hence a link to dance. It is known to date back to at least the twelfth century CE, but this is much later than the third century BCE date of Asoka's reign, so the film may not be historically accurate. Nevertheless, this fighting system does genuinely belong to the Indian subcontinent.

Peter Brook's *Mahabharata* is a dramatization of India's central religious text, a compilation of holy books equivalent to the Bible but fifteen times as long as both Testaments put together. It is a story of a gambling debt that turns to warfare on a massive scale, between the Kaurava and Pandava cousin clans, leading up to the battle of Kurukshetra. The film broadly conveys the essential sacred elements of the warrior ethos, usefully flagged up for us in a conversation between Krishna and Kunti (mother of three of the Pandavas, including Arjuna).

Krishna has made every conceivable effort to prevent the war, and finally asks Kunti: "What right have we to destroy our bodies?" He is convinced that if the war goes ahead massive slaughter will ensue. Kunti replies:

> I would tell my son, your body is beautiful, your body is noble. But if you live with the fear of death, why were you given life? Burn like a torch, if only for an instant.

It is poignant that these words come from a woman, and a reminder that it is a mistake to think of the warrior ethos as the province of men alone. But Kunti's words point to two essential elements of sacred warrior culture: firstly that one is given life to conquer the fear of death, and secondly, that a heroic stand, even if risking death, is better than a life of tedium: burn, instead, "like a torch."

But what is really sacred about a warrior culture? A pacifist, politically correct Western educated consciousness finds it hard to reconcile the sacred and killing, and one of the first objectors to the fact that the *Bhagavad Gita* contains the entire effort of Krishna to persuade Arjuna to fight was Mahatma Gandhi. He loved the book so much that he made a translation of the *Gita* into Gujarati, but his pacifism meant he was deeply conflicted over its explicit call to war. His implausible solution was to say that it was merely an *allegory*,[10] but if we follow that road, then there is no insight possible into what we call here a spiritual warrior ethos. Instead, Brook's film, whatever its shortcomings, does give us glimpses of how war can have a sacred dimension. Early in the film the boy warrior Ekalavya declares that Drona—the martial arts instructor to both clans of cousins—is his Master, and, when rejected, retreats into the forest to make an idol of him. It is a shame that Brooks chose a Japanese actor to play Drona, thus subliminally transferring the martial arts sensibility to the Japanese context. But India, as in all ancient cultures, had a sacred art of fighting of its own, and the young Ekalavya demonstrates it as a form of hatha yoga.

The film *Ghost Dog: The Way of the Samurai* takes us straight to the heart of our dilemma: How can a spiritual tradition becomes the framework for a career of killing? The spiritual tradition here is Zen Buddhism and the moral code that of Bushidō, the ethical system of the Japanese samurai. In *Ghost Dog*, it is a black American hitman, moodily played by Forest Whitaker, who adheres to this system of another culture, another age. Ghost Dog lives in a rooftop shack with his pigeons, and in honor of the mobster Louie who saved his life as a young man he agrees to kill a gangster. Unfortunately, this backfires on the mobster and he turns his men on Ghost Dog. After much killing, Ghost Dog is confronted by Louie, but will not defend himself, so he dies. Throughout the film Ghost Dog reads extracts from the *Hagakure*, a basic text of samurai Bushidō. His life is governed by its principles, and he carries out his martial arts exercises, which is his meditation, in front of a makeshift shrine on his rooftop, and pursues his daily life and killings in its spirit of serenity.

Ghost Dog's first killing in the film is crucial. It is not in self-defense, it is on the orders of Louie. We are prepared for this by a passage from the *Hagakure*, appearing shortly after the killing as an intertitle:

> A devotee of the Nembutsu recites the Buddha's name with every incoming and outgoing breath in order never to forget the Buddha. A retainer, too, should be just like this in thinking of his master. Not to forget ones master is the most fundamental thing for a retainer.

Buddhism regards life as sacred, and to kill as one of the worst transgressions. How could its original message be so lost as to now—admittedly at several removes—allow for a killing, not even in self-defense? But the above passage makes the link: a devotee must never forget the

Buddha, so a retainer must never forget his employer. Ghost Dog does this because of the moral debt he owes Louie. Through the *Hagakure* Ghost Dog is put in constant touch with the basic tenets of Buddhism, in this case in its Mahayana variant. A crucial extract, presented as another intertitle, goes like this.

> Our bodies are given life from the midst of nothingness. Existing where there is nothing is the meaning of the phrase, "Form is emptiness." That all things are provided for by nothingness is the meaning of the phrase, "Emptiness is form." One should not think that these are two separate things.

Ghost Dog appears to live by this idea, at least to some extent. His beautifully executed swordplay and karate practice is undertaken with the serenity born of the realization that the precision of their form arises out of emptiness, and he strives for the appropriate inner emptiness in his execution of the movements. His demeanor is self-effacing, and on his face is etched the sorrow—or *dukkha*—central to the Buddhist understanding of the world as a place of suffering. He has no possessions beyond his basic needs and that of his profession, and he expresses his compassion for life through friendships with a little girl in the park— to whom he lends a copy of *Rashomon and Other Stories* received from the girlfriend of his first killing—and with an ice-cream vendor. Above all he cares for his pigeons. All of this is spiritual practice. The question is this: Does the realization that form is emptiness—a central idea in Mahayana Buddhism—give him the moral justification to kill? *Le Samouraï* is a similar film, to which *Ghost Dog* is something of an homage to. It also involves a lone contract killer following a samurai code, though in this case it is a fictional text called *The Book of Bushido*. It raises the same kind of doubts as *Ghost Dog*, but is told in a more sparse style.

Let us turn now to samurai stories located closer to their original setting. Kurosawa's *Seven Samurai* is considered one of the best and most influential films of all time, and is set in late–sixteenth-century Japan when masterless samurai, called ronin, were plentiful due to the breakdown of earlier feudal systems. This leaves the village at the center of the story exposed to bandits, having no lord to provide protection in return for tithes. The samurai recruited by the villagers are typical Kurusawan characters, and we don't see much of their martial arts as *practice* except when the sixth and most skilled swordsman of the samurai, Seiji Miyaguchi, is briefly seen practicing by a stream in the rain. Rather, it is put into action in the battle at the end, or in training the villagers. Neither is there anything notably Buddhist about their worldview or stance in life. But the ethos of these samurai is clear: they operate out of a basic code of honor, and, what is more, often perform acts of compassion.

The Last Samurai makes an interesting contrast to Kurosawa's samurai film. It is a hybrid of modern American preoccupations and historical Shogunate samurai action, in which Tom Cruise plays an American soldier, Nathan Algren, drawn into samurai culture in the late nineteenth century. It is something of a *Dances with Wolves* for Japan, where the Samurai take the place of the Native Americans. In the same way as the protagonist of *Dances with Wolves* is alienated from his own kind, Algren finds himself sympathetic to the samurai who are resisting Western modernization. At one point another American asks Algren, "What is it that you hate so much about your own people?" The film Americanizes history by replacing the historical French and English influence and trade negotiations of the period with fictional America versions. The lead character is actually based on a French officer. Nevertheless, it introduces the Bushidō code and martial arts practice.

Yukio Mishima, the Japanese novelist, wrote a non-fiction work on the *Hagakure* as part of his commitment to bushidō. He was obsessed with the samurai, and, in what is known as the "Mishima Affair" of 1970, he committed *seppuku*—ritual suicide—after a failed coup attempt. *Mishima: A Life in Four Chapters* is the film version of his life directed by Paul Schrader, and written by Schrader and his brother Leonard. It uses theatrical sets to dramatize scenes from three of Mishima's novels, intercut with more conventional live-action, particularly towards the end in the climax of the failed coup. While *Taxi Driver* and *The Last Temptation of Christ*, with screenplays by Schrader, will be considered in later chapters, here we can usefully consider his *Mishima* in terms of martial spirituality and also transcendent style. What *is* spiritual in Mishima's militarism? What *is* transcendent in the style of the film?

Schrader contrasts sparseness with abundance as a way to pare away films which fail to be spiritual, but does sparseness automatically create the confrontation necessary for a spiritual transformation in the viewer? Schrader considers *Mishima* the best film he has directed: "It's the one I'd stand by—as a screenwriter it's *Taxi Driver*, but as a director it's *Mishima*."[11] So, according to Schrader himself, *Mishima* is the key film to see whether his theories work in practice.

Firstly, is it "sparse" in Schrader's sense? Certainly, if we compare it to the average Hollywood fare, whether action-adventure or romantic comedy or tragedy. He achieves this in two distinct phases, in slow camera moves over everyday objects, such as when Mishima dresses at the start of the film, and, more explicitly, in the dramatizations of scenes from Mishima's novels. In these scenes he uses the device of theatre-style sets, as does Lars von Trier in *Dogville*. Does this achieve his goal of creating confrontation instead of identification? Yes, perhaps, if they did not also distract the viewer with a certain anxiety over cultural dissonance. The sets in *Mishima* appear to derive from Japanese theatre traditions (Noh), but the overuse of color threatens their authenticity. In a similar way, Peter Greenaway's *The Pillow Book*, also set in Japan, fails to convince aesthetically where his Renaissance spectacles in *Prospero's Books* and *The Cook, The Thief, His Wife and Her Lover* are magnificently successful. Back to *Mishima*: is not the staging of the Golden Temple, as it opens up to him, a rather spectacular, *abundant* moment, regardless of its aesthetic lineage? Nevertheless, perhaps Schrader is right: his theatre-style sets, just as in *Dogville*, confront us, or at the very least, shock us out of our usual movie-going somnambulance.

But the central question is whether Mishima is intended to be the salvific character through confrontation with whom—not identification with whom—the viewer undergoes a spiritual transformation. Does he go, Zen-like, through the three stages of quotidian, disparity, and stasis, also understood as normalcy, crisis and transcendence? He is certainly an agonized character, and conflicted in a modern manner rather like Scorsese's Christ (as we will see). His romantic yearnings dwell on the aesthetic as eternal, but also as that which crushes, and from which freedom must be found; his militarism is Nietzschean and expresses itself in emperor adulation. Like Scorsese's Christ he finds himself to be a liar, and embroiled in a revolutionary movement. But the Christ of the Gospels is neither liar nor revolutionary, and the indigenous spiritual context of Mishima—Zen Buddhism and Shintoism—has salvific characters such as the Buddha or Zen Masters equally removed from Mishima.

We have to consider perhaps that perhaps the modern audience, and the filmmakers who serve them, cannot relate to the genuinely salvific, the genuine embodiment of Christ or the Buddha, but finds instead real confrontation with those who are Romantic, conflicted and nihilistic, who invert all values, make the Golden Pavilion (a Zen temple) a brothel, find resistance to capitalism impossible, and are left with only one choice: suicide.

In the second of the "four chapters" the film dramatizes scenes from Mishima's novel *Kyoko's House*, focusing on a sado-masochistic relationship between an actor and a woman who "buys" him to absolve his mother of debt. No normal relationship with a woman is possible, and their double suicide anticipates Mishima's own end. Each stage of the film is confrontational, but is this really through sparseness? Mishima tells us: "Men wear masks to make themselves beautiful, but, unlike a woman's, a man's determination to become beautiful is a desire for death." The image of Saint Sebastian, pierced by spears appears several times in the film, an image central to Derek Jarman's *Sebastiane*, and with a similar homoerotic overtone. But it is Mishima's militarism which is central to his character: he conceives of the Imperial Guard as a spiritual army opposed to corruption, modernization, Western ideas, foreign intervention and capitalism, just as the warriors and then Nathan Algren do in *The Last Samurai*. The hero in the dramatization of the third book *Runaway Horses*, Isao Iinuma, plots to overthrow the collaborationist government, but is captured and interrogated. He is told that he is young and pure but will have to tone down his attitude, to which he responds by saying, "If purity's toned down it is no longer purity." The interrogator tells him, "Total purity is not possible in this world." "Yes it is," responds Isao, "if you can turn your life into a line of poetry written in blood." Poetry written in blood? This is the theme of Jarmusch's *Dead Man*, itself an interesting reflection on the confrontation between a machine culture and an ancient way of life. But does this Nietzschean sentiment have anything to do with the spiritual life? Clearly many scholars of religion and film think so, and from this perspective they laud both Schrader and Scorsese.

In the fourth chapter, all of these elements come together in parallel with Mishima's own finale: the dramatic moment when he holds hostage a military camp commander and demands that the garrison assemble and listen to his speech. His words do not move them, however, and the film segues into a sequence in a fighter plane. The voiceover proclaims a typically Nietzschean militaristic vision of spirituality:

> Never in action had I discovered the chilling satisfaction of words. Never in words had I experienced the hot darkness of action. Somewhere there must be a higher principle reconciling art and action. That principle, it occurred to me, must be death. The upper atmosphere, without oxygen, is surrounded by death. To survive in this atmosphere, man, like an actor, must wear a mask. Flying at 45,000 feet, the silver phallus of the fuselage floated in naked sunlight. My mind was at ease, my thought process lively. No movement, no sound, no memory. The closed cockpit and outer space were like the spirit and body of the same being. In this stillness was a beauty beyond words. Before my eyes was the sight of the clouds and the sun. It was all part of me. There were no boundaries. No more body or spirit. Pen or sword.

So are these scenes *really* sparse when they culminate in this finale? Schrader even uses the famous *Vertigo* shot: a simultaneous zoom out and dolly in to dramatize this moment (also used in *Jaws*), and intercuts with the dramatic endings of the three novels portrayed in the earlier chapters, the burning of the Golden Pavilion by the crazed monk, the double suicide of the actor and his female purchaser, and the suicide by *seppuku* of Isao Iinuma. And, magnificently, the score by Philip Glass. But is there really transcendence here, captured in the final utterances: "There were no boundaries. No more body or spirit. Pen or sword?"

By the end of the film, we understand Mishima's opening statement that he wanted to transcend the gulf between words and action, pen and sword. Like Ghost Dog, he wants his swordplay to be in the service of the Buddha, or his representative on earth, the Emperor. As indentured to the cause his militarism is sacred. As a writer he wants to go beyond the body; and, as one yearning for the sacred, he wants to transcend the distinctions of word and body.

But all of these yearnings ultimately yield only the fruit of death and destruction: the kamikaze pilot may be transported by the beauty of the moment in his solitary plane, but, on plunging his "silver phallus" into the bodies of his enemies, he stands judged by the Buddha: you have harmed sentient beings.

Words. This is the central issue: both Schrader and Mishima have fallen for the myth of the Romantic. It is no coincidence that Mishima talks in the film of the key influences on him: Rodin, Oscar Wilde, and Rainer Maria Rilke. He is thrilled to learn that Byron had an army of three hundred men. His favorite writer is Thomas Mann, the person he'd most like to be is Elvis Presley. He is in thrall to the West and to its Romantic tradition. The search for the spiritual is lost, again, in art. Militarism *isn't* spiritual. Suicide *isn't* transcendent. Yes, all convention is turned upside down as mountains become rivers and rivers become mountains. But Mishima, and by extension Schrader, choose to stay in that dramatic, aesthetic world of jumbled-up imagery: they don't push through to the last stage described by Schrader, but which—it seems—he has not fully understood, when mountains become mountains again. The third, crucial, stage is missing.

Warfare appeals to the dramatic mind, the Romantic mind. *Ghost Dog* exemplifies in many ways the exhilaration and popular appeal of Eastern martial arts practices, though his executions are carried out with a gun. The close relation between many martial arts forms and dance—found explicitly in the *kata* routines of karate for example—gives scope for the balletic choreography of fight sequences not found in Western fighting styles. The exhilaration of such choreography soon found technical assistance in the use of "wires"—a catchall for the techniques used to fling actors gracefully through the air, involving harness, wires, and an off-screen soft landing. One of the early examples of this is found in *A Touch of Zen*. The story is an example of the *wuxia* genre: fiction concerning the adventures of martial artists set in ancient China. But any spiritual element present in the story is somewhat confused: the life of its protagonist Ku having perhaps some moral development. The fight scenes often involve the actors performing gravity-defying leaps, taken to an artistic peak in the later *wuxia* film *Crouching Tiger, Hidden Dragon*. The Buddhist credentials of the latter film are just as slight, as indicated early in the film when one protagonist tells the other, "I hear you have been studying deep meditation. It must be so relaxing. I am so envious you have no idea." A distinction was made earlier between concentration meditation and awareness-meditation. While either of these major forms may well bring about relaxation in the practitioner, this is only a byproduct and not the intention. Particularly not of *deep* meditation. A long-term practice of deep concentration may well make the practitioner tense, or at least intense, and the long-term practice of awareness meditation will, in the early stages, make the practitioner aware that their mind is a cesspool, and in the later stages bring them to under standings that most would find grim: this is not the anodyne pursuit of relaxation. *Crouching Tiger, Hidden Dragon*—sometimes satirized as "flying actors, hidden wires,"—is a feel-good action movie with no understanding either of the realities of meditation or the realities of the martial arts. It is, of course, exhilarating, as are the martial arts scenes in both volumes of *Kill Bill*. These involve more "wire-fu" which also features extensively in the *Matrix* trilogy.

Summary

This chapter has allowed us to consider films located within specific faith traditions, looking out for what kinds of spiritual practice have become part of the lived spiritual life. It is notable that, whereas the Western context of filmmaking with its largely secular framework has made a journey into various religious heartlands and thrown up good films of Jewish, Christian, and Buddhist practice, the same is not true of Hinduism and Islam. In India the Western techniques of filmmaking rapidly served a vast audience for popular entertainment, with apparently little appetite for the exploration of India's diverse religious history. Bollywood made billions out of a limited formula. In the exclusively Muslim world of Arab nations, resistant to so much of Western cultural production, it seems that no formula has been stumbled upon that yields up much world cinema at all, let alone a luminous cinema of Islamic practice. The injunction against the representation of living things is perhaps too deeply ingrained. Despite this, we do get glimpses of Sufi practices in *Meetings with Remarkable Men* and in *Monsieur Ibrahim*, and we get a glimpse of the Ethiopian Zār tradition in *Exiles*, all of which settings have a Muslim context. Perhaps these films suggest a way forward.

The films we have of Jewish, Christian, and Buddhist practice, even if the practice is incidental to the main thrust of the film, are often luminous. If one has anything like a sympathetic ear to religion—if one is "musical" to it—then one cannot fail to find in the synagogue scenes of *The Chosen* or *Kadosh* something of beauty; also the dance scene at the end of *The Quarrel*, or the silhouetted scenes of Jewish practice in *Trembling Before G-d*. Sonny's first service in the renovated church in *The Apostle* is deeply in the Christian tradition with its roots in poverty and simplicity, and is a glimpse of American Christianity at its best, while rather naturally the whole of *Into Great Silence* is a poetic essay in Christian monastic practice. Pasolini's *The Gospel According to St. Matthew* with its lyrical cinematography, ecstatic music, and a young Spanish trades union activist as Jesus, stands the test of time as the best Jesus film made to date.

The Buddhist films we looked at are mostly documentaries on Tibetan Buddhism or dramatizations of the life of the Dalai Lama such as *Kundun*, with the exception of *Why Did Bodhidharma Leave for the East?* and *Spring, Summer, Autumn, Winter, ... and Spring*. *Enlightenment Guaranteed* also stands out as a fictional but serious look at Zen from the point of view of "beginner's mind." Taken collectively, one glimpses the general nature of Buddhist practice, often luminous, sometimes embedded in shamanic cultures, and often contrasted with the modern world in both its capitalist and communist manifestation. A serious major film to convey any aspect of Hinduism has yet to be made perhaps, but *Jai Santoshi Maa* conveys something of the popular *bhakti* or devotional tradition, while if one can subtract the Freudian secularism of Ray's *Devi* there is a potentially deeper picture to be gained of essential Hindu spirituality and religious practice.

More generally, we looked at practices that cross religious boundaries, such as religious song and dance, and then at a specific religious practice with huge implications: the martial arts. *Whale Rider* and *Ghost Dog* stand out as portraits of individuals who pursue a martial arts practice as a spiritual practice, and in whom the idea of a spiritual, physical discipline has an almost luminous intensity.

"Almost" is an important caveat, as we shall explore in the next chapter. The question that arises is: How is a martial arts practice compatible with the spiritual life if it is a training for violence? Or, in Mahayana Buddhist terms: Does the realization that form is emptiness allow one to take life, at least under exceptional circumstances?

10
Violence, Compassion, Forgiveness and Atonement

We saw in the previous chapter that spiritual practice in the world's traditions may include physical activities such as dance, yoga, or the martial arts. While the martial arts may be cultivated solely to keep fit, or for spiritual or aesthetic purposes, they are of course a form of violence when put into practice, whether defensive or offensive. But religion and violence have many other points of contact, particularly in the justifications for war from religious thinkers—such as Augustine's "just war"—or in the compassionate interventions in the aftermath of violence, or even during it.

When one person has harmed another, two deeply spiritual issues arise: that of forgiveness and that of atonement. How does the wronged individual, perhaps afflicted with fear, rage and the lust for vengeance, overcome these passions and find the generosity to forgive? And can one forgive on behalf of loved ones wronged? In turn, how does the perpetrator, after succumbing to evil intent, or simply acting mistakenly or by accident, find inner peace after harming another? What is the journey of atonement or redemption? How does compassion arise in the midst of all this?

At a purely secular level the common saying "What goes round, comes round" is an expression of the realization that all acts have consequences. When this is taken at a deeper level it reveals the profound connectedness we have with other people, animals, the environment and eventually existence itself, a profound connectedness which some people describe through the abstract term "God."

Cinema provides countless examples of violence offered up merely as entertainment, generally on the excuse that the "bad guys" are on the receiving end and deserve what they get. There is no question of attempting to find understanding and forgiveness. But there are also significant films which begin to pose the questions just outlined and provide memorable dramatic journeys of illustration. We will look first at the issue of war and pacifism, and then contrast the subtly different nature of Christian and Buddhist compassion. We then turn to films of forgiveness, followed by one of the key themes associated with film and religion: atonement and redemption. These terms may have specifically religious or Christian connotations, but in our ordinary lived lives they are often present if only on a small scale.

Finally, in this section we look at films where atonement is false and violence unconvincingly justified. Such films could be ignored perhaps if it were not for the disturbing frequency with which they receive critical acclaim. This means that the issues are indeed difficult to resolve and therefore worthy of attention.

Violence and Pacifism in Religion

Costume dramas of Old Testament stories, of the *Mahabarata*, and of the birth of Islam, for example, have no choice but to present violence as sanctioned by religion. But religion has also been the traditional advocate of peace, for example among the Quakers, Amish, Buddhists and Jains.

Tolstoy wrote one of the most uncompromising books ever on pacifism, *The Kingdom of God is Within You*, in which he sets out the case for an *absolute* pacifism. Shunned in Russia and by most of religious tradition since then, it was Gandhi who took up its principles, corresponded on them with Tolstoy, and became a self-declared disciple of the Russian literary giant. Tolstoy opens his exploration of pacifism with an acknowledgment of his debt to the Quakers. He says that they had "established beyond doubt the duty for a Christian of fulfilling the command of non-resistance to evil by force, and had exposed the error of the church's teaching in allowing war and capital punishment."[1] Hence, it is appropriate to start this section with a film about Quakers tested in the American Civil War.

Friendly Persuasion stars Gary Cooper as Jess Birdwell, head of a family firmly embedded in their Quaker community. The film is something of a period costume drama, and also uses populist humor to give it wider appeal, all of which belies its serious potential. A contemporary remake in a more serious style—such as in the pacifist film *To End All Wars* (discussed next)—could provide a more realistic picture of Quaker tradition. Nonetheless, towards the end of *Friendly Persuasion*, as family members and the Quaker meeting are confronted in their pacifist principles with the reality of civil war, the film does get serious. We are prepared for the difficulties of this when a Union officer attends Meeting for Worship (the Quaker equivalent of Sunday church service) and tells them: "Would you men stand by while others die to protect you?" Jess's son Josh—played by a young Anthony Perkins—gives the honest answer, "I don't know," which enrages a Quaker elder. "Nothing can move me to violence, nothing!" But when their homes are looted and burned by Confederate forces, it is this same elder who is the first to demand that the menfolk of the Birdwell family fight.

At the end of the film, when waves of war lap around their homestead, Jess and his wife debate with Josh: it is clear that the young man is thinking seriously of taking up arms. "Thou shalt not kill," his mother reminds him, and makes him promise at bedtime to let the Lord's voice speak to him before making up his mind. But in the morning Josh descends with his rifle, his intent clear. The mother pleads with Jess to stop his son, but Jess shakes his head. "I'm just his father, not his conscience." This is perhaps the most revealing statement of the Quaker tradition: while insisting on non-violence it is at the same time clear that this is a matter of individual conscience.

To End All Wars is a more generalized film of Christian pacifism, with a dramatic setting almost identical to that in *The Bridge on the River Kwai*. The almost half-century between the two films allows for a very different sensibility to be pursued in the later film. Patriotic questions now in the distant past, *To End All Wars* explores how a small group of POWs, enduring the most terrible conditions, could retain their faith in life itself, whether through Christianity, or some other route such as philosophy or literature. It also represents the struggle between Old

Testament and New Testament understandings of violence. The film follows the efforts of Ernest Gordon to rise above the horrors of the camp—which include the crucifixion of one of the prisoners—and offer hope to inmates and forgiveness to their captors. His commanding officer, Major Ian Campbell, insists on the Old Testament "eye for an eye," but it is Gordon who prevails. In the "jungle school" that they set up they read the few books they have: Plato, Shakespeare, the Bible, and ask themselves the question: "What is Justice?" They also consider the issue of mercy. "It's the last bastion of cowards!" erupts Campbell. The Japanese tolerate the school, but when the camp commander reads the pacifist words of Jesus in the Bible he is as full of contempt as Campbell, and calls the book "superstition." He throws the image of the suffering Christ back in the inmates' faces when he orders the crucifixion of Dusty, a soldier who offers to die in the place of the Major—an act which is in turn inspired by the Japanese moral code. In the end, when the camp is mistakenly strafed by the Allies, the contradictions are too much for the Major, and in the ensuing mayhem he dies where Gordon lives on to apply his principles to wounded Japanese soldiers.

The Amish are a Christian group as committed to pacifism as the Quakers, so it is of interest to find in the film *Witness* several scenes which bear on this issue. In this film, the violence of the policeman's world meets the pacifism of the Amish somewhat halfway: both seem to learn from each other. Amish men were used to being mocked in their local town, but when bullies tackle the group containing Book, the cop, he is not willing to turn the other cheek. There are similar scenes in *Friendly Persuasion* which see the *pater familias* dunk a bully in an apple barrel, much to his wife's indignation. This is not quite Tolstoy's vision, however, but rather the earthly realities of attempting to live by pacifist principles and giving oneself some wiggle room here and there.

Turning now to the Indian subcontinent, we find a series of cultures with a long tradition of pacifism, despite of, or some say because of, its own history of warfare. It is no surprise that Tolstoy's message fell on more receptive ears in India than in Russia or most of the West. While the *Bhagavad Gita* is controversial among pacifists because its key dramatic element is the persuasion by Krishna of Arjuna to fight in the forthcoming battle of Kurukshetra— and also caused Gandhi much mental anguish, as we saw—there is generally far less violence in the Indian scriptures and more exhortation to pacifism than in the Western Bible.

In this context it is interesting to examine the film *Asoka* for the turning point in his life when he was transformed from a normally bloodthirsty leader of empire to a pacifist one. *Asoka* is no less a costume drama than *Friendly Persuasion* and unfortunately it does not dwell enough on the anguish of conversion. Legend has it that Asoka was stricken by the sheer scale of the bloodshed involved in conquering a neighboring kingdom, and so underwent an almost overnight conversion to Buddhism, as speedily as the emperor Constantine was converted to Christianity. In Asoka's case, and probably Constantine's, this is exaggerated: we know that Asoka's wife was a Buddhist, and her influence over a longer period would have affected him. But the film version prefers the more dramatic account. Asoka has conquered Kalinga—and is referred to by now as the "evil Asoka" for his brutality—but is told by an aide Vitasoka that he is "only" an emperor. "You have won the tears of widows," says Vitasoka bitterly, "the cries of orphans and enflamed bodies. You have won it all."

Perhaps the battlefield of Kalinga occupies the same place in Indian imagination as that of Kurukshetra: it is visualized in *Asoka* as a scene of devastation, burning and enslavement. Asoka wanders through it looking for his beloved, trips in blood and is then moved to bring water to an injured and dying soldier. He then finds his betrothed (Kaurwaki, who is known historically to have been his second wife), and their dead son. He renounces violence and throws his famous sword in the river. It's all too unhistorical and all too fast: the psychology of it is missing.

In *The Warrior* we find another telling of the rejection of violence by a warrior of the Indian subcontinent. But the British secular and designer-conscious culture in which it was made has already rejected the two principal elements of warrior-spirituality: the belief in the supernatural and the belief in warfare as religiously justified. The film is also ungrounded in any specifics of history, though vaguely set in "feudal" India. Uncoupled from the religious setting that informs *The Mahabharata* and *Asoka*, *The Warrior* becomes an expression of contemporary *unconsidered* pacifism. The left-leaning, politically correct modern mind mostly found within contemporary cultural production dramatizes its discomfort with war in a variety of ways, such as in this film.

As discussed above, *Seven Samurai* is a film containing violence, but by contrast carefully set in its period, and in which there is a continued undercurrent of non-violent thought. Near the start the chief samurai Kambei offers reflectively: "I got nothing out of fighting. I'm alone in the world." But it is the seventh and "fake" samurai Kikuchiyo whose antiwar polemic is the most heartfelt, applicable to any period or culture. Kurosawa has led up to this moment carefully. The newly recruited samurai are initially angry on receiving a lukewarm reception from the villagers, many of whom fear that their daughters will be seduced. Once this hurdle is overcome there arrives another challenge: Kikuchiyo discovers a cache of samurai amour, from which the genuine samurai deduce that the villagers are in the habit of capturing and killing samurai retreating in defeat from battle. "With bamboo poles!" says one in disgust. Kikuchiyo then launches into an extensive portrayal of the farmers as deceitful, miserly, cowardly, mean, stupid and murderous people, listened to in silence by the others. But then he turns on them. "But who made animals of them? You did! You damned samurai! Whenever you fight, you burn villages, you destroy crops, take away food, rape women, enslave men, kill them if they resist. Do you hear, you damned samurai?"

What follows next is pure Kurosawa. As Kikuchiyo sobs after his outburst, the six samurai look on in silence. Slowly they drop their heads. This is a scene inconceivable in Western cinema: the heroes are first of all doing nothing, but much worse is that they are at a loss for words, at a loss for what to do, and are contemplating with sorrow the genuine harm that their "heroism" entails. Here is an action film where for a period the audience just looks at thoughtful men with bowed heads. The camera cuts to a close-up of Kambei, whose expressive features Kurosawa so often puts to good purpose. He looks up slowly. "You're a farmer's son, aren't you?" he asks. Kikuchiyo acknowledges this by running out of the hut, only to encounter the village elder, come to rescue what he can out of the damning discovery of the amour. The samurai are still sitting with bowed heads. "Is anything the matter?" the old man asks, as he takes in the scene. "No," say the samurai ruefully.

It is possible that few viewers of the film remember its antiwar credentials, but they are there again at the end when the surviving three samurai, mourning their lost comrades, are placed in contrast with the rejoicing villagers planting next year's rice crop. "Again we are defeated," says Kambei. "The farmers have won. Not us." Few other samurai films can be said to contain within them such a critique of the samurai way of life.

The Thin Red Line and *Saints and Soldiers* are two more films that show a contemporary unease with the violence of war, transposing a certain liberal sensibility into a war setting of an era where objections to war, if made then, mostly had a different flavor. *The Thin Red Line* is a fictional story set during the Battle of Guadalcanal in World War II. In the middle of the film, various philosophizing takes place, without which it would just be an action movie, as the thoughtfulness is entirely verbal, unlike in *To End All Wars* where it is translated into physical acts of compassion. *Saints and Soldiers* is set just prior to the Battle of the Bulge in World War II and allows for a set of moral quandaries to develop. It ends with a scene of forgiveness as a U.S. soldier treats the wounds of a German officer he had several encounters with.

Waltz with Bashir is a very different kind of film, being mostly an animated derivation of live action, and dealing with the Sabra and Shatila massacres by Lebanese forces following the assassination of President-elect Bashir Gemayel in Beirut. The culpability of the Israeli military in the massacre has long been in dispute, and the film follows the memories of an Israeli soldier who took part in the event. The film is clearly an exercise on the boundaries of atonement. But culpability is unclear, and the process of acknowledgment, remorse, recompense, God's forgiveness and reformation is barely traversed. The abrupt ending—the switch to live-action newsreel of the aftermath of the massacre—also diverts the course of the film from the personal journey to the historic facts, and is as jarring as the change in aesthetic. However, the film has an extraordinary look to it, and speaks volumes about the issue of personal guilt in the aftermath of war.

Compassion

Pacifism is a stance towards violence that may be merely doctrinaire—as some of the old Quakers demonstrated in *Friendly Persuasion*—or it may arise out of deep compassion. Compassion is perhaps the broader stance or emotion, in that it seeks what is good for others and agonizes when that good is not clearly understood or obtainable without further suffering.

Kurosawa's significance for the world of religion and film lies in a specific kind of compassion—almost invisible—discussed already in its emergence as pacifism in *Seven Samurai*. We return to this film and also look at two more of his early films, *Drunken Angel* and *Ikiru*, that share the same actor, Takashi Shimura, who played Kambei the lead samurai. Kambei's compassion for the farmers is triggered after he has first refused their request for armed protection, and then hears the sobs of one of the farmers and the ridicule heaped on them by other men staying in the hostel: "The farmers might as well hang themselves." Takashi Shi mura's face is expressive of empathy and compassion in a way that Kurosawa deploys knowingly. In the scene described earlier, when the samurai are confronted by the farmer's son, Kikuchiyo, it is Shimura's face that most vividly represents the encountering of a generous spirit with unwelcome facts. Compassion is shown again when the youngest of the samurai give his precious rice to the village girl he now courts. She gives it in turn to her grandmother who lives alone and neglected, which the warriors find saddening, but again is a prompt for compassionate action. It is instructive to compare *Seven Samurai* with the American remake *The Magnificent Seven*. The film has a similar plot and ends with the same sentiment: "Only the farmers won. We lost. We always lose." There is also a similar sharing of food with the villagers. But there is nothing like the scene of silent contrition in *Seven Samurai*. Western culture requires either a more immediate sense of right and wrong, or a more immediate resolution to indeterminate issues.

It is in Kurosawa's *Drunken Angel* that Takashi Shimura's expressive features are put to an even more sustained compassionate purpose: here he plays a doctor who is concerned about the health of a gangster. Doctor Sanada is an alcoholic and Matsunaga, the gangster he attempts to help, has much less still to recommend him. But, as Matsunaga's tuberculosis develops, the film suggests through Sanada's gruff and flawed compassion that even the life of a criminal is important in the scheme of things.

Kurosawa's *Ikiru* features Takashi Shimura again, this time as Kanji Watanabe, a middle-aged bureaucrat who is diagnosed with stomach cancer. He is naturally devastated, but then finds one possible way of dealing with it: spending time with a female junior former employee whose gaiety and love of life he finds deeply appealing. However, before long she makes it clear that she cannot be his support in facing death: she belongs to the living. A theme running through the film is the uselessness of bureaucratic life, where the local government office creates paperwork out of every citizen's request, only in order to refer the petitioner to another department. One such request, long shunted around by the system, is for a children's park, and when this issue returns to Watanabe's desk he looks at it anew. With six months to live, he decides that he will back the project, despite his low standing, and the prevailing culture of prevarication. He succeeds in the end, and the film finishes with a widely acclaimed scene of him sitting on a swing and contemplating the joy it will bring to local children in the austerities of the postwar period.

Dodes'ka-den was Kurosawa's first film in color and a departure from previous work, including the use of new actors. It follows the lives of impoverished people living by a city dump in a kind of shack city, an environment hinted at in the river scenes in *Drunken Angel*. It has no central character through which we can follow any ideal of service or compassion, but instead it is the empathy with which the daily lives of these people are followed that marks out the film. Its title is a rendering of the sound made by a retarded man in his daily fantasy of being a tram driver: in English it would be the "clackety-clack" of metal wheels on rail-joints. Buddhism makes an explicit, though brief, appearance: the mother of the retarded man chants at her little Buddhist shrine in her home.

But why suggest that the compassion in Kurosawa's films has a Buddhist source, when Buddhism is almost never explicitly present in his films? And how can a universal emotion like compassion be either "Christian" or "Buddhist?" The answer lies perhaps in the role of *anger*. In the positive sense anger, as outrage at the injustices of the world, both informs Western compassion and drives the seeking for a better world in practical action. This anger is normally creative not destructive, and forms a counterpart to the Christian love that seeks to help others. When the world obstinately refuses to change, this anger can become frustration, or a merely intellectual position adopted by academics for example, who might rail in their works against capitalism or the state but draw a fat salary paid for by the same state and its capitalism. But the Buddhist East refracts its compassion and love for others with less conviction that the world is "wrong" and must be changed. The West has traditionally understood this as fatalism. But in Kurosawa's hands the compassion of the East becomes an unflinching look at what actually *is*, with less judgment or blame. This is the true quality of *Dodes'ka-den*, leaving the viewer to be angry or just moved at the circumstances of life. In Kurosawa's own childhood, he toured the aftermath of the Great Kantō earthquake of 1923, walking through heaps of piled corpses. His brother urged him not to turn his head away, but to look at the frightening scene, to absorb it fully. At thirteen, then, Kurosawa acquired perhaps a stance of unflinching compassion for the suffering of others which permeates all his films.

If we compare *Dodes'ka-den* with *City of God*, a 2002 film about slum people in Rio de Janeiro, then East-West differences could not be more starkly presented. In *City of God* there is a continual voyeuristic element in its subtle glamorizing of gang violence, thus placing the audience at a remove from a poverty that remains incomprehensibly other. While the film might arouse anger and indignation, it does not resemble the unflinching encounter with horror as in Kurosawa's childhood, but more a sanitization or even glamorizing of suffering.

If Buddhist compassion has a coolness about it which the West observes as segueing into indifference, then Christian compassion has a heat about it which the East observes as segueing into mania. A good representation of this in Western cinema lies in the Robin Williams canon. In *Good Will Hunting, Awakenings, Patch Adams, Dead Poet's Society* and *The Fisher King*, Robin Williams is typecast in the role of the compassionate teacher, therapist, doctor, or would-be doctor. His enthusiasm to help others often leads him into conflict with authority: his roles become an emblem of an instinctive response to the needs of others. But the roles are all couched in secular terms, and in the context of secular institutions such as schools, hospitals and the probation service. Hence, his compassion is no more explicitly Christian, than Kurosawa's is explicitly Buddhist: it is simply located in a specific cultural background. In *Good Will Hunting, Awakenings* and *Patch Adams* (based on a true story), Williams plays roles comparable with Doctor Sanada in *Drunken Angel*. In *Good Will Hunting*, it is Sean Maguire, called in to help a troubled young genius, Will Hunting. Sean has to work hard to reach the young man, a little as Sanada has to work at the gangster Matsunaga. In *Awakenings* and *Patch Adams*, Williams plays doctors relentlessly driven by their desire to heal. In *Awakenings*, Williams is Dr. Malcolm Sayers, modeled on the early life and work of neurologist Oliver Sacks. Sayers discovered that L-Dopa—a drug that was new at the time—helped catatonic patients wake up. These patients are still conscious, but trapped in entirely unresponsive bodies. Sayers visits the doctor involved in the original epidemic from forty years earlier that left the victims catatonic and, on seeing early film footage of them, asks "What are they thinking?" "They're not," comes the reply. "The virus didn't spare their higher faculties." "You know that for a fact." "Yes." "Because?" "Because ... the alternative is unthinkable." But Sayers thinks the unthinkable, and is motivated to try the experimental treatment with L-Dopa. It seems that the patients can be influenced by the will of another human being, simply by being given attention, and through this Sayers comes to believe that they lie intact as persons in their living tombs. The new drug works his longed-for miracle, and soon the hospital staff has to cope with a quite different set of problems, as the patients come to life again. The treatment is only a temporary fix however, and side effects manifest which make it impossible to continue it. As the patients return to their previous catatonic states, Sayers is naturally downcast. However, he learns his own lessons of life from the episode, and indeed, at the heart of the film is a celebration of life and of the caring that doctors can provide to restore it.

Robin Williams has the perfect temperament for these roles, so much so that the British film press uses him as a template of how not to act—the British find "emotion" difficult and are too quick to dismiss his performances as maudlin. But compassion is not maudlin, and Williams contains within his performances a very Western passion to help and to change the world. The Christian tradition may have had its roots in an apolitical and anti-science sensibility, but its encounter with the Enlightenment has made it activist and a believer in progress. Hence, the doctors played by Williams are culturally a world removed from Doctor Sanada as played by Takashi Shimura. In fact, Christianity and activism are now so intertwined that Ian

Maher says (as we saw in the Introduction), "In *Awakenings*, whilst Dr. Sayer does not convey any overt theological stance it is arguably that an implicit theology of liberation is at work in him."

Compassion can be overwhelmed by the sufferings in the world, and, if so, then madness looms. It is the *manic* element in Williams that hints so well at this, and perhaps the best example of it is in Terry Gilliam's surreal *The Fisher King*.

In *Fearless*, introduced earlier, Max and Carla survive a plane crash, though her baby does not. Max then takes it upon himself to help her through her despair, being the one person she can turn to. He can do this because of the shared terrors of the event, but in doing so he alienates his wife. We can all identify with the wife's experience as one who loves her husband but cannot find the necessary depth of compassion in what seems to be a burgeoning love between her husband and another woman. She cannot empathize deeply enough, because she did not share the experience. In the end, Max helps Carla by subjecting her to an outrageously risky stunt: he gives her a heavy object to hold and deliberately drives his car into a brick wall so as to show her that she could not have saved her baby. On impact she is restrained by the seat belt but the object eludes her grasp, just as her baby did in the plane. He imaginatively enters that part of their shared disaster which went beyond his own experience, and his gamble pays off: her guilt is assuaged or becomes manageable, and she is able to pick up her life's threads again, as is he.

Forgiveness

An enraged person who is violent towards inanimate matter may not harm anyone else, and indeed may find the action therapeutic. But a person prone to rage is likely to harm other sentient beings at some stage—and in Buddhism the stance of rage itself is considered "unskillful." So is rage when it is accompanied by intelligence and cunning, in which case even more harm may result, perhaps in the pursuit of revenge. The violence that comes of rage can be done in "hot" or "cold" fashion. But whatever the fate of the aggressor, either at the hands of other people, culturally sanctioned or vigilantist, or through cosmic forces such as karma or the will of a deity, the *victim* is placed under the moral and spiritual dilemma of forgiveness.

Filmic treatments of forgiveness are much rarer than those of revenge, the latter forming an endless fascination as justified violence in vigilante and revenge films. Alexandre Dumas's *Count of Monte Cristo* is an early example of a revenge story as a cold form of justified violence; Charles Bronson's vigilante films represent the hot end of the spectrum. But when forgiveness does become subject to filmic treatment it is especially memorable.

The Fisher King is a film of moral development with parallels to *Groundhog Day*, in which the aspects of compassion and forgiveness deserve a closer look. Peter Hasenberg introduces the film thus:

> "I am the janitor of God," says the mad tramp Brian Parry in Terry Gilliam's *Fisher King* (1991), thus hinting clearly—though incidentally—at a religious dimension to the film ... *The Fisher King* is a serious comedy, above all a story of guilt and redemption, with comedian Robin Williams as the wise fool, the spiritual guide of the guilt-ridden hero.[2]

Jeff Bridges plays an insufferable smart aleck called Jack, whose catastrophe and moral regeneration is witnessed and benchmarked by the female romantic interest. His moral development unfolds through a karmic entanglement with Parry. This character walks the typical

Williams tightrope between the compassionately moral and the maudlin. Instead of the single supernatural device of *Groundhog Day*, *The Fisher King* veers instead towards a surrealism typical of Gilliam's other work. Parry is apparently a derelict prone to hallucinations which take the memorable shape of a red knight on horseback lit up in flames. The core moral issue of the film is that Jack, as a radio DJ, has inadvertently tipped a loner over the edge by taunting him in his radio phone-in, where the man had needed compassion and support. The resulting gun rampage had killed Parry's wife in front of him in a fashionable restaurant, the kind of place where Jack had taunted the would-be gunman that sophisticated women went who were beyond his romantic reach. Jack has the moral insight to realize his complicity in this tragedy, but descends into a self-pitying booziness, oblivious to the love of his new but long-suffering girlfriend Anne. His journey to atonement begins in a chance encounter with Parry, who in turn finds in Jack a reason to start his own climb out of dereliction and despair. Parry had been a teacher—a typical Williams nurturing role—at Hunter College prior to his breakdown, and the film finishes with his leading the inmates of his mental ward in a rousing rendition of "How About You?"

Jack's compassion grows out of his guilt, while Parry's is merely liberated by his new role as derelict, a position forced on his conscious mind by the impossibility of absorbing his loss. Parry's compassion is symbolized by the "fool" who wanders into the castle of the wounded Fisher King—he is relating this to Jack under the moon in Central Park—and who doesn't see a king but a man in pain. In tending to the simple need of the king for water, the act becomes the outpouring of the Holy Grail and the king is healed. Although Parry and Jack never directly discuss Jack's role in the death of Parry's wife, Parry's forgiveness of Jack is implicit throughout. But the roles of healing are intertwined, as it is Jack who brings Parry his imagined "Holy Grail" and allows him to face his loss and move forward. Jack's journey, because it is long, and also suffers a hubristic reversal, is a more convincing portrait of atonement than Mendoza's in *The Mission*.

The Son is typical of the "social realism" film oeuvre of Jean-Pierre and Luc Dardenne: low-budget, often using non-professional actors. Spare and unjudgmental, their films follow ordinary people in their Belgian small-town settings. In the case of *The Son*, it is carpentry instructor Olivier whose routine is provoked when he is asked to take on a young offender recently released from juvenile detention. At first refusing, he then relents. We don't initially understand Olivier's mixed emotions, but through encounters with his ex-wife we realize that the young man had killed their baby son. The film builds up an intolerable tension as to Olivier's motives. From the wife's reaction we gather that he is following a course of forgiveness, a coming-to-terms with the young man's own plight as convicted killer, and the fostering of empathy for him. Such a course is unthinkable in popular terms, and there is no evidence that Olivier is religious. "Who do you think you are?" asks the wife. "Nobody would do this. So why you?" She is right at one level to say this: mainstream wisdom demands "justice" as revenge or at the very least anathematization of the perpetrator. She would naturally feel betrayed. On the other hand, in the monotheistic traditions, the privilege of forgiveness lies in the hands of the deity. Is Olivier therefore playing God?

Towards the end of the film, during a trip to a timber yard, we are left confused: is Olivier in fact planning some horrible revenge? When he finally confronts the young man with the fact that he is the father of the murdered infant, the offender is confused and fearful. Naturally, he attempts to flee, and in the chase and final subduing of the boy the audience is torn between the still-open possibilities. But the struggle finishes with no attempt at revenge. As Olivier straddles the boy, the young man has submitted now, and Olivier's hands are on his neck. The camera moves up to his face, but, although Olivier is breathing heavily there is no visible surge of hatred and aggression. His shoulders indicate movement, but it is only when the camera pans down again that we see Olivier's hands now placed to support him on either side of the boy's head.

Forgiveness takes a course in the woodland by the sawmill, under lowering Belgian skies, in a setting of banality but at the same time of astonishing beauty. The boy looks up into Olivier's eyes; they are both panting with no words left to express their situation. They sit up in the leaf-strewn woods, still breathing heavily. Olivier is the first to rise, wordless, and goes back to loading timber into his pick-up; the other follows him after a while and goes to join him in the work. They stare at each other, but as the boy picks up a plank, a little hesitantly at first, mingled with the faint defiance of one who has nothing to lose, and then loads it up, we can see that he is taking the place of the lost child under the severity of Olivier's instructional gaze. Kurosawa would have understood the scene: both protagonists are bound together by a horrific act, but some unfathomable instinct of love makes Olivier rise above popular convention, unaided by a shred of religious observance or belief, to confront the meaning and reality of forgiveness. This is extraordinary filmmaking. Neither its genre, nor the directors' oeuvre as a whole, prepares one for this austere, dry-eyed scene of forgiveness, framed by the sentiment of Olivier's wife: "Who do you think you are? Nobody would do this. So why you?" There is no answer to that question.

Into the Wild is based on the true story of Christopher McCandless, a young man who rejects the path set out for him by his parents and bums around America until settling into an abandoned bus in the Alaskan wilderness. Some way into the film there is an interesting scene where McCandless, liberated from convention, is taken in by an old man who makes leather goods. The two provoke each other in constructive ways. He tells the old man that "the core of man's spirit comes from new experiences," and challenges him to climb up a steep mountain path. He tells him further: "You're wrong if you think that the joy of life comes from human relationships. God's placed it all around us, it's in everything." The old man receives this with an open mind, but has a wisdom of his own to share as he probes McCandless' background. He is sorrowful that the young man has not been reconciled to his parents. He starts off tentatively: "There's some kind of bigger thing we can all appreciate, and it sounds like you don't mind calling it 'God.'" This is worth commenting on in terms of the delicacy with which the older man hears the term "God." He may be religious, but he doesn't want to burden their conversation with any assumptions, any kind of sermonizing that would destroy the mood between then. This is what he wants to say, however: "But when you forgive, you love. And when you love, God's light shines through you."

"Holy shit," responds McCandless, and they both laugh. But there is no doubt that something very real has passed between the two men.

Forgiveness isn't perhaps the cinema that most audiences are looking for, hence its rarity. In David Lynch's *The Straight Story*, we encounter something more familiar: ordinary rows which leave family members—in this case, siblings—estranged from each other. One party has to make the first move, and in *The Straight Story* it is Alvin who sets off to cross states on his lawnmower to offer the olive branch to his brother. It is a journey of atonement and forgiveness, when it finally comes, is simple and undramatic. The film is based on the true story of Alvin Straight, and is rather different from the rest of Lynch's oeuvre. Alvin hears that his brother has had a stroke, but as Alvin is not able-bodied enough to hold a driver's license, he makes the 240-mile journey on a modified lawn tractor. Rather like McCandless, he is liberated from his daily round, and encounters all kinds of things along the way, a pilgrimage of atonement perhaps, but one appropriate to a secular world. When he finally arrives, there is little outward emotion. His brother just looks at the lawnmower and says, "You ride that thing all the way out here to see me?" "I did, Lyall," answers Alvin, and no more is needed.

In *Dead Man Walking*—introduced earlier—a TV personality exhorts "get tough on sentencing," as Helen Prejean watches. Get tough on parole, get tough on judges who pass lenient sentences ... he receives applause. A figure like Prejean who wants to abolish the death sentence in America is fighting a system that reflects its voters. And the voters are with the families of the victims of murder, who largely want a justice that brings retribution, not forgiveness. When Prejean visits the father of the boy murdered by Poncelet, his first question is, "Are you a communist?" Forgiveness, it seems, is a concept so foreign to Americans that it might as well have its source in what they fear as much as forgiveness, communism. It does not strike them, it seems, to have a source in their religion. The father tells her: "When you lose a child all the memories get sealed in a place. Sealed like a shrine." Prejean has no answer to that, but pursues her campaign to commute the death sentence. When she visits the parents of the murdered girl, they ask, "What made you come round to our side?" They had assumed that her visit signaled her approval of the death sentence and withdrawal as Poncelet's spiritual advisor, and are shocked that she intends to go ahead. "How can you do that?" they ask, bewildered. "How can you sit with that scum?" All that Prejean can say, overwhelmed by their anguish, is that she is trying to follow the example of Jesus. But they will have none of it. "You brought the enemy into this house, sister," says the mother and tells her to go. As time goes on, the murdered boy's father is more willing to relate to Prejean, and in the end, strapped to his gurney, Poncelet asks his forgiveness, while for the other parents he simply says that he hopes his death gives them some relief.

We saw earlier that in *21 Grams* the bereaved woman Cristina is initially too numbed in her grief to press charges against the hit-and-run driver Jack who killed her husband and children. As grief turns to rage she asks of her new boyfriend Paul that he kill Jack. Although he is reluctant to do so at first, he agrees in the end. He goes through the motions, but perhaps in a way that helps us consider the nature of forgiveness: he is no natural vigilante, and in the end his compassion for Jack—and his impossible situation—means that he turns the gun on himself. It is worth mentioning that Sean Penn plays both Jack and Poncelet in these films, and directed *Into the Wild*. There is something in his work that forces the viewer to take a deeper look at things. Within this, luminous moments can emerge.

Atonement and Redemption

What are the key features of Western religion that distinguishes it from the East? There are many, but the idea of atonement and redemption features large. The West paints good and evil more starkly black and white than does the East—one only has to watch the films of Kurosawa and Miyazaki to realize that—and so the concept of atonement for evil deeds takes on more importance. In the East, where the ideas of karma and reincarnation are more common, atonement is spread out over the longer timescale of many lifetimes. In Christianity, however, atonement is a matter of urgency. Jesus becomes the focus of the impulse to atonement, and under the rubric of "Jesus died to save us from our sins" a powerful image exists to fuel the drive for atonement. However, in the films we now look at none of the characters are "saved" in this passive sense. It is not through faith in Christ and his resurrection that they find atonement: instead they undergo their own arduous journey of redemption, of suffering willingly borne, their own crucifixion.

In *Dead Man Walking*, Poncelet comes to some kind of atonement in the end, the crucial step being the final breakdown of his denial of the crime. In *Levity*, a murderer has discovered that there are actually five stages of atonement. Manual Jordan, played by Billy Bob Thornton, murdered a teenager, Abner Easley, and much later is granted parole from his life sentence. It seems that he felt remorse from the outset, and has convinced the parole board that he is no danger to anyone. But he is haunted by his actions, and early in the film tells us:

> I read a book that was written in the eleventh century. A man said that there was five steps toward making amends. The first involved acknowledging what you did. The second involved remorse. The third involved making right with your neighbor. Like if you stole his chicken, you'd have to go and bring him another. Only then were you able to go to step four, which was making it right with God. But it wasn't until step five that you could really get redeemed. It had to do with being at the same place and the same situation. That as it goes, you'd go and do something different. Only I can't bring Abner Easely back like he was some stolen chicken. Certainly made sure of that twenty-three years ago. And I don't believe in some God that's gonna open His arms to me even if I did. So there goes steps three and four. And as for step five, time makes sure we're never in the same place twice, no matter how much we wish it. Which is why, for me, I know I'll never be redeemed.

So, the five stages are: acknowledgment, remorse, recompense, God's forgiveness, and reform. Jordan has passed through the first two stages, but now, suddenly given his freedom into a world that doesn't know him, he is weighed down by the impossibility of recompense, forgiveness and reform. But whether he or the audience believes in God or not, a form of recompense opens up unexpectedly. He befriends the sister of the murdered boy, who is drawn to Jordan. However, just as in *21 Grams*, once she discovers that there is a pre-existing link between them the romantic possibilities are compromised. What saves Jordan is his role in preventing her son going the same route he did: falling in with gangs and their gun culture. The implication is clear: one can indeed never be in the same place twice, but life seems to have this odd habit of throwing up something that serves as its proxy. He could not bring back the life of the woman's brother, but he saves the life of her son. In Christianity, the symbol of this miracle is Jesus, in the East it is karma. With this recompense Jordan can now feel forgiven, to some extent at least, and can start to believe that he has changed: that he is not forever a murderer.

Manual Jordan spends years in jail, full of remorse for his killing, and agonizes throughout *Levity* as to whether he is redeemable. In *Bad Lieutenant*, the nameless protagonist (Harvey Keitel) is merely corrupt but is led to a sudden act of redemption that perhaps surprises him as much as us. The lieutenant is called in on a rape case. The victim is a Catholic nun, raped by the very boys her mission had set out to help. She says:

> Those boys were sad, raging boys. They came to me as the needy do. Like many of the needy, they were rude. Like all the needy, they took. And, like all the needy, they needed.... Jesus turned water into wine. I ought to have turned bitter semen into fertile sperm. Hatred to love. And maybe to have saved their souls. They did not love me, but I ought to have loved them. For Jesus loved those who reviled him. And never again shall I encounter two boys whose prayers are more poignant, more legitimate, more anguished.

But the lieutenant is absorbed in a shallow corrupt world where he uses the authority of his office to force women to fellate him, take drugs from dealers for himself and run a gambling ring on baseball. He has initially no idea of the nun's world where the compulsion is for others and the striving to forgive. In the church where she prays he kneels down with her and furtively offers to "beat the system" to provide "real justice" for her. The kids will get off lightly, he thinks, and in his genuine care for her, he wants to give her the vengeance he thinks she deserves. She simply says, "I have already forgiven them." He persists: "Come on, get with the program. How can you forgive these motherf ... these guys, 'scuse me. How could you? Don't you want them to pay for what they did to you?"

She repeats, "I forgive them."

The lieutenant is right in a sense: How can this woman not "get with the program?" Why isn't she like Olivier's wife? The lieutenant is the living embodiment of the "program," the legalized system of vengeance, and he can make it work for her behind the backs of the politically correct. So he pushes his creed: "But, do you have the right? You're not the only woman in the world. You're not even the only nun. Your forgiveness will leave blood in its wake. What if these guys do this to other nuns? Other virgins.... Can you bear the burden, sister?"

But she just tells him to talk to Jesus, and leaves him in the church. Left alone, he rants against God in a kind of delirium, gradually coming to the point of confessing all the bad things he has done. This is the crucial scene in the film: it is a *sudden* epiphany as opposed to the long sad atonement of Manual Jordan. The encounter with the essence of Christianity in the person of the nun breaks down his casual dismissal of the Catholic Church—*his* church—as a "racket." His well-meaning offer to help her is exposed as dirty, his corrupt soul is made clear to him in the mirror of her faith. The scene, while containing hallucinatory or perhaps magical realism elements, is convincing because the lieutenant's corruption is per haps only the surface of the man: all it took was the train-crash moment of his encounter with the nun to shatter his adopted cynical values and expose the truth of what it is to be human. His life had always been leading up to this moment. At least, this is one interpretation of the film.

As with the Belgian carpenter, we are at first unsure of what he is up to next when he regains his senses. He seeks out the boys, and there is every possibility that he is in fact intent on revenge. But no, he knows in fact that the streets will do the job for him: to rape a nun outrages even the gangs, and the boys are legitimate targets for the warped morality of hoodlums. He offers instead their salvation: money and a ticket on a bus out of town to start a new life elsewhere. "Your lives ain't worth shit in this town," he explains to them. But in doing so and neglecting other concerns he knows that he makes himself a target for gangsters. Peter Hasenberg is right to say that "Abel Ferrara's *Bad Lieutenant* is a most unusual example of a spiritual thriller."[3]

Atonement is a film version of Ian McEwan's novel of the same name. The film is beautifully produced, if something of a costume drama, and deals with the guilt of a thirteenyear-old girl from a wealthy English family over her false accusation of rape. Briony claims that Robbie, the son of the housekeeper, raped a fifteen-year-old girl staying at the house. The accusation sticks and Robbie is only released from jail on the condition that he serves in the war. Briony's elder sister Cecilia, in love with Robbie, later concludes that Briony did not take up her place at Cambridge because she felt guilty over her actions, and instead joins the nursing corps. Now eighteen, she is beginning to grasp the full implications of what she did. The film follows Briony's nursing and Robbie's soldiering, both the outcome of her mistaken identification.

Briony is haunted by her guilt, and is finally confronted by Robbie in a scene of great intensity as he boils over at the suffering she had brought him. Rapists do not have a good time in jail, and the war is no picnic either. All she can say in her defense is that she was thirteen at the time. But there is one thing she can do: she can write down the truth, give it to a solicitor, and clear his name.

But in the postmodern denouement of the film we cut to an aged Briony—played by Vanessa Redgrave—who is being interviewed on television about her latest novel, *Atonement*. She is overcome by emotion as she reveals that the scene of accusation in which Briony is confronted with her guilt and given a way to make amends is mere fiction. In reality, Robbie died at Dunkirk and Cecilia died in an air-raid. But what purpose would such a sad ending serve in a novel? What the film hints at is that atonement and reconciliation are indeed rare. Or perhaps, for the secular mind, that they are an outdated fantasy.

We have encountered long-term guilt for Manual Jordan, sudden exposure to moderate guilt for the Lieutenant, and a guilt only fictionally expunged for Briony. In *The Kite Runner*, there is long-term, nagging guilt for minor childhood transgressions: a guilty secret of nastiness made worse as the consequences for the victim become clear over time. As with previous examples, redemption comes through atonement via proxy. The "kite runner" of the film title is Hassan, who is Amir's servant and performs the traditional role of retrieving kites in the annual kite fighting competition in Kabul, prior to the Soviet invasion of Afghanistan. Both are teenage boys, close friends, but the differences of class become the source of tragedy. Hassan is beaten and raped by a gang of bullies while Amir looks on, horrified, but unwilling to act. This is enough to give him a sense of guilt, but, in his immature mind, it also causes him to worry that his father will favor Hassan. Perhaps because of this, or perhaps to eliminate the daily reminder of his cowardice, he frames his friend as a thief. If both boys had been born equal then, perhaps, Amir would not have got away with it, but Hassan and his father are dismissed. They belong to the Hazara ethnic group, which have often faced discrimination in Afghanistan. Not long afterwards Amir and his father Baba flee to America, and so Amir has little idea of what happens to Hassan. Amir grows up in California, and it is not until he is married and an established author that a family friend invites him back to Kabul because "there is a way to be good again." Amir discovers that Hassan was employed to look after their property after they had travelled to America, and both Hassan and his wife had died defending it against the Taliban. An even worse revelation is to follow: Hassan was Amir's illegitimate half-brother. In other words the betrayal was of his own brother.

As with Manual Jordan's murdered young man, there is no way to bring back the dead Hassan. Instead, Amir's atonement is offered through the proxy of Hassan's son, languishing in an orphanage. Amir pursues a course of great daring to rescue the boy, who has become the favorite of a Taliban leader. The guilt of his childhood cowardice now expiated, Amir returns to America with the boy, and a rehabilitation of the traumatized child begins. The rescue isn't very plausible but atonement has another poignant illustration in this film.

Spring, Summer, Autumn, Winter ... and Spring, its precursor *Why Did Bodhidharma Leave for the East?*, and *The Mission* involve atonement. In both of the Buddhist films, it is a child who transgresses, as described earlier, though much younger in fact than the teenage Amir in *The Kite Runner*. The context is now changed from a cultural history of Christian redemption to that of Buddhist belief in karma and reincarnation. Yet in both these films atonement takes place in this life, just as in *The Mission*. By chance the latter film and *Spring, Summer* also involve the protagonist dragging heavy objects up a mountain: in *The Mission* it is Mendoza's amour, while in Spring, Summer it is a millstone. It is a good filmic image.

Haibane Renmei is an animated made-for-TV series of thirteen episodes following the life of the Haibane or "charcoal feathers"—a group of beings with angel-like characteristics. The series, while clearly located in the cultural setting of both Miyazaki and the *Pokémon* franchises, has a soft and wistful quality that makes it unique. The series focuses on two Haibane girls: Rakka, named after "falling," and Reki, named after "stones," who is older and cares for Rakka and the others. They are born via strange cocoons that descend into a world constructed for them, the Old Home and Town. They stay in this bounded world as they complete some kind of journey of redemption or atonement, until their "Day of Flight" when they are released, perhaps to an afterlife or to be reincarnated. Rakka is temperamentally bound from the start to the posture of atonement, and in the end achieves it through her caring in general and her specific act of kindness to a bird—a creature she is linked with and perhaps has harmed in her previous existence. Reki, on the other hand, is temperamentally one who fights her circumstances, and her path to atonement is obstructed by her willfulness. It is hinted that she may have committed suicide under a train, as in *Maborosi*, while her self-destructive tendency is also apparent in her chain-smoking. In Susan Napier's thoughtful discussion of the series she tells us that "Reki" in a different ideogram means not "little stones" but a vehicle running over a body. She adds: "Reki, therefore, is a suicide victim, as are, potentially, all the other Haibane.... The Old Home and the Town may thus be considered a form of Purgatory, but one that the dwellers can escape from as long as they expiate their sins."[4] The creator Yoshitoshi ABe [*sic*], gives an illuminating interview on the series. He says that the characters are all part of him and represent experiences he went through as a teenager. Odd then, that he chose *girls* to dramatize these experiences—making this *shōjo* anime—but the notion of redemption requires perhaps a feminine principle of submission. When asked what the message of the film is, he simply says: "salvation." He adds enigmatically: "I have memories of going through a similar experience myself."

There are many more films where atonement in some form plays a role in the story. In *American Beauty*, Lester is saved from inappropriate hedonism in the crucial scene in the film, when the apparently mature schoolgirl friend of his daughter admits that she is a virgin. Eric Wilson comments on his sudden transformation: "He has consumed his development not in selfish eros but in generous *caritas*."[5] Lester had fallen in with the young woman's self-delusions of sexual sophistication, but when she utters the simple words "Be gentle with me, it's my first time," he suddenly realizes that she is young enough to be a daughter, and that as a father-figure he is better off fixing her a sandwich than having sex with her. In this case "caritas" is closer to the mark, and in this simple paternal act he is redeemed of all his inappropriate sexual fantasies. In Bergman's *Virgin Spring*, a father kills the rapists and killers of his daughter, but immediately offers to build a church of stone as his penance. And we saw in *The Apostle*, Sonny hospitalizes a man who subsequently dies, goes on the run, and attempts to atone by good works and rebuilding a church. When the police finally catch up with him he surrenders willingly to the process of the law.

False Atonements and Unconvincingly Justified Violence

The human being is a creature torn between higher and lower impulses—this is a picture drawn by all the religions, whether animist religions of the Native Americans, or the monotheist religions, or the Eastern religions. The great insight of Freud was that religion— in its cultural manifestation in late nineteenth century Vienna—had made it impossibly difficult to own the lower impulses. One could say that the most prominent characteristic of secular culture springs from the effort to reconnect with suppressed or sublimated impulses: those of sexuality and aggression. In the films so far examined in this section, we have explored portrayals of the higher impulses of pacifism, compassion, forgiveness, and of the journey of atonement or redemption. These films often have a background that makes these higher impulses stand out, for example the lack of forgiveness from one set of parents in *Dead Man Walking* makes Prejean's stance all the more striking.

Human nature is tricky: it would like to claim as a higher impulse something that is actually quite selfish; it would like to ease its conscience without the long journey of atonement. Hence, in this section we look at films where the basest of human acts—the taking of human life—is massaged into appearing selfless or noble, where the justifications are highly dubious, but where the cultural context perhaps goes back to Freud's liberation of the lower impulses.

An accident of Western religious history has placed the Old Testament at the heart of its literature, especially in the Protestant world. Gore Vidal memorably called the Old Testament a "barbaric Bronze Age text"[6]; J. S. Mill calls it "in many respects barbarous, and intended only for a barbarous people"[7]—a characterization that would seem a little extreme if one did not have the great religious literature of the East to compare it with: *The Dhammapadda*, *The Bhagavad Gita* (despite its call to arms), *The Upanishads*, the *Tao Te Ching*, and so on. The violence in the Old Testament is relentless, and should perhaps be properly separated from its religious content by declaring it as merely the history of an obscure tribe attempting to survive in a violent period. Perhaps that is not possible, but the end result of the Old Testament's overwhelming cultural significance for Christian theologians is that a form of mental gymnastics is required to reconcile the message of love and peace that Jesus undoubtedly brings, with the violence—often on religious grounds—which is all-pervading in the Old Testament, and, as we have seen, returns in Revelation. This contradiction quite naturally spills into the arena of religion and film.

Eric S. Christianson, writing in the context of the *Godfather* films, says, "I have long had an interest in the seemingly mass appeal of stylized (one might say, rhetorical) and extreme violence in a morally ambiguous context. ... My question for investigation here is, What ethics are at work in the presentation of screen violence?"[8] Christianson then usefully introduces the Hays production code, a voluntary practice for the American film industry that was followed until the 1960s. Most interesting is his admission that, as a theologian, he struggles with the issue of violence and moral compromise in reading the Old Testament:

> And this leads me to contrast a final parallel. The way we "read" *The Godfather* films is of particular interest to me as a Bible exegete, for we bring our reading ethic to other "texts" and reading the Bible presents us with some surprisingly similar moral quandaries.[9]

The parallel he wants to draw between the Old Testament and *The Godfather* films—and by extension much of cinematic violence—is "the refusal of the Bible's narrators to guide our assessment of the moral actions of its protagonists." This ought to astonish anyone who associates religion with morality, but a quick sampling of the Old Testament confirms Christianson's point. In film it is also a widely agreed tenet of criticism that it is for the viewer to make the moral assessment of the protagonists. A film should not preach. Of course, for a cultural conservative like Michael Medved, this idea is wrong-headed: at the very least a film should show morally uplifting characters. We start this section with the antithesis of such a character: Travis Bickle from *Taxi Driver*.

Everyone who takes a long hard look at the scum of society—the murderers, the rapists, the criminals, pimps and drug-pushers—at some level just wants to blow them away, right? Isn't that okay? This seems to be the underlying stance not only of many films properly dismissed as escapist pap, but also of serious films attracting the highest level of critical acclaim. Martin Scorsese's *Taxi Driver* is one of them: a film that does not pass judgment on a vigilante killer, Travis Bickle. But the film and its critical reception appear to demonstrate something more than a studious neutrality: Bickle actually becomes admirable. His desire to kill another human being, instead of understood as a contemptible impulse, becomes laudable. The lower impulse is massaged as a higher impulse. How does this come about?

Scorsese himself compares Bickle to a saint who wants to clean up both his life and his mind. Also, Bickle attempts suicide at the end of the movie as a way to mimic the Samurai's "death with honor" principle. In the film he is a depressed loner who cannot sleep, taking up the job of taxi driver on the night shift and attending porn screenings during the day. His thoughts turn to violence, leading first to the shooting of a grocery-store robber, and then an attempt to assassinate a senator. His disappointment in romance, and his interest in an underage prostitute, leads him to shoot her pimp, and finally a bloodbath of shooting in a brothel. He attempts to kill himself but has run out of ammunition. Early in the film we are given what is the justification for all this violence, when Bickle tells us while cruising the streets: "The animals come out at night. Whores, skunk pussies, buggers, queens, fairies, dopers, junkies. Sick, venal. Someday a real rain will come and wash this scum off the streets." This leads us to the extraordinary proposition put forward by a number of scholars that the violence in the film is "redemptive." This will be the argument for elevating the worst of human crimes to live with the best of its impulses. For example, David John Graham says, by way of introduction to Scorsese's films:

> I want to use some of his films to explore the concept of violence, and in particular the possibility that it can have a redemptive quality. The notion of redemptive suffering is probably a familiar one; can redemptive violence be as valid?[10]

Can redemptive violence be as valid as redemptive suffering? This is the disturbing question posed by Graham and by another academic, Christopher Deacy. The question asks whether an individual can experience redemption, not by submitting to violence, but by *perpetrating* it. Graham continues:

> The "savior"-figures are often anti-heroes, and their own vicissitudes are all too apparent, while not, however, preventing the element of hope amidst the despair from being seen. Scorsese has commented that the anti-hero of *Taxi Driver*, Travis Bickle, is "spiritual," but "it's the power of the spirit on the wrong road," like Charles Manson.[11]

Deacy also considers Bickle to be a "savior" figure when he says that "alienated and dysfunctional *noir* protagonists may be seen to undergo a process of being redeemed, reborn and resurrected through violence, destruction (often self-destruction) and a confrontation with the propensity towards sin that characterizes human existence."[12] He then poses the possibility that a man like Bickle can be compared to Jesus:

> Whether or not an actual film audience will come to formulate a correlation between the protagonist in a *film noir* and the figure of Jesus Christ, humiliated and enduring immense physical suffering on the Cross, it is the inherently human experience that the protagonist undergoes, and

which has the capacity to resonate with the lives and experiences of the audience members, that enables such films to be read in theological terms.[13]

This is open to challenge, firstly because Christ committed no sin, and, apart from a natural dismay at the onset of proceedings against him, and his famous cry "My Lord, why hast thou forsaken me," he was not disturbed in his mind, desperate, lost, or fallen; and secondly because the point of Christ as Redeemer is that by having love and faith in him, one is redeemed by proxy. Only a righteous man unjustly accused and condemned who does not resist his fate has a parallel with the life of Jesus, but even then this does not redeem us, because we are not invited to believe in anyone other than Jesus as the "Son of God."

Deacy is careful to avoid the charge that *film noir* is essentially escapist fantasy and therefore cannot bear the weight of theological parallel. He insists: "If *film noir* is therefore to constitute a site of redemptive activity that is analogous to the process at work in Christianity then there has to be a sense in which a redeemer-figure—a functional equivalent to Christ—performs an integral function in the redemptive process." One may not argue with this as a principle, but when Deacy chooses to focus on Travis Bickle the thesis begins to creak at the seams. Bickle carries out a vigilante murder. Astonishingly, by the law of America, and by the law of almost any developed nation, Bickle is not even investigated for murder, but is, instead, feted in the newspapers. There is even a hint in the ending that he might no longer be the sexual failure he seemed to be earlier in the film. The murder of the pimp cannot be called anything other than cold-blooded murder, because Bickle first engages him in conversation, giving him no chance to see death coming and to defend himself. But Deacy draws this conclusion:

> The carnage at the end of the picture, in which we witness Travis murdering "Sport" and his associates and attempting his own suicide, could be said to constitute a baptismal, cleansing bloodbath which shows the extent to which Travis is prepared to sacrifice himself on behalf of the endangered Iris and the sinful world in which she has become enmeshed. ... Only by engaging with, and confronting, the "filth" that has suffused the city can Travis's redemptive mission be fulfilled, in a manner analogous to—albeit ontologically different from—Jesus' becoming incarnate and bearing the sins of humanity in order to fulfill his redemptive mission.[14]

Deacy's only moderation of his comparison between Jesus and Bickle is that their missions are "ontologically different." But is not every element of Bickle's mission the antithesis of Jesus's—and does not the culmination in murder stand as a negation of everything that Jesus stood for? Where has love thy neighbor gone? Where has forgive "seventy time seven" gone? Where has turn the other cheek gone? To call the bloodbath "baptismal" and "cleansing" is to pervert the specifically Christian act of baptism, and perhaps all religious rituals of ablution. Deacy wants to argue that Bickle puts himself in harms way to save a prostitute, and that his "sacrifice" is redemptive. But countless madmen have decided that God wanted them to murder any number of different kinds of public figures in order to "cleanse" the world, and Scorsese himself is right to cite Charles Manson here, though one could pick the Oklahoma bomber, the Unabomber, and—most pertinently—John Hinkley who took a shot at Ronald Reagan.

Christ is redeemer in the Christian tradition precisely because he put himself in harm's way by *not* using violence on his enemies. If Deacy wants us to believe in an analogous way in Travis Bickle, then this is more than an "ontological difference"—surely it is the negation. He also suggests that "John Doe"—the mad ex-priest serial killer in the film *Seven*—could perform this role: Where does one stop? Where else is one to find a "functional equivalent to Christ"— in Hitler, Pol Pot and Saddam Hussein? Or in the man who hanged Saddam Hussein?

The point of investigating Deacy's thesis is not to disprove it—because it is absurd in the first place—but merely to indicate some of the steps in the justification of violence. It must be obvious that Travis Bickle undergoes no moral development at all: rather, he merely carries through the aggressive male rite-of-passage fantasy that many American men perhaps secretly dream of.[15]

Surely it is sobering to know that John Hinkley, a loner much like Bickle, attempted to assassinate Ronald Reagan after watching *Taxi Driver*. In turn, Paul Schrader, who wrote the screenplay, was inspired by the diaries of Arthur Bremer who shot and badly injured presidential candidate George Wallace in 1972. Schrader himself was experiencing a depression and loneliness which gave him material for Bickle's character, but also for another screenplay *Light Sleeper* (directed by Schrader). The latter film stars Willem Dafoe (who played Jesus in Scorsese's *Last Temptation*) as John LeTour, a drug dealer who "cleanses" himself and the world by murdering another drug dealer.

Perhaps these two screenplays—*Taxi Driver* and *Light Sleeper*—suggest more than anything that Schrader's wide reading of mysticism, and his lucid use of it to construct his "transcendent" film style, has actually missed the point of the transcendent: the discovery of profound connectedness. It is this deep vision of connectedness that makes for what Schrader has abstracted as a "style"—a coolness perhaps, an authenticity—but also makes it impossible to contemplate Bickle or LeTour's path as one of redemption. But yet another positive analysis of these films is presented by Jason Ambrosiano in his discussion of *Light Sleeper*:

> To free himself from his existential paralysis, LeTour must neither passively accept fate nor actively oppose it. He must, by participating in that fate, help transform it into grace, bring meaning to what was previously arbitrary.... As neo-noir hero himself, LeTour attains grace by moving past these elements, by shifting from existential detachment to sacred involvement.[16]

Ambrosiano gives us a clue perhaps as to why this perverse reading is made of the films: it is the element of *initiation* that perhaps stirs this instinct for violence. Most rites of male initiation in tribal societies involved some elements of risk, danger and violence, and perhaps there is an atavistic yearning for the bloodbath of sanctified vengeance as a means of moving beyond depression and existential crisis. But, in real life, there can be no "sanctified vengeance"—the killings undertaken by Bickle and LeTour, once stripped of cinematic glorification, are merely banal and tawdry.

Woody Allen's *Crimes and Misdemeanors*—mentioned earlier—is another film that can be considered alongside Bergman's films of exhausted Christianity. Allen says that "the only religion that I feel I can write about with any kind of accuracy is the Jewish religion. I have no feel for the details of Christianity."[17] But Allen explores the space vacated by faith as much as the Bergman he admires (and in *Crimes and Misdemeanors* even uses Bergman's cinematographer, Sven Nykvist). Judah Rosenthal is a successful ophthalmologist—and in America this means being surrounded by the cocoon of wealth and privilege—who decides to murder his inconvenient mistress. Allen tells us that "*Crimes and Misdemeanors* is about people who don't see. They don't see themselves as others see them. They don't see the rights and wrongs of the situation."[18] He contrasts Judah with Cliff—played by Allen himself— who does do the right thing, more or less, and is therefore the loser (of the love interest, in this case). Judah has a rabbi client called Ben, who is actually going blind, but is the only one with faith—blind faith.

Allen tells us that existential subjects are the only ones worth dealing with, and in *Crimes and Misdemeanors* this involves the different characters' understanding of what the nature of real life—a phrase that crops up a lot in the film—actually is. But Allen doesn't really pose this as an open question, because he has already decided: it is empty: "at best the universe is indifferent. At best!"[19] This is Allen's philosophy, a sophisticated post–Jewish or post–Holocaust nihilism, and in this world Judah not only remains undiscovered as the instigator of murder, but so pretty much does his conscience. In the final scene where he mulls over his story with Cliff he tells it in the third person:

> Suddenly it's not an empty universe after all, but a just and moral one, and he's violated it. Now he's panic-stricken, he's on the verge of a mental collapse, one inch away from confessing the whole thing to the police. And then, one morning he awakens. The sun is shining and his family is around him. Mysteriously the crisis has lifted. He takes his family on a vacation in Europe and it comes to pass that he is not punished. In fact he prospers. The killing is attributed to another person.... Now he's scot-free back to his protected world of wealth and privilege.

What is astonishing about this is that he "awakens" to a guilt-free world; he has an epiphany in reverse that wipes out his conscience, the organ of the human soul that connects us to others. This is even more radical than the "awakening" of Travis Bickle in *Taxi Driver*, whose murder spree was at least nominally on behalf of the oppressed prostitute he befriends. For the characters in *Crimes and Misdemeanors* Judah's insight is that *this is reality*. But it is not, and it is a religious question, *re-ligare*, to be joined again, which is inverted in its usual course here: Judah's trajectory is to be sundered not joined with the absolute.

Allen's film was well received, as was *Taxi Driver*, yet both are exceptional in filmmaking in that their characters get away with murder, not just judicially, but psychologically. In Allen's case, we can perhaps best understand the film as pursuing a nihilism that may have common ground with Bergman's, but differs sharply in not being truly anguished. Instead we have a New York, Jewish comedy of manners, which by definition does not ask of the audience that it seriously engages with existential questions. Yet Kathryn Bernheimer says *Crimes and Misdemeanors* is "a complex morality tale that ranks as the cinema's most rigorous exploration of Jewish values and ethics. ..."[20] And Clive Marsh writes: "As director, Allen manages to produce a rewarding, enjoying and challenging film, without providing a happy ending. He maps out clearly why, in exploring what it means to be human, human beings also need to examine what it might mean to be redeemed."[21] Marsh adds that he finds it strange that *21 Grams* is called a more hopeful film.[22] How odd! *Crimes and Misdemeanors* does have a happy ending for the murderer, and it nowhere explores the need for redemption. For the secular nihilist crime pays. Why not? But for the more serious secularists, as the characters in *21 Grams* portray, acts have moral weight no less than the weight of the soul itself.

The American writer on culture Allan Bloom insists that American nihilism is an empty nihilism, because it has no high-culture basis. He says "American nihilism is a mood, a mood of moodiness, a vague disquiet. It is nihilism without the abyss."[23] Bloom applies this idea to Allen's film *Zelig*, and another American writer on these themes, Christopher Lasch, who is equally skeptical of Woody Allen, could easily be writing about *Crimes and Misdemeanors*: "The confessional form allows an honest writer like Exley or Zweig to provide a harrowing account of the spiritual desolation of our times ... [but] the narcissist's pseudo-insights into his own condition, usually expressed in psychiatric clichés, serves him as a means of deflecting criticism and disclaiming responsibility for his actions."[24] This assessment is a valid explanation of why both Allen's films, and those of the New Age, fail to be serious explorations of the spiritual life.

The roots of American violence and its worship of the gun are readily traceable to the frontier culture of pioneering days, and so we really need to see the roots of American film violence in the American Western. The film *Shane* is a typical Western that attracts religious comments on its violence, such as the following from Robert Banks:

> Shane is therefore a variation on the Christ figure [because he saves a community] ... filling a similar role to the knights of the medieval legends. ... The medieval knight, however, is already in part a Christ-figure, so speaking of Shane this way still leaves us with the question of whether he is a compromised Christ-figure or a rather a legitimate blend of types appropriate to his context. Another set of figures with whom Shane has been compared is the Old Testament judges.[25]

It is true that Alan Ladd as Shane is less overtly macho than most gunslingers-out-of-retirement, and has in fact a surprisingly vulnerable manner to him. But the story is so tired now, reprised for example in Eastwood's *Unforgiven*: the old warrior reluctantly fights one more time, on behalf of the oppressed, and then rides off into the mountains as the lone hero. What on earth is comparable here to the life and message of Jesus? The term "savior" can be used for both, but that is merely a quirk of language, that the term can be used in either an entirely secular context or an entirely religious one. Peter Francis ruminates further on the Western (as we saw in the Introduction):

> Why should a practical theologian bother with Westerns or, indeed, any popular film? It is certainly not from any desire to "baptize" films or give Christian readings of secular stories. It is not to dole out an imprimatur to films that are morally uplifting, nor is it to utter condemnation of particular movies that are deemed morally dubious.[26]

One does rather wonder what the theologian is doing with film if it is not to use them to examine moral questions. Has the theologian abandoned this role to the moral philosopher and the cultural conservative? But Francis goes on to say: "In *High Plains Drifter* and *Pale Rider* we are offered theological themes and characters but they deliver a bogus view of God: a vengeful unpleasant God."[27]

Eric S. Christianson suggests a parallel with the typical hero of the Western film and the Old Testament figure of Ehud, a lone assassin who kills by deceit and whose act is described in obscene detail (Judges 3.13–30):

> Ehud is a loner, a trait recognized by the commentators. After delivering his tribute, he slips away from the crowd, suggesting that he must do the business alone [assassination]. While there may be good strategic and political reasons for this solitary action, there remains a certain heroic toughness about his task—he is a James Bond, a Dirty Harry—he is the law. The fact that he works alone is indicative of his status as God's deliverer and even hints at his special, deceptive, abilities. Like the Man [Eastwood], Ehud has no qualms about winning the "shoot-out" with deceit. Indeed, there is little that Ehud does in the story that does not involve deception.[28]

In the end one has to take such an approach to religion and violence as perhaps a uniquely American phenomenon, born out of its Puritan instinct for the Old Testament over the New, out of its war of independence and civil war, and out of long violence meted out to its indigenous inhabitants.

The Pornography of Violence

In *Seven Samurai*—unlike in the implausible scenarios in many samurai-film derivatives—Kambei is realistic that two samurai could not fight off forty bandits. He also adds that defense is more difficult than attack, a sobering piece of advice. "Pornographic" violence never contains this level of realism. A pornography of violence can be defined something like this: "emotionally arousing material that focuses on doing harm to people in a way that, perhaps tacitly, seems to condone that behavior in order to gratify the viewer."[29] Violence, as we have suggested, is condoned an infinite number of times in film when its victim is a *bad person*. Quite who gets to make that judgment is a crucial issue in law, but film violence likes to forget the legal niceties as the protagonist, such as Travis Bickle, gets to make that executive decision. What makes the resulting violence a pornography is the gratification, not in the first instance of the viewer, but of the screen perpetrator. The violent person may even carry a resigned air—I really wish I didn't have to do this—up to the point of execution, but once launched into violence the audience needs to believe that the protagonist is grimly enjoying the slaughter. What's more, they are clearly *fulfilled* by it.

What turns mundane screen violence, then, into a pornography of violence is the clear gratification or fulfillment of the perpetrator. In *Enter the Dragon*—the martial arts film that made Bruce Lee famous—his discipline has the sanctified air of a spiritual practice, much as Ghost Dog's. And the eventual targets of his one-man whirlwind massacre are clearly bad persons, including his nemesis Han, a disgraced Shaolin student. But what tips this piece of well-crafted escapism into a pornography of violence at times is Lee's expression as, for example, when he crushes a man underfoot. The camera lingers on his face, which has a beatific expression of intense concentration, verging on the orgasmic.

But it falls to Quentin Tarantino to provide perhaps the ultimate in mainstream pornographic violence in the two *Kill Bill* films. They are a natural extension of *Pulp Fiction* as a treatment of violence as an *aesthetic*, an art form which refers only to itself. This at least is how such a film is justified: it is only make-believe, and in its multiple references to other martial arts films going all the way back to *Enter the Dragon* perhaps it subverts the genre with its comic-book extremes and even questions violence. But that is too sophisticated a view: the fact is that *Kill Bill* is a vengeance story, and the female protagonist known only as "the Bride," clearly relishes every moment of the slaughter. "Relish" actually isn't quite right, as the Bride conveys a sense of discipline and duty, crossing off names on her list once they are dispatched in a variety of gory ends. Rather, it is something more subtle: a sense of exultation, an adrenalin rush, matched by Tarantino's skilful use of high-energy contemporary music. It is not orgasmic as Bruce Lee so creepily conveys with his little moans, but it is a *high*. And the gore is endless as it is delivered through the hands of Uma Thurman's character, who ultimately can only be seen as rather creepy. The fighting involves implausible wire-fu, as discussed earlier, but also has a considerable spiritual Bushido-style context. The Western God is also roped in—the Old Testament one that is—when she says at one point in the first film: "When fortune smiles on something as ugly as revenge, it seems proof like no other that not only does God exist, you're doing his will." A thousand revenge and vigilante films are justified by this sentiment. But mostly the on-the-hoof philosophizing in *Kill Bill* has an Eastern flavor, as in: "Suppress all human emotion and compassion. Kill whoever stands in the way, even if that be Lord God or Buddha himself." In the second film we return in time to her period as a martial arts trainee with a ridiculous parody of the Eastern Master, Pai Mei. She later kills another woman disciple of his who admits to having poisoned the old man. The Bride's swordplay overwhelms her, and in her rage over the killing of her Master she plucks out the woman's only good eye, squelching it under her toes. But it is Bill that she is after, the assassin who killed her husband and nearly killed her. The finale is particularly lame, and in Bill's own incoherent philosophizing we learn that he thinks her a "natural born killer." Perhaps it is a remark like this that allows for the self-referential nature of this cultural production to be divorced from actual questions of violence.

Ultimately is such an artistic confection of a film a pornography of violence or merely a tongue-in-cheek escapist aestheticization of violence? For the vast majority of well-adjusted viewers a film like this is enjoyed and forgotten as pop culture; it's not going to persuade them even to take up the discipline of a martial art, let alone kill anyone. But at some level it must be deadening, because the feminist, politically correct adrenalin rush of it makes an equation between killing or maiming and an exalted or expansive state. In reality such actions lead to a shrinking of the spiritual self—perhaps to the size of a pea as the grandfather of Little Tree says.

We can return now to briefly reconsider the case of Ghost Dog, whose violence is not at all pornographic in the sense just explored, and whose adherence to the Bushido code is not undermined by crass caricature and comic-book slaughter. His killings serve no purpose of his own, instead they are a repayment of a debt to his boss, who saved his life as a young man. There is a big "but," however, though we cannot be sure of Jarmusch's intentions here: Ghost Dog was perhaps mistaken. In a brief flashback we learn that Louie did not shoot Ghost Dog's assailant to save the young man, but in his *own* self-defense. There was no debt, and in the end Ghost Dog is shot by Louie, though not before he gives away *Rashomon* to him. This is highly significant: it is symbolic of the fact that the two men remember their fateful first encounter differently. Ghost Dog may be thoughtful, even mournful, about the deaths he engenders, but Tolstoy's argument holds here: one cannot be absolutely certain either that someone is going to kill you, or that you owe your life to them. *All* justifications for killing are spurious because we have no access to complete certainty. Which in the end leaves Ghost Dog no better justified than the Bride: form may be emptiness but this nowhere in Buddhism legitimizes the violent destruction of form.

There might be a plausible objection to this, the one raised by Kunti, the mother of three of the Pandavas, when she says to Krishna that, effectively, to turn away from the fight is to live in the fear of death. This is ignoble. Hence, *courage* is lauded in all spiritual traditions, and the overcoming of the fear of death is regarded as a spiritual attainment. Ghost Dog shows courage; Travis Bickle shows courage of a sort—does this not rescue them for the spiritual life? Eric S. Christianson as Bible exegete finds Ehud admirable in a James Bond, Dirty Harry, Clint Eastwood-kind of way—characters that work alone and show courage and resourcefulness. Isn't that spiritual somehow?

But the answer to this question lies in the fact that they are *assassins*, and Christianson is clear that they work with deceit, or at the very least stack the odds in their favor through superior weapons, stealth and cunning. The large-scale version of this is the U.S. policy of "overwhelming force," related to the so-called Powell doctrine of warfare. But when Krishna accepts Kunti's argument—one that he already knows as a member of the warrior caste— and persuades Arjuna to fight as the only honorable course open to him, he does not believe in "overwhelming force," deceit or stealth. He ensures that the war is as fair as possible. If battle is an honorable test of a person's courage and integrity in the face of death or injury, then that battle must be a fair fight if killing in it is to have *any* claim to spiritual legitimacy. A duel, for example, is a fair fight. But *assassination* is no such thing—and, of course, Tolstoy would point out that in any case a "fair fight" is not what war usually is, because Krishnas do not exist to make it that way.

Summary

Tolstoy came to the conclusion that the term "Christian soldier" was a total contradiction if meant literally, and a reading of the Pali Canon shows that the Buddha in turn could not possibly have condoned any form of killing, whether in self-defense or to protect others. Many attempts were made on his life, and he resisted none of them, escaping either through luck or the display of fearlessness and compassion that changed the mind of his assailant.

This section has examined some of the most difficult issues in the spiritual life surrounding violence. All kinds of wonderful-sounding precepts or spiritual injunctions are easy enough to accept in theory, but when the harsh reality of conflict catches up with one, these can be abandoned with disheartening rapidity. In other words, the situations portrayed in the films in this section put the spiritual life to the test. The first of these was faced by the Quakers in *Friendly Persuasion*, while in Kurosawa's *Seven Samurai* it is clear that compassion can flourish in the midst of violence. Kurosawa's work, including *Drunken Angel* and *Ikiru*, provides the context for contrasting Buddhist with Christian compassion, using films featuring Robin Williams to illustrate the latter.

Where there is violence, there can be forgiveness and atonement. Cinema offers few such films, but those that are available show again the extraordinary nature of film for conveying the profoundest of human emotions, even if ostensibly the film's narrative is elsewhere. Forgiveness and atonement cross all religious boundaries, and are as likely in an entirely secular context as in a spiritual one. In *Bad Lieutenant* it comes out of the blue for a corrupt police officer, while in the Islamic setting of *The Kite Runner* it has nothing to do with Islam. Perhaps the most poignant and beautiful meditation on atonement is in the anime series *Haibane Renmei*, a slow-moving but luminously gentle exploration of redemption. *The Fisher King*—perhaps through its surreal imagery of the unconscious—is also a luminous film of compassion and redemption. *To End All Wars* memorably places forgiveness in the context of armed conflict.

We finished this section with an unsparing critique of the pornography of violence, in films such as *Kill Bill*, and a return to a film not so easy to dismiss: *Ghost Dog*. Is the way of the samurai ever justifiable in spiritual terms? Is it truly a Buddhist path?

But the most surprising story perhaps is the Dardenne brothers' *The Son*, in which a man forgives the killer of his baby boy. Why? He subscribes to no religious system at all. Under a bleak winter Belgian sky, in a completely unremarkable woodland, a man with every opportunity for revenge does not take it. Instead, he allows the young offender into his consciousness, sternly perhaps, but, it seems, as the living embodiment of both Buddhist and Christian precepts of compassion, of all compassion.

11
East vs. West

East and West are rather loose categories, though they have been used so far in this book to point out some differences in filmmaking across the globe. This section pulls together such strands and so needs to revisit what the distinction might mean here for the spiritual life. As a first approximation, the West can be defined in terms of two features: monotheism and industrialism, while the East becomes whatever is not monotheism, and whatever is usually described as "developing." This definition is unconventional and would place many Middle Eastern countries in an indeterminate position where Islam is the monotheist religion and industrialization has not reached Western levels. However, few of the films under consideration here are the product of those cultures.

In spiritual terms it is clear that monotheism, mostly Christianity, has been the cultural background in which filmmaking developed. Less obvious is Max Weber's thesis that industrialization itself was a direct outcome of the Protestant religious ethic,[1] but at the very least it is clear that the spread of industrialization went hand in hand with Christian missionary work, and hence the spread of monotheism. So to some degree at least the movie camera and monotheism spread together. But to simply divide the world's religious and spiritual traditions into "monotheism" and "the rest" would be to fall into the trap of early Christian thought which used the term paganism to cover all that was not Christianity. Instead the films examined in this book have often been chosen to illustrate a wide range of non–Christian spiritualities, alongside those of the three monotheisms. Hence, animist, shamanic, Shinto, Hindu, Buddhist, New Age and also quite secular films have all been presented as conveying different and equally important contexts for issues in the spiritual life.

Having said this, it remains clear that the East as a general concept does present a set of issues in the spiritual life that are different to those of the monotheist West, and at times antithetical. It is also true that since the time of Schopenhauer ideas of the East have penetrated Western thought, though in a rather asymmetrical way. Schopenhauer was able to find resonances within the Western tradition for the new ideas from India he was reading, but his synthesis was short-lived, as it depended on some version of dualism in philosophy. As this became increasingly discredited in the scientific era, the East found no permanent toe-hold in Western philosophical theory. Rather, the opposite happened: Western scientific reductionism travelled with its materialism to the East, and provided the cultural framework within which so many Eastern filmmakers have been operating.

However, at a popular level Eastern ideas found a home in New Age spiritualities that had their origins in such ideas as Theosophy and Anthroposophy, and which flowered from the 1960s on. Hence, the lived spiritual or religious life in the West has acquired terms like "guru," "karma," and "nirvana" which beg of the thoughtful practitioner some response. The point was made earlier that the Western mind in comparison to the Eastern mind appears to be the mind of the drama queen, and that Tarkovsky captures this well when he says that the West is always saying "I! Mine! Me!" while the East "is totally absorbed into God, Nature, Time." Once alerted to this idea we can see it in the contrast between the Buddhist films discussed above and conventional Western dramas, or in contrasting the two Mongolian films, *The Story of the Weeping Camel* and *The Cave of the Yellow Dog*, with Western films that also have a Nature setting, such as *Into the Wild* and *Grizzly Man*, for example.

Also easy to spot is the dominance of monotheist assumptions in Western filmmaking, even when the setting is secular or atheist: they are part of the cultural landscape. Buddhism itself is a continual challenge to these assumptions and has drawn a range of criticisms from Western theologians who find it impossible to conceive of a religion without God. One strategy adopted by certain Western thinkers and theologians is to deny that Buddhism is a religion or, like Martin Buber, to suggest that if the Buddha is pursuing religion its goals are not "ours." Buber, writing at a time when the East was a more foreign religious presence in the West, was confident that the goal of the Buddha was not the same as that of Christ.[2] But who can really say that "the kingdom of heaven" is not the same as "nirvana?"

In the first instance films by Westerners about the East often suffer from what is known as "exoticization," so we start by looking at some films that demonstrate this, including also the attempt by Peter Brook to "de-exoticize" the *Mahabharata*. Next, we look at Western seekers in Eastern traditions and in one case how this is seen through Eastern eyes. However, it is the Western impact on Eastern religious values that are most significant here as the movie camera travelled east with its Western cultural loadings. Two films then show how this ramifies within Eastern communities living in the West.

Very often Eastern filmmakers are either trained in the West or absorb Western values as part of their apprenticeship in film, and this is then explored through the theme of the afterlife, and finally in two films already introduced: *The Cave of the Yellow Dog* and *The Story of the Weeping Camel*.

Exoticization

Frank Capra's 1937 *Lost Horizon* was perhaps one of the first significant films to exoticize the East, in this particular case a place in the Himalayas, and given the fabled name of Shangri-La, based on Shambhala, a mystical city in Tibetan Buddhist tradition. Nothing of any genuine Buddhist thought is present in the film; instead, it is a 200-year-old Belgian who is the spiritual leader of the community, and who spouts kindly utopian nonsense. Perhaps the next film venture to rehash the mysterious north of India as a place of spiritual utopianism is Edmund Goulding's 1946 version of *Razor's Edge*, the Somerset Maugham story introduced earlier. Neither in this nor in John Byrum's 1984 version, starring Bill Murray, does much of India's spiritual power come over. The Byrum film was a real lost opportunity, as Murray was committed to it, but the film is not that well made, and despite several references to the *Upanishads* it could not begin to show how this text, and the spiritual impact of India, could shape the protagonist's search for meaning after the horrors of World War I. In the original film all we really know is that "something strange" happens to him in the mountains, as it does to the nuns in *Black Narcissus*. In this film and in *Walkabout*, *Picnic at Hanging Rock*, and *Passage to India*, it is not just the exotic people of the Far East who are mysterious, but the very land itself.

All of these films to one degree or another display the features of what Edward Said has castigated in the West as a tendency to "orientalism"—a white man's fantasy of the non–Western cultures shaped by the prevailing imperialism and anthropology of the day. Perhaps *Passage to India* was the last gasp of this type of filmmaking, in which its lamentable exoticization of India is overlooked in the applause for the film's genuine indictment of the Raj. But its central event, in which a repressed, educated white woman is somehow so overcome by emotion in a mountain cavern—overwhelmed by its otherness, its mystery, its sheer, raw, natural or even sexual power—that she flees in complete hysteria, is an absurdity. An almost identical event is supposed to have overwhelmed the missing schoolteacher and female pupils in *Picnic at Hanging Rock*. Perhaps it arises from the fear held in the Western subconscious about untamed Nature, and about so-called "primitive" peoples who lives are closer to the earth.

David Jasper makes interesting comments on both *Passage to India* and the second of Satyajit Ray's Apu trilogy, *Aparajito*.[3] He shows that Lean, in building up the difference between the ordinariness and even tedium of the British enclave compared to the anarchic native Indian town, misses what Ray provides in his trilogy: an authentic India. Jasper criticizes Lean for not dwelling enough on the hatred towards the British in his film, but this is a little unfair: there is enough native public anger around the trial of Dr. Aziz to convey at least the fact of it. Jasper is more telling in his criticism of Lean for eliding Hindu-Muslim differences—as is even more the case in *Lagaan*—and rightly critical of the casting of Alec Guinness as Dr. Godbole. While Guinness is a superb actor, he becomes a joke as the "mystic" Indian with his ramblings about reincarnation: it is a spiritual miscasting as grating as Vittorio Mezzogiorno playing Arjuna in the *Mahabharata*, or Willem Dafoe as Jesus in *The Last Temptation*—as we shall see. Guinness is merely lugubrious where any Indian actor would instinctively have had a vast culture of punditry to draw on, that peculiarly Indian mixture of genuine mysticism and irritating conviction that is the polar opposite of British post–Christian secularism and culturally ingrained diffidence.

The *Mahabharata* was examined earlier from the perspective of the martial arts as spiritual practice. But it represents a challenge to Western filmmakers: to avoid the charge of exoticization it must avoid trivializing the piece or resorting to stereotyping of the kind just described. Peter Brook tackled this problem by drawing on mythology in an undeniably art-house production. The highbrow nature of the film derives partly from its look and feel as a theatre production, on which it was based. But it is Brook's solution to the cross-cultural problem that makes the film unique: he chose to use a determinedly international cast. Despite the Indian origin of the story, he drew on a wide range of national types for his actors, thus giving the film internationalist credentials. Brook uses a Japanese actor to play Drona, the royal guru and martial arts instructor to both the Kauravas and the Pandavas, as mentioned before. Ira Bhaskar points out that the martial arts in the film were "divorced from the respective contexts in which the martial arts were ways of life, homogenized into an image of the ancient East in general."[4] This is not just a case of the martial arts style, but of the entire religious system which gave rise to it, and so all the other imaginative castings, such as an Italian actor to play Arjuna, also create dissonances. No character in this drama is more uniquely and significantly Indian and, if played by the right Indian actor, would have been more authenticated as a result. Mezzogiorno is actually a suitable heroic actor, with jutting jaw; it is just that it juts in a quintessentially Italian way, not Indian. He is a post–Renaissance mid–European soldier, not an Aryan warrior-prince. The arrogance—in the best sense of the word—of a warrior is not universal, any more than modalities of the spirit can be conflated into a single stream. But the real significance of Arjuna is that he is the recipient, in the *Bhagavad Gita*, of Krishna's sacred teachings: a recapitulation of India's religious history, its extraordinary spiritual pluralism. Every path to the divine is held equal, and each of these is recounted to the recalcitrant Arjuna as the religious basis for resolving his moral crisis. An Italian, whose stage presence hauls in whether intended or not the entire history of Catholicism, cannot be this recipient. For Krishna, too, a totally Indian actor is needed, but with a feminine side, one whose body and voice dance, the dance that gives all Indian gods the unique curved body posture. The middle–England thespian earnestness of Bruce Myers, however talented he is on home ground, shrieks cultural and spiritual dissonance. Thirty years on no one would consider making the film in the same way, because Western audiences are now mostly expected to watch Eastern cultural productions untransposed into the Western framework.

Western Seekers in Eastern Systems

Despite the large-scale phenomenon of the hippie-era travels to the East, there are only a few films that deal with the subject. We look now at Jane Campion's *Holy Smoke* from the perspective of a Westerner seeking Eastern spirituality. Its opening scenes form a continuum with *The Doors*, though the spirituality in that film centered mostly on American homegrown esotericism and New Age ideas. In *Holy Smoke*, we start with westerners in India tripping out and dancing to "Holly Holy," by Neil Diamond. The film concerns Ruth (Kate Winslet), who, according to her sister, was "just like everyone else in India ... [she] wanted to find a live guru." They participate in the obligatory darshan in an Indian ashram initially just for a laugh, but "it was so scary. Some sort of freaky hypnotism happened." Ruth, it seems, is transfixed by the eyes of the guru, becomes a disciple, and burns her air ticket home. Ruth's awakening is visualized in psychedelic style and with appropriate orgasmic-style panting; again, this could be from *The Doors*.

Ruth's mother flies out to meet her, and is overwhelmed by India and the incomprehensibility of Ruth's Western friend, now called "Rahid." "It's her sannyasin name," Ruth explains. Her mum tries to trick her with a story of her father dying. Ruth cries and then says, "Maybe next time." "What do you mean: next time?" "You know, in another life." Worse is to come: Ruth herself has a new name, Nazni, and won't be moved to return. So her mother has to attend a ceremony at the ashram, and to do so must wash her hair. In a reference, perhaps, to the Rajneesh ashram of the 1980s, all visitors have their hair sniffed by guards, though no explanation is offered for this (later in the film there is a clip of Rajneesh himself, in his Rolls Royce, perhaps the symbol for the West of a corrupt guru). But mum can't stand it, runs off in a panic and has an asthma attack which requires her to be airlifted home. Ruth goes with her.

The film's proposition however is that the exit counselor, P. J. Waters, hired to cure Ruth of her devotions, is as much of a guru as her Indian guru. She is tricked into the outback and into his regime, furious at first. Her mother explains: "We think you have been manipulated, maybe even drugged." She finally agrees to three days in isolation with the exit counselor on the condition that if he can't change her mind she gets a ticket back to India.

He starts by talking about her mind. "It will seek the truth and the truth will set you free. John VIII 32. We're talking about your soul here. Have you ever thought about the damage that could be done to your soul, to your very center ... if you hand it over to someone else? To the wrong someone else?" He quotes his secular heroes including Socrates. Asked what her guru teaches she responds with: "It is. It is. It is." Waters then quotes the passage from the Upanishads where this phrase is found. But it turns out that he has had a bad experience of gurus himself, in India, naturally. Later, he shows her family video clips of infamous gurus: Rajneesh, Moon, Koresh, Manson, Jones (of Jonestown mass suicide) and Applewhite (of Heaven's Gate). This material breaks her down, and she burns her sari. But, to complete the guru analogy, Waters then sleeps with Ruth in her vulnerable state of tearful breakdown. From here on the film becomes an essay—verging on comedy—in sexual politics, and religion is more or less forgotten. But the message is the same: men as authority figures, whether religious or psychotherapeutic, abuse their power to sleep with women. Women's power on the other hand always trumps that of a man in the end. "You win," Waters tells Ruth as she finally humiliates him.

Ruth's interest in Eastern spirituality is not new: Westerners may have popularized it in the hippie sixties but, as we saw in *Meetings with Remarkable Men*, the Greek-Armenian Gurdjieff was in pursuit of the same spiritual sources much earlier, perhaps arriving in Tibet in the early years of the twentieth century. As a man born in late–nineteenth-century Armenia, he effectively looked West at a Christian industrial society, and East towards a pre-industrial religious world in which many esoteric traditions flourished. His early instinct as a *seeker* made the East more interesting than the West however, as the seeker in the West had long been driven underground by a mainstream Christianity that had burned Giordano Bruno and others at the stake, and a secular world within which the "seeker" had become an object of ridicule. Yet when he set up as a spiritual teacher near Paris between the wars he attracted exactly those Westerners who were serious seekers in Eastern traditions. His influence is said to extend to, among others, Frank Lloyd Wright, Alan Watts, Timothy Leary, Jacob Needleman, Kate Bush, and the filmmakers Alejandro Jodorowsky and Peter Brook (as we saw earlier). Hence, the film of Gurdjieff's autobiography was a natural project for Brook, who also had privileged access to the dances described earlier.

Like the *Mahabharata*, *Meetings with Remarkable Men* is really an impossible project for a filmmaker. Brook cast many English actors in the various roles that made up Gurdjieff's early life, including Warren Mitchell—known in Britain at the time for his role as Alf Garnett—as his father (whose performance is actually substantial). Most grating are the various spiritual masters he encounters, as they deliver their homilies in Shakespearian style. The young and mature Gurdjieffs also bear no resemblance to the original because both lack the steely esoteric discipline of the real man. They are too sweet, too wistful, as is the whole film. Having said that the film is attempting the impossible, it remains perhaps the only significant attempt to portray the life of a serious spiritual seeker.

As we have seen, the two film versions of Maugham's *Razor's Edge* follow an American seeker of truth, Larry Darrell, in the interwar years. Maugham is present in the novel—and one of the films—as a man with an avuncular interest in Darrell, but with enough distance from him so as to become the objective reporter of the story. From early on, Darrell is painted as a man out of sympathy with the materialist West, and with some inner depth. His girlfriend eventually gives up on him despite sympathizing with what was a common experience among demobbed soldiers after World War I: a post-trauma distress that needed to be assuaged by the finding of some deeper meaning to life. They agree that he will take a year out to start with, in which he will be a seeker of truth. "And what will you do with all that wisdom?" she asks. "If I ever acquire wisdom I'll be wise enough to know what to do with it," is his reply.

So Larry takes the hippie trail long before hippies came into being, and finds himself on a mountain in India with a guru. The problem of presenting an Indian guru to an American film audience has no more convincing solution here than in *Meetings with Remarkable Men*, but this is anyway a "before-and-after" story, where the mechanics of the transformation are passed over. The holy man that he meets in India is played in the 1946 version by the English actor Cecil Humphreys. Larry, played by Tyrone Power, in what looks like a stage set from the Shangri La of *Lost Horizon*, is told that God is the only guide—a Westernization of the Indian guru tradition made obvious by Humphreys speaking without even the type of foreign accent that Warren Mitchell adopts fairly successfully as Gurdjieff's father. In his flawless BBC English, the Indian guru gives Larry a kindly pep talk, telling him that the road to salvation is a narrow one, as difficult as the sharp edge of a razor. But towards the end of the interview the old man says, "We Indians believe that there are three paths to God," and proceeds to outline what are known in India as the *bhakti*, *jnani* and *karma* yogas, that is the paths respectively of love, wisdom or good works. Larry has chosen the path of knowledge, wisdom, so he retreats to a high peak in the mountains where his transformation is effected. All we know of this is the moment when his teacher visits and recognizes it in him. Larry and God had been for a brief moment one, and he had found the wisdom he had been looking for.

What makes the story and the film worthwhile is the attempt at critical distance with the device of the worldly-wise society gent that is Maugham, who doesn't himself go in for the spiritual search, but who recognizes the sincerity of it in Larry. In the end—this is still the 1946 version—Maugham tells us: "Larry found what we are all looking for. No one fails to become kinder, better and nobler through knowing him. Goodness is the greatest force in the world, and he's got it."

In the 1984 version with Bill Murray in the lead role, Maugham curiously disappears from the film. Larry is working as a coal-miner in France when his roommate asks him incredulously: "You've never read the Upanishads?" This is the moment in the story when Larry decides to go to India. With modern film budgets and transport Murray actually does go to India, in stunning settings. This time it appears to be a Buddhist temple that he, as Larry, enters. But the problem of a spiritual exchange with a non–Western teacher, in this version a lama, is avoided completely: there are no homely platitudes, there are no teachings at all. Larry retreats to a shelter high in the mountains and finds inner liberation. The response of the lama on his return is: "I'm sad because I am losing my cook." However, he is obliged to deliver the razor's edge line—as that is the film's title—and with that Larry returns to the West.

Haré Raama Haré Krishna is about the hippie adoption of Eastern religion, this time as seen through the eyes of an Indian man attempting to rescue his sister from a crowd of drug-taking Western-influenced people in Kathmandu. It is of interest because it shows the East-West divide through Eastern eyes. The film starts with a voice-over:

> This resounding chant of Hare Rama Hare Krishna has been spread by our gurus, teachers and swamis across the seven seas to Europe and America's western culture. The culture that had been oppressed by machines of its own manufacture and economic successes, that had forgotten the peace of progress and tranquility, were ever restless for the peace of the soul.

This is narrated as the camera pans across a map of the world, reaching European shores, and then zooming into Britain and a map of London. A Hare Krishna procession is moving down what looks like Oxford Street in the 1970s. We then jump to Montreal where we look through the windows of a modern house at a party. The narrator continues: "Who are these, who without understanding the meaning of the sacred chant Hare Rama Hare Krishna, have made their own tune for it and in its shelter are swinging and rollicking to it?" We see a record player at a party with a mini-skirted female dancing. Youths smoke dope on the floor. The narrator is introducing us to the social class we now know as hippies, and into which Jasbir has migrated from her traditional Indian family. Jasbir, the female protagonist of the film, has been mistreated as a child by her stepmother, and hence has rejected the values of her entire cultural heritage. One of these values is love between brother and sister, which bond is further broken when the father remarries and she stays in Canada and her brother returns to India with her mother. The main part of the film then deals with the siblings in adulthood as her brother attempts to extract her from the hippie scene in Kathmandu. Yet despite deploring the Western trivialization of Eastern spirituality, the film itself entirely revolves around a secular drama of family relations. In *Bee Season*, the Hare Krishnas again become the backdrop to failing family relations, though more interestingly the Hinduism in it is contrasted to the Jewish faith of the family.

India and the West

If there is a filmmaker most likely to be mentioned in the same breath as Bergman, Tarkovsky and Kurosawa, it is Satyajit Ray, and Jasper is right when he suggests that Ray's films give us an authentic India. But Jasper misses something here: he quite rightly cites the broad cultural background of Ray, including the films of Jean Renoir and the music of Mozart,[5] but omits the corollary, that of Western enculturation comes Western secularization. British rule meant that British secular culture dominated Indian thought, but there was also something un–British in the mix: a Marxist kind of socialism, which Ray clearly subscribes to. Hence, a secularized Ray becomes the darling of socialist cineastes. Unfortunately, his stupendous cinematography— comparable at times with that of Tarkovsky— doesn't necessarily even mean average cinema from a spiritual point of view, and it certainly avoided the slightest possibility of conveying the living religious cosmos and spiritual richness that is India: it merely—as Hindus objected to at the time—presented it as materially poor. Although the Apu trilogy gets better in each film, the last outing completes the picture of a Westernized filmmaking. In it, Apu follows a trajectory marked out by Rousseau, Coleridge, Goethe and Marx, rather than one marked out by the Vedas, the Upanishads, the Advaita and the devotional Shaivite renaissance.

In *The Stranger*, Ray's last film, the secularization of his cultural references is complete. Only Tagore gets a look in as a cultural hero of India: otherwise we learn of Socrates, Plato, Aristotle, Aristophanes, Freud, and NASA, with Darwin hovering in the background. We saw a similar phenomenon with *Mishima*: Western influences heavily outnumber indigenous ones. Ray's story concerns a long-lost uncle who is received with some suspicion as guest into a middle-class Bengali family. He brings something fresh and wild, a bit like the stranger who turns Pasolini's middle-class family upside down in *Theorem*. He has seen the world, studied Western anthropology, and finds in Indian tribal societies something more authentic than contemporary Bengali culture, the comedies of which he berates for not rising to the standards of Aristophanes. He is casually atheist about the conventional Western God. "It is hard to believe in a benevolent God these days," he says, "the daily papers alone make us question that belief." But what about Kali, the deity to which the great Bengali Ramakrishna devoted himself to, and which has no likeness to the Western God? Why is it that Ray can overlook the religious heritage relevant to his story and simply assume Western, middle-class atheism as a norm?

On the other hand, what the uncle does introduce to the family, and to us as viewers, is an Indian tribal dance. This is one of the genuine surprises of the film, as is the moment when the uncle encourages his niece to join in the dancing. But the appreciation of this derives from Western anthropological thinking and its recent discovery of ethnic "authenticity," and not at all from India's own animist past and its refraction into broader Hinduism. Ray Kancharla considers that the film takes on a "strange mystic magical quality," and understands it as an attack on the arrogance of technological living.[6] It is ironic that the attack has a broadly secular basis however.

This, it seems, is the fate of much Eastern filmmaking, and it is in Ray's *The Goddess* (*Devi*) that the betrayal of India is complete. This 1960 film comes early in Ray's career, though after his famous Apu trilogy. A young woman called Doya is declared by her father-in-law to be the incarnation or avatar of the goddess Kali, which she comes to believe after initial doubt. A child is "miraculously" cured in her presence, and so devotees gather to worship her, but later a child of the family dies despite all entreaties. Doya, overcome by the contradictions of it all, appears to lose her mind and wanders off into the mists, in a setting quite possibly on the holy river Ganges. The actress who played Doya, a descendent of Rabindranath Tagore, was fourteen at the time. Apparently, at one point while filming in Calcutta, an old man just wandered in on the set and made prostrations to her, which she found to be eerie and strange, but a help in understanding Doya. We could say that it helped her understand Ray's understanding of Doya, which portrays a young woman merely bowled over by the mysterious attention from others. From a spiritual point of view however—one sympathetic to the devotional and with a knowledge of the life of Ramakrishna (a Kali devotee installed as priest of the temple at Dakshineswar on the banks of the Ganges)—a quite other understanding is possible. Spiritually, the young woman could have undergone a genuine religious awakening like Ramakrishna, or for that matter Mother Meera, from which followers naturally arise. For Ray, his film is about superstition dispelled by the Freudian science of hysteria. For us, his film is possibly the greatest squandered opportunity in religious Indian filmmaking: it shows the false of which the true is denied. At least half of it leaves the viewer open to the religious possibilities in it, however, conveying through Ray's beautiful cinematography a world of Indian spirituality long overshadowed by anti-superstitious, anticolonialist and anti-paternalistic secular preoccupations. The Freudianized ending is of its period and consistent with anything in Bergman, but leaves us with a sense of loss.

Mother India, from a quite different director and perspective, represents more explicitly the Marxist consciousness in Indian filmmaking, and was indeed an Indo-Russian collaboration during the cold war. As an early Bollywood-style production it shows Indian religious life only as a stylized outer formalism. The film is more interesting in parading its socialist credentials. It was made at a time when industrial solutions to poverty were unclouded by issues of environment, so it follows the making of a canal for the better irrigation of crops.

Melanie Wright suggests that "for students of religion and film Bollywood presents distinctive problems and rewards. It provides a route into the visual culture that is vital for understanding Hinduism."[7] The problem, as suggested earlier in the discussion on *Jai Santoshi Maa*, is that Bollywood, particularly in its song-and-dance routines which so define its distinctive visual style, has largely forgotten the religious devotional context: *kirtan*. For example, *Lagaan* is a colonial cricket drama set in the Victorian Raj in which its obligatory song-and-dance scenes have nothing of the genuine devotionality of *Jai Santoshi Maa*. Villagers are oppressed by high taxes imposed by the British, and when they complain they are offered to chance to be freed of taxation for three years if they win at cricket. Hence, it becomes a liberation movie where the underdog has to undergo trials to succeed. There are some religious scenes in a local Radha-Krishna temple, but the protagonist is no more religious than Shane or the Terminator. The film also elides—presumably in the interest of religious harmony—the differences between Hindu and Muslim religious observance and social grouping.

Iran and the West

To set the context for some Iranian filmmaking it is worth first visiting a Western-made film about Iran. In *Not Without My Daughter*, Moody, an Iranian doctor, lives the American dream: a house by a lake, opera on the radio, a beautiful wife and intelligent child, but he faces anti–Iranian prejudice at work and misses his family. He wants to go home for a vacation and promises to his American wife, Betty, on the Koran that she and their daughter will be safe, despite the turmoil in 1984 Iran. Once there he finds that much has changed since the Revolution, and that Betty will have to wear Islamic dress after all. This is not Betty's first shock: next she has to step over a slaughtered goat, and then witness Friday prayers from her balcony. The worshipers are making the customary prostrations, but on the wall in front of them are Revolutionary depictions of the struggle against the West, Russia and Israel. "Allah Akbar" echoes across the courtyard. At the crack of dawn, the whole family prays together, and, when shopping a little later, a machine-gun toting, chador-clad woman with military backup forces Betty to tuck her hair under her headscarf. One of the relatives berates her: "Every single hair that is not covered is like a dagger aimed at the heart of our martyrs."

Betty finds it all "primitive," to which Moody replies: "All religious beliefs seem primitive when they're not your own." We learn that his family are country people, very religious, and after the Revolution threw all their Western-style furniture away. They sit on the floor at mealtimes, men and women separate. In a beautiful mosque the call to prayers is made via a cassette tape. It blares out over Tehran every day, so there is no lie-in for Betty. But the real shock is to come: Moody hasn't told her that he lost his job back in the Sates, and now wants to stay—and bring up his daughter as a Muslim. It turns out that the overthrow of the Western-backed Shah had come as great news to him: "For the first time, we could say to everyone: 'This is our faith. This our way of life. This is who we are.'"

Moody is no longer the man she knew, and she is now trapped. At a Koran school she meets another American wife, who has converted to Islam and accepted her new culture, but Betty can't do that. The rest of the film deals with her escape with her daughter. There is no doubt that the film intends to disparage the Islam of the Iranian Revolution, but in Moody we can recognize something valid: a person brought up in a deeply religious manner who finds in America an empty dream. As we will see in the films of Afghanistan, one cannot avoid the observation that if the West had not interfered so much in the political and religious life of Muslim countries, then the kind of retrenchment represented by the Iranian Revolution might either not have taken place, or might have been more rapidly overtaken by modernizing elements.

The Iranian film *Gabbeh* by Mohsen Makhmalbaf deals with tribal herdsmen whose livelihood happens to additionally revolve around the making of carpets, the Iranian word for which gives the film its title. There is little in it that is directly religious—it certainly has no reference to Islam—but its lyrical cinematography of nature and allegorical structure suggest a distant resemblance to *Anchoress*. The nomadic way of life is infinitely fragile when seen on film like this, brought to us by Western technology, but speaking through Makhmalbaf of a joyous simplicity in life: colors, tents, donkeys, goats, a wedding. He deliberately eschews the political, believing that films about exploitation do nothing to end it; instead he says that "one of the things I am trying to do is speak of relativism in a society that has individualistic and fundamentalist tendencies."[8] For him, to speak for relativism is to extol community, and this is palpable in *Gabbeh*.

The animated film *Persepolis* is a French realization of an Iranian graphic novel, and takes us full circle to the themes of *Not Without My Daughter*. It tells the story of Marjane Satrapi's growing up under the Revolution, her schooling in Vienna to prevent clashes with the authorities, her return to Iran and the mounting difficulties which led her to take permanent exile. Her inspiration, which comes at one point to her in a dream, is the figure of Karl Marx, and it is the longing for Western freedoms that eventually leads her to leave the country. The Westernization of the story is even more complete than in *Not Without My Daughter*, for one cannot glimpse at any time the religious counterweight to the polemic.

Afghanistan and the West

Turning now to Afghanistan, we look first at *Osama*, a film about life under the Taliban regime, as seen through the eyes of a young girl. Life is terrible for everyone, but particularly so for women in this film. "Osama" is the name assumed by a small girl sent to work as a boy because her mother and grandmother are not allowed to. Inevitably the subterfuge is exposed, and she is lucky to get away with her life. Osama's first job is for a compassionate shopkeeper, who on being thanked for taking her on, responds, "God is merciful." The mother responds, "God is clement." On parting they both say, "God bless you." To what extent are such exchanges merely by rote? Or is there something here that a secular culture has forgotten, the complete immersion in a spirituality of thankfulness, even in extreme poverty and danger? In this lies the potential for understanding Islamic resistance to the West, which it sees as atheistic. As Osama starts her first day of work, a Taliban crier knocks roughly on the shop door to say it is time for prayers. The shutters go up.

A central part of the film revolves around the ablutions that are an integral part of worship in Islam. Osama is taught by the shopkeeper how men wash and pray. But before long Mullah Sahib visits the shop and states flatly, "You are coming with me." The shopkeeper's protests are in vain, and Osama is taken with many other boys to train for war. They recite the Koran, rocking-fashion, wear the white headdress, and play and fight as boys do. They are then rigorously schooled in the ablutions proper to men by a kindly old instructor. Washing of the private parts is carried out modestly with pitcher and towel, and is a difficult skill to master, he tells them. The instructor spots Osama hiding, and tells her to proceed, unaware that she is a girl. He is almost completely immersed in a stone tub, and says, "it really is a wonderful feeling."

Ablutions as part of the lived spiritual life is a foreign concept to the West—beyond that of baptism, of course—and is just one of the practices that mark Islam as separate to Christianity. But no idea in the spiritual life is ever unique it seems, because the same idea of physical purity by water is found in the Japanese religion of Shinto,[9] and is perhaps the basis for Miyazaki's *Spirited Away*. Its Islamic form is seen again in *Monsieur Ibrahim*, when the old man takes Momo to the baths. At one point they are seated there and the old man listens to the boy, who has just lost his girlfriend. The old man explains to him that she cannot take his love away from him: "What you give is yours for good. What you keep is lost forever." He is Momo's spiritual teacher, and the water stands for purification. The Jewish form of ablutions is seen in *Kadosh*, where the women spend time in the baths, a female attendant taking the role of general advisor, and is also seen briefly in *A Price Above Rubies*, another film set in a Jewish *haredi* or conservative context.

We have examined the film *The Kite Runner* from the perspective of atonement, which is the film's central theme. However, it also reveals some aspects of life in Afghanistan, including how the middle-class family of Amir were able to leave the country during war, while the servant-class Hazaras stayed on to look after the family house. What is also of interest is the attitude of Amir's father, an educated man, to religious subjects. Amir is comment ing, as his father drinks alcohol, that "the mullahs at school say drinking is a sin. They say that drinkers will pay when the Reckoning comes." His father responds that he will never learn anything of value from those "bearded idiots." The boy asks, "The mullahs?," to which his father responds, "I piss on the beards of those self-righteous monkeys." He objects that they recite a book written in a tongue that they don't understand (presumably Arabic). But his interesting contribution is that he offers a Western model of religious thought: the route taken by a man who thinks for himself. "There is only one sin," he says earnestly and with conviction, eye-to-eye with his son, "and that is theft." For him, all other sins are variations on that one. One can work this out: to kill is to take a life that is not one's own, to rape is to take gratification that is not one's own, and to commit the crime that Amir does before long is to steal from his boyhood friend his honor. But within all this there is no crime in drinking, in insulting religious leaders, and, presumably, in blasphemy of any kind. Clearly, Amir's father cannot stay on under the Taliban: there is too much of the West in him.

Kandahar again documents life in Taliban-controlled Afghanistan: young boys learns the Koran by rote, interrupted only to answer questions on the purpose of the saber and machine gun, which are to cut off heads and hands, and to kill the enemy. The film follows an Afghan woman who has made a new life in Canada, returning to Afghanistan to prevent her sister from committing suicide. She makes a terrible journey to Kandahar across the desert, aided by a boy expelled from Koranic school and an African American Muslim convert who had originally fought the Russians and is now a doctor with a false beard. Effectively the country's tragedy is seen again through Western eyes.

In *Buddha Collapsed Out of Shame*, a small girl in the village of Baniyam—made famous by the Taliban's destruction of its giant Buddha statues—wants to go to school. Made by Hana Makhmalbaf, Mohsen Makhmalbaf's daughter, it shows how the Taliban have reacted to Western values, such as the schooling of women, by retreating to fundamentalist ideas.

All of these harrowing films set in Afghanistan return one to the question posed earlier: What if Islamic religious life had been able to develop without the presence of the West? Without war and the poverty it brings, and particularly without the natural retrenchment that societies make when dominated—and even humiliated—by an alien culture? One asks this question because even in this small set of films one can glimpse the hidden side of Islam: compassion, gentleness, and a devout way out life.

Buddhism and the West

Here we look briefly at three films where Western values have a visible impact on Eastern Buddhist communities, though in the first one the setting is also shamanic. In *Himalaya* "scientific" ideas erode the authority of the shaman; in *The Cup* it is football that dominates a Buddhist monastery, and in *Travelers and Magicians* it is the rock guitar that displaces older religious preoccupations.

Himalaya depicts a whole way of life that is shamanic, but at the same time Buddhist in context. The film opens with the aging Nepalese Tinle (played by Thilen Lhondup), confronted with the dead body of his chieftain son, brought home by Karma. Tinle then explains to young Tsering, the would-be chieftain and son of the dead man, that his father's spirit will be reborn in the realm of Padmasambhava, which is the name of the most revered founder of Tibetan Buddhism, and which religion is followed in the mountains states of the northern Indian subcontinent. Tinle continues that that the soul of Tsering's father will float over the various hells and then reach the paradise of the Buddha, teachings that are expounded in the *Tibetan Book of the Dead*, as examined earlier. "We all have to die," says the bereaved but apparently serene Tinle. The face and voice of actor Thilen Lhondup embodies, as does that of Maksim Munzuk (Dersu Uzula), a far eastern mode of shamanism, interesting to compare with that of Chief Dan George and Ted Thin Elk in the Native American traditions or David Gulpilil of the Aboriginals. The boy asks his grandfather how long one stays dead, to which the old man replies, "Everything that lives must die, then be reborn and die again." The child is not so much interested in metaphysics as in a more pressing question: "How many lives does it take to become chief?" The family have long been chiefs, and it might be his turn next.

But the old man's grief and anger are just below the surface, fuelled by his certainty that Karma had lied about the circumstances of his son's death: his son knew the mountains too well to make a mistake. And here is the central theme of the film: a life-or-death relationship with the mountains that is mediated through the spirits, the existence of which is challenged by the more Western-leaning Karma. The village makes a living by mining salt which they trade for rice and other essentials, and the success of their annual caravan is crucial. Its timing is what comes into question: Tinle, as guardian of the shamanic traditions of divination, needs to be sure that the spirits of the mountain will grant them good passage. (The religious rites of Nepal are divided between lamas and shamans—called bombo—in which calendrical functions are more normally performed by the lamas.[10])

The sky-burial of Tinle's son then proceeds, with the old man dismembering the body in a time-hallowed and deeply shamanic ritual, making available the carcass in pieces small enough for the vultures. Although different to the sky-burial of the Native Americans, the underlying shamanic significance is clear: the body is returned to Nature via the most spiritually significant of animals, the bird. As the birds feed, the ceremonially robed villagers play drums and chant.

Tinle demands to lead the caravan this year, but the role should more naturally fall to Karma, who ought to be leader during the minority of Tsering. The lamas set the date for departure, after lengthy astrological considerations, but Karma is impatient with their ancient ways, anxious that winter is approaching. Meanwhile, Tinle visits a Buddhist monastery, where the monks are engaged in traditional chanting: a glimpse into the religious heartland of these mountain kingdoms. He wants to persuade his lama son Norbou to take the place of Karma. But Norbou points out that "I don't know anything about mountains, yaks, or salt." In Tinle's absence, Karma sets off with half the village, the other half sticking to the traditional date-setting, and waiting for Tinle. One man who is staying behind shouts, "If you leave early, you'll be plagued by demons!"

The film then follows the two caravans, symbolizing in Karma's leadership a more secular Westernized worldview, and in Tinle's leadership the ancient animist bond with the mountains. There are no outward signs of modernity, but perhaps Karma represents the first rustle of the giant wind of change that blows up from the West and into every remote shamanic corner of the earth. Tinle says, on discovering that mostly only the old men are left with their salt, "The gods are with us. The mountains will recognize us. They're our allies."

In every mountainous part of the world the ancient peoples spoke with the spirits of the mountains as allies. Only the secular West could have invented the idea of "conquering" them, and apparently, in Japan to this day there is still a reluctance to walk up to the very peak, as if this would offend the mountain. But the mountains can also speak to the secular Westerner, for example in the life and work of Norwegian eco-philosopher Arnie Nees, or to the Austrian Heinrich Harrer, subject of the film *Seven Years in Tibet*.

But the real drama plays out in the face of old Tinle, whose imperious ways are drawn from the very rocks of the mountain, and carry sway over men and yaks. At every step in the dramatic landscape we understand the deep harmony he personifies, that exists between man, mountain, and the twin religious streams of shamanism and Buddhism that illuminate his mind. They catch up with Karma, who then saves the old man's life in bad weather. Tinle is reconciled to him and makes him chief, reminding him however: "A chief commands his men. But receives his orders from the gods." This way Karma is brought back to the old ways. But one knows that Karma's fascination for Western thought represents the future of his society: the reconciliation is just temporary.

The Cup is a film of the Tibetan diaspora, this time a Tibetan monastery in India which succumbs to World Cup soccer mania. Western values in the form of football impinge on an ancient Eastern tradition, already uprooted from its homeland through a Chinese invasion that brought Marxist thought. What this film does beautifully is to show how adaptable an ancient religion can be when faced with the new. To start with the football craze is felt most strongly by the youngest of the monks, and the abbot and other elders are naturally dubious of it. But as the crucial final game in France approaches the day of its broadcast, all are swept up in the enthusiasm and the practical challenges of hooking up a satellite dish.

It is hard not to make a comparison here between the Islamic reaction to Western values in Iran and Afghanistan as shown on film, and the reaction of the Tibetan Buddhists. There is no doubt a tolerance in Buddhism that goes back to its founder, and, perhaps even more importantly to Asoka, who ensured that it was respectful of local religions as it swept both East and West from its source in India.

Travelers and Magicians is perhaps most directly a culture-clash film between Eastern and Western values. It features a young government official in Bhutan who is bored of village life and plays American pop music when he can. He sets off on his planned journey to America, but misses the only bus of the day. Forced to walk he meets all kinds of characters on the way, including a Buddhist monk who tells him, "You know, the Buddha said hope causes pain." It is hard to find a statement more indicative of the profound difference between Christianity and Buddhism. "Hope" is a future-oriented emotion and the driving force behind all progress and development. Yet is also proves to be a powerful force that militates against a real knowledge of the present. *Travelers and Magicians* does not explore the depths of these philosophical ideas, but, like the director's previous film *The Cup*, it explores the East-West divide with gentle humor. Whether resisted with humor or resisted with insurgency, the values of the West encroach on the East, and the films discussed here are a valuable record of that.

The East in Western Enclaves

My Son the Fanatic and *East is East* are two films starring Om Puri as Pakistani-born Muslims in typical British immigrant enclaves: one is a taxi driver and the other runs a chip-shop. In both films he is the father of a family attempting to negotiate the tension between tradition and integration. In *My Son the Fanatic*, Puri plays Parvez, a tolerant secular Muslim, while in *East is East* he plays George, a traditionalist. An asset in watching these films is the book *The Islamist*, which is an autobiographical account of Ed Husain's upbringing in the East End of London by Muslims of a mystical orientation, i.e., non-political.[11] Husain was then radicalized by Hizb Ut Tahrir—an internationalist Islamic group—and led a university Islamic society into protest action. He made a full circle in the end, however, after his group was involved in the death of a student and he was de-radicalized as he took up a Sufi mystical path, though not exactly that of his parents. The book is a vital contrast to the two films in the section because it shows just how much filmmaking of this type plays on stereotypes and fails to reveal the kind of realities facing Husain. Nevertheless, behind the stereotypes one glimpses many of the inevitable clashes of philosophy between a deeply religious culture and that of secularist Western youth, clashes resolved by Husain for himself, and hopefully for those influenced by the foundation he since set up.

Melanie Wright comments on *My Son the Fanatic* that "whilst the broad trend in such writing is to evaluate the film positively, regarding it as a source of information and insight on British Islam, other critics bemoan the film's handling of religion."[12] This is true of both films in that Islam here has two aspects, firstly as culture and secondly as a collective spiritual life. Few films, it seems, are able to penetrate the otherness of the first aspect and all the culture-clash dramas that arise out of it, in order to reach the second.

Afterlife East and West

The afterlife is differently conceived East and West, as discussed earlier. We can return again to comments by Susan L. Schwartz to help sum up these differences. She says most tellingly of *What Dreams May Come* that it "is a work of imagination (film) about a work of imagination (life and death), constructing a western illusion about an eastern illusion, all the while addressing western apocalyptic paranoia at the end of the millennium, which is, of course, irrelevant in the east."[13] The "Eastern illusion" is reincarnation and karma theory. Schwartz continues:

> I propose that the crafters of this film were well aware that its insights into the nature of the imagination and its impact on reality, both in life and in death, are South Asian in origin and character. They chose to compensate for, and perhaps obscure that fact, by using a visual palette composed entirely of Western romantic artwork.

The film actually follows a largely Western conception of the afterlife—an Orphic story—until the end where the husband and wife agree to reincarnate in Jersey to fall in love. Schwartz's comments usefully remind us that Western notions of the afterlife in mainstream culture have in the century of the cinema become far more a product of the Romantic tradition than the Christian one. However, films of the East, while retaining their traditional images of reincarnation here and there, are also succumbing to the Romantic.

Mongolia and the West

We have seen in this chapter that the impact of Western filmmaking on non–Western filmmakers has mostly been one of secularization. However Miyazaki, although a triumphant borrower of Western tropes—and commercial success—is shown to have substantially retained Japanese spiritual elements, as perhaps Kurosawa does in a more muted way. We finish this chapter with a look at two films by Byambasuren Davaa, who also seems to use the Western system without succumbing to its ideology.

The Story of the Weeping Camel and *The Cave of the Yellow Dog* are remarkable docudramas of the last of the Mongolian herdsmen in contemporary times. Davaa is Mongolian-born and pursued film studies in Germany, a country much more sympathetic to Nature-oriented ways of life than the Anglo-American axis. These two films convey a quieter kind of drama than is generally a product of the Western mind. They are set in different parts of Mongolia: *Yellow Dog* in the lush Western mountains, while *Camel* in the more Eastern plains. If shamanism per se is the product of hunter-gatherer cultures, then it was much moderated in the later cultures that domesticated animals. The Mongolian herdsmen pursue a religion that is a mixture of this moderated shamanism and the later Buddhism, in a form that is not much different to the practices in Tibet, Nepal and Bhutan, as portrayed to some extent in the films described earlier.

Neither of the films have any direct reference to shamanism, excepting in that they portray a people in a deep relationship with their animals. Anyone who has absorbed the stereotype of the camel as a stubborn creature prone to spitting will be surprised at how gentle and loveable the Mongolian camel is. In *The Story of the Weeping Camel*, the whole extended family, or clan, take the trouble to arrange and perform an ancient ritual (which may just have some shamanic origins) to persuade a she-camel to nurse a calf that she has rejected at birth.

In *The Cave of the Yellow Dog*, Byambasuren Davaa has achieved something very rare in a documentary filmmaking: the apparent construction of a coherent and rounded story out of the unprompted daily life of the subject family. The story revolves around reincarnation, and a yellow dog that is at first suspect because it may have learned the ways of the wolf. Davaa comments that it was impossible to construct a shooting schedule, because each day was taken as it came, the signs of the weather considered, and then action taken accordingly. The herdsmen very much live in the present, and in a world which is unchanging: nothing of a Western teleology, whether Biblical, New Age, Darwinian, or in the modern sense of progress, could enter their consciousness. Of course, the films also hint at how that consciousness is probably doomed to disappear as it encounters Western-style technologies and the lure of the city.

What is important in these two films is that Western filmmaking can be mastered by those in the Far East, and used to preserve older more religious ways of life without distorting them through Western assumptions. Such an effort ought everywhere to be encouraged, rather like the efforts to secure biodiversity through collecting and archiving rare animal and plant lines. The glamour of progress, whether presented through Western democratic belief systems, or Eastern Marxist ones, or even through New Age beliefs in the evolution of spirituality, threatens the ancient treasures of the spiritual life and its variety. Davaa's films, along with documentaries such as *Into Great Silence*, represent a welcome new departure in filmmaking.

Summary

Although "East" and "West" are rather loose terms, it turns out that visions of the spiritual life found in many films are usefully examined under these categories, and particularly in films where the mutual impact of their very different spiritual values creates engaging drama. It makes sense to talk of Western seekers in Eastern traditions and also of the impact on Eastern ways of life of Western values. Sometimes these become stories of Western materialism set against Eastern spirituality or Western exoticization of Eastern culture.

The examples in this chapter confirm the idea that Western filmmaking usually brings, along with Western technology, a set of cultural assumptions. These are principally secular, but also monotheistic. Hence, a truly luminous spiritual cinema of the East risks losing the specific voice of its own heritage. Along the way however we have found a number of Eastern films that are true to their heritage and contain luminous moments. Some thirty films with Eastern settings have been touched on here of which the important must-see movies have mostly been introduced earlier. The films that remain may not be individually outstanding, but collectively form a spiritual world cinema the viewing of which is an effective interfaith exercise. Many small glimpses of unfamiliar spiritualities, even if exoticized or placed within a context of conflict or poverty, are expansive of one's own spiritual practice and vision.

The secular-spiritual divide across West and East became obvious in this set of films: Eastern filmmakers are naturally interested in social change, and much of that comes from the dual forces of Western technology and Western democratic ideals, including freedom for women and toleration of sexual and religious difference. In the next and final chapter we look more deeply at how the secular-spiritual divide plays out in film, mostly in the West, and particularly in the realm of religious and sexual politics.

12
Secular vs. Spiritual

Anyone pursuing the spiritual or religious life in the broadly Western context does so in a prevailing culture of secularism. Unless somehow ghettoized within a specific religious group, one is likely to have encounters with humanists, agnostics, atheists or those who are in one way or another skeptical of spirituality and religion, or encounter such views in the media. Although the secular-spiritual divide can be deep, intelligent people can make friendships across that divide and learn from each other. There are many instances of this worth looking at in film (for example, the conversations between Catholic nun Sister Miriam and secular lawyer Dr. Martha Livingstone in the film *Agnes of God*). Science is at the heart of the Western discomfort over religion, so it is interesting to look at films that attempt to chart the science-religion debate, given that science itself is a domain that filmmakers may have as little experience of as religion. Committed religionists may also find themselves in the realm of politics, hence many people who have both a religious life and a political life will recognize various filmic depictions of sometimes well-known figures torn between their loyalties across this particular divide. In South America it often takes the form of a clash between Marxist principles and Roman Catholicism, while in Tibet the clash was between Buddhism and Maoism. In the U.S. it might be a religious conviction pursuing activism against poverty or the death penalty. But perhaps nowhere is the secular-religious divide more agonized than in the arena of sexual politics, and there is no lack of filmic treatment of the issue.

Hence, this chapter looks at a range of films—some of them already introduced—to discover dialogues across the divide, the arguments against religion from science, the tension between politics and religion, and the fraught arena of sexuality and religion. It finishes on the theme of secular cynicism, but uncovers an antidote to it from an unexpected source.

Constructive Encounters Across the Divide

Agnes of God was introduced earlier as presenting a sympathetic portrait of a mother superior, one with full awareness of the secular world. Here we look at some of the exchanges between the lawyer Dr. Martha Livingston and Mother Miriam Ruth, and also between Martha and Agnes, the accused nun. As Martha gets to know the young nun that she is to represent, they have this conversation:

>   MARTHA: You're very pretty.
>   AGNES: No, I'm not.

MARTHA: Hasn't anyone told you that before?
AGNES: Let's talk about something else.
MARTHA: What would you like to talk about?
AGNES: I don't know.
MARTHA: Anything. The first thing that comes into your mind.
AGNES: God ... but there is nothing to say about God.
MARTHA: The second thing that comes into your mind.
AGNES: Love.
MARTHA: Have you ever loved anyone?
AGNES: Yes.
MARTHA: Who?
AGNES: Everyone.

Agnes—and with no learning whatsoever—conveys two central elements of Christianity: firstly, that there is nothing one can say about God, and secondly, that love is what is extended to all, not to the romantic one. In fact, all three monotheisms contain within their history strenuous efforts to point out that there is nothing one can say about God—this is known as the *via negativa* or the negative theology.

Another scene from this film should stick in the mind of anyone who has ever glimpsed the meaning of religion: the Mother Superior is concerned that the young nun is not eating enough. "I don't think the communion wafer has the recommended daily allowance of anything," Miriam tells Agnes sternly. "Of God," whispers Agnes, her eyes shining, looking directly at her Mother Superior. Miriam's face softens, she smiles. "Of God," she has to agree.

But these moments would have less impact without Martha's chain-smoking reductionist Freudianism as the counterpoint. In the exchanges between Martha and Miriam, these essentials of the religious life are pitted against the "science" of Freud. The first interview given by the Mother Superior to the investigating court psychiatrist does not go well. Miriam is driven to say: "Look, I don't know how to tell you this politely, but I don't approve of you ... not you personally. ..." Martha completes the sentence for her: "the science of psychiatry." "Exactly," says Miriam, grim-faced. "I want you to deal with Agnes as speedily and easily as possible. She won't hold up to any kind of cross-examination." Martha retorts: "I'm not from the Inquisition," to which Miriam responds quickly: "And I'm not from the Middle Ages." Frowning with disapproval, Miriam finishes their interview with: "I know what you are. I don't want that mind cut open."

As the investigation develops, Martha concludes that Agnes is a hysteric, like many others who might have shown symptoms such as the stigmata over the centuries. Miriam is adamant that the psychiatric approach is wrong. "Agnes belongs to God," she says. Martha responds defiantly: "And I intend to take her away from Him." But Martha's certainties begin to dissolve. After Agnes accuses her of attempting just what she had threatened earlier, to take her away from God, Martha is shaken. It is one thing to make the bland assertion, quite another to see the enormity of what it means to the young nun. Miriam confronts her: "You hate us. You hate nuns." "I hate ignorance and stupidity," says Martha defensively. In the argument that ensues, she becomes angry however and puts the whole case for the secular life that she wants Agnes to experience: "She has a right to know there is world out there filled with people who don't believe in God and aren't any worse off than you, Mother! People who have gone their entire lives without bending their knees once, to anybody. And people who fall in love and have babies, and occasionally are very happy! She has a right to know that!"

Miriam then turns and confronts Martha with the fact that she had been married for twenty-three years with two daughters. She was a failure as a wife and mother. The implications are clear: she has known the secular world as deeply as anyone, but has made a deliberate choice for God. "And don't tell me that I am making up for past mistakes, Dr. Freud!" she shouts. But their mutual unburdening is the beginning of their friendship, as both try to find a way out for Agnes, under suspicion of murdering her baby. The exchanges between them now fall into a pattern: sometimes angry, at other times full of understanding for each other's very different lives. Towards the end Martha has to reiterate her own faith as the facts surrounding Agnes's pregnancy are further confused: "She is not an enigma, Mother. Everything she has done is explainable through modern psychiatry—one, two, three right down the line." "Is that what you believe she is," retorts Miriam, "the sum of a psychological process?" Martha replies, "That's what I have to believe!" While the film's conclusion is somewhat unsatisfactory, the encounter between Martha and Miriam remains convincing.

The Exorcism of Emily Rose is rather different from other possession stories, such as The *Exorcist*, *Carrie*, and *The Omen*. Emily Rose insists that her problem is "spiritual," and so her family call in a priest to exorcise her and they end her medication for suspected epilepsy. The film is a courtroom drama with flashbacks to the actual events, and features a lawyer, Erin Bruner, placed in a position rather like Martha Livingston in *Agnes of God*. This time Erin is hired to defend the priest, who is held responsible for the death of the girl. Erin herself begins to doubt the case of conventional medicine and engages a professor of anthropology, Dr. Sadira Adani, to testify on the "reality" of possession. This part of the film is reminiscent of the trials in *Audrey Rose* and *Switch*, where the case for reincarnation is put to a court by an expert witness. In all three cases the "spiritual" account is rejected. Interestingly, Dr. Adani draws on the notion of a "separate reality" made popular in the books by one-time anthropologist and then cult author Carlos Castaneda. It is also of interest that Tarkovsky had planned a film about Castaneda, but died before he could make it.[1] Although it contains few of the exchanges that make *Agnes of God* such an important film, *The Exorcism of Emily Rose* stands out from the horror genre as a film genuinely trying to grapple with a difficult subject. Erin's summing up includes these lines: "Is it a fact that Emily was beloved of God? And that after her exorcism she chose to suffer till the end so that we might believe in a more magical world? A world where the spiritual realm really exists?"

The Nun's Story, *Black Narcissus*, *The Song of Bernadette* and *Elmer Gantry* are also interesting for including secular characters engaged in some way with religious protagonists. Unlike Dr. Martha Livingstone, these characters have prior insight into religion that makes their secularism quite often a source of insight rather than conflict. In *The Nun's Story*, Sister Luke struggles over her loyalties to her two callings: religion and medicine. While recovering from her tuberculosis in the jungle mission of the Congo, Dr. Fortunati tells her that her illness is a symptom of her inner conflict. He is worldly wise and perhaps a little jaded, but he understands both the concept of a "calling"—his own is to medicine—and religion. One can be secular-minded yet retain an honest and open respect for religion. Fortunati can see, however, that Sister Luke's ultimate calling is not to religion: he tells her that she is "worldly" and will never be the kind of nun her convent wants her to be.

Black Narcissus features a secular-minded Englishman who has "gone native" in Northern India: the local agent, Dean. At one point in the film he stands with Sister Clodagh in front of an Indian holy man seated in the lotus posture and the recipient of constant attention from devotees. He has told her of the holy man's background as a decorated general and benefactor, and speaker of several languages including perfect English. Now he never speaks. She would like to get rid of him, but really doesn't know what to do. "What would Christ have done?" asks Dean. She turns sharply to look at him, her face full of indignation, but he is sincere. She has no answer to his question, but it is a good one: it forces the religious person to haul the founder of their religion down from their mythologized sanctum to be standing flesh and blood under the hot Indian sun and gaze upon a holy man. It is, of course, an impossible image for Sister Clodagh—the implications are staggering—but this is just the gift that the secular world can bestow on the spiritual life in empathetic encounters across the divide.

In his first encounter with the nuns, as they open their convent, Dean wants to know if they are a contemplative order, but no, he is told, they are active: school, dispensary, very busy. "Good," he says, "you'll be doing me a great favor when you educate the local girls, sister." "We have heard that you don't like to be alone" is the retort. He turns out to be sympathetic and helpful: his worldliness ultimately perhaps a better religion than their impractical optimism. But he is also the catalyst for disaster as two of the nuns fall for him. Ivan Butler has this to say about the film:

> As usual, Powell and Pressburger incurred certain critical censure on the grounds of vulgarity and sensationalism, but in fact this is a ravishingly beautiful film, and as sincere in feeling as many higher-claiming religious epics, even if some of the situations (e.g., "frustrated" sister going off her head) are becoming familiar.[2]

The Song of Bernadette appears to be simply a biopic, or one of Butler's "higher-claiming religious epics," of Louise Soubirous, the village girl whose visions of the Virgin Mary led to her home town of Lourdes becoming a place of pilgrimage. Soubirous's visions take place in the year 1858, and she is subjected to two skepticisms in the film: a religious one from church authorities, and a secular one from civic authorities including Imperial Prosecutor Vital Dutour (Vincent Price). Dutour is probably portrayed as more cynical and anti-religious than the historical character may have been, but his character is very recognizable for a 1940s audience. The faith of Soubirous is contrasted right to the end with Dutour's atheism, as is the healing properties of the spring against his continued running nose. At the end of the film, when the grotto at Lourdes is now host to thousands of candle-bearing supplicants, Dutour approaches the bars that protect the spring and thinks aloud:

> I am a stranger here. I am not like these thousands of souls flickering brightly and hopefully in the darkness. My pride has always stood between them and me. The pride of being a superior human being. But now I know that we are all a wretched, animal species, distinguished from the insects only by nerve centers and false reasonings. A hungry cancer is feeding at my throat. Tomorrow, I'll crawl back to Languedoc, hide in some hole of death and be heard of no more. I'll be alone, alone and desolate. And why not? It's logical. I'll be alone because I have loved no one, no one and nothing, not even myself. Nothing. Nothing.

A 1940s audience could identify with both Bernadette and Dutour, but since that time Dutour would no longer find himself a stranger in society, as his doctrine has largely prevailed over Bernadette's. The secular mind barely knows its estrangement now. As for Bernadette, she dies painfully of cancer of the bone in a convent, where she faces the opposite problem to that of Suzanne Simonin: she has too much faith, not too little, and is the butt of cruelty from other nuns for that reason. But Bernadette has remained an inspiration for pilgrimage to this date, and the Jewish daughter in *Bee Season* watches a short extract of the film on the hotel room TV before one of her competitions.

In *Elmer Gantry*, it is journalist Jim Lefferts who is the foil to Gantry's religious fervor—which is anyway suspect—and who makes for a good disputant in argument. "What is a revival?" Lefferts ponders thoughtfully in the middle of dictating his front-page article on the big-tent religion of Sister Sharon Falconer. He wants to know if it is a religion or a circus. When Falconer and Gantry confront him over his scandalizing article, Lefferts demands to know who ordained them. "How did you get God's approval?" he asks. Falconer has no answer, so Gantry steps in and drives Lefferts to admit that he does not believe in the Bible. Gantry presses home his questioning: "Do you believe Jesus Christ can give us life everlasting?"

Modern atheists like Richard Dawkins or Sam Harris would answer with an immediate "no," because such atheists take the question literally. But when understood as the mystics do, then the question has a poignancy no one can ignore. It means, simply, Is there a longing in you for the infinite, for the eternal? Does not some organ in you palpitate at the question? For the modern atheist this is ridiculous, but for Lefferts it is not, and Gantry, charlatan to some degree perhaps, nevertheless knows it. Lefferts soberly replies, "I'd love to believe it." "But you don't," asks Gantry. "No." As the exchange develops Lefferts says that he has doubts over the divinity of Jesus. Accused of blasphemy by another party, he is indignant: "To doubt is not blasphemy. When you say 'blasphemy' you mean 'Don't dare disagree. Don't think. Don't doubt.'" He pauses, then continues, his face serious: "But Tolstoy, Darwin, Jefferson, Lincoln—they had the same doubts."

Lefferts's point is well-made, and, in another kind of film, might have led to a debate on Deism. Instead Gantry uses his advantage to secure radio time to preach his gospel of faith, as opposed to Lefferts's "poison of doubt and disbelief" which Gantry claims he has learned from atheists like Mencken (who wrote satirically on the Scopes trial), Ingersoll (the famous agnostic reviled as an "injured soul") and Sinclair Lewis (a humanist writer of great warmth). The latter is an ironic reference to the author of the book on which this film is based. Lewis was awarded the Nobel Prize in Literature, and it is by no means certain that he was an atheist in the angry sense at least. But Lefferts finds this fair, and looks on amused as Gantry drives his bargain with the media proprietor. Later, when Gantry is accused by a prostitute friend, it is Lefferts who sticks by him. Gantry is then attacked by an outraged public. Everything has gone horribly wrong, and Gantry stands amidst the ruined props in his tent. Lefferts comments thoughtfully: "The mob don't like their gods to be human." Gantry tells him, "You do the best you can, and you leave the rest to the Lord." Lefferts tips his head and says with affectionate curiosity, "You really do believe in the Lord, don't you?" "You're damn right I do," comes back Gantry. "It does a man good to get down on his knees once in a while." This is just the insight that Dr. Livingstone denied to Mother Miriam.

Witness has been mentioned before; here we look at the secular-spiritual encounter which is at the core of the story. Peter Weir consistently engages with themes that verge on the religious and here he does so explicitly, in the encounter between a Philadelphia cop, John Book, and a recently widowed Amish woman, Rachel Lapp. The contrast is between a secular Philadelphia policeman whose job it is to meet violence with violence and a religious community whose founding principle is pacifism. *Witness* is bookended with the elements of a homicide drama, a murder witnessed by Rachel's son Samuel, a small boy in his first visit to the big city. The term "witness" has both a secular meaning, as in eyewitness to the crime, and a specific

Christian meaning. What the film shows, however, is not any doctrinal exposition of religious "witness," but Christianity as a way of life, as understood by those attempting to come close to its origins. The gospels quite naturally have nothing to say about cars, electricity, the telephone, insurance and government assistance—all of which the Amish eschew—but Jesus does extol a life of poverty and simplicity, and also exhorts us to turn the other cheek "seventy time seven" times. While many films deal with the corruption of Christianity, or are skeptical of its supernatural foundations, *Witness* engages with the Amish, and their attempt to live by these values, with considerable respect.

In *The Quarrel*, the two Jewish men go their separate ways at the end of the film, but not before Hersh shares a little story with Chaim. Hersh had been on a train when a woman tells him that she gets angry whenever she sees a Jew dressed like him in the style of another century. "You make the rest of us look ridiculous." "Madam," he says to her, "you are making a mistake. I am not Jewish. I am Amish." The woman is confounded and apologizes profusely: she gushes how she has *such* respect for the Amish and the way they keep their traditions. Chaim laughs, but the point is serious: the prejudices around religion are peculiar and unexpected.

Returning to *Witness*, early in the film, when Detective Book drives a protesting Rachel Lapp and her witness son to identify a possible suspect, she tells him, "We want nothing to do with your laws." Book replies, "It doesn't surprise me. A lot of people I meet are like that." At this point he has no conception of the world she comes from, but she is clear about his: she wants nothing to do with a man who carries a gun. But when the boy identifies the killer as another policeman, their lives become bound together as corrupt officers now target Book, Rachel and Sam. Book is injured in a gunfight, realizes that all three of them are in mortal danger, and drives Rachel and her son to her Amish community. Book risked everything to return them home, and to erase all trace of their testimony, but when he tries to drive off his injury gets the better of him and he crashes his car. His moral stance in this is the beginning of the reciprocity between those who are otherwise representatives of opposing lifestyles. Aware that Book must not be discovered, or Samuel would then be in danger, the community nevertheless shelters him, and Rachel nurses him to health. The film gets into its stride here, as Book encounters the religious world of the Amish. Their way of life as a continuous religious observance is a world away from his modern secularism, and he beholds it at first bemused, and then with wonder. They are literally foreign to him in that, as descendents of the original Swiss-German Anabaptists, they speak a dialect of German—and refer to him as "the English." Book's first shock is when young Sam discovers his loaded gun in the drawer, and has to explain to him never to touch a loaded gun. Rachel discovers them as Sam is handling the unloaded weapon, and demands that while Book is in her house, he should respect their customs. He meekly hands over the gun for safekeeping, symbol of the ethical gulf that apparently divides them. In the next scene Sam's grandfather Eli is explaining to Sam that the gun is for taking life; that it is wrong to take life; and that only God has that privilege (for the sake of good filmmaking, all this discussion is in English). Looking at the gun on the table, the old man tells the boy, "What you take into your hands, you take into your heart. 'Wherefore come out from among them and be ye separate,' saith the Lord." This piece of religious instruction is conveyed gently, and, as the boy now declares that he would kill a bad man, because he has seen a bad man kill, there is a genuine debate to be had. The boy has entered into the world of Book, while the old Amishman is explaining why their community has separated themselves from the mainstream: they have never followed the call to arms.

Next, Rachel offers Book the clothes of her dead husband, explaining that the jacket has no buttons because it is "hochmut"—vanity—to wear such ornamentation. It is these small reminders that make Amish observance interesting in the film. Book turns out to have some skills in carpentry, and is put to work in a barn-raising, a scene that epitomizes the Amish collective way of life. It is here that one might want to criticize Weir for exoticizing the Amish a little, in the same way that he exoticizes the landscape in *Picnic at Hanging Rock* or the Aboriginals in *The Last Wave*. The barn-raising scene is an epitome of early American Christian community, is set in idyllic landscape and to stirring classical music. The men swarm over the timber-framed construction—a reminder perhaps of Walt Whitman's celebration of the house-framing as religious an act as any sacrament[3]—while the women prepare food and make quilts. The large collective meal is prefaced as usual with prayer. But Weir's filmic purpose is to make stark the contrast with what then follows: the intrusion of Book's violent police world into the community. This is not before Eli warns Rachel that "there is talk" about her and Book, and that if it goes any further there will be a "shunning." Book and Rachel are attracted to each other, but it is Book who sums it up after they almost lose themselves in passion: "If we'd made love last night, I'd have to stay, or you'd have to leave."

We saw earlier that in *Jesus of Montreal* an actor just named Daniel plays the part of Jesus in a radical retelling of the Passion, a theatrical staging commissioned by the Catholic Church and then repudiated by it for being "inaccurate." Daniel himself appears confused and is perhaps a microcosm of secular incomprehension towards Christ, as his identification with his stage role grows apace. After a scene where he acts violently towards the producer of a commercial—a parallel to Jesus overthrowing the tables of the moneychangers in the Temple—he is assessed by the court psychiatrist. But the encounter between psychiatrist and would-be religious figure produces nothing luminous as in the case of Martha and Sister Agnes. Instead—and amusingly—the psychiatrist just suggests to Daniel that, for someone with a drama degree, it must be a bit demeaning to have to play the role of Jesus. What is missing throughout is what Agnes reminds us of, as the core of Christianity: the love of God and the love of others. Daniel is merely the "angry young man" who sees the same rebelliousness in Jesus, and precious little else. Jesus here is mostly claimed for art, or for Marx.

Returning to *The Quarrel:* Chaim is the secular novelist who encounters his boyhood friend, the deeply religious Rabbi Hersh, who had always been the more religious of the two, and had followed the principle enunciated by Jewish teachers like Reb Saunders that to have eyes for the world is to forfeit one's life. But the circumstances of the Holocaust changed him:

> You accused me of hiding in my room from the temptations of the world. You were right. I spent most of my youth with my eyes on the ground, so I wouldn't be tempted. But then in 1941 a young German soldier grabbed me by my Jewish beard, and pulled my head *up*, and forced me to look up into his eyes, and I saw the World there. And I haven't put my head down since.

He now sees the Nazis as the "real" face of the world. He cannot believe in the secular values of Chaim, a man who makes the world his primary reality, because however fine the world may be at this moment the "Nazis" of any kind can rear up again. The "World" is a place of betrayal. He begs Chaim to return to his faith in the most moving of terms: this is a priest reaching out to one who has closed his being to the music of religion. It is this scene where Chaim finally responds with depth of feeling: "If I were to return to God it would be for the sake of *your* passion." He adds that "it is a blessing to share this day with you." Then he pauses, and says, "But, there is another chapter to your story." He tells of an old Lithuanian woman he met in Paris who smuggled Jews to save their lives, but was an atheist. Of course, they cannot resolve these issues, nor can they overcome the guilt of surviving when others, including close family perished.

Rabbi Hersh gives us a vivid picture of the renunciative spiritual life—one that can be called *via negativa*—as one lived with one's eyes to the ground, avoiding the open gaze that allows the world in, with its beauties and its temptations. Even more vivid is the image of the soldier who grabbed his beard and forced his eyes up, though for Hersh they stayed up only to contemplate with sorrow the ugliness of the "World." The image is reminiscent of a passage from Hegel where he suggests that in ancient times—and this would have been in the Judaeo-Christian world prior to Aquinas—the eyes of men sought only what was beyond the "World," just like Hersh. Hegel then says: "The eye of Spirit had to be forcibly turned and held fast to the things of this world...." (It is Hersh's tragedy that it was a Nazi that forced him to do this.) According to Hegel, it took a long time for the things of this world to come into focus, but in the modern period the problem is the opposite: "sense is so fast rooted in earthly things that it requires just as much force to raise it."[4] One could say that the essence of Jewish religious practice is the raising of its eyes from the world to God, balanced however by an intense family life, which in turn is the place where religious feeling finds expression in the "World."

The Holocaust has prompted diametrically opposed responses in the two men: in one the "eye of Spirit" is turned to God, in the other to the world. They are sheltering from the rain in an old garage and the Rabbi speaks:

> What is it, really, that separates us? We look at people, you see their potential for good, I look at people, the *same* people, I see their potential for evil. You believe that if people would only follow their reason that would be in the best interests of everyone. I believe that if people followed their reason it would lead to disaster. ... The wise men of Athens. Ever since the Greek philosophers people believed that reason alone could lead to morality. How could this be? Reason alone is amoral. To the most moral Greek it seemed perfectly reasonable to take a newborn baby that was unhealthy and put it outside to die. In other words reason is a tool. ... So, how do we protect ourselves if reason fails us? By relying on something higher than reason. If a person does not. ... If there is no Master of the Universe, then who is to say that Hitler did anything wrong?

Here, in a short speech, is encapsulated the ancient argument between the Hebraic and Hellenic worldviews. When the Greek mode of thought re-emerged in the Renaissance it slowly came to dominate the Western worldview, culminating in Enlightenment rationalism. We saw how Umberto Eco dramatized one aspect of this in *The Name of the Rose*; here is another playing out of the same cultural tension.

Religion vs. Science

We turn now to some films that make explicit the alleged faultlines between science and religion. *Inherit the Wind* is a 1960 film about Darwinism versus faith, dramatizing the historical events of the 1925 Scopes "Monkey" Trial. The film is based on the 1955 play of the same name (which was revamped for the British stage by Kevin Spacey in 2009). The clash of Darwinism and Biblical creationism has rumbled on since 1925, more in America than elsewhere, until the "New Atheism" debates triggered by 9/11which have pitted twenty-first century atheists such as Richard Dawkins and Sam Harris against the "new defenders of faith" which include, for example and rather ironically, the leader of the human genome project Francis

Collins.[5] Hence, Spacey's Old Vic production is a response to its times as much as the dusting down of an old classic.

The trial itself resulted in the conviction of John Scopes for teaching Darwinism to a high school science class, forbidden by Tennessee state law at the time, but the play—a fictionalized version of the trial—was intended just as much as an indictment of anti-communist McCarthyism of the 1950s, much like *The Crucible*. One of the playwrights was later to comment that "it's not about science versus religion. It's about the right to think." It is just the right to think that is often center-stage in the religion-versus-science debate, particularly in its rekindling in the early twenty-first century. In the 1960 film version, the fictional characters Matthew Harrison Brady, Henry Drummond, Bertram Cates and E. K. Hornbeck correspond to the historical figures of William Jennings Bryan, Clarence Darrow, John Scopes, and H. L. Mencken. We saw that Elmer Gantry mentioned H. L. Mencken as a contemporary journalist who spread the "poison" of atheism: it was Mencken who gave the name "monkey" to the trial. Scopes was the schoolteacher at the centre of the row, Bryan the former Secretary of State who headed up the prosecution, and Darrow the attorney for the defense. Scopes was found guilty and fined $100, but on appeal the verdict was overturned. In the film version, Hornbeck (the Mencken equivalent) is a wise-cracking reporter whose paper hires Drummond (Darrow) for the defense.

Inherit the Wind is that rare American film: one in which ideas take a central place, whether or not one reads it as an allegory of McCarthyism, and hence about communism, rather than Darwinism. Either way, the fact that the young teacher is jailed throughout the trial is shocking: even Galileo was not jailed, but placed under house arrest. But when Brady (Bryan) says over dinner that "the way of scientism is the way of darkness," he anticipates the "new defenders of faith" by eighty years. What the film shows so well is that mainstream American Christianity, in struggling against a scientism that provides only a materialist reductionist philosophy, could only defend religion by attacking the science. It is probably a futile strategy.

When one of Cates's (Scope's) pupils gives testimony as to what he had learned about evolution, Brady (Bryan) is jubilant: "He has been taught that he wriggled up like an animal from the filth and muck below." The clumsiness of the Christian attack on Darwinism is painful, and the film clearly sides with enlightened reason. If science shows that we "wriggled up" from the mud, it is absurd to ridicule it. But while the Christians might be clumsy, they are merely groping to find a way of saying that the human being, whatever the biological origins, also partakes of what is sacred. Science has nothing to say about the sacred, but *scientism*—the creed that makes science the only arbiter of human experience—eliminates it. So the religionists are following a sound instinct: that the sacred needs advocacy in the public sphere. But the secularists are also right. When Drummond (Darrow) cross-examines the boy, the judge intervenes: "The right to think is not on trial here." Drummond disagrees, and that ultimately is the stance of the film: the right to think has to take priority over possible offense to religion.

It must be galling to atheists like Dawkins that one of America's top scientists and head of the human genome project, Francis Collins (as just mentioned), should be a Christian in the C. S. Lewis mold. This is not so difficult to understand if we see Collins as a practitioner of good science but not a believer in *scientism*. There are many scientists who happen to believe in God and many who don't.

This, and the social implications of belief, are nicely illustrated in the science-fiction film *Contact*: two scientists, one religious the other not, volunteer for an experiment. *Contact* is a film about the search for extra-terrestrial intelligence (SETI), based on the novel by scientist and science writer Carl Sagan. His work is itself a good example of scientism—the leakage of science into the domain of culture and the promotion of scientism's central tenet that it should remain our sole source of understanding. *Contact* shares some common ground with the New Age book *Chariots of the Gods?*, by Erich von Däniken, and the various films derived from it. Däniken's idea is that religion is the human response to encounters with aliens of vastly higher intelligence, and in *Contact* the same mystical fervor surrounds the discovery of an alien message to humanity. However, religious fundamentalists oppose the efforts to return the contact much as they opposed Darwinism in *Inherit the Wind*. The role of scientism in these scenarios is the proposition that an exponential increase in intelligence somehow takes life or mind into the realm of the sacred. This is simply a complete misunderstanding of religion: we only have to think of Reb Saunders in *The Chosen*, as an illustration of the certainty that mere computational "intelligence" is in fact the obstacle to true religion. Also, we saw that in *Lawnmower Man* the scientific mind is just as likely to imagine accelerated intelligence taking the form of accelerated aggression. But *Contact* exposes interesting cultural perspectives on religion, despite its origins in scientism. Firstly, the issue of intelligence and religion is brought to the fore. Secondly, the easy arousal of fundamentalist religion to oppose anything new is well illustrated. Lastly, the two scientists who are desperate to become the first humans to make contact with the aliens are divided over religion but the one who is an atheist is turned down for the job in favor of the religious one. This is not, however, a triumph for religion, but merely a comment on power in modern scientific America—atheism does no favors for those who wish high office. Indeed, it is still said that while a Catholic has been President, and a Jew may yet become one, an atheist has no chance.

Contact is a reasonably well-made film and Jodie Foster is good as the SETI scientist, Eleanor Arroway. She does get to have contact in the end as the first big machine built to achieve this is destroyed by a religious fanatic—and with it, her rival—but the ending degenerates as all fantasies of this kind must into some kind of *deus ex machina*. Transported to another planet or dimension, the "alien" appears to her as her father, and so neither science nor religion wins in the end, but Freud.

The Body was introduced earlier as a film containing good dialogue across the religious-secular divide. A Jesuit priest, Matt, encounters an archaeologist, Sharon, of secular bent as they grapple with the possibility that the bodily remains in question are that of Jesus Christ. At one point Sharon says, "I don't understand why it would be a disaster for the Catholic Church if these were the bones of Christ? Isn't it enough that he was an exceptional man who founded an exceptional way of life that's good and compassionate and understanding?" Matt responds: "Right.... The power of his message is love, you're right on that. But at the same time salvation and resurrection. He's God. He's not only God for me, he's God for millions of people.... If you take away his resurrection you kill the God Jesus and with him the dreams of millions of people who believe He is all they have." Quite naturally she objects: "Are you manipulating me, Matt?" She doesn't want the responsibility of it. "What about the truth?" he asks. "The truth will set you free," she intones. "You ask me to see *your* truth," he replies, "to think like a scientist. Now, I ask you to experience *my* truth. To think with your heart. Can you do that for me?"

The God Who Wasn't There is a non-fiction film by Brian Flemming which has a broadly atheistic basis. More specifically, it pursues the idea of Jesus as myth, rather than historical figure, and features interviews with a range of believers and non-believers. Among the prominent atheists appearing are Sam Harris in interview and Richard Dawkins in a voice-over. The film is almost as crude an anti-religious tract as the *Left Behind* film series is a pro-religious tract. Indeed, Tim Lahaye and Jerry B. Jenkins, authors of the "Left Behind" book series, are among those shown early on in *The God Who Wasn't There*, along with Charles Manson and David Koresh, as Christians, along with short quotes. Lahaye and Jenkins are overtitled with: "Look forward to the day when all non-Christians are thrown into a lake of fire, 'howling and screeching.'"

In *The God Who Wasn't There*, the story of Jesus is first summarized through film extracts from old B-movie costume-dramas, going back as far as 1905. Flemming then begins his presentation of gaps, inconsistencies and contradictions in the story, again illustrated by costume-drama extracts. He focuses on Paul's testimony asking the question: "If Jesus was a human who had recently lived, nobody told Paul." Paul also seems ignorant of much of what is present in the Gospels. Now, much of this ground is already covered in a wide variety of works of varying scholarly quality. Flemming's film raises many questions, but the continued use of old film extracts seems designed to prejudice the viewer against the conventional account, though at the same time it reinforces the point that the religious costume drama is generally a poor vehicle for religion. Whether the historical status of Jesus matters or not depends on one's point of view: no doubt the arguments will continue for centuries as evidence either way is slight.

Flemming concludes: "Modern Christianity makes no sense." As a scientific system, perhaps not. As a system of propositional philosophy, perhaps not. But it is perhaps the comment by the atheist Sam Harris about the Rapture that is most telling. Harris says that "it is perfectly maladaptive to planning for a sustainable future." This may be true, but none of the old religions had encountered the problem of sustainability, and, more important, the Rapture and its associated apocalyptic beliefs are not what define Christianity or any other religion. They are beliefs at the margins.

The documentary represents some attempt at dialogue across the religious-scientific divide, and there is no doubt that Christians are better off for considering the inconsistencies in the accounts of their religious founder. But the film sticks to the territory occupied by many atheists, which is to attack religion on the basis of its worst manifestations. This would be like attacking science on the basis of such things as Chernobyl, Hiroshima, Nagasaki, thalidomide, pollution, or for that matter all the aggressive uses that the invention of Alfred Nobel and the armaments industry has been put to. In contrast, some of the films discussed earlier have a more balanced dialogue between these apparently opposing world views.

Expelled: No Intelligence Allowed is a non-fiction film at the intersection of science and religion: this time, on the subject of evolution. Produced to much higher standards than *The God Who Wasn't There*, it takes a little while to realize what its propaganda actually is. Written by and starring the American actor Ben Stein, it is simply a rather manipulative vehicle for his belief in Intelligent Design, a pseudo-scientific theory of evolution which leaves open the possibility of a creator God as the intelligent designer of Nature.[6] We learn that a number of American academics and journalists have had their careers damaged by holding to Intelligent Design, or perhaps even for including it in a survey of evolutionary thought. No doubt this shows an ugly side of big science, but the real problem of the film is that it does not even begin to explain the rationale for Intelligent Design, or put forward its best theories, which are about the genuine gaps in the science of evolution. Hence, the viewer has no chance to form an opinion either way, despite the interesting thinkers that are interviewed. Instead, highly emotive scenes are flashed onto the screen, including from the Berlin Wall, Nazi Germany, and a quick excerpt from *Inherit the Wind*. This is a slick and dishonest use of the filmic medium for the purposes of religious propaganda, and shows us how not to further the spiritual life on film. Inconsistencies in the scientific account of evolution and inconsistencies in the story of Jesus are equally *interesting*, but neither of these last two films presents a worthwhile debate over those issues.

Secular vs. Religious Politics

Buñuel writes, "I have always been impressed by the famous photograph of ... ecclesiastical dignitaries standing in front of the cathedral of Santiago de Compostela in full sacerdotal garb, their arms raised in the Fascist salute ... God and country make an unbeatable team; they break all records for oppression and bloodshed."[7] Tarkovsky writes about Buñuel's approach: "His protest—furious, uncompromising and harsh—is expressed above all in the sensuous texture of the film, and is emotionally infectious. The protest is not calculated, not cerebral, not formulated intellectually. Buñuel has too much artistic flair ever to fall for political inspiration, which in my view is always spurious when it is expressed overtly in a work of art."[8]

The important point in these quotes by serious filmmakers is that political inspiration, just like religious inspiration, is spurious when it dominates a film. Confessional polemics of any kind make bad films, but, as Tarkovsky is clear, the protest is valid if it is part of the "sensuous texture" of the film. We now look at films where the secular-religious divide takes a political dimension, firstly with Marxist themes, and then with the theme of Liberation Theology. With this background we are then finally prepared to analyze Scorsese's *The Last Temptation of Christ*. In all of these films we can be on the alert for spurious polemics, i.e., films that close down dialogue instead of opening it up.

My Night with Maud is a wonderful example of cinema that explores ideas without either laboring them or proselytizing. It simply reflects the complex cultural currents that swirl around individuals, who for reasons of temperament respond to this powerful eddy or that. Being set in provincial France, a culture not embarrassed by the intellectual, it picks out with great delicacy two crucial strands in French cultural history: the religion of the Catholic Church and the revolution of Marx. Jean-Louis is a Catholic mathematician meeting up with an old school friend Vidal, a socialist. Their opposing belief systems are focused on Pascal's "wager." Pascal is a natural thinker for Jean-Louis to consider, and in the early part of the film he introduces Pascal's works for us. The wager of Pascal is that one should believe, because, after death, even if there is only a remote chance that God is true, then one is bound for heaven. If God doesn't exist, then nothing is lost. Pascal is usually remembered for this, rather than for the extraordinary night of mystical experience which taught him that the "God of the philosophers" was merely an intellectual construct.[9] The wager appeals to the intellect, and so more easily becomes part of philosophical culture than the mystery of Pascal's religious experience. So, Jean-Louis tells Vidal: "I'm just re-reading him. I'm very disappointed. I know him almost by heart, yet he tells me nothing. Empty. I'm a Catholic. It's because I am a Christian I resent his severity. If Pascal represents Christianity then I'm an atheist."

But Jean-Louis is no atheist, and in his church attendance we also glimpse something of the power of a well-attended service in which a priest can say something as radical as this: "Christianity is an adventure of sanctity." How else should one describe the spiritual life? Yet "adventure" is the last thing that a secularist sees in religion. It falls to Jean-Louis's Marxist friend to defend Pascal. Vidal says, "To a communist, Pascal's wager is very real." For Vidal, religion is a foreign land, but he has translated the term "God" into what Marxists consider their highest value: "history." For the Marxist tradition—considered by many Western thinkers to have the outward form of a teleological religion[10]—"history" is an inevitable movement towards a future state of salvation where the proletariat ushers in the classless society of abundant means. This is not so different in its vision to that of apocalyptic Christianity: it is a future state which explains both the misery of the present one, and excuses the violence of revolution. Vidal makes it clear that the wager on "history" is what justifies his life. Though this might be the central, rather amusing theme, there is also much else in this film that makes for a valuable meditation on the place of religion in the life of French people in the 1960s and of the uncomfortable place of the intellect in Christian tradition.

For Marxist historians, the revolution Marx hoped for took place in the wrong country, Russia. It then leaped to another wrong country, China, and in one of China's first acts as a revolutionary state, it invaded Tibet. We have already discovered the terrible impact that this had on Tibetan Buddhism, but this was a natural outcome of two elements in Marx's thought: his loathing of religion and his love of violent revolution. The conflict of values between Tibetan Buddhism and revolutionary Marxism are epitomized in the meeting between the young Dalai Lama (Kundun) and Mao Tse Tung. In the film *Kundun* it is dramatized in the following exchange (a little condensed here):

> MAO: You have fallen behind, and we want to help you. ... You know, my mother was a Buddhist. I have a great respect for your Lord Buddha. He was anti-caste, anti-corruption, anti-exploitation. For some, religion and politics can mix.
> KUNDUN: I think socialism and Buddhism have some things in common.
> MAO: I understand you well. But you need to learn this: religion is poison. Poison. Utter poison. It weakens the race, like a drug. It retards the mind of people and society. The opiate of the people. Tibet has been poisoned by religion, and your people are poisoned and a failure.

A little later, Kundun is in discussion with general Tan:

> GENERAL: We are here to heal the people of Tibet. We are here to liberate you.
> KUNDUN: No. Buddha is our physician General Tan, he will heal us. Wisdom and compassion will set us free. ... You cannot liberate me General Tan, I can only liberate myself.

What is at stake here is two quite different interpretations of the word "liberation." Just as Romer's two Frenchmen understand Pascal's wager as relevant to their different belief systems, so do the Dalai Lama and Mao understand "liberation" quite differently in their belief systems. For the socialist, the "self" is the sum total of human interactions and these are in the first instance economic. Liberation is therefore economic liberation. For the Buddhist, the "self" is an illusion, liberation from which brings truth, compassion and wisdom. There appears to be no possible common ground here, as the continued anguish of Tibet and the exile of its spiritual leader show.

The documentary film *Tibet: Cry of the Snow Lion* covers much of the events of the Chinese invasion, including brief archive footage of the meeting between the Dalai Lama and Mao, as in *Kundun*. The narrator tells us that the Dalai Lama was impressed by Chinese industrialization and was initially optimistic, but "his hopes for a constructive relationship with communist China were dashed when, during their last meeting, Mao told him 'religion is poison.'" The film also shows how Tibetan peasants initially viewed the Chinese positively, until land was taken from the landlords and redistributed to them. The problem for the Chinese was that the landlords were Buddhist religious officials, and, when these monks were humiliated and beaten, this alienated the peasantry.

We have seen in a number of films that South America provides another context for the encounter between Marxism and religion, this time between socialists wanting to improve the lot of the ordinary people and the Roman Catholic authorities who wanted the same thing but via another route. Put bluntly, the church was in bed with capitalism, and favored the long route to working-class prosperity so vividly described by former British Prime Minister Margaret Thatcher as "trickle-down." South America did better than Tibet, however, because some synthesis between Marx and religion was possible, and developed in what is known as "Liberation Theology." It was a movement that grew in Latin America during the 1950s–1970s, and some of its leading proponents, such as the Franciscan Leonardo Boff, were accused of being Marxists. Boff was silenced for a year by Cardinal Joseph Ratzinger, later Pope Benedict XVI, and the same threat over his environmentalism led Boff eventually to leave the church. We saw that Pasolini found in the Gospel of Matthew no real contradiction with his Marxism, and more generally that the Christianity of St. Paul is one that promotes the welfare of the poor. Recent developments in what is called "engaged Buddhism"[11] have similar origins as Liberation Theology, but have come too late to have made any compromise possible in Tibet. The *potential* was there between the Dalai Lama and Mao, but Mao could not understand that the peasants of Tibet, much like the working poor in Latin America, lived a religious life that meant everything to them, and that economic improvement was not their only goal.

It is in this context that we briefly revisit the film *Romero*. It was made by the Catholic production company Paulist Productions, which also made *Entertaining Angels: The Dorothy Day Story*, to be considered shortly. Romero was chosen by the Roman Catholic Church to be archbishop of El Salvador. "He's a good compromise choice," is said of him in the film. "He'll make no waves." But he did because the right-wing forces in the country were responsible for human rights violations that he witnessed and spoke out against. Romero was no supporter of either Marxism or capitalism, but said simply, "Our faith requires that we immerse ourselves in the world." What the El Salvadorian world presented, as in many other South American countries, was a Cold War by proxy, where left-wing and right-wing ideologies battled for power. The nub of it was put clearly in a debate that Romero attended. A right-winger says: "We only want to have what North Americans have, to live as they do." It sounds like an innocuous enough aspiration, but this sentiment allowed the Chicago School of laissez-faire economics, backed by the U.S. government, to force harsh economic changes on many South American countries.[12] Romero was assassinated, perhaps by a right-wing death squad. At his funeral, which was attended by a quarter of a million mourners, there was more killing. Rather telling of the secular context of Western filmmaking, the original plan was to make *Romero* as a TV movie but three major networks turned it down as "too depressing, too controversial, and lacking in love interest." Margaret Miles adds that its director commented "'as if ... Romero's love of God wasn't a love interest.'"[13]

The film *The Crime of Father Amaro* gives a similar picture of church authorities aligning themselves with reactionary forces, and of resistance at grassroots level. The problem for makers of films like these is that the political has dramatic potential easily translated into engaging cinema, while the love interest in God is much harder to convey—or sell. As Miles points out of *Romero*, it is in the first instance an "adventure" film,[14] as is *The Crime of Father Amaro*, much sweetened in this case by a human love interest. Indeed, Padre Amaro's "crime" is to fall in love with a young woman. Liberation Theology is not just a South American phenomenon however, but an idea that travels and adapts. We saw when looking at *Priest* earlier that Greg, the priest in question, has a superior who adheres to it. Greg himself is involved in the most direct way possible with the poor of his parish, an outcome, not in the first instance of Marx but of St. Paul.

In *Entertaining Angels: The Dorothy Day Story*, a biopic of the founder of the Catholic Worker press and soup kitchens, the setting is Depression-era New York. Like Romero, Day is a candidate for beatification on account of her work with the poor. However, as the film shows, all did not go smoothly with the Catholic hierarchy: at one point she was asked to remove the word "Catholic" from her organization, and her refusal alienated clerical leaders. *Entertaining Angels* suffers from the problems of all biopics however: trying to cram a whole life story into a short period. It is also a costume drama in the way that *Kundun* somehow avoids being, perhaps because 1930s New York is already a filmic stereotype. Hence, despite much gritty detail of poverty and the difficulties of looking after people who have fallen to the lowest social stratas, the film has a glossy feel that makes Day herself rather remote. But she, and the film, will always be remembered for her stinging rebuke to the American mainstream: "If you feed the poor, you're called a saint, but if you ask why they're poor, you're called a Communist." For that alone the film is worth seeing.

Religious politics is not always about poverty. In the film *Amen.* (note that the full stop is part of the title) the criticism is of the Roman Catholic Church's perceived acquiescence to the Nazis in World War II. The film dramatizes the course taken by the Christian Nazi Kurt Gerstein, who becomes head of "Technical Disinfection Services" in the SS, and witnessed the mass killing of Jews through this agency. Appalled by what he saw, he attempted to report it through various, obviously problematic, channels. Within the Catholic hierarchy he finds no outrage or sympathetic ear, until finally a young Jesuit priest Riccardo Fontana takes up the cause. The common theme with the other films here is that of church hierarchies aligning themselves with temporal power. One of the best comments on it in film is one we encountered in *The Mission* when the cardinal—after destroying the hopes of the indigenous peoples for freedom from slavery—is comforted with the sentiment "the world is thus." His response was, "No, thus have we made the world." In an interview with Costa-Gavras, the director of *Amen.*, he denies that the film, and others such as *The Magdalene Sisters*, and *The Crime of Father Amaro*, are "Catholic bashing." His very pertinent point is that the Catholic Church is unique because "it is the only one organized as a state, with a centralized power."[15] It is the church as state that is being criticized here, not religion itself.

Arnold Toynbee said that Marx "created the fourth Judaic religion."[16] The idea that Marxism actually is a religion is held by a number of contemporary thinkers, including the British novelist Philip Pullman and public intellectual John Gray. A good rebuke to such thinkers is by British philosopher A. C. Grayling, who points out in his review of Gray's *Black Mass*: "This empties the word 'religion' of any meaning, making it a neutral portmanteau expression like 'view' or 'outlook.'"[17] Hence, it is better instead to understand Marxism as an all-pervasive worldview which merely has an analogy with religion in how it is held and dictates responses to ideas and events. The films just examined juxtapose Marxism and religion in varied ways, but cannot really convey how deep Marxist assumptions run in those who acquire it as a form of intellectual culture. Once a Catholic, always a Catholic, they say, and one never really abandons belief in God or communion. Once a Marxist, always a Marxist, is also true, and one never really abandons belief in "history" or planning—or, perhaps, the idea that religion is poison.

While neither Scorsese nor Schrader—who put Kazantzakis's *The Last Temptation of Christ* onto celluloid—were Marxists, Kazantzakis was, and this intellectual climate shines through in the film. One could say that an "ism" is a doctrine which, if adhered to, frames one's outlook on everything. In this sense it is fair to claim that Kazantzakis adhered to Marxism, even if he was more inspired by Lenin, and definitely repulsed by Stalin. His book is Marxist because it frames the life of Jesus in terms of the specific kind of revolutionary politics found in the Marxist tradition, even if the divergence between Marx, Trotsky, Lenin and Stalin—to give some examples—are considerable. In Scorsese's film, with its screenplay by Schrader, the Marxist subtext of the story is retained, even if the screenwriters were more interested in the Freudian angle.

With these introductory remarks, we can now explore the proposition that, if Pasolini's is perhaps the greatest Jesus film, then Scorsese's is perhaps the most deranged—Mel Gibson's *The Passion of the Christ* notwithstanding. In fact, there are some similarities between *The Last Temptation of Christ* and *The Passion of the Christ*, oddly, because Scorsese's derives from extensive secular interpolations, while Gibson's derives from devoutly religious exaggeration. The extremity of their positions in both cases makes them works that fail Tarkovsky's test: they fall for what he calls "political inspiration," a polemic laid too thick on the "sensuous texture" of a film.

The suggestion here is that Scorsese's film is deranged because it is the product of the pressure-cooker Christian tradition inverted through secular revisionings, due equally to Marx and Freud. Most of this derives from Kazantzakis's 1951 novel, which so enraged the Catholic Church that it placed the book on its Index of Forbidden Books, not long before the practice was finally abandoned. But added to this are the preoccupations of Scorsese as director and Schrader as screenwriter, and so *Last Temptation* becomes an important crossroads of discovery when it comes to film and religion. As we have seen, Scorsese is high on the list of directors cited as "spiritual," as is Schrader, both as director in his own right and because of his seminal book *Transcendental Style*. To fling "deranged" at Kazantzakis, Scorsese and Schrader needs some justification then.

Firstly, it is clear that *Last Temptation* is a deeply serious work, attempting something similar to *Jesus of Montreal*, but pushing far harder at the issues. Its premise is that Jesus is part of the "resistance" to Roman occupation, a completely baseless assumption if one goes on the Gospels and what scant historical material is available. In the film his position is further compromised by the voices in his head which drive him to pursue a quite bizarre tactic to silence them: the making of crosses for the Romans, and the assistance in crucifixions of other "messiahs." To complete a picture which has no foundation whatsoever in the New Testament, Judas is the principled and passionate objector to Jesus as collaborator, almost beating him up, smashing up a cross just made and shouting at him: "The Romans can't find anyone to make crosses except you. You are worse than them!" But why does Jesus make crosses for the Romans, when he is part of the "resistance?" He reveals this to us after one of his nightmares: "God loves me. I know he loves me. I want him to stop. I can't take the pain. I want him to hate me. I make crosses so he will hate me. I want to crucify every one of his messiahs."

So far, so Ingmar Bergman. Whether one accepts the Gospels as literal truth, or as documents selected and modified by committees intent on building a church to suit the Roman

Empire—and even if one includes the non-canonical Gospels discovered at Nag Hammadi—then *Last Temptation* is so far an independent fiction. In the *Gospel of Judas*, discovered in 1970 in Egypt, there is a source for the idea, now widespread, that Judas was required by Jesus to betray him, in order to fulfill prophecy. This idea appears later in the film, but it still gives no ground for the opening of *Last Temptation*. However, the idea of Jesus as a political revolutionary is probably at least a hundred years old, and emerged quite naturally as secular minds attempted to re-write the Jesus story according to the strictures of Marxism. Likewise, Freud's legacy has also been written into Jesus interpretations for nearly as long: D. H. Lawrence wrote a short story called "The Escaped Cock" in 1929 in which Jesus, surviving the crucifixion, realizes how wonderful bodily life is, has sex with an island priestess, and gives up messianic duties with relief. Naturally, *Last Temptation* stands in the line of such imaginings, and has Jesus, after his outburst about the making of crosses, visit a brothel, where he queues patiently with the other clients. In fact, he only wants a chat with Mary Magdalene, who says she hates both him and God: "You're pitiful. ... You never had the courage to be a man. If you weren't hanging onto your mother, you were hanging on to me." Jesus, it seems, is a failure both politically and sexually.

But none of this makes the film so far completely deranged. A secular account of Jesus is plausibly constructed of three elements: a Marxist requirement that he be a political revolutionary, a Freudian requirement that he is sexually repressed, and a psychiatric diagnosis that he is a paranoid schizophrenic who hears voices. Instead of the luminous figure of Pasolini's *Gospel of Matthew*, whose contradictory utterances are at every stage magnificently authoritative—whatever interpretation one makes of them—Scorsese's Jesus therefore becomes a whimpering coward, weak-willed and just like any one of us, or perhaps just another Travis Bickle, the anti-hero of *Taxi Driver*. Jesus in *Last Temptation* is played by Willem Dafoe, a fine actor often associated with Scorsese and Schrader, and he is convincing in the next scene when he tells us: "I'm a liar. A hypocrite. I am afraid of everything. I don't steal, I don't fight, I don't kill, not because I don't want to, but because I am afraid. You look inside me and you only find fear." It is convincing as an account of *homo freudiensis*, the inauthentic man of twentieth century western civilization.

Judas, on the other hand, is the epitome of the fearless freedom fighter, killing Romans when he can, and sent to kill Jesus at the start of the film because he is so useless. Instead of killing him he decides to give him a chance, but warns him, holding his fingers a short distance apart, "If you stray this much from the path, I'll kill you." The path of course is Marxist revolutionary struggle. So far, so plausibly secular. "The Escaped Cock" and *Jesus of Montreal* do similar work and leave it at that. What makes *Last Temptation* so extreme, and ultimately deranged, is when the starkness of this secular construction of Jesus then encounters the equally stark and unmistakably supernatural messianic role into which he grows. "Magical realism" is a dubious ploy in literature and cinema if used in films this serious: it belongs to heart-warming romances like *Amelie* or quasi-political escapism like *Pan's Labyrinth*. In fact, the part of *Last Temptation* where the characters around Jesus begin to wonder if he really is "the One" is reminiscent of similar scenes in *The Matrix* where Neo—an anagram of "One"—is likewise touted for messiah-hood. This would just be Western narcissism, but *Last Temptation* has now veered into the supernatural, and the suspension of disbelief about God.

When Jesus then starts to preach, Dafoe's American enthusiasm, contrasted with the equally American disillusion that plays so wonderfully over his features—and to good effect in so many other films—becomes laughably earnest, and horribly reminiscent of Brian in the Monty Python film. It is no surprise then that David Jasper concluded that most Jesus films were "subverted by the far more serious comedy" of *The Life of Brian*, as we saw earlier. Wonderfully deranged, too, in *Last Temptation* is David Bowie as Pontius Pilate. An ex–British-public-schoolboy, coke-addled aesthete is a bizarre choice for Pilate, and his script is equally unsupported in scripture: "You're more dangerous than the Zealots." This inverts what Pilate so famously found in Jesus: nothing worth crucifying, no threat to the Roman state at all—as *The Life of Brian* correctly had it. Finally, on the cross, more magical realism. It is just a dream, but an angel-child leads him away to have sex with all the female characters: Mary and Martha, and, as in Lawrence's version, to enjoy the ordinary life of the family. He even gets to contradict St. Paul, who, taken aback at first in meeting the actual Jesus, then declares he is glad because he can get on with creating Christianity without any worries that it relates to the actual Christ. But his abandoned disciples catch up with him, and finally so does Judas, who is really angry now. All of this is just a dream, however, and the film ends with him on the cross, "ashamed of the wrong way he looked for God."

Scorsese himself tells us that Pasolini had made the Jesus film he had always wanted to make, but when he read the Kazantzakis novel "with its magnificent language and its restlessly probing spirit—that tone, at once so frank and tender—I felt I'd found another way of approaching Christ."[18] Scorsese tells us that he feels he has not only honored Kazantzakis's book, but that he had also faithfully interpreted Christ. It was not an attack on faith: "As if belief and faith were that flimsy. As if the image of Christ could not withstand interpretation." But Scorsese misses the point: all readings of Christ are interpretations, but there are religious interpretations—of admittedly bewildering variety—and secular interpretations. If the secular categories of Freud and Marx are brought to bear on Christ—as Scorsese and Kazantzakis set out to do—then the result is inevitably an attack on faith, because that is what Freud and Marx explicitly pursued. It is not that faith is flimsy, but that the doctrines of Freud and Marx have *replaced* it in the modern mind. The result is bizarre, like interpreting football through knitting or architecture through science fiction. The pure despair of Bergman gains American Marxist testosterone, abyss-free nihilism, pop–Freudianism and inappropriate magical realism. Hence, it has hard to find a better term for this mishmash than "deranged."

Is *Last Temptation* important to the interdiscipline of religion and film? Yes, not just because Scorsese and Schrader are important to it, but because the film—whether we regard it as deranged or perhaps simply a film of its time—usefully represents almost the whole spectrum of secular assumptions about religion. Perhaps we might remind Schrader of his own words, used to criticize the maker of costume dramas of Christ: "He has not lifted the viewer to Christ's level, he has brought Christ down to the viewer." This is *exactly* what the film does. Christ has been brought down to a level lower even that of Travis Bickle, because Christ can't even kill Romans: he hasn't the courage.

We are now in a position, after the critiques earlier of *Taxi Driver* and *Mishima*, to finally answer the proposition put by David John Graham at the start of this book: that Schrader arguably "later became the leading exponent of what he describes" in his book on transcendental style. The answer appears to be no, he has not. His book, with deep understanding and sympathy for mystical traditions, and a well-honed argument on how Zen in particular can underpin a "transcendental style," simply never translates into film. The secular forces acting on him are too powerful.

Religion and Sexual Politics

One of the most intense encounters between the religious and secular worlds is over sexuality, homosexuality and lesbianism. Generally speaking, in the Western context, it is plain as day to most secularists that religion is centuries behind in its sexual politics, and for many this is sufficient reason to reject the entirety of spirituality and religion. It is no surprise to find a good number of films dealing with these issues.

There is much evidence that in the Mediterranean prior to warrior invasions from the North there existed goddess cultures in which women held high social status and in which religion was shaped more by women than men.[19] Pasolini's *Medea* gives us a glimpse of such a goddess culture, but only at the point of its overthrow. The film is a loose adaptation of Euripides's play, and stars Maria Callas, the opera singer, in the lead role. One might say that the play portrays the transition from an earlier nature-religion to a more complex religion whose pantheon of deities better met the needs of the city-state at war and the needs of warrior males. In making Medea the central character, rather than Jason, Euripides's play is also considered to be perhaps the first feminist work in Western history. What Pasolini brings to this is quite extraordinary: from one perspective, a clumsy, low-budget production with many first-time actors or, from another perspective, a luminous vision of an ancient world and its shifting religious sensibilities.

The film opens with the centaur guardian of the infant Jason, telling him that all of Nature is sacred, and that when Nature becomes "natural" all will be finished, "and something else will begin. Farewell sky, farewell sea." Pasolini has started the story much earlier than Euripides, and we begin to see what he intends with it: he is setting the scene for Medea's exile from, not just her own country, but her own way of religion. The centaur is telling the boy that every way he looks there is a god hidden in the water, the sky, the trees, and in the animals. "Yes," he concludes, "all is sacred, but holiness is also a curse. The gods that love can also hate." This might almost be the essence of polytheism: a pluralist, animist world, rooted in a shamanic past, but with spirits that are not so much ontologically "real" as rapidly becoming psychic forces, abstractions of the forces of nature.

Pasolini clearly draws on Sir James Frazer and other anthropologists of the early-to-mid twentieth century in the construction of the first part of the film. The centaur tells Jason that the seed planted by primitive man was seen by him as undergoing a resurrection, an account that is close to Frazer's interpretation. We now cut to the world of Medea, which is preparing for a human sacrifice to make the crops grow. Medea looks at the victim, a young man, hung by his hands, and awaiting his gruesome fate. After he is hacked to death, portions of his blood are collected by the villagers, in order to sprinkle on the fields. Medea officiates over the burnt remains, and chants: "Give life to the seed and be reborn with the seed." Dancers with huge rabbit masks participate in the festivities, a reminder of the shamanic roots of this religion, and reminiscent of scenes in *The Wicker Man*. Later, Medea is garbed for her prayers by her female attendants, and a fire lit, to the accompaniment of ethnic music that included cymbals, conches and deep trumpets. She enters and rolls around in the shallow fire, and screams as she becomes the medium for oracular powers. Thus purified she worships at the base of the sacred golden ram—whose fleece Jason is on the way to steal. But it is not his power as a warrior that overwhelms her, but his beauty: symbolic perhaps of how women surrendered their power to men in that crucial historical transition.

The key moment in the film follows the theft of the fleece and her flight with Jason (the success of which is ensured only by her killing her brother): the arrival at her new home, that of "civilized" Greek culture, and far away from her "barbarian" birthplace. The men disembark and build camp, but Medea stares at them from the Argo in growing bewilderment. At last she bursts out:

> This place will sink, because it has no foundation! You do not call god's blessings on your tents. You speak not to god. You do not seek the centre; you do not mark the centre. No! Look for a tree, a post, a stone!

Her grief is like Ishi's. But the men just look at her amused, and she runs distraught into the fields, crying aloud:

> Speak to me Earth, let me hear your voice, I have forgotten your voice. Speak to me Sun. Where must I stand to hear your voice? Speak to me Earth. Speak to me Sun. Are you losing your way, never to return again? Grass, speak to me. Stone, speak to me. Earth, where is your meaning? Where can I find you again?

This scene, for which there is no source in Euripides's play, is extraordinary: Pasolini has somehow intuited the essence of what the goddess religion entails in the very moment of its overthrowing. Also remarkable is the similarity to Ishi's anguish: he, too, said words to the effect: "Earth, where is your meaning?" It is the mirror-image of Christine's rapturous return to Nature in *Anchoress* after she frees herself from the church. Medea has lost all contact with the earth, not because she is losing her touch, but because she is plunged into a new world, constructed by the masculine temperament, and in which the deities are cut lose from their moorings: from now on they are psychological, not animistic. She gains one small consolation, however: in the new land, her gifts as a "barbarian" oracle and healer mean fame and respect. At least this is what Jason tells her after he betrays her. Her revenge on him and her killing of her children as part of that are well-known, but Pasolini makes another interesting interpolation in the story when the old centaur appears again to Jason. This is in a vision where there are now two centaurs, the old one representing the old world, and the new one representing the new; one sacred and one desecrated. The new centaur, the one of the man, not the child, engages him in this discussion about the old centaur:

> CENTAUR: Despite all your schemes and interpretations, his influence causes you to love Medea.
> JASON: Love Medea?
> CENTAUR: Yes. Also you pity her. You understand her spiritual catastrophe. A woman of an ancient world, confused in a world which ignores her beliefs. She experienced the opposite of a conversion and has never recovered.
> JASON: What use is this knowledge to me?
> CENTAUR: None. It is a reality.

Pasolini has summed it up in the simple phrase: Medea's *spiritual catastrophe*, the "opposite of a conversion." And Jason's response is to ask what use this knowledge is to him. At that time it was no use, one might say, but, at the beginning of the twenty-first century, this knowledge is perhaps again important, or even vital. The sexual politics of the late twentieth century was often a politics of liberation *from* religion. But for women who pursue both liberation and a spiritual life there may be difficulties: Where do they turn? Medea gives one possibility: to turn back to goddess cultures and try and reconstruct a modern religion out of the little data that exists, as modern "witches" such as Starhawk (spiritual activist Miriam Simos) have attempted.[20] The film *Anchoress* is a film of nature spirituality, despite its protagonist being located in a Christian world. It can be seen as documenting the completion of what was begun in *Medea*: the *spiritual* subjugation of women. In reality, Christine Carpenter has had to wait for Starhawk and other modern religious feminists for her liberation.

Returning to Tarkovsky's *Andrei Rublev*, it is clear that the bulk of the film deals with Christian issues. However, it has a most interesting interlude—dated as 1408—where Rublev encounters a pagan group in the woods, who tie him up in order to prevent him alerting the authorities to their celebrations. As in *The Wicker Man*, the assumption is that paganism involves unlicensed sexuality, and women in prominent ritual roles. More important here is the specific nature of the male rejection of women's spirituality. Rublev has heard something by the river, and quickly realizes that the people bearing torches are practicing "witchcraft." Tarkovsky enhances the strangeness of the scene with church music played backward. Just like the Calvinist policeman Howie in *The Wicker Man*, Rublev enters the night to discover naked couples running off together, his Christian sensibilities outraged. His capture comes just as he witnesses a young woman repeatedly jumping over a small fire, reminiscent of a similar scene in *The Wicker Man*. "I saw you, black vermin, lurking there," his male captor tells him, as offended by Rublev's obvious priesthood as Rublev is by their "witchcraft." He is tied up for the night to prevent him interfering with their sacred rites, but a woman takes pity on him and engages him in talk. She wants to know why he has threatened them with Judgment Day, understanding it as a curse of fire. "Because it is a sin to run around naked and do things like that," he replies. "This is the night when everyone should love," is her response. "Is loving a sin?" She tells him that he is tied up so as to prevent him alerting the authorities: "You want to convert us by force. Do you think it is easy living in fear like us?" But Rublev doesn't consider their cavorting naked in the woods as love. He tells her: "You fear because you either don't love at all, or you love shamelessly, bestially, not with the heart."

Rublev is about to make the crucial distinction that, for him, sets Christianity above "paganism"—the idea that love should be brotherly. This is a reference to the early Christian idea of *agape*, a love that is wholly religious and expresses itself between those who have taken vows of retreat from the world, as we have seen earlier. But she simply says that it is all love, and kisses him. She unties him, and the camera follows his gaze towards the revelers and lingers on a crucial part of their rituals: the launching of a corn dolly in a crude boat. It has a single lit candle placed centrally in the sheaf of wheat stalks, and naked men and women standing in the water guide its course down the river. As Rublev retreats in confusion, his face scratched by a branch in the woods, the young woman who released him gazes after him. Tarkovsky's camera draws into her face and lingers there, as if to say: this beauty represents a form of religion you cannot understand. The following morning Rublev passes couples lying together, with small corn wreaths and other symbols of their Nature religion hanging over them from the eves of barns; fires are dying out. The cock crows—symbolically—and Rublev walks back, sobered, to his group of fellow-travelers. As they ask him where he had been, we see the crude little boat with nothing more than a wisp of smoke emerging from it, as it floats past their camp. As he talks, the little boat bumps into their craft, and we see the burned out corn dolly. A little later, the revelers of the night before are chased out of the woods by the authorities, hunted down like animals. A woman escapes by swimming naked across the river: she is in her element.

The details of the corn dolly sacrifice could have come from Frazer, as could the corn dolly scene in *Anchoress*, but what is valuable here is the simple juxtaposition between a religion invented by men for men—the Greek version of Christianity—and an older religion where, at the very least, men and woman were equal.

Turning now to *Whale Rider*, we saw in the chapter on the martial arts as spiritual practice that the young Maori girl in the film, Pai, fights for an equal role in a man's world. Pai is a modern girl growing up within a Western technological lifestyle, and absorbs a key lesson: that women are equal to men. She has a claim to be the new chief by descent, though this has never gone to a woman before. Her claim is not just as temporal leader, but as spiritual leader. After much struggle and setback in which her grandfather is torn between his love for her and his adherence to patriarchal tradition she wins through two portents: firstly her heroic riding of the whale, and secondly her discovery of a whale tooth. The dances she learns in school are sacred dances, and although her culture might have elevated the masculine elements of warfare, she now brings something of the spiritually feminine to the tradition.

If Medea and Ayesha represent the fearsome side of the goddess stereotype, and Pai represents a woman capable of mastering the fighting arts, then it is interesting to consider the inversion of such status—women as the ultimately vulnerable. This is because vulnerability is an essential element of the spiritual life, and its opposite is *armored*. The armored self is defended against all hurt, but this move also denies any sense of connectedness, let alone the profound connectedness that is at the heart of the spiritual life, and in which suffering cannot be shut out. Women represent a certain kind of vulnerability in which love is manifest, and is of permanent fascination to men, particularly when men are inculcated in the cultural norms of patriarchal aggressive masculinity.

As mentioned before, Lars von Trier has written and directed a number of harrowing films featuring women abused and degraded in a largely male environment, including *Breaking the Waves, Dancer in the Dark, Dogville* and *Antichrist*. Perhaps no other director has so relentlessly pursued this theme, excavating some of the darkest emotions in gender conflict. The degradation of the women in each film takes a different course. In *Breaking the Waves*, a vulnerable young woman is made a religious outcaste for her love of a man who becomes sexually crippled and forces her into paid sex as some kind of proxy for their lost love life. She has to die in the end. In *Dancer in the Dark*, the singer Bjork plays a vulnerable woman forced into a murder. She, too, dies in the end. In *Dogville*, Grace (Nicole Kidman) ultimately recovers the all-conquering power of a Medea or Ayesha, and annihilates the community that humiliated her: hell hath no cold fury as the woman scorned. But in *Antichrist*, the idea is driven full cycle: the female protagonist has become evil, beyond the reach of masculine rationality, a conclusion that she has herself reached in her dissertation studies on witchcraft. What is going on with von Trier in this sequence, one may ask? Has he confronted the issue of female vulnerability again and again, only to give up in the end, shake his head and just posit that women are intrinsically evil? Whatever one makes of it, there are spiritual implications in this sequence, particularly in *Breaking the Waves*. This is the most cited of von Trier's films of vulnerable women in the religious context. Iena Makaurshka opens her analysis of the film with this point: "It is tempting, as many critics have done, to read the character of Bess (Emily Watson) in *Breaking the Waves*, a film written and directed by Lars von Trier, as yet one more Christ-figure, Mary Magdalene, or Joan of Arc."[21] But why should we take this film as religiously or spiritually significant in the first place? Makarushka's concerns are mostly feminist, though she says "it differs from that of some feminist critics who have argued that von Trier, like the sadistic, misogynist deity with whom Bess speaks, creates a failed religious fable of woman as sacrificial victim."[22] Bess is vulnerable to God in the film and vulnerable to her husband, and to the male authority figures in her life. Towards the end of the film, Bess responds to the priest who seems to follow only the Word and the Law—illustrating the Old Testament–Jewish leanings of Protestantism—by saying, "You can't love the Word. You can only love a person." When questioned about this Lars von Trier explained:

> The priest talks about loving the Word and the Law. That was the only thing you had to obey. That's what would make a person complete. But Bess twists the concepts and says that the only thing that can make a person complete is loving another person. This is really the formulation of the film's moral.[23]

If this is the film's moral, then it is a secular one: the essence of a devotional religion, in contrast, is that the love of God is what makes a person complete, though earthly loves, seen as an adumbration of that divine love, are not a contradiction of it. Interestingly, in the same interview, von Trier says that he became a Catholic in order to have a sense of belonging to a community, and because his parents were committed atheists.

The spiritual feminists' dilemma is here: to love is to be vulnerable twice over: in the first instance to the male, whose agenda is foreign, indifferent and ultimately lethal, and in the second instance to God, as conceived and interpreted through the agenda of men. Yet for von Trier it seems that the fascination with female vulnerability is unresolvable, as *Antichrist* shows: he seems to give up on the equation of "love equals vulnerability." The woman in *Antichrist*, despite all male sensitivity and kindness, represents only death, and so "love equals death" is the ultimate equation that he wants to draw.

In addition to the cycle of films just described von Trier also made a TV version of *Medea* in 1998, which again explores the theme of the wronged woman. Von Trier pursued an aesthetic within it rather similar to that in *Anchoress*, though as it was shot on video, it on the one hand loses definition but on the other gave him the opportunity to experiment with blue-screen style compositing to good effect. He drew on a version of the Euripides play scripted by fellow Dane Carl Theodore Dreyer, and there is even a legend that von Trier was in telepathic contact with Dreyer during the making of the film. But von Trier's version lacks the insight that Pasolini brought to the story of Medea: that she was a woman who had suffered a *spiritual* catastrophe. Instead, the film becomes estranged both from the spiritual dimension, and from the Greek setting. Where Pasolini used the pitiless sun of a Greek summer, von Trier uses the endless rain of Danish marshlands and pine forest; where Paso lini casts a passionate Greek woman (though American-born) in the lead role, von Trier casts a dour Danish actress Kirsten Olesen; where Pasolini retains Medea's mythical supernaturalism, von Trier has her carry out her revenge by a poisoning compatible with secular science.

Where von Trier does help us conceive of Medea as more than a woman dumped by her husband is in the videography: the continued recourse to natural elements of water, grasses, dunes and sky work, as in *Anchoress*, to suggest that "woman" is primordial, and perhaps, linked to the sacred. The final scene, where Medea shakes out her hair onboard the vessel that sails her into exile, intercut with Jason's frenzy of grief, uses a high shot of him rolling around in windswept long grasses: he is enmeshed in the elemental forces of her revenge. But there is nothing *explicit* about Medea as a functionary of the goddess religion, which Pasolini so intuitively and forcefully put to screen.

Cinema presents other heartbreakingly vulnerable women, of course: for example, Gelsomina in *La Strada* and Viridiana in Buñuel's film of the same name. Bazin, in writing on *La*

Strada, is concerned with questions of social realism and concludes that Gelsomina's breakdown is the key part of the film: "The stupid, obstinate, and brutish Zampanò can't realize how much he needs Gelsomina, and above all he can't sense the eminently spiritual nature of the bond between them. ... Thus one can look at *La Strada* as a phenomenology of the soul, perhaps even of the communion of saints, and at the very least as a phenomenology of the reciprocal nature of salvation."[24]

We have looked at Godard's *Hail Mary* from the perspective of aesthetics, but it makes also makes an interesting comparison with von Trier's cycle. Both directors are men exploring the mystery of women through their chosen art, and often verging on the religious or mystical in doing so. Where *Hail Mary* differs from the von Trier films is that Mary's vulnerability contains within it an infinite strength: Joseph at no time attempts to break down her virginity. In *Kadosh*, however, the women are all broken against the wheel of implacable monotheistic tradition, and in Dreyer's harrowing *Day of Wrath* an old woman is tortured and burned at the stake, in the wake of which a young woman's strength and innocence eventually fails to prevent her capitulating to the same fate: she even comes to believe in her own evil. Derek Malcolm comments:

> Dreyer's measured pace and stark visuals—long horizontal pans and close-ups of riven faces—accompanied as they are by acting of intense realism, makes this a morality play of enormous power. And the scenes of torture and burning, though discretely handled, are almost unbearable, at least partly because the torturers and burners are not mere hysterics but stolidly convinced they have divine justice on their side.[25]

The problem for all ancient faith traditions, and especially so for monotheisms with their reliance on textual sources, is: how do you update it? In his book on Jewish mysticism, Gershom Scholem demonstrates the extent to which Judaism has changed over the centuries.[26] But, while all faiths change, the pace of change demanded by the encounter with progressive humanism creates massive contradictions, particularly for Judaism as it has one of the oldest textual scriptures in the world.

Where the *legitimate* sexual yearnings of a young woman in *Day of Wrath* led her to be burned for witchcraft—for how else could she have won the attentions of the pastor's son?—what happens when sexual leanings are deemed "illegitimate?" What happens to lesbians and gays under old religion? We saw that in *Kadosh* the women suffer mutely, but in *Trembling Before G-d* the gay men and lesbian women fight their tradition. In *Eyes Wide Open*, a rabbi has an affair with a young man, new to an Orthodox Jerusalem community, but in the end the homosexual interloper is cast out as having brought "evil" to the rabbi. In *Priest*, Father Greg faces prosecution after he is arrested for public indecency in a car, but returns to his church at the request of his superior. However, when they jointly distribute the Eucharist, the congregation shuns Greg, and he finally only receives a kind of absolution from the female parishioner who was herself subject to sexual abuse and who found no support from the church.

If men and women have differences of approach to religion—as Luce Iragaray is confident of[27]—then what about gays and lesbians? While there is a substantial history of religious friendship either misperceived as homosexuality, or perhaps drifting into it, there are no films that present accounts of, for example, Whitman's life, or that of Socrates, Rumi or Ramakrishna, which would explore the relationship between male teacher and male disciple, where a love exists that perhaps crosses the line into the carnal. Instead, we have a handful of films that deal with the problems faced by gay people who are adherents of faith traditions that implicitly or explicitly condemn non-heterosexual relationships. These films are about religious communities that struggle to accept their gay or lesbian congregants, and the crises of faith that this provokes in them.

In *Latter Days*, four Mormons move in next door to gay party-boy Christian Markelli in Los Angeles. Mormon Elder Aaron Davis, to the horror of his three brethren, turns out to be a closet gay and becomes involved with Christian. The director and writer of the film, C. Jay Cox, based both characters on himself at different stages in his life. The film's opening is not promising: it seems to stereotype gays and play to sensation-seekers. However, as the film develops and settles into its serious themes, the opening seems a legitimate gambit, both in its place in an artistic whole, and as a ploy to draw in an audience that might not initially want to grapple with the issues. So, how *do* you deal with these two powerful forces in your life: religion and homosexuality? The film treats both as legitimate, real, and integral to personality. Aaron is devout, expresses his faith in good works and ministry, and represses his homosexuality. Christian is a hedonist with no thought for religion, characterized thus by Aaron after their first intimacy: "You're so pretty and colorful on the outside but on the inside you're nothing but fluff ... a walking, talking marshmallow human: there's nothing about you that's not skin deep." Christian is stung by this, and the two young men make journeys towards each other. The film is not merely an American production making a calculated nod to religion's wide social standing in America: it has moments of real religious insight, both in passing and central to its story. For example, early on Aaron encounters Christian's restaurant-owner boss, in tears after hearing of the death of a dear friend of hers. He is a complete stranger to her, but in the enactment of his calling, he pushes gently past her initial rejection of his offer of comfort. He starts talking about cartoons and how he was amazed as a kid that when he put his face right up to them they were just a mass of dots: "I think life is like that sometimes, but I like to think that from God's perspective life, everything, even this, makes sense: it's not just dots, we're all connected, and it is beautiful." She smiles through her tears. Someone has reached out to her, and she is bigger for accepting his offering.

Christian loses Aaron for a while as the young Mormon is sent home in disgrace and enrolled in a gay deprogramming course. But in the denouement Christian catches up with him and speaks eloquently of their love, painting a compelling image of it as profound as the trumpets of angels. Together again, Aaron asks Christian in bed, "What God do you believe in?" Christian replies, "It's not just God. It's everything." Along the way we also learn of how Christian was abandoned in the snow to die by a father who could not accept his homosexuality, and how a mountain ranger saved his life with his bodily warmth. The religious life everywhere, it seems, is about the interaction of strangers whose "family" is everyone.

In *Saved*, Mary is a student at an American Christian school, where uniforms, moral conformity, and a devotion to Jesus are the norm. When her boyfriend tells her he might be gay, she is alarmed and later has a vision of Jesus, from which she understands that it is her mission to "cure" him of his homosexuality by having sex with him and converting him to the conventional path of heterosexuality. It doesn't work, so he is sent off to a program for degayification—as Aaron was in the previous film—and she falls pregnant. While not directly about homosexuality, what the film achieves is what Christianity everywhere needs to make haste for: an updating of its stance on gender and sexuality issues without losing its first principles. After all, if sexual misconduct were so dreadful, why did Jesus make a point of not condemning the adulteress in the Gospel of John? If homosexuality was an issue that he thought was important, why did he never mention it? He does say that sexual immorality among other things makes a man unclean (Mark 7:20–23), but in *Saved*, it is clear that the only sexual immorality present in the film is the wrong-headed attempt to de-gayify a gay man.

Secular Cynicism

We saw in films like *Agnes of God*, *Black Narcissus*, *The Nun's Story*, *Elmer Gantry*, *Witness*, *Jesus of Montreal* and *The Quarrel* debates across the secular-spiritual divide that gave about equal weight to arguments on both sides. This is good filmmaking, whatever one's stance, because both sides are informed and speaking in good faith. But there is a way of being informed about the spiritual life that is in bad faith: its aim in exploring the subject is only to disparage, mock or titillate. Films that research religion in order to titillate—and we have included *The Da Vinci Code* and *The Ninth Gate* as examples—are only escapism. But those that mock or disparage in earnest are more interesting as they may hide within them some real insights into the spiritual life, if only by negating the truths of them. Cynicism may at least have some intelligence behind it.

In *Enduring Love*, the protagonist is a middle-class British male, Joe Rose, who has to endure religion and a very working-class enthusiasm wrapped up in the same antagonist, Jed Parry. Based on the novel by Ian McEwan, it pursues a more intense anti-religious polemic than *Saturday*, one of his best-known works. *Enduring Love* is a satire on devotional religious love. As a bulwark to middle-class British atheism the device might not invite much attention, but to those versed in the devotional mystics the satire is disturbingly accurate in places. Jed "falls in love" with Joe after a ballooning accident, and stalks him. Joe is a science journalist, whose career has taken a few unexpected twists, but is a middle-class professional, whereas Joe, an English-language teacher who now lives on his inheritance feels working-class even if only for his religious evangelism and his rural accent. Ostensibly *Enduring Love* is about a man suffering obsessive love for another man, under the compulsion of a neurotic disorder called de Clérambault's Syndrome. But McEwan has added a dimension that was not required by the overall story arc: this love is religious.

Jed is a delusional obsessive stalker of his quarry, reading confirmation of Joe's love in each alternating exasperated rejection and attempt to reason with him. But a deranged homosexual stalker would be enough to cause a rift in Joe's heterosexual relationship, given that the other main plot element revolves around a ballooning accident which had resulted in the death of an onlooker, who, like Joe, had intervened to save a boy's life. The rift between Joe and his girlfriend Clarissa is potentially like that in the film *Fearless*, where the protagonist survives a plane-crash, an experience his wife has no way of identifying with.

Isn't the provocation to Joe's settled love life and professional career from the twin disruptions of being drawn into a fatal accident and the delusional world of a sex stalker enough? As Joe has to draw on the resources of his middle-class rationality to cope with these, so perhaps McEwan wanted to further heighten its triumph by the even starker contrast with evangelical religion. What gets confused in the process is whether Jed wants to convert Joe or become his lover. What can be made out of it however is an analogy between the derangement which finds love in another man "in the teeth of evidence" and the alleged derangement of those who find love in God, whose existence is again clung to "in the teeth of evidence"—according to atheists, that is.

It is an interesting journey from *Razor's Edge* to *Enduring Love*, both films based on novels by leading British authors of their age. Somerset Maugham read the mystics and imagined a protagonist who lived their teachings as benign truth. Ian McEwan read the mystics—or at least has mastered the language in which they speak—and imagined an antagonist who lived their teachings as pathological delusion. What we learn from *Enduring Love* is that religious devotional love is now truly a love that dare not speak its name. Maugham and Russell belonged to an older world where such things, although perhaps equally foreign to their temperaments, held respect. McEwan belongs more to the world of Sartre where cynicism towards mysticism and religious love is universally sanctioned.

Holy Smoke, discussed in the previous chapter, does usefully raise the question of *charisma* in the religious context. It is a personality trait found in many fields and commands attention, loyalty, fascination and devotion in others. All the gurus and preachers in the films of Chapter 7 have this quality. For our purposes, *Holy Smoke* fails to make a direct engagement with questions of religion, though it presents an inventive plot device which is promising for such an exploration. As we saw, a young Australian woman called Ruth finds a guru in India, takes initiation and burns her return air ticket. Her family contrives a plot to bring her home, and then effectively confine her with a religious de-programmer P. J. Waters. The argument that develops between them could have become a dialogue across the secular-spiritual divide, but instead the dialogue becomes a gender power play, which is the real theme of the film: a feminist critique of male power whether wielded for religion or against. But the male power, whether that of the guru or the anti-guru, is seen as charisma, born out of deep convictions. The charisma is quintessentially masculine.

In a film that is strange even by Pasolini's standards, *Theorem* becomes an exploration of the impact of a charismatic stranger on a single family. Terence Stamp plays the nameless visitor who wreaks havoc on a bourgeois family by exposing their hidden desires, perhaps sexual, perhaps spiritual. Made in 1968, *Theorem* can be seen as part of the extraordinary cultural upheavals of that year, which included student revolts and the assassination of Martin Luther King. It is also stylistically bound up with the Surrealist and Theatre of the Absurd traditions, though the strange ending where the maid floats up into the heavens is more magical realism than anything else. While its atmosphere is religiously haunting at times, it suffers from the same problem as *Holy Smoke*: the exploration of charisma as a plot device serves both religious and non-religious purposes, in this case socialism rather than feminism. Hence, what could be religious questions are rather drowned in the clamor of other, more fashionable discourses.

The purpose of the charismatic stranger in exposing bourgeois weakness is also the theme of Polanski's 1966 *Cul-de-sac*. Here it is a criminal who arrives at the castle home of a trendy couple on the tidal island of Lindisfarne (Holy Island) off the coast of Northumberland, England. There is no religious element in the film, but the psychology of charisma is well-explored as an entirely negative force. In *Holy Smoke* and *Theorem*, charisma could have been a way in to explore the genuine spiritual problem of how and why one person affects another religiously, but the more secular concerns of power—perhaps in a Foucauldian sense—prevail. Religion is treated with skepticism. The real contrast is with the curé in *Diary of a Country Priest*: he had no charisma at all, but reached out with some unstoppable force to the countess.

We conclude this section by returning to the film that most cheerfully, brilliantly, and memorably embodies secular cynicism towards religion, *Monty Python's Life of Brian*, and will compare it with a film that raised just as much adverse reaction from conservative religion,

Dogma. The former is quintessentially British comic genius, while the latter is typically crass American vulgarity—or so it would seem. In reality, *The Life of Brian* as a satire of religion is utterly disengaged. It is the end-product of a cultural process begun in Marx and Freud, whose skepticism towards religious was total, and whose demonstration of it as an illusion had become the cultural climate of the Monty Python generation. It had become a culturally received but unexamined orthodoxy. What the *Life of Brian* does so brilliantly is create a series of comic images to cement it in the popular mind. *Dogma*, on the other hand, while irredeemably scatological, constructively engages with a number of essential ideas in monotheism, including the issue of Old Testament violence, idolatry and the gender of God.

The Life of Brian is useful in that, as in *Jesus of Montreal*, we are provided with a picture of how the secular mind might imagine Jesus. In this case Brian becomes a religious teacher by accident, when he imitates one of the countless deranged prophets in Jerusalem in an attempt to hide his identity from the Romans. An adoring crowd soon gathers when he stops mouthing meaningless platitudes and implores him to impart the teachings he is keeping back from them. His protests that he is not the messiah are merely met with the conviction that only the messiah would deny his divine status. The portrait of a religious leader here is in the end not particularly cynical; instead the cynicism is directed at the ignorant and sycophantic crowd that constructs such leaders.

By contrast, *Dogma* is very American and very knowing about the Western religious tradition. Where the latter film is perfect in its own terms, but religiously uninteresting, *Dogma* is a huge missed opportunity. There is intelligence in the portrayal of two fallen angels as prone to Old Testament violence of the kind that needs questioning in the Western tradition. There is intelligence in the portrayal of the grotesque violence they mete out to the "idolaters" who, as the boardroom executives of a media company trading under "Mooby, the Golden Calf," deserve a hideous death ... according to the Old Testament. The satire here is probably more instructive about idolatry than the rather solemn attempt to explore the issue in *My Father My Lord*, as we saw earlier. *Dogma* further shows intelligence in the satirizing of the cult of the Jesus bloodline, when the female protagonist, Bethany Sloane, learns of her status from the "Metatron," and, although made much before the film of the *Da Vinci Code*, the latter could easily be the target of *Dogma*'s satire.

Finally, the choice of the popular singer Alanis Morissette to play God is pure genius. In the culminating scene, God is released from a clever contemporary trap just in time to save the day as the angels run amok, and, although we are already told that God is a woman, Morissette's appearance is remarkable. She is potentially all that the goddess religion would make a deity to be, yet is stern, righteous, and terrifying. She both embodies Otto's *mysterium tremendum et fascinans* while having the caring qualities of a mother. And finally, when Her natural order is restored, She performs handstands in the flowerbeds. If the rest of the film was not so irredeemably crass, this would have been a truly luminous moment.

While both films appear equally cynical to start with we can say that *Dogma* represents an informed secular engagement with religion, whereas *Brian* represents an uninformed secular disengagement. Robert K. Johnston makes these comments on *Dogma*:

> When Kevin Smith's irreverent yet God-affirming movie opened at the New York Film Festival in October 1999, it did so over the objections of Cardinal John O'Connor and Mayor Rudolf Guiliani. That the movie exuberantly affirms the existence of God and tells the story of a woman's recovery of faith, or that Smith is a practicing Catholic, was thought irrelevant.... Here is a movie that is not agnostic or un–Christian in its viewpoint, even if it is sacrilegious and sexy in its design. After

all, as Smith commented, if he were to talk about God to his generation, he wouldn't make *The Song of Bernadette* (1943).[28]

Dogma is God-affirming because it is *engaged*. As Smith says, one can't make *The Song of Bernadette* for this generation, or for that matter *The Diary of a Country Priest* or *The Gospel According to Matthew*. However, *Dogma* is insufficient to withstand the cynical onslaught of films like *The Life of Brian* and *Enduring Love*. Instead, we need more films as creatively intelligent about religion as *Dogma*, more Morissettes cartwheeling in flowerbeds, and less toilet humor.

Summary

Unexpectedly, the story of filmmaking across the secular-spiritual divide often turns out to be religiously interesting. For Satyajit Ray and many other Eastern filmmakers, there could be no dialogue between a religious feudal past and a modern secular democracy—the urgency was in social reform, quite probably hindered by all vestiges of traditional religion. For the West, despite its invention of secular atheism, its relative material and democratic advances mean that older questions return to the table—questions of the spirit. In the films in this section we have many examples of secular cynicism which are actually rather well

informed about religion, but, more interestingly, many dialogues across the divide which are a real meeting of minds.

Whether it is in *The Song of Bernadette* of 1943, *Elmer Gantry* of 1960, *My Night with Maud* of 1969, or *Agnes of God* and *Witness* of 1985, the encounter across the spiritual-secular divide is often even-handed: we are not required to take on a belief system or a belief in the supernatural, but to consider spiritual community as a reality. We also found that the seemingly unbridgeable Marxist-religious divide—which had such a devastating impact on the spiritual life of Tibet, never mind China itself—is bridged in Liberation Theology and similar conjunctions of Catholicism and social action: the films *Romero* and *Entertaining Angels: The Dorothy Day Story* being two exemplars of this. Sexual politics, on the other hand, fares less well in film: the negative legacy of patriarchal religion still hinders women's spirituality, and almost all old religions have failed to adapt to gay rights. Filmmakers, often angry about this, are also angry for their protagonists—real or fictional—who are denied the church or religious grouping they love on the grounds of sexual discrimination. *Latter Days* is a good example of this. Secular filmmaking provides vivid polemics against the dead weight of tradition, for example *Dogma*, though its crassness will for many obliterate its genuine critique of Old Testament violence and its genuine revisioning of God as a popular female singer doing handstands in a flower bed.

Conclusions: A Luminous Cinema of the Spirit

Nearly four hundred films have been discussed in the preceding chapters, investigating their relevance to the spiritual or religious life. The themes chosen for those chapters have given a broad coverage, throwing up many interesting surprises along the way. In the chapter summaries, attention has been drawn to the best of these films—those that have something luminous about them. Pulling these together yields a list of around sixty outstanding films, which comprise nothing less than the "must-see" films of the spiritual life, a canon of religion and film. These are found in the Appendix, along with short descriptions.

It is tempting, as sixty is rather a large number of films, to then select a "top ten" from them or similar small number of films and declare these to be all-time greats, a canon of religion and film that could comfortably be watched in a week or two. However, the problem is that it would leave out so many important films. No reduced set of films covers enough ground to adequately portray the spiritual life in the round. Instead, it is better to declare that the spiritual life on film is a matter of gathering up a host of smaller clues, rather than a single great revelation. The sixty films selected for the Appendix should therefore be seen as *collectively* illustrating many, perhaps most, of the important features of the spiritual life.

But what do the final sixty films have in common that would suggest a method of filmmaking particularly fruitful for the spiritual life? Is it to do with genres, directors, writers, or actors, or all of these? To take genres first, some were eliminated from the start, including the costume drama and the saintly biopic, as suggested by serious thinkers on religion and film such as Bazin. In addition, no preference was made across the populist/art-house division, though escapist fantasy was rejected on the grounds that any serious attempt to live the spiritual life begins where escapism ends. This decision above all else has perhaps given these sixty films a rather serious quality to them, but they are by no means all art-house films, and we have discovered along the way that "highbrow" is anyway no guarantee at all of a luminous film, even if the theme is a religious one. This brings us to the question of directors and screen-writers, who between them are mostly responsible for the nature of a filmic production, even granting the recent insistence of the "auteur" theory that film production hides important contributions from the whole production team. Because this is such a key question, we have looked carefully at stellar directors and screenwriters such as Ingmar Bergman, Stanley Kubrick, Akira Kurosawa, Hayao Miyazaki, Pier Paolo Pasolini, Paul Schrader, Martin Scorsese, Satyajit Ray, Andrei Tarkovsky and Peter Weir. Mostly we found that they were no more likely to produce a luminous film or moment than a complete unknown, though the relatively less well-known director may not match them in originality, production standards, cinematography—or for that matter, budget. Among these auteur directors, we have discovered that Ingmar Bergman, Paul Schrader, Martin Scorsese and Satyajit Ray, despite various pointers to the spiritual, leave us oeuvres that are mostly "dull" in our terminology. And it turns out that where a director does make a luminous film, with the spiritual life central to its theme, the next film may have nothing to offer.

This is an interesting discovery, but perhaps only to be predicted: there appears to be no necessary path from art to the sacred. Scorsese's *Kundun* is a must-see film for the spiritual life, while his *Last Temptation* is only of interest as an illustration of period secular preoccupations, and his *Taxi Driver* a highly dubious celebration of the vigilante killer. Bresson's *Diary of a Country Priest* contains perhaps the most luminous illustration of the Christian idea of grace to date, but lives within an oeuvre that is autistic, or at the very least emotionally cold. Pasolini's *The Gospel According to St. Matthew* stands far above his other films. *Thunder heart* happens to usefully convey many elements of the Native American religious sensibility within an action drama format, but Michael Apted has made nothing else—apart perhaps from the companion documentary *Incident at Oglala*—with similar content. Wim Wenders made the marvelous *Wings of Desire*, but the sequel, *Faraway, So Close!*, which pursues the same theme, is dire. Jim Jarmusch thoroughly researched Native American culture for *Dead Man*, but did this have a lasting impact on his filmmaking? Not really—despite hints of it in *Ghost Dog: The Way of the Samurai*—and why should it, for the artist in Jarmusch, as in most filmmakers, is drawn to a variety of themes.

This is an observation made many years ago by Colin Wilson in his book *The Outsider*, when he pointed out that novelists such as Sartre and Hemingway were not permanently concerned with the problem of the "Outsider"—which for Wilson is a spiritual problem. He says, "The measure of their unconcern lies in the fact that they passed on to other subjects."[1] Yes, this is the job of the artist, whether painter, novelist, or director: to be *artists*, not specialists in the spiritual life. What attracts a director to a spiritual theme is a text: a novel, play or existing screenplay—or in Pasolini's case a gospel—in which they see dramatic potential. Of course, some directors are also religious, and may attempt a film that proselytizes their religion or spiritual beliefs. Mostly these don't work, though Bertolucci's *The Little Buddha* might be an exception. However, it seems that the best films for the spiritual life are made by directors who are usually completely fresh to the spiritual content and who then move on to other subjects. But what makes their religious films a success? Did Pasolini and Bresson really know what they were doing? Any more than the curé knew what he was doing? Yes, of course, in an artistic sense, but perhaps not in a religious sense. In both cases these two secularist directors drew on an existing text which they could never have imagined into being, but then, that was not their role here (though many of the great films cited in this book were indeed written by the director). Somehow, perhaps only by chance, they apply the methods of filmmaking to a text that is then illuminated by the process: an actor, a scene, a luminous quality of light, a judicial choice of music. What results is *more* than the text: it is a luminous cinema.

One fares little better trying to find a group of actors whose presence might guarantee a film of spiritual significance, though what we do find here is that a certain type of face can help convey certain kinds of spiritual orientations or sensibilities. There are of course interesting stories concerning actors and the spiritual life: for example, Linus Roache, who acted in two films discussed here, *Priest* and *Pandaemonium*, met the American spiritual teacher Andrew Cohen in 1994, joined his organization, and now serves on the Advisory Board for Cohen's center in New York. Shirley MacLaine, who acted in *Being There*, wrote an intensely personal and somewhat controversial account of her spiritual journey, including beliefs in reincarnation and aliens.[2] As mentioned earlier, Steven Seagal, the American film star, has been recognized by as a reincarnated tulku. Also mentioned was Sean Penn's appearance as an actor in some interesting films and his interesting directorial debut, *Into the Wild*. But the presence of any of these actors in a film is simply no guide as to their spiritual content, less even than with directors.

Of course, sometimes actors are typecast, and so we have suggested that Robin Williams often becomes the face of Christian compassion, while Takashi Shimura becomes the face of Buddhist compassion in a number of Kurosawa films. Native American actors such as Chief Dan George become the face of Native American spirituality while David Gulpilil becomes the face of Australian aboriginal spirituality. Maksim Munzuk as Dersu Uzula conveys the Siberian animist sensibility. When Graham Greene as Ishi in *The Last of His Tribe* breaks down as he remembers the loss of his people and their connection with the land, it is hauntingly memorable because Greene is a Native American. The presence of these actors has contributed to some outstandingly luminous scenes on film.

The mixed ethnicity of this group of actors gives us a clue as to the special role of film in the religious or spiritual life: while it might convey and make deeper our understanding of a religious path we already know, it also gives us an extraordinary glimpse into the spiritual lives of those apparently remote from us. What mere book could capture for the outsider the beauty of Judaism as seen through some of the films here? What mere book could illuminate for the outsider Christian grace, Buddhist meditation, or the spirituality of indigenous peoples? What mere book could pursue moral issues so vividly as in *Groundhog Day*, *The Son*, or *Bad Lieutenant*? None of us are outsiders to those problems, even if they are intensified in these dramas beyond the everyday. Through the special qualities of film—that is a dramatic medium expressed through moving light—and in the faces, movements and gestures of gifted actors, we are taken into the very depth of spiritual experience in its total variety. Although the medium itself—the directors, writers, actors and cinematographers— passes on to other subjects, when it does linger on spiritual-religious themes we can say for its contribution to the spiritual life: film is a quite astonishing medium.

Filmography

About Schmidt. Directed by Alexander Payne. 2002.
Afterlife. Directed by Hirokazu Kore-eda. 1998.
Agnes of God. Directed by Norman Jewison. 1985.
Agora. Directed by Alejandro Amenábar. 2009.
Akira Kurosawa's Dreams. Directed by Akira Kurosawa. 1990.
Altered States. Directed by Ken Russell. 1980.
Amélie. Directed by Jean-Pierre Jeunet. 2001.
Amen. Directed by Costa-Gavras. 2002.
American Beauty. Directed by Sam Mendes. 2000.
An American Werewolf in London. Directed by John Landis. 1981.
Anchoress. Directed by Chris Newby. 1993.
Andrei Rublev. Directed by Andrei Tarkovsky. 1969.
Angel Heart. Directed by Alan Parker. 1987.
Antichrist. Directed by Lars von Trier. 2009
Aparajito. Directed by Satyajit Ray. 1956
The Apostle. Directed by Robert Duvall. 1997.
Artificial Intelligence: AI. Directed by Steven Spielberg. 2001.
Asoka. Directed by Santosh Sivan. 2001.
At Play in the Fields of the Lord. Directed by Hector Babenco. 1991.
Atanarjuat: The Fast Runner. Directed by Zacharias Kunuk. 2001.
Atonement. Directed by Joe Wright. 2007.
Audrey Rose. Directed by Robert Wise. 1977.
Awakenings. Directed by Penny Marshall. 1990.
Babette's Feast. Directed by Gabriel Axel. 1987.
Bad Lieutenant. Directed by Abel Ferrara. 1992.
Baraka. Directed by Ron Fricke. 1992.
Battlefield Earth. Directed by Roger Christian. 2000.
A Beautiful Mind. Directed by Ron Howard. 2001.
Becket. Directed by Peter Glenville. 1964.
Bee Season. Directed by Scott McGehee, David Siegel. 2005.
Being There. Directed by Hal Ashby. 1979.
The Believers. Directed by John Schlesinger. 1987.
Birth. Directed by Jonathan Glazer. 2004.
Black Narcissus. Directed by Michael Powell and Emeric Pressburger. 1947.
Black Robe. Directed by Bruce Beresford. 1991.
Blair Witch Project. Directed by Daniel Myrick and Eduardo Sánchez. 1999.
Blithe Spirit. Directed by David Lean. 1945.
Blue Velvet. Directed by David Lynch. 1986.
The Body. Directed by Jonas McCord. 2001.
Breaking the Waves. Directed by Lars von Trier. 1996.
The Bridge on the River Kwai. Directed by David Lean. 1957.
Buddha Collapsed Out of Shame. Directed by Hana Makhmalbaf. 2007.
Carrie. Directed by Brian De Palma. 1976.
The Cave of the Yellow Dog. Directed by Byambasuren Davaa. 2005.
Chances Are. Directed by Emile Ardolino. 1989.
Chocolat. Directed by Lasse Hallström. 2000.
The Chosen. Directed by Jeremy Kagan. 1981.
City of Angels. Directed by Brad Silberling. 1998.
City of God. Directed by Fernando Meirelles. 2002.
Close Encounters of the Third Kind. Directed by Steven Spielberg. 1997.
Contact. Directed by Robert Zemeckis. 1997.
Conversations with God. Directed by Stephen Deutsch. 2006.
The Cook, the Thief, His Wife, and Her Lover. Directed by Peter Greenaway. 1989.
Cries and Whispers. Directed by Ingmar Bergman. 1972.
The Crime of Father Amaro. Directed by Carlos Carrera. 2002.
Crimes and Misdemeanors. Directed by Woody Allen. 1989.
Crouching Tiger, Hidden Dragon. Directed by Ang Lee. 2001.
The Crucible. Directed by Nicholas Hytner. 1996.

Cul-de-Sac. Directed by Roman Polanski. 1966.
The Cup. Directed by Khyentse Norbu. 1999.
Dancer in the Dark. Directed by Lars von Trier. 2000.
Dances with Wolves. Directed by Kevin Costner. 1990.
Dark City. Directed by Alex Proyas. 1998.
The Dark Crystal. Directed by Jim Henson. 1982.
The Da Vinci Code. Directed by Ron Howard. 2006.
Day of Wrath. Directed by Carl Theodor Dreyer. 1943.
Dead Again. Directed by Kenneth Branagh. 1991.
Dead Man. Directed by Jim Jarmusch. 1995.
Dead Man Walking. Directed by Tim Robbins. 1995.
Dead Poet's Society. Directed by Peter Weir. 1989.
Dean Spanley. Directed by Toa Fraser. 2008.
Dersu Uzula. Directed by Akira Kurosawa. 1975.
Devi (The Goddess). Directed by Satyajit Ray. 1960.
Devil's Advocate. Directed by Taylor Hackford. 1997.
Diary of a Country Priest. Directed by Robert Bresson. 1950.
The Diary of Anne Frank. Directed by George Stevens. 1959.
Dodes' ka-den. Directed by Akira Kurosawa. 1970.
Dogma. Directed by Kevin Smith. 1999.
Dogville. Directed by Lars von Trier. 2004.
Donnie Darko. Directed by Richard Kelly. 2001.
Don't Look Now. Directed by Nicolas Roeg. 1973.
The Doors. Directed by Oliver Stone. 1991.
Doubt. Directed by John Patrick Shanley. 2008.
Drunken Angel. Directed by Akira Kurosawa. 1948.
East Is East. Directed by Damien O'Donnell. 1999.
Education of Little Tree. Directed by Richard Friedenberg. 1997.
Edward Scissorhands. Directed by Tim Burton. 1990.
Elmer Gantry. Directed by Richard Brooks. 1960.
Enakkul Oruvan. Directed by S. P. Muthuraman. 1984.
Encounters at the End of the World. Directed by Werner Herzog. 2007.
End of Days. Directed by Peter Hyams. 1999.
Enduring Love. Directed by Roger Michell. 2004.
The English Patient. Directed by Anthony Minghella. 1996.
The Enigma of Kaspar Hauser. Directed by Werner Herzog. 1974.
Enlightenment Guaranteed. Directed by Doris Dörrie. 2000.
Enter the Dragon. Directed by Robert Clouse. 1973.
Entertaining Angels: The Dorothy Day Story. Directed by Michael Ray Rhodes. 1996.
Excalibur. Directed by John Boorman. 1981.
Exiles. Directed by Tony Gatlif. 2004.
Existenz. Directed by David Cronenberg. 1999.

The Exorcism of Emily Rose. Directed by Scott Derrickson. 2005.
The Exorcist. Directed by William Friedkin. 1973.
Expelled: No Intelligence Allowed. Directed by Nathan Frankowski. 2008.
Eyes Wide Open. Directed by Haim Tabakman. 2009.
Eyes Wide Shut. Directed by Stanley Kubric. 1998.
Faraway, So Close! Directed by Wim Wenders. 1993.
Fearless. Directed by Peter Weir. 1993.
Fiddler on the Roof. Directed by Norman Jewison. 1971.
Fifth Element. Directed by Luc Besson. 1997.
Fight Club. Directed by David Fincher. 1999.
The Fisher King. Directed by Terry Gilliam. 1991.
Fluke. Directed by Carlo Carlei. 1995.
Forrest Gump. Directed by Robert Zemeckis. 1994.
Friendly Persuasion. Directed by William Wyler. 1956.
Gabbeh. Directed by Mohsen Makhmalbaf. 1996.
George Harrison: Living in the Material World. Directed by Martin Scorsese. 2011.
Gerry. Directed by Gus Van Sant. 2002.
Ghost. Directed by Jerry Zucker. 1990.
Ghost Busters. Directed by Ivan Reitman. 1984.
Ghost Dog: The Way of the Samurai. Directed by Jim Jarmusch. 1999.
The Gift. Directed by Sam Raimi. 2000.
The God Who Wasn't There. Directed by Brian Flemming. 2005.
The Godfather. Directed by Francis Ford Coppola. 1972.
Gods and Monsters. Directed by Bill Condon. 1995.
The Golden Compass. Directed by Chris Weitz. 2007.
Good Will Hunting. Directed by Gus Van Sant. 1997.
The Gospel According to St. Matthew. Directed by Pier Paolo Pasolini. 1964.
Grizzly Man. Directed by Werner Herzog. 2005.
Groundhog Day. Directed by Harold Ramis. 1993.
Guge: The Lost Kingdom of Tibet. Directed by David Kerstein. 2008.
The Guru. Directed by Daisy von Scherler Mayer. 2002.
Jaws. Directed by Steven Spielberg. 1975.
Haibane Renmei. Directed by Yoshitoshi Abe. 2002.
Hail Mary. Directed by Jean-Luc Godard. 1985.
Haré Raama Haré Krishna. Directed by Dev Anand. 1971.
Harry Potter and the Chamber of Secrets. Directed by Chris Columbus. 2002.
Harry Potter and the Goblet of Fire. Directed by Mike Newell. 2005.
Harry Potter and the Prisoner of Azkeban. Directed by Alfonso Cuarón. 2004.

Harry Potter and the Sorcerer's Stone. Directed by Chris Columbus. 2001.
Heart and Souls. Directed by Ron Underwood. 1993.
Heaven Can Wait. Directed by Ernst Lubitsch. 1943.
Heaven Can Wait. Directed by Warren Beatty. 1978.
Henry Poole Is Here. Directed by Mark Pellington. 2008.
The Hidden Fortress. Directed by Akira Kurosawa. 1958.
High Plains Drifter. Directed by Clint Eastwood. 1973.
Himalaya (Caravan). Directed by Eric Valli. 1999.
Holy Flying Circus. Directed by Owen Harris. 2011.
Holy Smoke. Directed by Jane Campion. 1999.
The Hours. Directed by Stephen Daldry. 2002.
Hulk. Directed by Ang Lee. 2003.
I Heart Huckabees. Directed by David O. Russell. 2004.
Igby Goes Down. Directed by Burr Steers. 2002.
Ikiru. Directed by Akira Kurosawa. 1952.
Illusion. Directed by Michael A. Goorjian. 2004.
In the Mood for Love. Directed by Won Kar Wai. 2000.
Incident at Oglala. Directed by Michael Apted. 1992.
Indigo. Directed by Stephen Deutsch (Simon). 2003.
Inherit the Wind. Directed by Stanley Kramer. 1960.
Into Great Silence. Directed by Philip Gröning. 2005.
Into the Wild. Directed by Sean Penn. 2007.
Ishi: *The Last Yahi.* Directed by Jed Riffe. 1992.
It's a Wonderful Life. Directed by Frank Capra. 1946.
Jacob's Ladder. Directed by Adrian Lyne. 1990.
Jai Santoshi Maa. Directed by Vijay Sharma. 1975.
Jaws. Directed by Steven Spielberg. 1975.
Jesus of Montreal. Directed by Denys Arcand. 1989.
Jesus of Nazareth. Directed by Franco Zeffirelli. 1977.
Kadosh. Directed by Amos Gitai. 1999.
Kagemusha. Directed by Akira Kurosawa. 1980.
Kandahar. Directed by Mohsen Makhmalbaf. 2001.
Karz. Directed by Subhash Ghai. 1980.
Karzzzz. Directed by Satish Kaushik. 2008.
Kill Bill: Vol. 1. Directed by Quentin Tarantino. 2003.
Kill Bill: Vol. 2. Directed by Quentin Tarantino. 2004.
The Kite Runner. Directed by Marc Forster. 2007.
Koyaanisqatsi. Directed by Godfrey Reggio. 1982.
Kundun. Directed by Martin Scorsese. 1999.
Lagaan. Directed by Ashutosh Gowariker. 2001.
The Last of His Tribe. Directed by Harry Hook. 1992.
The Last Samurai. Directed by Edward Zwick. 2003.
The Last Supper. Directed by Tomás Gutiérrez Alea. 1976.
The Last Temptation of Christ. Directed by Martin Scorsese. 1988.
The Last Wave. Directed by Peter Weir. 1977.
The Late Great Planet Earth. Directed by Robert Amram. 1979.
Latter Days. Directed by C. Jay Cox. 2003.
Lawnmower Man. Directed by Brett Leonard. 1992.
Leap of Faith. Directed by Richard Pearce. 1992.
Left Behind. Directed by Vic Sarin. 2000.
Left Behind II: Tribulation Force. Directed by Bill Corcoran. 2002.
Left Behind III: World at War + interview. Directed by Craig R. Baxley. 2005.
Left Luggage. Directed by Jeroen Krabbé. 1998.
Levity. Directed by Ed Solomon. 2003.
A Life Less Ordinary. Directed by Danny Boyle. 1997.
The Life of Brian. Directed by Terry Jones. 1979.
The Life of the Buddha. Directed by Martin Meissonnier. 2004.
Light Sleeper. Directed by Paul Schrader. 1992.
Little Big Man. Directed by Arthur Penn. 1970.
Little Buddha. Directed by Bernardo Bertolucci. 1993.
Lost Horizon. Directed by Frank Capra. 1937.
The Lost World of Tibet. Directed by Emma Hindley. 2006.
The Love Guru. Directed by Marco Schnabel. 2008.
Love Liza. Directed by Todd Louiso. 2002.
Luther. Directed by Eric Till. 2003.
Maborosi. Directed by Hirokazu Koreeda. 1995.
Madhumati. Directed by Bimal Roy. 1958.
The Magdalene Sisters. Directed by Peter Mullan. 2002.
The Magician. Directed by Ingmar Bergman. 1958.
The Magnificent Seven. Directed by John Sturges. 1960.
Mahabharata. Directed by Peter Brook. 1989.
Mahal. Directed by Kamal Amrohi. 1949.
A Man Called Horse. Directed by Elliot Silverstein. 1970.
A Man Called Peter. Directed by Henry Koster. 1955.
A Man for All Seasons. Directed by Fred Zinnemann. 1966.
Masada. Directed by Boris Sagal. 1981.
The Matrix. Directed by Andy Wachowski and Lana Wachowski. 1999.
Matrix Reloaded. Directed by Andy Wachowski and Lana Wachowski. 2003.
Matrix Revolutions. Directed by Andy Wachowski and Lana Wachowski. 2003.
A Matter of Life and Death. Directed by Michael Powell and Emeric Pressburger. 1946.
Medea. Directed by Pier Paolo Pasolini. 1969.
Medea. Directed by Lars von Trier. 1988.
Meet Joe Black. Directed by Martin Brest. 1998.

Meetings with Remarkable Men. Directed by Peter Brook. 1979.
Megiddo: The Omega Code 2. Directed by Brian Trenchard-Smith. 2001.
Metropolis. Directed by Fritz Lang. 1927.
Michael. Directed by Nora Ephron. 1996.
Microcosmos. Directed by Claude Nuridsany and Marie Pérennou. 2003.
The Milky Way. Directed by Luis Buñuel. 1968.
Million Dollar Baby. Directed by Clint Eastwood. 2004.
The Mirror. Directed by Andrei Tarkovsky. 1975.
Mishima: A Life in Four Chapters. Directed by Paul Schrader. 1985.
The Missing. Directed by Ron Howard. 2003.
The Mission. Directed by Roland Joffé. 1986.
Mr. Ya Miss. Directed by Antara Mali. 2005.
Monsieur Ibrahim. Directed by François Dupeyron. 2003.
Monty Python and the Holy Grail. Directed by Terry Gilliam. 1975.
Mother India. Directed by Mehboob Khan. 1957.
Mulholland Drive. Directed by David Lynch. 2001.
My Father My Lord. Directed by David Volach. 2007.
My Neighbor Totoro. Directed by Hayao Miyazaki. 1988.
My Night with Maud. Directed by Eric Rhomer. 1969.
My Son the Fanatic. Directed by Udayan Prasad. 1997.
The Mystic Masseur. Directed by Ismail Merchant. 2001.
Name of the Rose. Directed by Jean-Jacques Annaud. 1986.
Naqoyqatsi. Directed by Godfrey Reggio. 2002.
Nausicaä of the Valley of the Wind. Directed by Hayao Miyazaki. 1984.
Nazarín. Directed by Luis Buñuel. 1959.
The Ninth Gate. Directed by Roman Polanski. 1999.
Northfork. Directed by Michael Polish. 2003.
Nostalgia. Directed by Andrei Tarkovsky. 1983.
Not Without My Daughter. Directed by Brian Gilbert. 1991.
The Nun's Story. Directed by Fred Zinnemann. 1959.
Of Gods and Men. Directed by Xavier Beauvois. 2010.
Oh God! Directed by Carl Reiner. 1997.
Om Shanti Om. Directed by Farah Khan. 2007.
The Omega Code 1. Directed by Robert Marcarelli. 1999.
The Omega Code 2. See *Megiddo: The Omega Code 2*.
The Omen. Directed by Richard Donner. 1976.
One Flew Over the Cuckoo's Nest. Directed by Milos Forman. 1975.
Once Were Warriors. Directed by Lee Tamahori. 1994.
Open Your Eyes. Directed by Alejandro Amenabar. 1997.
Ordet. Directed by Dreyer. 1955.
Orphée. Directed by Jean Cocteau. 1950.
Osama. Directed by Siddiq Barmak. 2003.
The Others. Directed by Alejandro Amenábar. 2001.
The Outlaw Josey Wales. Directed by Clint Eastwood. 1976.
Paap. Directed by Pooja Bhatt. 2003.
Pale Rider. Directed by Clint Eastwood. 1985.
Pandaemonium. Directed by Julien Temple. 2000.
Pan's Labyrinth. Directed by Guillermo del Toro. 2006.
Paradise Now. Directed by Hany Abu-Assad. 2005.
The Party. Directed by Blake Edwards. 1968.
A Passage to India. Directed by David Lean. 1984.
The Passion of the Christ. Directed by Mel Gibson. 2004.
Patch Adams. Directed by Tom Shadyac. 1998.
Pather Panchali. Directed by Satyajit Ray. 1955.
The Pawnbroker. Directed by Sidney Lumet. 1964.
Persepolis. Directed by Vincent Paronnaud and Marjane Satrapi. 2007.
Phenomenon. Directed by Jon Turteltaub. 1996.
Pi. Directed by Darren Aronofsky. 1998.
The Piano. Directed by Jane Campion. 1993.
Picnic at Hanging Rock. Directed by Peter Weir. 1975.
The Pillow Book. Directed by Peter Greenaway. 1996.
Pleasantville. Directed by Gary Ross. 1998.
Pocahontas. Directed by Mike Gabriel and Eric Goldberg. 1995.
Pokémon: The First Movie. Directed by Kunihiko Yuyama and Michael Haigney. 1998.
Poltergeist. Directed by Tobe Hooper. 1982.
Poltergeist II: The Other Side. Directed by Brian Gibson. 1986.
Powaqqatsi. Directed by Godfrey Reggio. 1988.
Powder. Directed by Victor Salva. 1995.
A Price Above Rubies. Directed by Boaz Yakin. 1998.
Priest. Directed by Antonia Bird. 1994.
Princess Mononoke. Directed by Hayao Miyazaki. 1997.
Prospero's Books. Directed by Peter Greenaway. 1991.
Pulp Fiction. Directed by Quentin Tarantino. 1994.
The Quarrel. Directed by Eli Cohen. 1991.
Rabbit-Proof Fence. Directed by Phillip Noyce. 2002.
Rain Man. Directed by Barry Levinson. 1988.
The Rapture. Directed by Michael Tolkin. 1991.
Rashomon. Directed by Akira Kurosawa. 1950.
The Razor's Edge. Directed by Edmund Goulding. 1946.

The Razor's Edge. Directed by John Byrum. 1984.
Reincarnation. Directed by Takashi Shimizu. 2005.
The Reincarnation of Peter Proud. Directed by J. Lee Thompson. 1975.
La Religieuse. Directed by Jacques Rivette. 1966.
Revelations (disk 1 and 2). Directed by David Seltzer. 2005.
Romero. Directed by John Duigan. 1989.
The Sacrifice. Directed by Andrei Tarkovsky. 1986.
Saints and Soldiers. Directed by Ryan Little. 2003.
Le Samouraï. Directed by Jean-Pierre Melville. 1967.
Saved. Directed by Brian Dannelly. 2004.
Schindler's List. Directed by Steven Spielberg. 1993.
The Sea Inside. Directed by Alejandro Amenábar. 2004.
Sebastiane. Directed by Paul Humfress and Derek Jarman. 1976.
The Secret of Roan Inish. Directed by John Sayles. 1994.
Seven. Directed by David Fincher. 1995.
Seven Samurai. Directed by Akira Kurosawa. 1954.
Seven Years in Tibet. Directed by Jean-Jacques Annaud. 1997.
Seventh Seal. Directed by Ingmar Bergman. 1957.
Shadowlands. Directed by Richard Attenborough. 1993.
Shane. Directed by George Stevens. 1953.
She. Directed by Robert Day. 1965.
Siesta. Directed by Mary Lambert. 1987.
Signs. Directed by M. Knight Shyamalan. 2002.
The Silence. Directed by Ingmar Bergman. 1963.
Silence of the Lambs. Directed by Jonathan Demme. 1991.
Silent Light (Stellet licht). Directed by Carlos Reygadas. 2007.
The Sixth Sense. Directed by M. Knight Shyamalan. 1999.
Snow Cake. Directed by Marc Evans. 2006.
Solaris. Directed by Andrei Tarkovsky. 1972.
Somewhere in Time. Directed by Jeannot Szwarc. 1980.
The Son. Directed by Jean-Pierre Dardenne and Luc Dardenne. 2002.
The Song of Bernadette. Directed by Henry King. 1943.
Spirit, Stallion of the Cimarron. Directed by Kelly Asbury. 2002.
Spirited Away. Directed by Hayao Miyazaki. 2001.
Spring, Summer, Autumn, Winter ... and Spring. Directed by Kim Ki-duk. 2003.
Stalker. Directed by Andrei Tarkovsky. 1979.
Star Wars. Directed by George Lucas.
The Story of the Weeping Camel. Directed by Byambasuren Davaa and Luigi Falorni. 2003.

La Strada. Directed by Federico Fellini. 1954.
The Straight Story. Directed by David Lynch. 1999.
The Stranger. Directed by Satyajit Ray. 1991.
A Stranger Among Us. Directed by Sidney Lumet. 1992.
Switch. Directed by Blake Edwards. 1991.
Tarnation. Directed by Jonathan Caouette. 2003.
A Taste of Cherry. Directed by Abbas Kiarostami. 1997.
Taxi Driver. Directed by Martin Scorsese. 1976.
The Terminator. Directed by James Cameron. 1984.
The Terrorist. Directed by Santosh Sivan. 1999.
Theorem. Directed by Pier Paolo Pasolini. 1968.
They Shoot Horses, Don't They? Directed by Sydney Pollack. 1969.
The Thin Red Line. Directed by Terrence Malick. 1998.
Thirteenth Floor. Directed by Josef Rusnak. 1999.
Three Colors: Blue. Directed by Krzysztof Kieslowski. 1993.
Through a Glass Darkly. Directed by Ingmar Bergman. 1961.
Thunderheart. Directed by Michael Apted. 1992.
Tibet: Cry of the Snow Lion. Directed by Tom Piozet. 2002.
Tibetan Book of the Dead. Directed by Barrie McLean. 2005.
Time of Favor. Directed by Joseph Cedar. 2000.
To End All Wars. Directed by David L. Cunningham. 2001.
Touch. Directed by Paul Schrader. 1997.
A Touch of Zen. Directed by King Hu. 1969.
Touching the Void. Directed by Kevin Macdonald. 2004.
Travelers and Magicians. Directed by Khyentse Norbu. 2003.
The Tree of Life. Directed by Terrence Malick. 2011.
Trembling Before G-d. Directed by Sandi Simcha Dubowski. 2001.
The Trial of Joan of Arc. Directed by Robert Bresson. 1962.
True Confessions. Directed by Ulu Grosbard. 1981.
Truly Madly Deeply. Directed by Anthony Minghella. 1991.
The Truman Show. Directed by Peter Weir. 1998.
21 Grams. Directed by Alejandro González Iñárritu. 2003.
2001: A Space Odyssey. Directed by Stanley Kubrick. 1968.
Unbreakable. Directed by M. Night Shyamalan. 2000.
Unforgiven. Directed by Clint Eastwood. 1992.
Ushpizin. Directed by Giddi Dar. 2004.
Vajra Sky Over Tibet. Directed by John Bush. 2006.
Vanilla Sky. Directed by Cameron Crowe. 2001.

Vertigo. Directed by Alfred Hitchcock. 1958.
Virgin Spring. Directed by Ingmar Bergman. 1960.
Viridiana. Directed by Luis Buñuel. 1961.
Waking Life. Directed by Richard Linklater. 2001.
Walkabout. Directed by Nicolas Roeg. 1971.
Waltz with Bashir. Directed by Ari Folman. 2008.
The Warrior. Directed by Asif Kapadia. 2001.
Westworld. Directed by Michael Crichton. 1973.
Whale Rider. Directed by Niki Caro. 2002.
What Dreams May Come. Directed by Vincent Ward. 1988.
What the Bleep Do We Know? Directed by William Arntz. 2004.
Where the Green Ants Dream. Directed by Werner Herzog. 1984.
Why Did Bodhidharma Leave for the East? Directed by Yong-Kyun Bae. 1989.
The Wicker Man. Directed by Robin Hardy. 1973.
Wide Awake. Directed by M. Night Shyamalan. 1998.
Wings of Desire. Directed by Wim Wenders. 1987.
Winter Light. Directed by Ingmar Bergman. 1962.
Wise Blood. Directed by John Huston. 1979.
Witness. Directed by Peter Weir. 1985.
World of Apu. Directed by Satyajit Ray. 1960.
Yeelen. Directed by Souleymane Cissé. 1987.
Yuga Purusha. Directed by Rajendra Babu. 1989.
Zabriskie Point. Directed by Michelangelo Antonioni. 1970.
Zelig. Directed by Woody Allen. 1983.

Appendix: Sixty Must-See Films for the Spiritual Life

1 *Agnes of God.* Norman Jewison, 1985.
A materialist-minded lawyer is hired to defend a young nun accused of killing her baby, but is soon confronted with a religiosity she cannot so easily dismiss. In her encounter with the determined Mother Superior the chain-smoking lawyer pits science and Freud against religion, but is deeply affected by the young nun's piety and the older nun's wisdom.

2 *American Beauty.* Sam Mendes, 2000.
A satire on affluent suburban America, in which a man's midlife crisis provokes not a nihilism but a rhapsodical appreciation of the beauty of ordinary life.

3 *Anchoress.* Chris Newby, 1993.
Stunning black and white cinematography conveys something of Nature and "goddess" spiritualities, though its setting is medieval Christianity. It follows the spiritual vocation of a young woman who firstly becomes an anchoress but then realizes that her true spirituality is with the religions of the earth.

4 *The Apostle.* Robert Duvall, 1997.
A Southern preacher in an American church is on the run after violence. As a journey of atonement "The Apostle" rebuilds an old church and inspires his congregation to follow in the footsteps of Jesus and St. Paul.

5 *Bad Lieutenant.* Abel Ferrara, 1992.
A corrupt officer is confronted with a nun whose forgiveness of her rapists jolts him out of his comfortable assumptions. A shocking drama that shows how layers of habitual corruption can be suddenly peeled back to discover integrity and the ability to act decisively for good.

6 *Baraka.* Ron Fricke, 1992.
Richly beautiful nature film with a debt to Reggio's *Qatsi* trilogy, but taken several steps further in its direct references to the spiritual life, and the contrasts with industrialized society.

7 *Cave of the Yellow Dog.* Byambasuren Davaa, 2005.
Gentle portrayal of the life of nomadic herdsmen in Mongolia, the film is shot in stunning landscape. A girl wants a dog as pet but the ramifications for the family are considerable. Will it reincarnate as a human, she asks? In subtle ways the shamanic–Buddhist background to their culture is portrayed.

8 *The Chosen.* Jeremy Kagan, 1981.
Two young Jews from different backgrounds grapple with their faith, modernity and the founding of Israel in a New York drama that provides some vivid insights into the essence of Judaism.

9 *Dead Man Walking.* Tim Robbins, 1995.
A docu-drama following the efforts of Sister Helen Prejean to save a man on death row. The killer is not easily likable and Prejean's New Testament conviction that State killings are wrong makes her few friends among the prison service or the victims' families. Yet her perseverance suggests that her Christianity is truer than that serving the needs of retribution.

10 *Dersu Uzula.* Akira Kurosawa, 1975.
Follows the life of a Siberian animist hunter who finds all things in Nature to be alive. Shot in scenes of outstanding natural beauty, it prompts reflections on an ancient form of spirituality.

11 *The Diary of a Country Priest.* Robert Bresson, 1950.

A young French priest takes up a post in a village that has no time for him, his religion, and his ill health, but against all odds he brings God's grace to a bitter old woman. As he declines further in health and struggles with his own doubts he realizes that everything is indeed grace. Extraordinary.

12 *Dogma.* Kevin Smith, 1999.

Bouts of toilet humor in this film should not disguise serious religious intent, in a story of angels punished for their Old Testament violence. Redeemed by a rendition of God as a woman capable of both dishing out ultimate justice and cartwheeling in the flower beds.

13 *Donnie Darko.* Richard Kelly, 2001.

Surreal meditation on the transition from life to death for a teenager who cannot conform, informed by a giant rabbit who insists that the world is about to end. It's not every day that a jet engine lands in your bedroom.

14 *Drunken Angel.* Akira Kurosawa, 1948.

A classic meditation on compassion, in which a doctor—who is no saint—attempts to treat a gangster with little gratitude or any other saving grace. A study in how lives are bound together by unexpected acts.

15 *Elmer Gantry.* Richard Brooks, 1960.

A showman who is not quite a charlatan turns to the religious life out of love for a lady preacher. Successful at first, he is brought low in the end, but not before his calling begins to convince. Includes thoughtful dialogue across the religious-secular divide.

16 *Enlightenment Guaranteed.* Doris Dörrie, 2000.

A wonderful story of two German brothers who set out for a Zen retreat in Japan. Their journey is beset by mishaps, and their encounter with enlightenment unconventional in a study of "beginner's mind."

17 *The Fisher King.* Terry Gilliam, 1991.

Surreal atonement and redemption story concerning a selfish radio DJ confronted with the man driven to vagrancy after losing his wife. Two men make journeys home under the benign shadow of the Red Knight and the Fisher King story.

18 *Friendly Persuasion.* William Wyler, 1956.

Costume drama story of American Civil War Quakers with a serious ending. The film becomes a fine study in the ethics of pacifism and the realities confronting its adherents.

19 *The Gospel According to St. Matthew.* Pier Paolo Pasolini, 1964.

The universally recognized "must-see" Jesus film. Beautifully shot in black and white with non-professional actors, superb music. Altogether an utterly unconventional approach that leaves the gospel to speak for itself.

20 *Groundhog Day.* Harold Ramis, 1993.

This is a story of the moral development of a caddish weather forecaster plunged into the nightmare of a repeated day. In a world that he no longer controls the only constant is the lovely Rita, who cannot understand his circumstances but rejects his repeated advances. Gradually all that changes ...

21 *Haibane Renmei.* Yoshitoshi Abe, 2002.

Gentle and beautiful TV anime series on the theme of purgatory and redemption. Young people arrive in a midway world in strange cocoons. Some are penitent in their nature, others less so, but all await "the day of flight."

22 *Hail Mary.* Jean-Luc Godard, 1985.

A beautifully filmed meditation on women's spirituality and the mysteries of conception by a reputed atheist. Set in a world of French basketball and petrol stations it retells the virgin birth story without either skepticism or theological correctness.

23 *Himalaya.* Eric Valli, 1999.

A glimpse into the animist-shamanic culture of Nepal in a story of rival leaders of the annual salt-caravan. One leans to the new ways of the West, influenced by changes blowing up from far away, while the other holds to tradition.

24 *Ikiru.* Akira Kurosawa, 1952.

A minor bureaucrat fights the system to create a small children's park in postwar Japan. He is dying and this is his gift to life.

25 *Into Great Silence.* Philip Gröning, 2005.

A poetic documentary about life in a Carthusian monastery in France. It follows the lives of the monks in their reclusive order, creating with its stunning cinematography of mountain and cloister the very silence that the initiates are seeking.

26 *Jacob's Ladder.* Adrian Lyne, 1990.

A film that defines the "rubber reality" genre. What, if anything, is real in Jacob's life, and why does his chiropractor quote Eckhart at him? This is a demanding but very rewarding journey through the "bardo" of dying.

27 *Jai Santoshi Maa*. Vijay Sharma, 1975.
A rare glimpse into Hindu goddess devotionality in a low-budget production that was a seventies hit in India. A young woman's path to betrothal despite the jealousies of her sisters-in-law is guided by her devotion to the goddess.

28 *Kundun*. Martin Scorsese, 1999.
Masterful portrait of the life of the Dalai Lama with many glimpses into the spiritual life of Tibet prior to the Chinese invasion. From his discovery as the reincarnated former lama to the moment of exile, the spiritual leader of Tibet is shown grappling with the contradictions of an ancient religion confronted with the forces of modernity.

29 *The Last Wave*. Peter Weir, 1977.
A glimpse into the spiritual world of the Australian Aboriginal as a lawyer faces the parallel inundation of his civilization through the forces of Nature and the invasion of his mind by an ancient culture that seems to call to him.

30 *Latter Days*. C. Jay Cox, 2003.
A gay Mormon and a Los Angeles gay party boy fall for each other in a film that is initially sensationalist but develops into a thoughtful exploration of how a gay Christian faces contradictions and prejudice, and also how religion touches the non-religious.

31 *Little Buddha*. Bernardo Bertolucci, 1993.
A story of the life of the Buddha interwoven with the search in America for a reincarnated Tibetan lama. How *does* an average couple cope with the idea that their boy is meant to be a religious leader in a tradition a world away from their own?

32 *Maborosi*. Hirokazu Koreeda, 1995.
A hauntingly beautiful Japanese film which meditates on loss, love and compassion. A widow remarries and moves to a remote fishing town where her new husband finds the few right words at the right time and in the right setting of sea and sky to bring her healing.

33 *A Man Called Peter*. Henry Koster, 1955.
Biopic of the Rev. Dr. Peter Marshall, a preacher who twice served as Chaplain of the United States Senate. His sermons have an edge that make him stand out.

34 *Meetings with Remarkable Men*. Peter Brook, 1979.
Film version of spiritual teacher G. I. Gurdjieff's autobiography follows his early years, culminating in his esoteric training in a remote monastery in the Middle East. Includes superb scenes of the sacred dances and movements that were to become an important part of his teaching.

35 *Monsieur Ibrahim*. François Dupeyron, 2003.
Delightful story of a Muslim shopkeeper in Paris who becomes guardian to a Jewish boy whose parents abandon him. The old man introduces the boy to the practice of Islamic ablutions and Sufi whirling, leaving him with a profound spiritual legacy.

36 *My Neighbor Totoro*. Hayao Miyazaki, 1988.
Enormously popular with children, this film gives insight into the Japanese empathy for Nature and its animist understanding of it as a world peopled by spirit entities. In their new house in the country a young family become acquainted with a variety of helpful spirits.

37 *My Night with Maud*. Eric Rhomer, 1969.
A very French exploration of the conflict and common ground between Catholicism and socialism, explored through the love lives of young people and the challenge of Pascal's wager.

38 *Nausicaä of the Valley of the Wind*. Hayao Miyazaki, 1984.
Animated film with profound animist implications, beautifully visualized. This is a story of humans, forests, and the spirit world in which the presence of good and evil in the protagonists is not clear-cut, and in which Nature claims dominance over such human concepts.

39 *Northfork*. Michael Polish, 2003.
A magical story of angels and a dying boy set in the mountains and plains of Montana. A hydroelectric scheme will sweep away a community, just as the white man swept away the world of the Native American. Perhaps.

40 *The Nun's Story*. Fred Zinnemann, 1959.
A nun's faith is challenged by war and by her commitment to medicine. A fine study of what it means to serve in a healing order when one's first loyalty is to medicine, not religion.

41 *Of Gods and Men*. Xavier Beauvois, 2010.
Based on the real-life story of Trappist monks endangered by Islamist forces in Algeria, we follow the choices made by each monk to stay and serve their community and their religion. A gripping insight into monastery life in the 21st century, and into the power of a genuine calling.

42 *Pi*. Darren Aronofsky, 1998.
A mathematical genius encounters corporate powers, the Kaballa, a 216-digit number that links an ancient religion with the stock market ... and an electric drill. An unusual exploration of the role of numbers in esoteric religious history, with an unexpected resolution.

43 *Powder.* Victor Salva, 1995.
A young man has paranormal gifts due to a lightning strike, which make him an outsider at school where all he wants is to fit in. But he helps people "see" their connection to other living things, which draws him close to some but further alienates authority.

44 *Princess Mononoke.* Hayao Miyazaki, 1997.
A spectacular parable of the battle between the Forest Spirit and the advancement of industrialization, this film conveys the Japanese sensitivity to Nature and its spirits along with the insight that no player in a drama is either wholly good or wholly evil.

45 *The Quarrel.* Eli Cohen, 1991.
Two survivors of the Holocaust meet after many years and dispute about religion, the war, and guilt. Many elements of the Judaic religion are present here. The world-renouncing rabbi and the secular Jew of literature cannot reconcile their differences, but are still bound by deep ties of religion and culture.

46 *The Razor's Edge.* Edmund Goulding, 1946.
Film version of Somerset Maugham's novel. It follows the spiritual journey of a demobbed World War I soldier unable to take up a purely material lifestyle, who travels to India in search of wisdom.

47 *Seven Years in Tibet.* Jean-Jacques Annaud, 1997.
The story of Austrian mountain climber Heinrich Harrer and his friendship with the young Dalai Lama. He instructs the Buddhist leader in Western ways, while absorbing the ancient religious traditions of the "roof of the world."

48 *The Son.* Jean-Pierre Dardenne and Luc Dardenne, 2002.
A Belgian carpenter is provoked into an extreme reaction when he takes on a young offender. Forgiveness is the theme of this somber film, a forgiveness made unforgettable yet having no obvious religious source.

49 *The Song of Bernadette.* Henry King, 1943.
Biopic of Louise Soubirous, the young woman whose visions of the Virgin Mary led to Lourdes becoming a place of pilgrimage. Notable for the rueful skepticism of the local Prosecutor, and the dynamics between them.

50 *The Sixth Sense.* M. Knight Shyamalan, 1999.
"I see dead people," confides a young boy to his psychiatrist. Together they take a gamble, that the spirits of the dead need understanding as much as if not more than the living. Will listening to them resolve their torment? They need to move on ... all of them.

51 *Spirited Away.* Hayao Miyazaki, 2001.
Extraordinary animated film of the spirit world inhabited by giant radishes, witches and frogs all serving in a bath-house for spirit guests. In stumbles young Chihiro whose integrity is her only resource as she negotiates this bizarre world, hoping to rescue her parents from a spell.

52 *Spring, Summer, Autumn, Winter ... and Spring.* Ki-duk Kim, 2003.
A meditation on the cyclical progress of the master-disciple relationship in Korean Chan Buddhism reflected in the changing seasons of Nature. Set mostly on a small floating temple in a lake fringed with forests and mountains it is also a poetic investigation of the laws of karma.

53 *Thunderheart.* Michael Apted, 1992.
A young FBI agent called to a Native American reservation becomes entangled in the past: visions of the Ghost Dance and a glimpse of a non-white identity give him insight into the tragedy and spiritual life of America's original peoples.

54 *To End All Wars.* David L. Cunningham, 2001.
The same setting as in *The Bridge on the River Kwai* provokes a Christian pacifist to argue for compassion over vengeance in a POW camp run by a harsh administration.

55 *21 Grams.* Alejandro González Iñárritu, 2003.
Meditation on culpability, bereavement, religion, life and death in an intertwined narrative of ordinary people confronted with tragedy and the violent emotions that follow. Life wins.

56 *Vanilla Sky.* Cameron Crowe, 2001.
A wealthy young man can afford to live in a virtual reality world which erases his disfigurement and elements of his past. But why does his beautiful girlfriend keep changing into another beautiful woman and cause him so much despair? His unconscious guilt erupts into his fake world and forces him to make an ethical choice.

57 *Whale Rider.* Niki Caro, 2002.
A young Maori girl challenges the sacred male tradition, secretly learning the martial arts forbidden to women. Her grandfather resists her right to be spiritual leader of their group until her action in saving a whale shows her power.

58 Why Did Bodhidharma Leave for the East. Yong-Kyun Bae, 1989.

An exploration of facets of Chan Buddhism in Korea, following teacher and pupils in a remote Zen temple. It contrasts the ancient wisdom of the Buddha in its application to the morality of a child and to the conundrum of the adult seeker in attempting a renunciation of modern life. Beautifully shot in natural settings.

59 *Wings of Desire*. Wim Wenders, 1987.

Astonishing meditation on the nature of angelic beings, their task in recording all that is of beauty, intellect and love in the human world of postwar Berlin, and the descent into human form of one of their kind, encouraged by a former angel: Peter Falk.

60 *Witness*. Peter Weir, 1985.

A Chicago cop is thrust into the world of the Amish, a religious group holding to 18th-century ways, who are in turn drawn into both the violence of the modern world and to learn respect for the policeman's integrity.

Chapter Notes

Introduction

1. Elizabeth Debold, "Spiritual but Not Religious: Moving Beyond Postmodern Spirituality," *What Is Enlightenment?* December 2005–February 2006.
2. See for example Carl Elliott and Tod Chambers, eds., *Prozac as a Way of Life* (Studies in Social Medicine) (Chapel Hill: University of North Carolina Press, 2004).
3. Bertrand Russell, *Mysticism and Logic* (London: George Allen and Unwin, 1963), pp. 15–16.
4. Mike King, *Secularism: The Hidden Origins of Disbelief* (Cambridge: James Clarke, 2007), pp. 193–196.
5. Jeffrey F. Keuss, "Reading Stanley Kubrick: A Theology Odyssey," in Eric S. Christianson, Peter Francis and William Telford, eds., *Cinema Divinité: Religion, Theology and the Bible in Film* (London: SCM Press, 2005), p. 83.
6. G. W. F. Hegel, *Phenomenology of Spirit* (Oxford: Oxford University Press, 1977), p. 5.
7. Jeffrey F. Keuss, "Reading Stanley Kubrick: A Theology Odyssey," in Eric S. Christianson, Peter Francis and William Telford, eds., *Cinema Divinité: Religion, Theology and the Bible in Film* (London: SCM Press, 2005), p. 90.
8. Mike King, *Secularism: The Hidden Origins of Disbelief* (Cambridge: James Clarke, 2007), pp. 64–66.
9. Andrei Tarkovsky, *Sculpting in Time* (London: Faber and Faber, 1989), p. 226.
10. Andre Bazin, "Cinema and Theology," in Alain Pierre and Bert Cardullo, eds., *Bazin at Work: Major Essays and Reviews from the Forties and Fifties* (New York: Routledge, 1997), p. 61.
11. David Martin, *On Secularization: Towards a Revised General Theory* (Aldershot: Ashgate, 2005).
12. Michael Medved, *Hollywood vs. America* (New York: HarperCollins, 1993), cover text.
13. Peter Francis, "Clint Eastwood Westerns: Promised Land and Real Men," in Eric S. Christianson, Peter Francis and William Telford, eds., *Cinema Divinité: Religion, Theology and the Bible in Film* (London: SCM Press, 2005), p. 182.
14. Danah Zohar and Ian Marshall, *SQ: Spiritual Intelligence, the Ultimate Intelligence* (London: Bloomsbury, 2000).
15. Mike King, *The American Cinema of Excess: Extremes of the National Mind on Film* (Jefferson, NC: McFarland, 2009), pp. 258–284.
16. Isaac Kramnick, ed., *The Portable Enlightenment Reader* (London: Penguin, 1995), p. 138.
17. Joel W. Martin and Conrad E. Ostwalt, Jr., eds., *Screening the Sacred: Religion, Myth, and Ideology in Popular American Film* (Boulder: Westview Press, 1995), p. 5.
18. See for example Daniel C. Dennett, *Breaking the Spell: Religion as a Natural Phenomenon* (London: Penguin, 2007), p. 43.
19. Andrei Tarkovsky, *Sculpting in Time* (London: Faber and Faber, 1989), p. 37.
20. Andrei Tarkovsky, *Sculpting in Time* (London: Faber and Faber, 1989), p. 113.
21. John R. May, "Contemporary Theories Regarding the Interpretation of Religious Film," in John R. May, ed., *New Image of Religious Film* (Kansas City: Sheed and Ward, 1997).
22. Melanie J. Wright, *Religion and Film: An Introduction* (London: I. B. Tauris, 2006), p. 5.
23. Melanie J. Wright, *Religion and Film: An Introduction* (London: I. B. Tauris, 2006), p. 16.
24. David John Graham, "The Uses of Film in Theology," in Clive Marsh and Gaye Ortiz, eds., *Exploration in Theology and Film: Movies and Meanings* (Oxford: Blackwell, 1997), p. 37.
25. Gerard Loughlin, *Alien Sex: The Body and Desire in Cinema and Theology* (Malden, MA: Blackwell, 2004), p. ix.
26. Andre Bazin, "Cinema and Theology," in Alain Pierre and Bert Cardullo, eds. and trans. *Bazin at Work: Major Essays and Reviews from the Forties and Fifties* (New York: Routledge, 1997), p. 64.
27. Joseph Cunneen, *Robert Bresson: A Spiritual Style in Film* (London: Continuum International, 2003), p. 85.

28. Paul Schrader, *Transcendental Style in Film: Ozu, Bresson and Dreyer* (New York: Da Capo, 1988), p. 165.

29. David John Graham, "The Uses of Film in Theology," in Clive Marsh and Gaye Ortiz, eds., *Explorationin Theology and Film: Movies and Meanings* (Oxford: Blackwell, 1997), p. 40.

30. David Jasper, "On Systematizing the Unsystematic: A Response," in Clive Marsh and Gaye Ortiz, eds., *Exploration in Theology and Film: Movies and Meanings* (Oxford: Blackwell, 1997), p. 238.

31. Gerard Loughlin, "Cinema Divinite: A Theological Introduction," in Eric S. Christianson, Peter Francis and William Telford, eds., *Cinema Divinité: Religion, Theology and the Bible in Film* (London: SCM Press, 2005), p. 1.

32. Mike Tucker, *Dreaming with Open Eyes: TheShamanic in 20th C Art and Culture* (San Francisco: Aquarian/HarperSanFrancisco, 1992), p. xxi.

33. Gaye Ortiz and Maggie Roux, "The *Terminator* Movies: Hi-Tech Holiness and the Human Condition," in Clive Marsh and Gaye Ortiz, eds., *Exploration in Theology and Film: Movies and Meanings* (Oxford: Blackwell, 1997), p. 146.

34. Gaye Ortiz and Maggie Roux, "The *Terminator* Movies: Hi-Tech Holiness and the Human Condition," in Clive Marsh and Gaye Ortiz, eds., *Exploration in Theology and Film: Movies and Meanings* (Oxford: Blackwell, 1997), p. 154.

35. Christopher Vogler, *The Writer's Journey: MythicStructure for Storytellers and Screenwriters*, 2d ed. (London: Pan Books, 1998), p. xvii.

36. Peter Malone, "*Edward Scissorhands*: Christology from a Suburban Fairy-Tale," in Clive Marsh and Gaye Ortiz, eds., *Exploration in Theology and Film:Movies and Meanings* (Oxford: Blackwell, 1997), p. 85.

37. Ian Maher, "Liberation in *Awakenings*," in Clive Marsh and Gaye Ortiz, eds., *Exploration in Theologyand Film: Movies and Meanings* (Oxford: Blackwell, 1997), p. 100.

38. Maria Consuelo Maisto, "Cinematic Communion? *Babette's Feast*, Transcendental Style, and Interdisciplinarity," in David Jasper and S. Brent Plate, eds., *Imag(in)ing Otherness: Filmic Visions of Living Together* (Atlanta: Scholars Press, 1999), p. 83.

Chapter 1

1. Kierkegaard, *The Essential Kierkegaard* (Princeton: Princeton University Press, 1990), p. 280.

2. F. Nietzsche, *The Birth of Tragedy* (London: Penguin, 1993), p. 32.

3. Marjeet Verbeek, "Too Beautiful to Be Untrue: Toward a Theology of Film Aesthetics," in John R. May, ed., *New Image of Religious Film* (Kansas City: Sheed and Ward, 1997), p. 175.

4. Dean Sluyter and Ean Sluyter, *Cinema Nirvana: Enlightenment Lessons from the Movies* (New York: Three Rivers Press, 2005), p. 5.

5. David L. Smith, "'Beautiful Necessities': *American Beauty* and the Idea of Freedom," *Journal of Religion and Film*, Vol. 6, No. 2 (October 2002), [3].

6. David L. Smith, "'Beautiful Necessities': *American Beauty* and the Idea of Freedom," *Journal of Religion and Film*, Vol. 6, No. 2 (October 2002), [9].

7. Sir James George Frazer, *The Golden Bough: Study in Magic and Religion*, Abridged (New York: Touchstone, 1996), chapters XLV–XLVIII.

8. http://www.princeton.edu/~csrelig/cinema/Scenario.htm, viewed 23 January 2009.

9. Francisca Cho, "Imaging Nothing and Imaging Otherness in Buddhist Films," in David Jasper and S. Brent Plate, eds., *Imag(in)ing Otherness: Filmic Visions of Living Together* (Atlanta: Scholars Press, 1999), p. 172.

10. Michael L. Gillespie, "Picturing the Way in Bae Yong-kyun's *Why Has Bodhidharma Left for the East ?*," *Journal of Religion and Film*, Vol. 1, No. 1 (April 1997), [28].

11. Graham Harvey, *Animism: Respecting the Living World* (London: Hurst, 2005).

12. Andrei Tarkovsky, *Sculpting in Time* (London: Faber and Faber, 1989), p. 168.

13. Nigel Savio D'Sa, "Andrei Rublev: Religious Epiphany in Art," *Journal of Religion and Film*, Vol. 3, No. 2 (October 1999), [8].

14. Nigel Savio D'Sa, "Andrei Rublev: Religious Epiphany in Art," *Journal of Religion and Film*, Vol. 3, No. 2 (October 1999), [18].

15. Reginald Lansing Cook, "The Nature Mysticism of Thoreau," in *The Concord Saunterer* (Middlebury, VT: Middlebury College Press, 1940), p. 9.

16. R. Jefferies, *The Story of My Heart* (London: Macmillan, 1968).

17. Walt Whitman, *Leaves of Grass* (Oxford: Oxford University Press, 1990), p. 27, "Starting from Paumanok," v. 15.

18. Stephen Brie and David Torevall, "Moral Ambiguity and Contradiction in *Dead Poets Society*," in Clive Marsh and Gaye Ortiz, eds., *Exploration in Theologyand Film: Movies and Meanings* (Oxford: Blackwell, 1997), p. 167.

19. Matthew McEver, "The Messianic Figure in Film: Christology Beyond the Biblical Epic," *The Journal of Religion and Film*, Vol. 2, No. 2 (October 1998), [14].

20. Christopher Deacy, *Christologies, Redemption and the Medium of Film* (Cardiff: University of Wales Press 2001), p. 45.

21. Susan L. Schwartz, "I Dream, Therefore I Am: What Dreams May Come," Journal of Religion and Film, Vol. 4, No. 1 (April 2000), [2].

22. Colin Wilson, *The Outsider* (New York: Penguin Putnam, 1982), p. 88.

23. Maria Consuelo Maisto, "Cinematic Communion? *Babette's Feast*, Transcendental Style, and Interdisciplinarity," in David Jasper and S. Brent Plate, eds., *Imag(in)ing Otherness: Filmic Visions of Living Together* (Atlanta: Scholars Press, 1999).

24. Kierkegaard, *The Essential Kierkegaard* (Princeton: Princeton University Press, 1990), p. 96.
25. Jean Schuler, "Kierkegaard at Babette's Feast: The Return to the Finite," *Journal of Religion and Film*, Vol. 1, No. 2 (October 1997), [6].

Chapter 2

1. Bertrand Russell, *A History of Western Philosophy* (London: Unwin Paperbacks, 1989), p. 489.
2. Mircea Eliade, *Shamanism: Archaic Techniques of Ecstasy*, Bollingen Series 76 (Princeton: Princeton University Press, 2004), p. 5.
3. Cited in S. Naifeh and G.W. Smith, *Jackson Pollock: An American Saga* (London: Pimlico, 1992), p. 337.
4. Michael Harner, *The Way of the Shaman* (San Francisco: HarperSanFrancisco, 1990), p. xi.
5. Jordan Paper, *The Spirits Are Drunk: Comparative Approaches to Chinese Religion* (Albany: State University of New York Press, 1995), p. 95.
6. Ake Hultkrantz, *The Religions of the American Indians* (Berkeley: University of California Press, 1979), p. 11.
7. Russell Means, *Where White Men Fear to Tread: The Autobiography of Russell Means* (New York: St. Martin's Griffin, 1995), p. 513.
8. Ake Hultkrantz, *The Religions of the American Indians* (Berkeley: University of California Press, 1979), p. 93.
9. Holger Kalweit, *Dreamtime and Inner Space: The World of the Shaman* (Boston: Shambala, 1988), p. 181.
10. Mike Tucker, *Dreaming with Open Eyes: TheShamanic in 20th C Art and Culture* (San Francisco: Aquarian/HarperSanFrancisco, 1992), p. 253.
11. Mark Schilling, "Pokemon, Miyazaki go head-to-head," *Variety*, May 30, 2008.
12. Susan Napier, *Anime from Akira to Howl's Moving Castle: Experiencing Contemporary Japanese Animation* (New York: Palgrave Macmillan, 2006), p. xiii.
13. Susan Napier, *Anime from Akira to Howl's Moving Castle: Experiencing Contemporary Japanese Animation* (New York: Palgrave Macmillan, 2006), p. 152.
14. Jolyon Baraka Thomas, "Shuko Asobi and Miazaki Hayao's *Anime*," in Jolyon Mitchell and S. Brent Plate, eds., *The Religion and Film Reader* (New York: Routledge, 2007), p. 185.
15. Motohisa Yamakage, *The Essence of Shinto: Japan's Spiritual Heart* (Tokyo: Kodansha International, 2006), p. 22.
16. Susan Napier, *Anime from Akira to Howl's Moving Castle: Experiencing Contemporary Japanese Animation* (New York: Palgrave Macmillan, 2006), p. xi.
17. Helen McCarthy, *Hayao Miyazaki: Master of Japanese Animation: Films, Themes, Artistry* (Berkeley: Stone Bridge Press, 2003), p. 134.
18. Susan Napier, *Anime from Akira to Howl's Moving Castle: Experiencing Contemporary Japanese Animation* (New York: Palgrave Macmillan, 2006), p. 242.
19. Susan Napier, *Anime from Akira to Howl's Moving Castle: Experiencing Contemporary Japanese Animation* (New York: Palgrave Macmillan, 2006), p. 235.
20. Motohisa Yamakage, *The Essence of Shinto: Japan's Spiritual Heart* (Tokyo: Kodansha International, 2006), p. 44.
21. Mircea Eliade, *Shamanism: Archaic Techniques of Ecstasy*, Bollingen Series 76 (Princeton: Princeton University Press, 2004), p. 462.
22. Holger Kalweit, *Dreamtime and Inner Space: The World of the Shaman* (Boston: Shambala, 1988), p. 133.
23. John Gregory, *The Neoplatonists: A Reader* (London: Routledge, 1999), p. 180.
24. Augustine (Saint), *Confessions*, trans. R.S. Pine-Coffin (Middlesex, England: Penguin, 1986), VII:9, p. 146.
25. Eric G. Wilson, *Secret Cinema: Gnostic Vision in Film* (London: Continuum, 2006), p. 4.
26. Kenneth Sylvan Guthrie, *The Pythagorean Sourcebook and Library* (Grand Rapids: Phanes Press, 1987), p. 30.
27. Arifa Akbar, "Christian Protests May Leave Philip Pullman's Trilogy as One of a Kind," *The Independent*, 18 July 2008.
28. Michael Harner, *The Way of the Shaman* (San Francisco: HarperSanFrancisco, 1990), p. 42.
29. Quoted in Phil Daoust, "A Life Out of Shot," *The Guardian*, 13 March 2010.
30. Stephen Simon, *The Force Is with You: Mystical-Movie Messages That Inspire Our Lives* (Charlottesville, VA: Hampton Roads, 2002).
31. Stephen Simon, *The Force Is with You: Mystical-Movie Messages That Inspire Our Lives* (Charlottesville, VA: Hampton Roads, 2002), p. 4.
32. Candace B. Pert, Molecules of Emotion: The Science Behind Mind-Body Medicine (New York: Scribner, 2003).
33. Mike King, *The American Cinema of Excess: Extremes of the National Mind on Film* (Jefferson, NC: McFarland, 2009), p. 115.
34. Several film versions exist of the book: Erich von Daniken, *Chariots of the Gods? Was God an Astronaut?* (London: Corgi, 1972).
35. Mario DeGiglio-Bellemare, "Signs," *Journal of Religion and Film*, Vol. 6, No. 2 (October 2002), [6].
36. Eric G. Wilson, *Secret Cinema: Gnostic Vision in Film* (London: Continuum, 2006), p. 4.
37. Donna Yarri, "Film Review: I ♥ Huckabees," *The Journal of Religion and Film*, Vol. 10, No. 1 (April 2006), [1].
38. For a longer discussion of speed as the stumbling block of the film see Mike King, *The American Cinema of Excess: Extremes of the National Mind on Film* (Jefferson, NC: McFarland, 2009), pp. 153–158.

Chapter 3

1. For example Mary Beard, "Exit Strategies," *The Guardian*, 21 March 2009.

2. John Burroughs, *The Last Harvest* (Boston: Houghton Mifflin, 1922), p. 288.
3. Walt Whitman, *Leaves of Grass* (Oxford: Oxford University Press, 1990), p. 77.
4. Chad W.D. Bolton, "Film Review: Henry Poole Is Here," The Journal of Religion and Film, Vol. 12, No. 2 (October 2008), [3].
5. W.Y. Evans-Wentz, *The Tibetan Book of the Great Liberation* (London: Oxford University Press, 1968).
6. Guillermo Arriaga with Warren Curry (interviewer), "Basic: An Interview with *21 Grams* Screenwriter Guillermo Arriaga," in Jolyon Mitchell and S. Brent Plate, eds., *The Religion and Film Reader* (New York: Routledge, 2007), p. 246.
7. Clive Marsh, *Theology Goes to the Movies: An Introduction to Critical Christian Thinking* (London: Routledge, 2007), p. 96.
8. Roy M. Anker, *Catching Light: Looking for God in the Movies* (Grand Rapids: Eerdmans, 2004), p. 367.
9. Mary Dodson, "Capturing C. S. Lewis's 'Mere' Christianity: Another Look at *Shadowlands*," *Journal of Religion and Film*, Vol. 6, No. 1 (April 2002), [2].
10. Elyse Sara, "Book Review: Finding Meaning at the Movies," *The Journal of Religion and Film*, [6].
11. Clive Marsh, *Theology Goes to the Movies: An Introduction to Critical Christian Thinking* (London: Routledge, 2007), p. 97.
12. David Breskin, "The Rolling Stone Interview," in Jolyon Mitchell and S. Brent Plate, eds., *The Religion and Film Reader* (New York: Routledge, 2007), p. 247.
13. Ingmar Bergman, "Introduction to *The Seventh Seal*," in Jolyon Mitchell and S. Brent Plate, eds., *The Religion and Film Reader* (New York: Routledge, 2007), p. 28.
14. http://en.wikipedia.org/wiki/Through_a_Glass_Darkly_%28film%29, accessed 10 December 2007.
15. Kierkegaard, *The Essential Kierkegaard* (Princeton: Princeton University Press, 1990), p. 280.
16. Susan L. Schwartz, "I Dream, Therefore I Am: What Dreams May Come," *Journal of Religion and Film*, Vol. 4, No. 1 (April 2000), [2].
17. Susan L. Schwartz, "I Dream, Therefore I Am: What Dreams May Come," *Journal of Religion and Film*, Vol. 4, No. 1 (April 2000), [11].
18. Mike King, *The American Cinema of Excess: Extremes of the National Mind on Film* (Jefferson, NC: McFarland, 2009), pp. 204–205.
19. Bhikku Nanamoli and Bhikku Bhodi, *The Middle Length Discourses of the Buddha: A New Translationof the Majjhima Nikaya* (Boston: Wisdom, 1995), Sutra 144, pp. 1114–116.
20. Joe Fisher, *The Case for Reincarnation* (Toronto: Collins, 1984), p. 125.
21. See for example Papus (Dr. G. Encausse), *Reincarnation: Physical, Astral and Spiritual Evolution*, trans. Marguerite Vallior (London: Martinist Press, n.d.), p. 70.
22. Joe Fisher, *The Case for Reincarnation* (Toronto: Collins, 1984), p. 125.
23. Robert K. Johnston, *Reel Spirituality: Theology and Film in Dialogue* (Engaging Culture) (Grand Rapids: Baker Academic, 2007), p. 230.
24. Abbas Kiarostami with Bill Horrigan (interviewer), "In Dialogue with Kiarostami," in Jolyon Mitchell and S. Brent Plate, eds., *The Religion and Film Reader* (New York: Routledge, 2007), p. 90.

Chapter 4

1. Clive Marsh, *Theology Goes to the Movies: An Introduction to Critical Christian Thinking* (London: Routledge, 2007), p. 143.
2. John Izod, *Myth, Mind and the Screen: Understanding the Heroes of our Time* (Cambridge: Cambridge University Press, 2001), p. 161.
3. F. Nietzsche, *Twilight of the Idols* (Oxford: Oxford University Press, 1998), p. 15.

Chapter 5

1. Bhikku Nanamoli and Bhikku Bhodi, *The Middle Length Discourses of the Buddha: A New Translationof the Majjhima Nikaya* (Boston: Wisdom, 1995, 72), p. 676 and p. 696.
2. Kenneth Sylvan Guthrie, *The Pythagorean Source book and Library* (Grand Rapids: Phanes Press, 1987), p. 71.
3. Papus (Dr. G. Encausse), *Reincarnation: Physical, Astral and Spiritual Evolution*, trans. Marguerite Vallior (London: The Martinist Press, n.d.), p. 11.
4. See for example R. Steiner, *Occult Science: An Outline* (London: Rudolf Steiner Press, 1986).
5. Roger Woolger, *Other Lives, Other Selves* (London: Bantam, 1988).
6. Joe Fisher, *The Case for Reincarnation* (Toronto: Collins, 1984), p. 167.
7. Joe Fisher, *The Case for Reincarnation* (Toronto: Collins, 1984), p. 75.
8. Max Erlich, *The Reincarnation of Peter Proud* (London: Corgi, 1975), p. 127. He cites Schopenhauer's *Parerga and Paralipomena*, II, Chapter 16.
9. Max Erlich, *The Reincarnation of Peter Proud* (London: Corgi, 1975), p. 56.
10. See for example J. Stearn, *Edgar Cayce: The Sleeping Prophet* (New York: Bantam, 1989).
11. For the interview see the extra features on the DVD release of the film.
12. Hugh Brody, *The Other Side of Eden: Hunters, Farmers, and the Shaping of the World* (New York: North Point Press, 2000), p. 134.
13. C. Trungpa, *Cutting Through Spiritual Materialism* (Boston: Shambhala, 1987).
14. Barbara W. Tuchman, *Bible and Sword: Englandand Palestine from the Bronze Age to Balfour* (New York: Ballantine, 1984), ch. xvii.

15. Susan Napier, *Anime from Akira to Howl's Moving Castle: Experiencing Contemporary Japanese Animation* (New York: Palgrave Macmillan, 2006), p. 252.

16. Clive Marsh, *Theology Goes to the Movies: An Introduction to Critical Christian Thinking* (London: Rout-ledge, 2007), p. 142.

17. See for example Timothy Freke and Peter Gandy, *The Jesus Mysteries: Was the "Original Jesus" a Pagan God?* (New York: Three Rivers Press, 1999).

18. Wheeler Winston Dixon, *Visions of the Apocalypse: Spectacles of Destruction in American Cinema* (London: Wallflower Press, 2003), p. 16.

19. Michael Northcott, *An Angel Directs the Storm: Apocalyptic Religion and American Empire* (London: I.B. Tauris, 2004), p. 66.

20. Heather Hendershot, "Waiting for the End of the World—Christian Apocalyptic Media at the Turn of the Millennium," in Jon Lewis, ed., *The End of Cinema as We Know It: American Film in the Nineties* (London: Pluto Press, 2002), p. 333.

Chapter 6

1. Paul Schrader, *Transcendental Style in Film: Ozu, Bresson and Dreyer* (New York: Da Capo, 1988), p. 38.

2. Irena Makarushka, "Transgressing Goodness in Breaking the Waves," in David Jasper and S. Brent Plate, eds., *Imag(in)ing Otherness: Filmic Visions of Living Together* (Atlanta: Scholars Press, 1999), p. 90.

3. Kim Newman, "Rubber Reality," in *Sight and Sound*, June 1999.

4. Eric S. Christianson, "Why Film Noir Is Good for the Mind," in Eric S. Christianson, Peter Francis and William Telford, eds., *Cinema Divinité: Religion, Theology and the Bible in Film* (London: SCM Press, 2005), p. 152.

5. Andrei Tarkovsky, *Sculpting in Time* (London: Faber and Faber, 1989), p. 193.

6. Eric G. Wilson, *Secret Cinema: Gnostic Vision in Film* (New York: Continuum International, 2006), p. viii.

7. Eric G. Wilson, *The Strange World of David Lynch: Ironic Religion from "Eraserhead" to "Mulholland Dr."* (New York: Continuum International, 2007), p. x.

8. Gregory J. Watkins, "Book Review: Teaching Religion and Film," *The Journal of Religion and Film*, [17].

9. This is the title of a sutra: Bhikku Nanamoli and Bhikku Bhodi, *The Middle Length Discourses of the Buddha: A New Translation of the Majjhima Nikaya* (Boston: Wisdom, 1995), 87, p. 718.

10. Walt Whitman, *Leaves of Grass* (Oxford: Oxford University Press, 1990), p. 76, "Song of Myself," v. 48.

11. Robert Jewett, "Stuck in Time: Kairos, Chronos, and the Flesh in *Groundhog Day*," in Clive Marsh and Gaye Ortiz, eds., *Exploration in Theology and Film: Movies and Meanings* (Oxford: Blackwell, 1997), p. 162.

12. Stephen Simon, *The Force Is with You: Mystical-Movie Messages That Inspire Our Lives* (Charlottesville, VA: Hampton Roads, 2002), p. 21.

13. Eric G. Wilson, *The Strange World of DavidLynch: Ironic Religion from "Eraserhead" to "Mulholland Dr."* (New York: Continuum International, 2007), p.155.

14. Eric G. Wilson, *The Strange World of David Lynch: Ironic Religion from "Eraserhead" to "Mulholland Dr."* (New York: Continuum International, 2007), p. 159.

15. Mike King, *The American Cinema of Excess: Extremes of the National Mind on Film* (Jefferson, NC: McFarland, 2009), p. 133 and 204–205.

16. Michael Brannigan, "There Is No Spoon: A Buddhist Mirror," in William Irwin, ed., *The Matrix and Philosophy: Welcome to the Desert of the Real* (Chicago: Open Court, 2002), p. 108.

17. Peter B. Lloyd, *Exegesis of the Matrix* (London: Whole-Being, 2003), p. 2.

18. Aude Lancelin, "*The Matrix* Decoded: Le Nouvel Observateur Interview with Jean Baudrillard," *International Journal of Baudrillard Studies*, Volume 1, Number 2 (July 2004).

19. John Shelton Lawrence, "Fascist Redemption or Democratic Hope?" in Matthew Kapell and William G. Doty, eds., *Jacking in to the Matrix Franchise* (New York: Continuum, 2004), pp. 80–96.

20. Mike King, *The American Cinema of Excess: Extremes of the National Mind on Film* (Jefferson, NC: McFarland, 2009), p. 305.

Chapter 7

1. Georg Feuerstein, *Holy Madness* (London: Arkana, 1990).

2. Paul Reps, *Zen Flesh, Zen Bones* (Middlesex, England: Penguin, 1976), p. 66.

3. Anthony Storr, *Feet of Clay: A Study of Gurus* (London: HarperCollins, 1997).

4. Mariana Caplan, *Halfway Up the Mountain: TheError of Premature Claims of Enlightenment* (Prescott, AZ: Hohm Press, 1999).

5. Mike Tucker, *Dreaming with Open Eyes: TheShamanic in 20th C Art and Culture* (San Francisco: Aquarian/HarperSanFrancisco, 1992), p. 257.

6. Bill Blizek and Ronald Burke, "'The Apostle': An Interview with Robert Duvall," *Journal of Religion and Film*, Vol. 2, No. 1 (April 1998), [10].

7. Ivan Butler, *Religion in the Cinema* (New York: A.S. Barnes, 1969), p. 82.

Chapter 8

1. Andre Bazin, "Cinema and Theology," in Alain Pierre and Bert Cardullo, eds. and trans. *Bazin at Work: Major Essays and Reviews from the Forties and Fifties* (New York: Routledge, 1997), p. 63.

2. Ivan Butler, *Religion in the Cinema* (New York: A.S. Barnes, 1969), p. 99.

3. Ivan Butler, *Religion in the Cinema* (New York: A.S. Barnes, 1969), p. 109.

4. Susan Jacoby, *Freethinkers: A History of American Secularism* (New York: Metropolitan, 2004), ch. 9.

5. André Bazin, *What Is Cinema? Vol. 1* (Berkeley: University of California Press, 1967), p. 137.

6. Susan Sontag, *Against Interpretation* (London: Vintage, 2001), p. 188.

7. Susan Sontag, *Against Interpretation* (London: Vintage, 2001), p. 179.

8. Tom Aitken, "Sacrilege, Satire or Statement of Faith—Ways of Reading Luis Buñuel's *Viridiana*," in Eric S. Christianson, Peter Francis and William Telford, eds., *Cinema Divinité: Religion, Theology and the Bible in Film* (London: SCM Press, 2005), p. 94.

9. Ivan Butler, *Religion in the Cinema* (New York: A.S. Barnes, 1969), p. 71.

10. Margaret Miles, *Seeing and Believing: Religion and Values in the Movies* (Boston: Beacon Press, 1996), p. 53.

11. Roy M. Anker, *Catching Light: Looking for God in the Movies* (Grand Rapids: Eerdmans, 2004), p. 162.

12. Michael Medved, *Hollywood vs. America* (New York: HarperCollins, 1993), p. 60.

13. Michele Desmarais, "Report from Sundance 2006: Religion in Independent Film," *Journal of Religion and Film*, Vol. 10, No. 1 (April 2006), [45].

Chapter 9

1. Andrew Rawlinson, *The Book of Enlightened Masters: Western Teachers in Eastern Traditions* (Chicago: Open Court, 1997), p. 98.

2. Karen Armstrong, *A History of God* (London: Mandarin, 1994), p. 226.

3. Lloyd Baugh, "The Masterpiece: *The Gospel According to St. Matthew*," in Jolyon Mitchell and S. Brent Plate, eds., *The Religion and Film Reader* (New York: Routledge, 2007), p. 203.

4. Lloyd Baugh, "The Masterpiece: *The Gospel According to St. Matthew*," in Jolyon Mitchell and S. Brent Plate, eds., *The Religion and Film Reader* (New York: Routledge, 2007), p. 206.

5. Clive Marsh and Gaye Ortiz, eds., *Exploration in Theology and Film: Movies and Meanings* (Oxford: Blackwell, 1997), p. 243.

6. Bhikku Nanamoli and Bhikku Bhodi, *The Middle Length Discourses of the Buddha: A New Translation of the Majjhima Nikaya* (Boston: Wisdom, 1995), p. 890.

7. Luce Irigaray, *Between East and West: From Singularity to Community* (New York: Columbia University Press, 2002), p. 85.

8. Philip Lutgendorf, "*Jai Santoshi Maa* Revisited: On Seeing a Hindu 'Mythological' Film," in S. Brent Plate, ed., *Representing Religion in World Cinema: Filmmaking, Mythmaking, Culture Making* (New York: Palgrave MacMillan, 2003).

9. Rachel Dwyer, *Filming the Gods: Religion and Indian Cinema* (London: Routledge, 2006), p. 47.

10. M. Gandhi, *The Collected Works of Mahatma Gandhi, Vol. XLI*, The Publications Division, Ministry of Information and Broadcasting, Government of India, Ahmedabad, 1970, p. 93.

11. Paul Schrader, *Schrader on Schrader and Other Writings* (London: Faber & Faber, 2004), p. 39.

Chapter 10

1. Leo Tolstoy, *The Kingdom of God Is Within You* (Mineola, NY: Dover, 2006), p. 1.

2. Peter Hasenberg, "The 'Religious' in Film: From King of Kings to The Fisher King," in John R. May, ed., *New Image of Religious Film* (Kansas City: Sheed and Ward, 1997), p. 41.

3. Peter Hasenberg, "The 'Religious' in Film: From King of Kings to The Fisher King," in John R. May, ed., *New Image of Religious Film* (Kansas City: Sheed and Ward, 1997), p. 51.

4. Susan Napier, *Anime from Akira to Howl's Moving Castle: Experiencing Contemporary Japanese Animation* (New York: Palgrave Macmillan, 2006), p. 191.

5. Eric G. Wilson, *Secret Cinema: Gnostic Vision in Film* (London: Continuum, 2006), p. 143.

6. Gore Vidal, "Monotheism and its Discontents," The Lowell Lecture, Harvard University, April 20, 1992, cited in Alister McGrath, *The Twilight of Atheism: The Rise and Fall of Disbelief in the Modern World* (New York: Doubleday, 2004), p. 229.

7. John Stuart Mill, *On Liberty and Other Essays* (Oxford: Oxford University Press, 1998), p. 55.

8. Eric S. Christianson, "An Ethic You Can't Refuse?—Assessing the Godfather Trilogy," in Eric S. Christianson, Peter Francis and William Telford, eds., *Cinema Divinité: Religion, Theology and the Bible in Film* (London: SCM Press, 2005), p. 110.

9. Eric S. Christianson, "An Ethic You Can't Refuse?—Assessing the Godfather Trilogy," in Eric S. Christianson, Peter Francis and William Telford, eds., *Cinema Divinité: Religion, Theology and the Bible in Film* (London: SCM Press, 2005), p. 121.

10. David John Graham, "Redeeming Violence in the Films of Martin Scorsese," in Clive Marsh and Gaye Ortiz, eds., *Exploration in Theology and Film: Movies and Meanings* (Oxford: Blackwell, 1997), p. 63.

11. David John Graham, "Redeeming Violence in the Films of Martin Scorsese," in Clive Marsh and Gaye Ortiz, eds., *Exploration in Theology and Film: Movies and Meanings* (Oxford: Blackwell, 1997), p. 94.

12. Christopher Deacy, *Christologies, Redemption and the Medium of Film* (Cardiff: University of Wales Press, 2001), p. 1.

13. Christopher Deacy, *Christologies, Redemption and the Medium of Film* (Cardiff: University of Wales Press, 2001), p. 9.

14. Christopher Deacy, *Christologies, Redemption and the Medium of Film* (Cardiff: University of Wales Press, 2001), p. 117.

15. For a fuller treatment of violence in American cinema see Mike King, *The American Cinema of Excess: Extremes of the National Mind on Film* (Jefferson, NC: McFarland, 2009), ch. 4.

16. Jason Ambrosiano, "'The Ties That Bind and Bless the Soul': Grace and Noir in Schrader's *Light*

Sleeper," The Journal of Religion and Film, Vol. 2, No. 2 (October 1998).

17. Woody Allen with Stig Björkman (interviewer), "Woody Allen on Woody Allen," in Jolyon Mitchell and S. Brent Plate, eds., *The Religion and Film Reader* (New York: Routledge, 2007), p. 241.

18. Woody Allen with Stig Björkman (interviewer), "Woody Allen on Woody Allen," in Jolyon Mitchell and S. Brent Plate, eds., *The Religion and Film Reader* (New York: Routledge, 2007), p. 242.

19. Woody Allen with Stig Björkman (interviewer), "Woody Allen on Woody Allen," in Jolyon Mitchell and S. Brent Plate, eds., *The Religion and Film Reader* (New York: Routledge, 2007), p. 243.

20. Kathryn Bernheimer, *The 50 Greatest Jewish Movies: A Critic's Ranking of the Very Best* (Secaucus, NJ: Birch Lane Press, 1998), p. 102.

21. Clive Marsh, Theology Goes to the Movies: An Introduction to Critical Christian Thinking (London: Rout-ledge, 2007), p. 95.

22. Clive Marsh, Theology Goes to the Movies: An *Introduction to Critical Christian Thinking* (London: Routledge, 2007), p. 99.

23. Allan Bloom, *The Closing of the American Mind:How Higher Education Has Failed Democracy and Impoverished the Souls of Today's Students* (London: Penguin, 1987), p. 155.

24. Christopher Lasch, *The Culture of Narcissism: American Life in an Age of Diminishing Expectations* (New York: W. W. Norton, 1991), p. 19.

25. Robert Banks, "The Drama of Salvation in George Steven's Shane," in Clive Marsh and Gaye Ortiz, eds., *Exploration in Theology and Film: Movies andMeanings* (Oxford: Blackwell, 1997), p. 63.

26. Peter Francis, "Clint Eastwood Westerns: Promised Land and Real Men," in Eric S. Christianson, Peter Francis and William Telford, eds., *Cinema Divinité: Religion, Theology and the Bible in Film* (London: SCM Press, 2005), p. 182.

27. Peter Francis, "Clint Eastwood Westerns: Promised Land and Real Men," in Eric S. Christianson, Peter Francis and William Telford, eds., *Cinema Divinité: Religion, Theology and the Bible in Film* (London: SCM Press, 2005), p. 197.

28. Eric S. Christianson, "A Fistful of Shekels: Ehud the Judge (Judges 3.12–30) and the Spaghetti Western," in Eric S. Christianson, Peter Francis and William Telford, eds., *Cinema Divinite: Religion, Theology and the Bible in Film* (London: SCM Press, 2005), p. 204.

29. Paraphrased from D. E. H. Russell, *Against Pornography: The Evidence of Harm* (Berkeley: Russell, 1993), pp. 3–12.

Chapter 11

1. Max Weber, *The Protestant Ethic and the Spirit of Capitalism* (New York: Dover, 2003).

2. Martin Buber, *I and Thou* (Edinburgh: T&T Clark, 1937), p. 120.

3. David Jasper, "'What Happened in the Cave?' Communities and Outsiders in Films of India," in David Jasper and S. Brent Plate, eds., *Imag(in)ing Otherness:Filmic Visions of Living Together* (Atlanta: Scholars Press, 1999), pp. 123–132.

4. Ira Bhaskar, "Postmodernism and Neo-Orientalism," in David Jasper and S. Brent Plate, eds., *Imag(in)ing Otherness: Filmic Visions of Living Together* (Atlanta: Scholars Press, 1999), p. 147.

5. David Jasper, "'What Happened in the Cave?' Communities and Outsiders in Films of India," in David Jasper and S. Brent Plate, eds., *Imag(in)ing Otherness:Filmic Visions of Living Together* (Atlanta: Scholars Press, 1999), p. 126.

6. Ray Kancharla, "India's Cinema: Home and the World, the Foci of Religion," in John R. May, ed., *New Image of Religious Film* (Kansas City: Sheed and Ward, 1997), p. 241.

7. Melanie J. Wright, *Religion and Film: An Introduction* (London: I.B. Tauris, 2006), p. 144.

8. Mohsen Makhmalbaf, "Once Upon a Filmmaker: Conversations with Mohsen Makhmalbaf," in Jolyon Mitchell and S. Brent Plate, eds., *The Relig ion and Film Reader* (New York: Routledge, 2007), p. 93.

9. Motohisa Yamakage, *The Essence of Shinto: Japan's Spiritual Heart* (Tokyo: Kodansha International, 2006), p. 89.

10. Shirley Nicholson, ed., *Shamanism* (Wheaton, IL: Theosophical Publishing House, 1987), p. 161.

11. Ed Husain, *The Islamist: Why I Joined RadicalIslam in Britain, What I Saw Inside and Why I Left* (Lon don: Penguin, 2007).

12. Melanie J. Wright, *Religion and Film: An Introduction* (London: I. B. Tauris, 2006), p. 125.

13. Susan L. Schwartz, "I Dream, Therefore I Am: What Dreams May Come," *Journal of Religion and Film*, Vol. 4, No. 1 (April 2000), [1].

Chapter 12

1. Mike Tucker, *Dreaming with Open Eyes:The Shamanic in 20th C Art and Culture* (San Francisco: Aquarian/HarperSanFrancisco, 1992), p. 262.

2. Ivan Butler, *Religion in the Cinema* (New York: A.S. Barnes, 1969), p. 97.

3. Walt Whitman, *Leaves of Grass* (Oxford: Oxford University Press, 1990), p. 67, "Song of Myself," v. 41.

4. G.W.F. Hegel, *Phenomenology of Spirit* (Oxford: Oxford University Press, 1977), p. 5.

5. Mike King, *Postsecularism: The Hidden Challenge to Extremism* (Cambridge: James Clarke, 2009), ch. 3 and 4.

6. See Mike King, *Postsecularism: The Hidden Challenge to Extremism* (Cambridge: James Clarke, 2009), p. 65 and pp. 88–97.

7. Tom Aitken, "Sacrilege, Satire or Statement of Faith—Ways of Reading Luis Buñuel's Viridiana," in Eric S. Christianson, Peter Francis and William Telford, eds., *Cinema Divinité: Religion, Theology and the Biblein Film* (London: SCM Press, 2005), p. 94.

8. Andrei Tarkovsky, *Sculpting in Time* (London: Faber and Faber, 1989), p. 51.

9. Blaise Pascal, *Pensées* (Harmondsworth: Penguin, 1980), p. 309.

10. See for example John Gray, *Black Mass: Apocalyptic Religion and the Death of Utopia* (London: Allen Lane, 2007).

11. See for example Stephen Batchelor, *Buddhism Without Beliefs: A Contemporary Guide* (London: Blooms bury, 1998).

12. See for example Naomi Klein, *The Shock Doctrine: The Rise of Disaster Capitalism* (London: Penguin, 2007).

13. Margaret Miles, *Seeing and Believing: Religion and Values in the Movies* (Boston: Beacon Press, 1996), p. 62.

14. Margaret Miles, *Seeing and Believing: Religion and Values in the Movies* (Boston: Beacon Press, 1996), p. 64.

15. Costa-Gavras, "Filming the Story of a Spy for God: An Interview with Costa-Gavros," in Jolyon Mitchell and S. Brent Plate, eds., *The Religion and Film Reader* (New York: Routledge, 2007), p. 210.

16. Arnold Toynbee, *Mankind and Mother Earth* (London: Book Club Associates, 1976), p. 573.

17. A. C. Grayling, "Through the Looking Glass," *New Humanist*, Volume 122, Issue 4 (July/August 2007).

18. Martin Scorsese, "On Reappreciating Kazantzakis," in Jolyon Mitchell and S. Brent Plate, eds., *The Religion and Film Reader* (New York: Routledge, 2007), p. 267.

19. See for example Marija Gimbutas, *The Language of the Goddess: Unearthing the Hidden Symbols of Western Civilization* (New York: Thames and Hudson, 1989) and Merlin Stone, *When God Was a Woman* (New York: Harcourt Brace Jovanovich, 1976).

20. Starhawk, *The Spiral Dance: A Rebirth of the Ancient Religion of the Great Goddess* (San Francisco: HarperSanFrancisco, 1999).

21. Irena Makarushka, "Transgressing Goodness in Breaking the Waves," in David Jasper and S. Brent Plate, eds., *Imag(in)ing Otherness: Filmic Visions of Living Together* (Atlanta: Scholars Press, 1999), p. 61.

22. Irena Makarushka, "Transgressing Goodness in Breaking the Waves," in David Jasper and S. Brent Plate, eds., *Imag(in)ing Otherness: Filmic Visions of Living Together* (Atlanta: Scholars Press, 1999), p. 62.

23. Lars von Trier, "Trier on von Trier," in Jolyon Mitchell and S. Brent Plate, eds., *The Religion and Film Reader* (New York: Routledge, 2007), p. 232.

24. Andre Bazin, "La Strada," in Alain Pierre and Bert Cardullo, eds. and trans. *Bazin at Work: Major Essays and Reviews from the Forties and Fifties* (New York: Routledge, 1997), p. 118.

25. Derek Malcolm, "A Century of Films: Day of Wrath," in Jolyon Mitchell and S. Brent Plate, eds., *The Religion and Film Reader* (New York: Routledge, 2007), p. 226.

26. Gershom Scholem, *Major Trends in Jewish Mysticism* (New York: Schocken, 1995).

27. See Luce Irigaray, *Between East and West—From Singularity to Community* (New York: Columbia University Press, 2002).

28. Robert K. Johnston, *Reel Spirituality: Theology and Film in Dialogue* (Engaging Culture) (Grand Rapids: Baker Academic, 2007), p. 59.

Conclusions

1. Colin Wilson, *The Outsider* (New York: Penguin Putnam, 1982 [1956]), p. 70.

2. Shirley MacLaine, *Out on a Limb* (London: Corgi, 1983).

Bibliography

Akbar, Arifa. "Christian Protests May Leave Philip Pullman's Trilogy as One of a Kind." *The Independent*, 18 July 2008.

Ambrosiano, Jason. "'The Ties That Bind and Bless the Soul': Grace and Noir in Schrader's *Light Sleeper*." *The Journal of Religion and Film*, Vol. 2, No. 2 (October 1998).

Anker, Roy M. *Catching Light: Looking for God in the Movies*. Grand Rapids: Eerdmans, 2004.

Armstrong, Karen. *A History of God*. London: Mandarin, 1994.

Augustine (Saint). *Confessions*. Middlesex, England: Penguin, 1986.

Batchelor, Stephen. *Buddhism Without Beliefs: A Contemporary Guide*. London: Bloomsbury, 1998.

Bazin, André. *Bazin at Work: Major Essays and Reviews from the Forties and Fifties*. Ed. and trans. Alain Pierre and Bert Cardullo. New York: Routledge, 1997.

_____. *What Is Cinema? Vol. 1*. Berkeley: University of California Press, 1967.

Beard, Mary. "Exit Strategies." *The Guardian*, 21 March 2009.

Bernheimer, Kathryn. *The 50 Greatest Jewish Movies: A Critic's Ranking of the Very Best*. Secaucus, NJ: Birch Lane Press, 1998.

Blizek, Bill, and Ronald Burke. "'The Apostle': An Interview with Robert Duvall." *Journal of Religion and Film*, Vol. 2, No. 1 (April 1998).

Bloom, Allan. *The Closing of the American Mind: How Higher Education Has Failed Democracy andImpoverished the Souls of Today's Students*. London: Penguin, 1987.

Bolton, Chad W.D. "Film Review: *Henry Poole Is Here*." *The Journal of Religion and Film*, Vol. 12, No. 2 (October 2008).

Brody, Hugh. *The Other Side of Eden: Hunters, Farmers, and the Shaping of the World*. New York: North Point Press, 2000.

Buber, Martin. *I and Thou*. Edinburgh: T&T Clark, 1937.

Burroughs, John. *The Last Harvest*. Boston: Houghton Mifflin, 1922.

Butler, Ivan. *Religion in the Cinema*. New York: A.S. Barnes, 1969.

Caplan, Mariana. *Halfway Up the Mountain: The Error of Premature Claims of Enlightenment*. Prescott, AZ: Hohm Press, 1999.

Christianson, Eric S., Peter Francis, and William Telford, eds. *Cinema Divinité: Religion, Theology and the Bible in Film*. London: SCM Press, 2005.

Cook, Reginald Lansing. "The Nature Mysticism of Thoreau." *The Concord Saunterer*. Middlebury, VT: Middlebury College Press, 1940.

Cunneen, Joseph. *Robert Bresson: A Spiritual Style in Film*. London: Continuum International, 2003.

Daniken, Erich von. *Chariots of the Gods? Was God an Astronaut?* London: Corgi, 1972.

Daoust, Phil. "A Life Out of Shot." *The Guardian*, 13 March 2010.

Deacy, Christopher. *Christologies, Redemption and the Medium of Film*. Cardiff: University of Wales Press, 2001.

Debold, Elizabeth. "Spiritual but Not Religious: Moving Beyond Postmodern Spirituality." *What Is Enlightenment?* December 2005–February 2006.

DeGiglio-Bellemare, Mario. "Signs." *Journal of Religion and Film*, Vol. 6, No. 2 (October 2002).

Dennett, Daniel C. *Breaking the Spell: Religion as a Natural Phenomenon*. London: Penguin, 2007.

Desmarais, Michele. "Report from Sundance 2006: Religion in Independent Film." *Journal of Religion and Film*, Vol. 10, No. 1 (April 2006).

Dixon, Wheeler Winston. *Visions of the Apocalypse:Spectacles of Destruction in American Cinema*. London: Wallflower Press, 2003.

Dodson, Mary. "Capturing C. S. Lewis's 'Mere' Christianity: Another Look at *Shadowlands*." *Journal of Religion and Film*, Vol. 6 No. 1 (April 2002) [2].

D'Sa, Nigel Savio. "Andrei Rublev: Religious Epiphany in Art." *Journal of Religion and Film*, Vol. 3, No. 2 (October 1999).

Dwyer, Rachel. *Filming the Gods: Religion and Indian Cinema*. London: Routledge, 2006.

Eliade, Mircea. *Shamanism: Archaic Techniques of Ecstasy*. Bollingen Series 76. Princeton: Princeton University Press, 2004.

Elliott, Carl, and Tod Chambers, eds. *Prozac as a Way of Life (Studies in Social Medicine)*. Chapel Hill: University of North Carolina Press, 2004.

Erlich, Max. *The Reincarnation of Peter Proud*. London: Corgi, 1975.

Evans-Wentz, W.Y. *The Tibetan Book of the Great Liberation*. London: Oxford University Press, 1968.

Feuerstein, Georg. *Holy Madness*. London: Arkana, 1990.

Fisher, Joe. *The Case for Reincarnation*. Toronto: Collins, 1984.

Frazer, Sir James George. *The Golden Bough: Studyin Magic and Religion* (Abridged). New York: Touchstone, 1996.

Freke, Timothy, and Peter Gandy. *The Jesus Mysteries: Was the "Original Jesus" a Pagan God?* New York: Three Rivers Press, 1999.

Gandhi, M. *The Collected Works of Mahatma Gandhi, Vol. XLI*. Publications Division, Ministry of Information and Broadcasting, Government of India, Ahmedabad, 1970.

Gillespie, Michael L. "Picturing the Way in Bae Yongkyun's *Why Has Bodhidharma Left for the East?*" *Journal of Religion and Film*, Vol. 1, No. 1 (April 1997) [28].

Gimbutas, Marija. *The Language of the Goddess: Unearthing the Hidden Symbols of Western Civilization*. New York: Thames and Hudson, 1989.

Gray, John. *Black Mass: Apocalyptic Religion and the Death of Utopia*. London: Allen Lane, 2007.

Grayling, A. C. "Through the Looking Glass." *New Humanist*, Volume 122, Issue 4 (July/August 2007).

Gregory, John. *The Neoplatonists: A Reader*. London: Routledge, 1999.

Guthrie, Kenneth Sylvan. *The Pythagorean Source-book and Library*. Grand Rapids: Phanes Press, 1987.

Harner, Michael. *The Way of the Shaman*. San Francisco: Harper & Row, 1990.

Harvey, Graham. *Animism: Respecting the Living World*. London: Hurst, 2005.

Hegel, G.W.F. *Phenomenology of Spirit*. Oxford: Oxford University Press, 1977.

Hultkrantz, Ake. *The Religions of the American Indians*. Berkeley: University of California Press, 1979.

Husain, Ed. *The Islamist: Why I Joined Radical Islam in Britain, What I Saw Inside and Why I Left*. London: Penguin, 2007.

Irigaray, Luce. *Between East and West: From Singularity to Community*. New York: Columbia University Press, 2002.

Irwin, William, ed. *The Matrix and Philosophy: Welcome to the Desert of the Real*. Chicago: Open Court, 2002.

Izod, John. *Myth, Mind and the Screen: Understanding the Heroes of Our Time*. Cambridge: Cambridge University Press, 2001.

Jacoby, Susan. *Freethinkers: A History of American Secularism*. New York: Metropolitan Books, 2004.

Jasper, David, and S. Brent Plate, eds. *Imag(in)ing Otherness: Filmic Visions of Living Together*. Atlanta: Scholars Press, 1999.

Jefferies, R. *The Story of My Heart*. London: Macmillan, 1968.

Johnston, Robert K. *Reel Spirituality: Theology and Film in Dialogue*. Engaging Culture. Grand Rapids: Baker Academic, 2007.

Kalweit, Holger. *Dreamtime and Inner Space: The World of the Shaman*. Boston: Shambala, 1988.

Kapell, Matthew, and William G. Doty, eds. *Jacking in to the Matrix Franchise*. New York: Continuum, 2004.

Kierkegaard. *The Essential Kierkegaard*. Princeton: Princeton University Press, 1990.

King, Mike. *The American Cinema of Excess: Extremes of the National Mind on Film*. Jefferson, NC: McFarland, 2009.

_____. *Postsecularism: The Hidden Challenge to Extremism*. Cambridge: James Clarke, 2009.

_____. *Secularism: The Hidden Origins of Disbelief*. Cambridge: James Clarke, 2007.

Klein, Naomi. *The Shock Doctrine: The Rise of Disaster Capitalism*. London: Penguin, 2007.

Kramnick, Isaac, ed. *The Portable Enlightenment Reader*. London: Penguin, 1995.

Lancelin, Aude. "*The Matrix* Decoded: Le Nouvel Observateur Interview with Jean Baudrillard." *International Journal of Baudrillard Studies*, Vol. 1, No. 2 (July 2004).

Lasch, Christopher. *The Culture of Narcissism: American Life in an Age of Diminishing Expectations*. New York: W. W. Norton, 1991.

Lewis, Jon, ed. *The End of Cinema as We Know It: American Film in the Nineties*. London: Pluto Press, 2002.

Lloyd, Peter B. *Exegesis of the Matrix*. London: Whole-Being Books, 2003.

MacLaine, Shirley. *Out on a Limb*. London: Corgi, 1983.

Marsh, Clive. *Theology Goes to the Movies: An Introduction to Critical Christian Thinking*. London: Routledge, 2007.

_____, and Gaye Ortiz, eds. *Exploration in Theology and Film: Movies and Meanings*. Oxford: Blackwell, 1997.

Martin, David. *On Secularization: Towards a Revised General Theory*. Aldershot: Ashgate, 2005.

Martin, Joel W., and Conrad E. Ostwalt, Jr., eds. *Screening the Sacred: Religion, Myth, and Ideologyin

Popular American Film. Boulder: Westview Press, 1995.

May, John R., ed. *New Image of Religious Film.* Kansas City: Sheed and Ward, 1997.

McCarthy, Helen. *Hayao Miyazaki: Master of Japanese Animation: Films, Themes, Artistry,* Berkeley: Stone Bridge Press, 2003.

McEver, Matthew. "The Messianic Figure in Film: Christology Beyond the Biblical Epic." *The Journal of Religion and Film,* Vol. 2, No. 2 (October 1998).

McGrath, Alister. *The Twilight of Atheism: The Rise and Fall of Disbelief in the Modern World.* New York: Doubleday, 2004.

Means, Russell. *Where White Men Fear to Tread: The Autobiography of Russell Means.* New York: St. Martin's Griffin, 1995.

Medved, Michael. *Hollywood vs. America.* New York: HarperCollins, 1993.

Miles, Margaret. *Seeing and Believing: Religion and Values in the Movies.* Boston: Beacon Press, 1996.

Mill, John Stuart. *On Liberty and Other Essays.* Oxford: Oxford University Press, 1998.

Mitchell, Jolyon, and S. Brent Plate, eds. *The Religion and Film Reader.* New York: Routledge, 2007.

Naifeh, S., and G.W. Smith. *Jackson Pollock: An American Saga.* London: Pimlico, 1992.

Nanamoli, Bhikku, and Bhikku Bhodi. *The Middle Length Discourses of the Buddha: A New Translation of the Majjhima Nikaya.* Boston: Wisdom, 1995.

Napier, Susan. *Anime from Akira to Howl's Moving Castle: Experiencing Contemporary Japanese Animation.* New York: Palgrave Macmillan, 2006.

Newman, Kim. "Rubber Reality." *Sight and Sound.* June 1999.

Nicholson, Shirley, ed. *Shamanism.* Wheaton, IL: Theosophical Publishing House, 1987.

Nietzsche, F. *The Birth of Tragedy.* London: Penguin, 1993.

_____. *Twilight of the Idols.* Oxford: Oxford University Press, 1998.

Northcott, Michael. *An Angel Directs the Storm: Apocalyptic Religion and American Empire.* London: I.B. Tauris, 2004.

Paper, Jordan. *The Spirits Are Drunk: Comparative Approaches to Chinese Religion.* Albany: State University of New York Press, 1995.

Papus (Dr. G. Encausse). *Reincarnation: Physical, Astral and Spiritual Evolution.* Trans. Marguerite Vallior. London: Martinist Press, n.d.

Pascal, Blaise. *Pensées.* Harmondsworth: Penguin, 1980.

Pert, Candace B. *Molecules of Emotion: The Science Behind Mind-Body Medicine.* New York: Scribner, 2003.

Plate, S. Brent, ed. *Representing Religion in World Cinema: Filmmaking, Mythmaking, Culture Making.* New York: Palgrave MacMillan, 2003.

_____, and David Jasper, eds. *Imag(in)ing Otherness: Filmic Visions of Living Together.* Atlanta: Scholars Press, 1999.

Rawlinson, Andrew. *The Book of Enlightened Masters: Western Teachers in Eastern Traditions.* Chicago: Open Court, 1997.

Reps, Paul. *Zen Flesh, Zen Bones.* Middlesex, England: Penguin, 1976.

Russell, Bertrand. *A History of Western Philosophy.* London: Unwin Paperbacks, 1989.

_____. *Mysticism and Logic.* London: George Allen and Unwin, 1963.

Russell, D. E. H. *Against Pornography: The Evidence of Harm.* Berkeley: Russell, 1993.

Sara, Elyse. "Book Review: *Finding Meaning at the Movies.*" *The Journal of Religion and Film.*

Scholem, Gershom. *Major Trends in Jewish Mysticism.* New York: Schocken, 1995.

Schrader, Paul. *Transcendental Style in Film: Ozu, Bresson and Dreyer.* New York: Da Capo, 1988.

Schuler, Jean. "Kierkegaard at Babette's Feast: The Return to the Finite." *Journal of Religion and Film,* Vol. 1, No. 2 (October 1997).

Schwartz, Susan L. "I Dream, Therefore I Am: *What Dreams May Come.*" *Journal of Religion and Film,* Vol. 4, No. 1 (April 2000).

Simon, Stephen. *The Force Is with You: Mystical Movie Messages That Inspire Our Lives.* Charlottesville, VA: Hampton Roads, 2002.

Sluyter, Dean, and Ean Sluyter. *Cinema Nirvana: Enlightenment Lessons from the Movies.* New York: Three Rivers Press, 2005.

Smith, David L. "'Beautiful Necessities': *American Beauty* and the Idea of Freedom." *Journal of Religion and Film,* Vol. 6, No. 2 (October 2002).

Sontag, Susan. *Against Interpretation.* London: Vintage, 2001.

Starhawk. *The Spiral Dance: A Rebirth of the Ancient Religion of the Great Goddess.* New York: HarperCollins, 1999.

Stearn, J. *Edgar Cayce: The Sleeping Prophet.* New York: Bantam Books, 1989.

Steiner, R. *Occult Science: An Outline.* London: Rudolf Steiner Press, 1986.

Stone, Merlin. *When God Was a Woman.* New York: Harcourt Brace Jovanovich, 1976.

Storr, Anthony. *Feet of Clay: A Study of Gurus.* London: HarperCollins, 1997.

Tarkovsky, Andrei. *Sculpting in Time.* London: Faber and Faber, 1989.

Tolstoy, Leo. *The Kingdom of God Is Within You.* Mineola, NY: Dover, 2006.

Toynbee, Arnold. *Mankind and Mother Earth.* London: Book Club Associates, 1976.

Trungpa, C. *Cutting Through Spiritual Materialism.* Boston: Shambhala, 1987.

Tuchman, Barbara W. *Bible and Sword: England and Palestine from the Bronze Age to Balfour.* New York: Ballantine, 1984.

Tucker, Mike. *Dreaming with Open Eyes: The Shamanic in 20th C Art and Culture*. San Francisco: Aquarian/ HarperSanFrancisco, 1992.

Vogler, Christopher. *The Writer's Journey: Mythic Structure for Storytellers and Screenwriters* 2nd ed. London: Pan Books, 1998.

Watkins, Gregory J. "Book Review: *Teaching Religion and Film*." *The Journal of Religion and Film*.

Weber, Max. *The Protestant Ethic and the Spirit of Capitalism*. New York: Dover, 2003.

Whitman, Walt. *Leaves of Grass*. Oxford, New York: Oxford University Press, 1990.

Wilson, Colin. *The Outsider*. New York: Penguin Putnam, 1982.

Wilson, Eric G. *Secret Cinema: Gnostic Vision in Film*. New York: Continuum International, 2006.

_____. *The Strange World of David Lynch: Ironic Religion from "Eraserhead" to "Mulholland Dr."* New York: Continuum International, 2007.

Woolger, Roger. *Other Lives, Other Selves*. London: Bantam, 1988.

Wright, Melanie J. *Religion and Film: An Introduction*. London: I. B. Tauris, 2006.

Yamakage, Motohisa. *The Essence of Shinto: Japan's Spiritual Heart*. Tokyo: Kodansha International, 2006.

Yarri, Donna. "Film Review: I ♥ Huckabees." *The Journal of Religion and Film*, Vol. 10, No. 1 (April 2006).

Zohar, Danah, and Ian Marshall. *SQ: Spiritual Intelligence, the Ultimate Intelligence*. London: Bloomsbury, 2000.

Index

Aboriginals, 47, 48, 63, 131, 203, 214, 249
About Schmidt, 68, 74, 75, 241
Advaita, 198
aesthetics, 6, 9, 19, 20, 21, 23, 24, 25, 27, 28, 29, 30, 31, 32, 33, 34, 35, 36, 50, 51, 52, 63, 69, 70, 76, 129, 164, 166, 168, 172, 189, 230
afterlife, 21, 33, 60, 65, 76, 80, 81, 82, 83, 84, 87, 88, 89, 90, 91, 92, 95, 101, 111, 181, 193, 205, 206
Afterlife, 21, 81, 82, 205, 241
agape, 115, 116, 142, 143, 145, 228
aggression, 9, 63, 113, 120, 121, 176, 182, 185, 217, 218, 229
Agnes of God, 136, 140, 146, 208, 210, 232, 236, 241, 247
agnostic, 9, 212, 235
Agora, 51, 241
Akashic record, 67, 88
Akira Kurosawa's Dreams, 33, 241
alchemy, 36, 50, 52
alienation, 7, 8, 9, 20, 30, 61, 105, 110
aliens, 9, 61, 62, 217, 239
Allen, Woody, 20, 105, 186, 187, 241, 246, 262
Altered States, 61, 63, 241
Ambrosiano, Jason, 186, 262, 266
American Beauty, 24, 25, 27, 33, 35, 70, 114, 182, 241, 247, 253, 268
American Transcendentalists, 29
American Werewolf in London, An, 61, 241
Amish, 99, 145, 169, 170, 212, 213, 214, 251
Anchoress, 24, 25, 27, 28, 35, 129, 201, 227, 228, 230, 241, 247
Andrei Rublev, 30, 31, 227, 241, 254, 266
Andrew Cohen, 7, 238
Angel Heart, 49, 50, 241

angels, 33, 42, 43, 71, 73, 80, 81, 82, 86, 87, 88, 89, 90, 91, 95, 113, 114, 181, 224, 232, 235, 248, 249, 251
animism, 10, 29, 36, 37, 38, 39, 41, 42, 44, 45, 46, 47, 49, 50, 55, 63, 64, 161, 182, 192, 199, 204, 226, 239, 247, 248, 249
anthropologists, 41, 226
anthropology, 41, 226
Anthroposophy, 37, 56, 93, 192
Antichrist, 57, 107, 229, 230, 241
Aparajito, 194, 241
apocalypse, 105, 106, 107, 108, 109, 136, 257, 266
Apostle, The, 127, 130, 154, 167, 182, 241, 247, 259, 266
Apted, Michael, 40, 238, 243, 245, 250
Aquinas, Thomas, 10, 89, 128, 215
Arsenyev, Vladimir, 44, 131
Artificial Intelligence AI, 241
Asoka, 161, 170, 171, 204, 241
astrology, 36, 50, 51, 52
At Play in the Fields of the Lord, 143, 241
Atanarjuat The Fast Runner, 97, 241
atheism, 9, 12, 27, 55, 72, 129, 134, 141, 199, 211, 216, 217, 233, 235
atheist, 16, 65, 69, 72, 90, 100, 128, 129, 134, 140, 153, 193, 198, 212, 214, 217, 218, 219, 248
atonement, 6, 125, 127, 129, 143, 168, 172, 176, 177, 178, 180, 181, 182, 191, 202, 247, 248
Atonement, 22, 168, 169, 171, 173, 175, 177, 178, 179, 180, 181, 183, 185, 187, 189, 191, 241
Audrey Rose, 92, 103, 109, 210, 241
Augustine, St., 10, 50, 51
autism, 13, 31, 53
autistic, 13, 66, 73, 74, 238
Awakenings, 19, 174, 241, 253

Bad Lieutenant, 179, 180, 191, 239, 241, 247
Baraka, 29, 35, 44, 74, 241, 247
bardo realm (in Tibetan Buddhism), 67, 70, 111, 113, 114, 116, 118, 248
Battlefield Earth, 154, 241
Baudrillard, Jean, 119, 120, 259, 267
Bazin, André, 12, 16, 20, 28, 133, 136, 137, 230, 237, 252, 259, 265, 266
Beautiful Mind, A, 52, 241
Becket, 20, 156, 241
Bee Season, 53, 198, 211, 241
Being There, 130, 239, 241
Believers, The, 49, 241
bereavement, 21, 29, 60, 62, 65, 66, 68, 69, 70, 71, 74, 76, 80, 82, 83, 102, 103, 250
Bergman, Ingmar, 17, 20, 71, 72, 73, 102, 126, 127, 129, 141, 182, 186, 187, 198, 199, 223, 225, 237, 238, 241, 243, 245, 246, 257
Bhagavad Gita, 96, 162, 170, 183, 195
Bhaskar, Ira, 194, 263
Birth, 102, 109, 241, 253, 268
Bishop of Southwark, 11
black magic, 49
Black Narcissus, 193, 210, 232, 241
Black Robe, 141, 241
Blair Witch Project, 32, 241
Blake, William, 30, 34, 59, 60, 89, 126, 130, 244, 245
Blithe Spirit, 58, 85, 241
Bloomsbury group, 75
Blue Velvet, 111, 114, 241
Body, The, 15, 105, 106, 217, 241, 252
Bollywood, 96, 149, 160, 167, 199
Breaking the Waves, 140, 229, 241, 259, 265
Bresson, Robert, 16, 20, 110, 138, 139, 140, 142, 143, 144, 146, 148, 153, 154, 238, 242, 245, 252, 259, 266, 268

Bridge on the River Kwai, The, 169, 241, 250
Brook, Peter, 124, 161, 193, 194, 196, 243, 244, 249
Brown, Dan, 53
brujería, 49
brujo, 49, 56, 63
Bruno, Giordano, 51, 55, 196
Buddha, 18, 19, 77, 92, 98, 99, 100, 113, 114, 121, 124, 137, 155, 157, 158, 159, 162, 163, 164, 165, 166, 189, 190, 193, 202, 203, 204, 220, 241, 249, 250, 257, 259, 261, 268
Buddha Collapsed Out of Shame, 202, 241
Buddhism, 6, 10, 11, 25, 28, 36, 38, 44, 45, 49, 59, 67, 77, 86, 97, 98, 99, 100, 112, 119, 120, 125, 144, 145, 147, 148, 149, 155, 156, 157, 158, 161, 162, 163, 164, 166, 167, 168, 170, 173, 174, 175, 181, 190, 191, 192, 193, 197, 203, 204, 206, 208, 220, 221, 239, 247, 250, 254, 259, 264, 266
Buñuel, Luis, 115, 139, 140, 153, 219, 230, 244, 246, 259, 264
Bushido code, 163, 189

Campbell, Joseph, 18, 120
Campion, Jane, 13, 195, 243, 244
Caouette, Jonathan, 11, 245
Capra, 15, 86, 193, 243
Caputo, John D., 10
caritas, 69, 142, 143, 182
Carrie, 20, 57, 58, 210, 241
Castaneda, Carlos, 210
catharsis, 142
Catholic Film Reviews, 15
Catholicism, 16, 28, 55, 90, 125, 128, 134, 135, 139, 140, 144, 195, 208, 220, 221, 222, 236, 249
Cave of the Yellow Dog, The, 97, 100, 193, 206, 241
Chan Buddhism, 28, 126, 157, 158, 250
Chances Are, 94, 95, 102, 104, 108, 241
charity, 27, 140, 142, 144
charlatanry, 8, 85, 102, 103, 124, 128, 212, 248
Cherokee, 41
Chief Dan George, 41, 42, 203, 239
Chief Ted Thin Elk, 38, 41
Cho, Francisca, 28, 254
Chocolat, 146, 241
Chopra, Deepak, 7
Chosen, The, 149, 159, 167, 217, 241, 247
Christianity, 10, 11, 17, 18, 19, 23, 24, 25, 26, 27, 28, 31, 35, 36, 37, 38, 39, 42, 47, 49, 50, 51, 52, 53, 55, 56, 57, 58, 67, 69, 70, 72, 73, 82, 83, 86, 87, 89, 92, 93, 105, 106, 107, 109, 113, 115, 116, 119, 127, 128, 129, 136, 137, 138, 139, 140, 141, 143, 144, 145, 146, 149, 152, 153, 154, 157, 167, 168, 169, 170, 173, 174, 178, 179, 180, 181, 183, 185, 186, 188, 190, 191, 192, 194, 196, 202, 204, 206, 209, 212, 213, 214, 215, 216, 218, 219, 220, 221, 222, 223, 224, 227, 228, 231, 232, 235, 238, 239, 241, 247, 249, 250, 255, 257, 258, 262, 263, 266, 267
Christianson, Eric S., 110, 183, 188, 190, 252, 253, 259, 261, 263, 264, 266
cinematography, 11, 12, 19, 20, 24, 28, 29, 35, 42, 68, 75, 112, 145, 146, 153, 155, 167, 198, 199, 201, 238, 247, 248
City of Angels, 71, 80, 89, 90, 241
City of God, 173, 241
clairvoyant, 56, 82, 94, 98
Close Encounters of the Third Kind, 94, 241
Cocteau, Jean, 32, 112, 244
Cohen, Leonard, 67, 156
Coleridge, Samuel, 11, 31, 75, 198
Comanche, 42
communism, 178, 216
compassion, 9, 19, 58, 60, 68, 75, 79, 80, 85, 89, 138, 140, 143, 144, 150, 163, 168, 171, 172, 173, 174, 175, 176, 178, 182, 189, 190, 191, 202, 220, 239, 248, 249, 250
connectedness, 7, 8, 9, 13, 17, 19, 29, 34, 57, 63, 71, 80, 108, 109, 130, 146, 168, 186, 229
Contact, 216, 217, 241
convent, 134, 135, 136, 144, 146, 210, 211
conversion, 62, 143, 144, 170, 227
Cook, the Thief, His Wife, and Her Lover, The, 51, 52, 241
corn dolly, 26, 228
costume drama, 16, 20, 21, 24, 27, 105, 153, 169, 170, 180, 218, 222, 225, 237
Cries and Whispers, 71, 73, 74, 80, 241
Crime of Father Amaro, The, 139, 140, 221, 222, 241
Crimes and Misdemeanors, 102, 186, 187, 241
crop circles, 61, 62
Crouching Tiger, Hidden Dragon, 166, 242
Crucible, The, 216, 242
Cul-de-Sac, 242
cultural autism, 13, 31, 52, 60, 78, 94, 139
Cunneen, Joseph, 16, 252, 266
Cup, The, 203, 204, 205, 242
cynicism, 126, 132, 208, 233, 234, 235

Da Vinci Code, The, 15, 51, 53, 54, 63, 106, 232, 242
Dalai Lama, 98, 99, 104, 123, 155, 156, 167, 220, 221, 248, 250
Dancer in the Dark, 140, 229, 242
Dances with Wolves, 163, 242
Dark City, 111, 242

Dark Crystal, The, 54, 242
Davaa, Byambasuren, 11, 97, 206, 207, 241, 245, 247
Davidic dance (Judaism), 159
Dawkins, Richard, 100, 212, 215, 216, 217
Day of Wrath, 230, 231, 242, 265
de Beauvoir, Simone, 8
Deacy, Christopher, 184, 185, 254, 262, 266
Dead Again, 103, 109, 242
Dead Man, 135, 136, 146, 165, 177, 178, 182, 238, 242, 247
Dead Man Walking, 135, 136, 146, 177, 178, 182, 242, 247
Dead Poet's Society, 32, 35, 174, 242
Dean Spanley, 104, 109, 242
demiurge, 111, 118, 119, 120
Dersu Uzula, 28, 35, 47, 63, 203, 239, 242, 247
Desiderata, 11, 148
Devi (The Goddess), 167, 199, 242
devotion, 5, 10, 21, 25, 53, 94, 140, 159, 160, 161, 167, 198, 199, 229, 232, 233, 248
Diary of a Country Priest, 136, 138, 141, 146, 147, 152, 234, 235, 238, 242, 247
Diary of Anne Frank, The, 152, 242
Diderot, Denis, 134, 135
Dionysius the pseudo-Areopagite, 19
Dogma, 90, 234, 235, 236, 242, 248
Dogville, 164, 229, 242
Donnie Darko, 67, 68, 113, 114, 116, 118, 122, 242, 248
Doors, The, 59, 60, 195, 242
Doubt, 144, 146, 242
Dreyer, 20, 110, 128, 230, 231, 242, 244, 252, 259, 268
Drunken Angel, 172, 173, 174, 191, 242, 248
Duvall, Robert, 127, 128, 129, 154, 241, 247, 259, 266

East Is East, 242
Eastwood, Clint, 41, 42, 78, 187, 188, 190, 243, 244, 246, 252, 263
Eckhart, Meister, 7, 113
Education of Little Tree, 100, 242
Edward Scissorhands, 242, 253
Ehrman, Max, 11, 148
Eliade, Mircea, 37, 255
Elmer Gantry, 128, 210, 211, 216, 232, 236, 242, 248
Emerson, Ralph Waldo, 25, 32
emotional intelligence, 13
Enakkul Oruvan, 96, 242
Encounters at the End of the World, 29, 242
End of Days, 108, 242
Enduring Love, 233, 235, 242
English Patient, The, 80, 242
Enigma of Kaspar Hauser, The, 130, 242

Enlightenment, 8, 10, 36, 61, 134, 156, 157, 167, 174, 215, 242, 248, 252, 253, 259, 266, 267, 268
enlightenment (Eastern concept), 25, 98, 123, 216
Enlightenment Guaranteed, 8, 156, 167, 242, 248
Enter the Dragon, 79, 189, 242
*Entertaining Angels
The Dorothy Day Story*, 221, 236, 242
eros, 115, 182
escapism, 15, 62, 112, 119, 121, 189, 224, 232, 237
eschatology, 105
esotericism, 36, 37, 51, 56, 57, 101, 195
Estève, Michel, 16, 20
eternal, 14, 51, 81, 82, 96, 101, 105, 115, 116, 118, 164, 212
eternal recurrence, 96, 115, 116, 118
ethics, 161, 183, 187, 248
Excalibur, 111, 242
Exiles, 48, 167, 242
existentialism, 13, 34, 63, 95, 110, 186, 187
Existenz, 111, 121, 242
exorcism, 57, 85, 86, 210
Exorcism of Emily Rose, The, 57, 210, 242
Exorcist, The, 20, 57, 63, 84, 85, 210, 242
*Expelled
No Intelligence Allowed*, 218, 242
Eyes Wide Open, 152, 231, 242
Eyes Wide Shut, 8, 52, 54, 242

familiar (spirit companion), 22, 30, 37, 55, 56, 89, 95, 96, 97, 103, 114, 115, 127, 134, 135, 155, 160, 177, 184, 211
Faraway, So Close!, 89, 238, 242
Fearless, 68, 80, 174, 233, 242
Fiddler on the Roof, 152, 242
Fifth Element, 61, 62, 242
Fight Club, 108, 242
film noir, 19, 110, 184, 186
Fisher King, The, 100, 115, 174, 175, 191, 242, 248, 261
Fluke, 104, 242
forgiveness, 129, 168, 169, 172, 175, 176, 177, 178, 179, 180, 182, 191, 247, 250
Forrest Gump, 130, 242
Frankfurt School, 14
Frazer, Sir James, 26, 226, 228, 253, 267
Freud, Sigmund, 9, 14, 39, 41, 72, 74, 101, 108, 129, 136, 148, 150, 167, 182, 183, 198, 199, 209, 210, 217, 223, 224, 225, 234, 247
Friendly Persuasion, 169, 170, 172, 191, 242, 248

Gabbeh, 201, 242
Gandhi, Mahatma, 162, 169, 170, 261, 267

Ganesh (Hinduism), 160
gematria, 52, 53
*George Harrison
Living in the Material World*, 60, 242
George Lucas, 18, 44, 245
Gerry, 29, 242
Ghost, 38, 39, 40, 58, 83, 90, 102, 104, 113, 116, 162, 163, 165, 166, 167, 189, 190, 191, 238, 242, 250
Ghost Busters, 116, 242
Ghost XE "*Ghost*"Dance, 38, 39, 40, 250
*Ghost Dog
The Way of the Samurai*, 162, 238, 242
ghosts, 58, 81, 83, 85, 86, 90, 91, 102, 113, 117
Gibson, Mel, 70, 223, 244
Gift, The, 56, 242
Gnostic, 6, 10, 18, 21, 62, 111, 118, 119, 122, 255, 259, 261, 269
God, 11, 14, 15, 19, 26, 28, 41, 51, 52, 53, 59, 60, 61, 62, 70, 71, 72, 73, 76, 78, 79, 80, 90, 93, 99, 101, 105, 106, 107, 114, 115, 116, 124, 128, 135, 137, 138, 139, 140, 141, 143, 146, 148, 149, 150, 151, 152, 154, 157, 160, 161, 168, 169, 172, 173, 175, 176, 177, 179, 180, 184, 185, 188, 189, 193, 197, 198, 199, 201, 209, 210, 212, 213, 214, 215, 216, 217, 218, 219, 221, 222, 223, 224, 225, 229, 230, 232, 233, 234, 235, 236, 241, 247, 248, 255, 257, 260, 261, 264, 265, 266, 267, 268
God Who Wasn't There, The, 217, 218, 242
Godard, Jean-Luc, 27, 28, 230, 242, 248
goddess, 10, 25, 26, 28, 160, 199, 225, 227, 228, 230, 235, 247, 248
Godfather, The, 183, 242
Gods and Monsters, 80, 242
Goethe, 32, 75, 198
Golden Compass, The, 37, 54, 55, 56, 242
Golem, 18
Good Will Hunting, 174, 242
Gospel According to St. Matthew, The, 27, 152, 154, 167, 238, 242, 248, 261
Gospels, 107, 108, 138, 164, 218, 223
grace, 16, 19, 91, 135, 136, 137, 138, 139, 147, 186, 238, 239, 247, 248
Graham, David John, 15, 17, 184, 225, 252, 262
Greenaway, Peter, 51, 52, 164, 241, 244
Greene, Graham (Native American actor), 38, 131, 239
Grizzly Man, 29, 193, 242
Groundhog Day, 6, 94, 115, 116, 118, 122, 142, 175, 239, 242, 248, 259
*Guge
The Lost Kingdom of Tibet*, 242
Gulpilil, David, 47, 48, 203, 239

Gurdjieff, G. I., 59, 124, 125, 159, 161, 196, 197, 249
guru, 7, 123, 124, 126, 127, 128, 133, 193, 194, 195, 196, 197, 233, 234
Guru, The, 126, 242

Haibane Renmei, 181, 191, 242, 248
Hail Mary, 27, 28, 35, 230, 242, 248
Haré Raama Haré Krishna, 197, 242
harmony, 10, 111, 200, 204
Harrer, Heinrich, 99, 204, 250
Harris, Sam, 212, 215, 217, 218
Harry Potter and the Chamber of Secrets, 54, 242
Harry Potter and the Goblet of Fire, 242
Harry Potter and the Prisoner of Azkeban, 54, 243
Harry Potter and the Sorcerer's Stone, 111, 112, 243
Hasidism, 52, 149, 150, 152
healing, 49, 87, 126, 129, 130, 132, 227
Heart and Souls, 84, 87, 90, 102, 243
heathenism, 25
Heaven Can Wait, 82, 84, 87, 243
Hegel, 8, 57, 215, 252, 263, 267
Henry Poole Is Here, 66, 243, 256, 266
Hermes Trismegistus, 54
Hermetica, 36
Hidden Fortress, The, 44, 243
High Plains Drifter, 188, 243
Himalaya (Caravan), 100, 203, 243, 248
Hinchi Indians, 62
Hinduism, 11, 99, 119, 120, 149, 159, 160, 161, 167, 192, 194, 198, 199, 200, 248, 261
hippie, 60, 61, 98, 195, 196, 197, 198
Holy Flying Circus, 12, 243
Holy Smoke, 195, 233, 234, 243
homosexuality, 80, 135, 140, 152, 153, 225, 231, 232, 233
Hopi, 29
horror film, 57, 62, 103, 210
horror film, 20, 37, 49, 50, 57, 62, 80, 85, 109
Hours, The, 75, 76, 80, 243
Hubbard, Barbara Marx, 7
Hulk, 62, 243
Hultkrantz, Ake, 43, 255, 267
hunter gatherers, 47, 131
Hypatia, 51

I Heart Huckabees, 62, 243
Idiots Savants, 59, 130, 132, 133
idolatry, 108, 151, 152, 234, 235
Igby Goes Down, 80, 243
Ikiru, 172, 191, 243, 248
Illusion, 67, 87, 88, 243
In the Mood for Love, 11, 243
Incident at Oglala, 40, 238, 243
India, 10, 39, 40, 41, 45, 49, 50, 58, 74, 76, 77, 96, 99, 101, 103, 104, 108, 116, 119, 126, 131, 142, 149, 155, 158, 159, 160, 161, 162, 167, 170,

171, 192, 193, 194, 195, 196, 197, 198, 199, 203, 204, 210, 211, 233, 248, 250, 261, 263, 267
Indian XE "India" dance, 126, 161
Indigo, 60, 61, 117, 243
Indigo (children), 60, 61, 117, 243
infinite, 2, 14, 26, 34, 57, 71, 118, 121, 188, 212, 230
Inherit the Wind, 215, 216, 217, 218, 243
Inipi, 38
interdiscipline, 13, 14, 225
Into Great Silence, 11, 28, 35, 145, 146, 154, 156, 167, 207, 243, 248
Into the Wild, 29, 177, 178, 193, 239, 243
Iran, 10, 77, 78, 105, 158, 200, 201, 204
Irigaray, Luce, 160, 261, 265, 267
Ishi
The Last Yahi, 131, 243
Islam, 6, 49, 79, 119, 144, 149, 150, 152, 159, 167, 169, 191, 192, 194, 200, 201, 202, 205, 249
Izod, John, 83, 257, 267

Jai Santoshi Maa, 159, 160, 167, 199, 200, 243, 248, 261
Jasper, David, 16, 17, 130, 154, 194, 198, 224, 252, 253, 254, 259, 263, 265, 267, 268
Jaws, 85, 165, 242, 243
Jefferies, Richard, 29, 32
Jesus, 7, 18, 19, 20, 70, 88, 92, 105, 106, 107, 108, 117, 128, 129, 133, 135, 136, 138, 140, 143, 152, 153, 154, 167, 170, 178, 179, 180, 183, 184, 185, 186, 188, 194, 212, 213, 214, 217, 218, 222, 223, 224, 225, 232, 234, 235, 243, 247, 248, 257, 267
Jesus Christ, 7, 9, 16, 18, 19, 20, 32, 54, 67, 70, 71, 88, 92, 105, 106, 107, 108, 117, 121, 127, 128, 129, 130, 133, 134, 135, 136, 138, 140, 143, 152, 153, 154, 157, 164, 167, 170, 178, 179, 180, 183, 184, 185, 186, 187, 188, 193, 194, 211, 212, 213, 214, 217, 218, 222, 223, 224, 225, 229, 232, 234, 235, 243, 247, 248, 257, 267
Jesus of Montreal, 70, 106, 214, 223, 224, 232, 234, 243
Jesus of Nazareth, 20, 243
Johnston, Robert K., 78, 235, 257, 265
Journal of Religion and Film, 15, 62, 128, 145, 253, 254, 255, 256, 257, 259, 261, 262, 263, 266, 267, 268, 269
Judaism, 11, 36, 51, 52, 53, 76, 77, 105, 149, 150, 151, 152, 159, 160, 161, 167, 186, 187, 198, 202, 211, 213, 214, 215, 231, 239, 247, 249, 262, 265, 266, 268
Julian of Norwich, 26
Jung, C. G., 18, 39, 47, 103

Kabbalah, 36, 51, 52, 53
Kadosh, 105, 150, 151, 167, 202, 230, 231, 243
Kagemusha, 243
Kalweit, Holger, 43, 255, 267
Kandahar, 202, 243
Kar Wai, Wong, 11
karma, 28, 46, 78, 83, 84, 93, 113, 116, 125, 175, 178, 179, 181, 193, 197, 205, 250
Karz, 96, 243
Karzzzz, 96, 243
Kazantzakis, Nikos, 222, 223, 225, 265
Keuss, Jeffrey F., 252
Kidman, Nicole, 55, 76, 102, 229
Kierkegaard, Soren, 10, 23, 24, 30, 32, 33, 34, 76, 143, 253, 254, 257, 267, 268
Kieslowski, 69
Kill Bill
Vol. 1, 243
Vol. 2, 243
kirtan (Hinduism), 159, 199
Kite Runner, The, 6, 181, 191, 202, 243
kodami, 45, 46
Koran, 200, 201, 202
Koyaanisqatsi, 29, 74, 243
Krishnamurti, Jiddu, 148, 149
Kroeber, Alfred, 131, 132
Kubrick, Stanley, 8, 9, 52, 237, 252
Kundun, 9, 47, 98, 109, 155, 156, 167, 220, 222, 238, 243, 248
Kurosawa, Akira, 17, 28, 33, 44, 47, 163, 171, 172, 173, 174, 177, 178, 191, 198, 206, 237, 239, 241, 242, 243, 244, 245, 247, 248

Lagaan, 161, 194, 200, 243
Lakota, 38
lama, 98, 99, 197, 203, 249
Last of His Tribe, The, 131, 239, 243
Last Samurai, The, 163, 165, 243
Last Supper, 17
Last Supper, The, 49, 243
Last Temptation of Christ, The, 88, 89, 156, 164, 219, 222, 223, 243
Last Wave, The, 47, 48, 63, 64, 214, 243, 249
Late Great Planet Earth, The, 107, 243
Latter Days, 231, 236, 243, 249
Lawnmower Man, 121, 217, 243
Lawrence, D. H., 120, 223, 224, 259
Lean, David, 85, 101, 241, 244
Leap of Faith, 127, 128, 129, 130, 140, 243
Left Behind, 107, 217, 243
Left Behind II
Tribulation Force, 243
Left Behind III
World at War, 243
Left Luggage, 152, 243
lesbianism, 151, 225, 231
Levity, 178, 179, 243

Lewis, C. S., 15, 70, 90, 121, 216, 257, 266
liberation, 15, 19, 67, 118, 120, 140, 174, 183, 197, 200, 220, 227
Liberation Theology, 19, 219, 221, 236
Life Less Ordinary, A, 87, 243
Life of Brian, The, 11, 12, 124, 130, 154, 224, 234, 235, 243
Life of the Buddha, The, 155, 243
Light Sleeper, 185, 186, 243, 262, 266
Little Big Man, 41, 243
Little Buddha, 92, 99, 104, 109, 238, 243, 249
London School of Economics, 12
Lost Horizon, 193, 197, 243
Lost World of Tibet, The, 156, 243
Loughlin, Gerard, 15, 17, 252, 253
Lourdes, 67, 211, 250
Love Guru, The, 126, 243
Love Liza, 75, 78, 80, 243
luminosity, 20
Luther, 16, 20, 243
Luther, Martin, 16, 234

Maborosi, 74, 75, 77, 78, 80, 182, 243, 249
Madhumati, 97, 108, 159, 243
Magdalene Sisters, The, 144, 146, 222, 243
magical realism, 25, 42, 48, 110, 112, 125, 140, 180, 224, 225, 234
Magician, The, 126, 243
Magnificent Seven, The, 172, 243
Mahabharata, 158, 160, 161, 171, 193, 194, 196, 243
Mahal, 97, 108, 243
Mahayana Buddhism, 77, 100, 125, 163, 167
Maher, Ian, 19, 174, 253
Maisto, Maria Consuelo, 20, 21, 33, 253, 254
Makaurshka, Iena, 229
Maksim Munzuk, 44, 203, 239
Malcolm, Derek, 230, 265
Malick, Terence, 29, 245
Man Called Horse, A, 41, 243
Man Called Peter, A, 127, 132, 243, 249
Man for All Seasons, A, 20, 243
Manichaeism, 10, 51
manifest destiny, 143
manitou, 41
Maoism, 28, 208, 220, 221
martial arts, 120, 158, 159, 161, 162, 163, 166, 167, 168, 189, 194, 228, 250
Martin and Ostwalt, 16
Martin, David, 12, 252
Marx, Karl, 7, 9, 30, 88, 107, 126, 148, 198, 201, 214, 219, 220, 221, 222, 223, 225, 234
Marxism, 14, 220, 221, 222, 223
Marxist, 14, 19, 38, 81, 119, 198, 199, 204, 207, 208, 219, 220, 222, 223, 224, 225, 236

Mary Magdalene, 54, 224, 229
Masada, 76, 77, 119, 243
Master (spiritual teacher), 32, 44, 45, 54, 99, 123, 124, 125, 126, 132, 150, 157, 158, 162, 189, 215, 255, 268
Matrix Reloaded, 243
Matrix Revolutions, 243
Matrix, The, 58, 77, 111, 119, 120, 121, 122, 224, 243, 259, 267
Matter of Life and Death, A, 82, 84, 87, 243
Maugham, Somerset, 8, 126, 132, 193, 233, 250
May, John R., 14, 252, 253, 261, 263
maya, 76, 119
McCarthyism, 216
McEwan, Ian, 180, 233
Means, Russell, 42, 48, 255, 268
Medea, 225, 226, 227, 228, 229, 230, 243, 244
medicine man, 38, 40, 49
meditation, 7, 29, 32, 60, 68, 74, 80, 91, 94, 148, 149, 156, 157, 158, 162, 166, 191, 220, 239, 248, 250, 251
Medved, Michael, 13, 16, 144, 183, 252, 260, 268
Meet Joe Black, 87, 90, 244
Meetings with Remarkable Men, 124, 132, 159, 167, 196, 197, 244, 249
*Megiddo
The Omega Code 2*, 244
Mennonite, 28, 145
Merchant, Ismail, 126, 244
metaphysics, 30, 203
Metropolis, 51, 244
Michael, 2, 13, 28, 40, 56, 90, 120, 144, 183, 238, 241, 242, 243, 244, 245, 246, 249, 250, 252, 254, 255, 257, 259, 260, 267, 268
Microcosmos, 29, 244
Miles, Margaret, 142, 221, 259, 264
Milky Way, The, 139, 140, 244
millenarianism, 105, 151
Million Dollar Baby, 78, 80, 244
Mirror, The, 30, 244
*Mishima
A Life in Four Chapters*, 77, 164, 244
Mishima, Yukio, 163
Missing, The, 49, 244
Mission, The, 141, 142, 143, 176, 181, 222, 244
Miyazaki, Hayao, 38, 44, 45, 46, 47, 55, 56, 63, 86, 178, 181, 202, 206, 237, 244, 245, 249, 250, 255, 268
monastery, 28, 53, 125, 139, 145, 146, 156, 157, 159, 203, 204, 248, 249
Mongolia, 11, 97, 155, 193, 206, 247
monks, 11, 132, 133, 139, 146, 148, 155, 156, 203, 204, 220, 248, 249
monomyth, 18, 120
monotheism, 10, 56, 93, 119, 141, 156, 192, 234
Monsieur Ibrahim, 159, 167, 202, 244, 249

Monty Python, 11, 14, 154, 224, 234, 244
Monty Python and the Holy Grail, 11, 244
moral development, 6, 95, 103, 115, 118, 122, 166, 175, 185, 248
Mormons, 231, 232, 249
Mother India, 199, 244
Mr. Ya Miss, 96, 101, 244
Muggeridge, Malcolm, 11
Muir, John, 32
Mulholland Drive, 112, 118, 244
Murray, Bill, 116, 126, 193, 197
Muses, 53
My Father My Lord, 151, 235, 244
My Neighbor Totoro, 45, 47, 64, 244, 249
My Night with Maud, 219, 236, 244, 249
My Son the Fanatic, 205, 244
Mystic Masseur, The, 126, 244
mysticism, 7, 8, 18, 19, 29, 30, 31, 32, 61, 66, 112, 113, 126, 138, 149, 186, 194, 199, 231, 233
mythology, 18, 37, 62, 194

Name of the Rose, 37, 53, 63, 156, 215, 244
Napier, Susan, 44, 45, 105, 182, 255, 257, 261, 268
Napier, Susan J., 44, 45, 105, 182, 255, 257, 261, 268
Naqoyqatsi, 29, 244
narcissism, 32, 117, 120, 122, 224
Native Americans, 10, 29, 38, 39, 40, 41, 42, 43, 47, 48, 49, 58, 59, 63, 87, 100, 131, 132, 141, 161, 163, 182, 203, 238, 239, 249, 250
Nature, 11, 21, 23, 25, 26, 27, 29, 31, 32, 33, 34, 35, 41, 42, 44, 45, 46, 47, 63, 92, 108, 125, 130, 134, 157, 193, 194, 203, 206, 218, 226, 227, 228, 247, 249, 250, 254, 266
Nausicaä of the Valley of the Wind, 56, 64, 244, 249
Nazarín, 115, 140, 146, 153, 244
negative theology, 209
Neoplatonism, 10, 18, 21, 36, 37, 39, 41, 43, 45, 47, 49, 50, 51, 52, 53, 54, 55, 57, 59, 61, 62, 63, 64, 88, 93, 111, 120, 122
New Age, 6, 7, 8, 13, 18, 21, 33, 36, 37, 39, 41, 43, 45, 47, 49, 51, 53, 55, 57, 58, 59, 60, 61, 62, 63, 70, 76, 93, 117, 120, 123, 157, 187, 192, 195, 206, 207, 217
New Testament, 107, 108, 109, 135, 136, 142, 143, 169, 223, 247
Newton, Isaac, 50
Nietzsche, Friedrich, 23, 88, 90, 96, 115, 253, 257, 268
nihilism, 20, 186, 187, 225, 247
Ninth Gate, The, 111, 112, 232, 244
nirvana, 157, 193
Northfork, 42, 43, 63, 67, 87, 91, 244, 249

Nostalgia, 24, 30, 34, 51, 244
Not Without My Daughter, 200, 201, 244
numerology, 52, 53
Nun's Story, The, 133, 134, 140, 146, 210, 232, 244, 249
nuns, 132, 133, 134, 144, 146, 180, 193, 209, 211
Nykvist, Sven, 20, 186

Of Gods and Men, 139, 146, 244, 249
Oh God!, 105, 244
Old Testament, 36, 52, 105, 107, 108, 135, 136, 169, 183, 187, 188, 189, 229, 234, 235, 236, 248
Om Shanti Om, 96, 244
Omega Code 1, The, 244
Omega Code 2, The, 244
Omen, The, 20, 57, 210, 244
omniscience, 116
Once Were Warriors, 161, 244
One Flew Over the Cuckoo's Nest, 80, 244
Open Your Eyes, 116, 117, 244
oracle, 47, 98, 227
Orage, Alfred Richard, 59
Ordet, 128, 129, 244
orenda, 41
organized religion, 6, 7, 9, 63
orientalism, 194
Orphée, 32, 35, 112, 244
orrery, 54
Ortiz, Gaye, 18, 252, 253, 254, 259, 261, 262, 263, 267
Osama, 105, 201, 244
Others, The, 85, 86, 244
Otto, Rudolf, 8, 112
Ouspensky, P. D., 59, 115
Outlaw Josey Wales, The, 41, 78, 244
Ozu, 11, 74, 110, 252, 259, 268

Paap, 96, 99, 108, 109, 161, 244
pacifism, 158, 162, 168, 169, 170, 171, 172, 182, 212, 248
pagan, 25, 26, 31, 51, 227
paganism, 25, 28, 89, 92, 192, 227, 228
Pale Rider, 188, 244
Pali Canon, 77, 92, 98, 158, 190
Pandaemonium, 2, 11, 31, 32, 34, 238, 244
Papus, 93, 257, 268
Paradise Now, 78, 244
paranormal, 54, 57, 94, 249
Party, The, 126, 244
Pascal, Blaise, 10, 137, 138, 219, 220, 249, 264, 268
Pasolini, Pier Paolo, 12, 27, 152, 153, 154, 167, 198, 221, 223, 224, 225, 226, 227, 230, 234, 237, 238, 242, 243, 245, 248
Passage to India, A, 101, 115, 244
Passion of the Christ, The, 69, 223, 244
Patch Adams, 8, 174, 244
Pather Panchali, 244
patriarchy, 26
Pawnbroker, The, 152, 244

peak experience, 10
Penn, Sean, 74, 136, 178, 239, 243
Persepolis, 201, 244
Pert, Candace, 61
Phenomenon, 61, 62, 63, 244, 252, 266
Pi, 52, 53, 63, 244, 249
Piano, The, 244
Picnic at Hanging Rock, 193, 194, 214, 244
Pico della Mirandola, 37
pilgrimage, 48, 156, 177, 211, 250
Pillow Book, The, 164, 244
Plate, Brent, 253, 254, 255, 256, 257, 259, 261, 262, 263, 265, 267, 268
Plato, 36, 37, 93, 170, 198
Platonism (see Neoplatonism), 51
Pleasantville, 111, 244
Pocahontas, 55, 244
Pokémon
The First Movie, 55, 56, 181, 244
Poltergeist, 47, 57, 58, 84, 244
Poltergeist II
The Other Side, 57, 244
polytheism, 10, 160, 226
pornography of violence, 188, 189, 191
postmodernism, 17, 68, 123, 180
Powaqqatsi, 29, 244
Powder, 58, 59, 63, 64, 84, 104, 112, 244, 249
prayer, 9, 38, 70, 146, 148, 150, 152, 155, 156, 157, 158, 214
preacher, 123, 124, 127, 128, 129, 130, 132, 133, 138, 154, 247, 248, 249
Prejean, Helen, 135, 136, 146, 177, 178, 182, 247
Price Above Rubies, A, 152, 202, 244
Priest, 2, 140, 141, 146, 221, 231, 238, 244
priests, 19, 72, 132, 133, 139, 141, 142, 143, 146
Princess Mononoke, 45, 47, 64, 244, 250
prophecy, 58, 105, 223
prophet, 7, 28, 94, 105, 107, 123, 154, 234
Protestant, 28, 34, 107, 135, 136, 183, 192, 263, 269
Prozac, 8, 111, 252, 267
psychedelic, 9, 195
psychotherapy, 63, 111
Pullman, Philip, 37, 54, 222, 255, 266
Pulp Fiction, 189, 244
Purgatory, 95, 182
Pythagoras, 36, 37, 50, 52, 53, 92, 93

Quakers, 7, 145, 169, 170, 172, 191, 248
Quarrel, The, 124, 151, 160, 167, 213, 214, 232, 244, 250

rabbi, 149, 150, 151, 152, 154, 186, 231, 250
Rabbit-Proof Fence, 48, 244
Rain Man, 13, 244
Ramakrishna, Sri, 160, 198, 199, 231

Rapture, 92, 106, 107, 218
Rapture, The, 106, 109, 244
Rashomon, 47, 163, 190, 244
Rashomon effect, 47
Rawlinson, Andrew, 148, 261, 268
Razor's Edge, The, 8, 116, 126, 132, 245, 250
redemption, 25, 30, 31, 32, 69, 72, 111, 118, 142, 168, 175, 178, 179, 181, 182, 184, 185, 186, 187, 191, 248
reductionism, 192
Reggio, Godfrey, 29, 243, 244, 247
reincarnation, 21, 36, 60, 65, 77, 78, 81, 82, 84, 92, 93, 94, 95, 96, 97, 98, 99, 100, 101, 102, 103, 104, 106, 108, 109, 178, 181, 194, 205, 206, 210, 239
Reincarnation, 21, 92, 93, 96, 99, 101, 103, 104, 107, 109, 245, 257, 267, 268
Reincarnation of Peter Proud, The, 93, 96, 102, 108, 245, 257, 267
Religieuse, La, 134, 146, 245
remorse, 142, 143, 172, 178, 179
Renaissance, 36, 37, 50, 51, 55, 164, 194, 215
resurrection, 18, 36, 65, 81, 82, 92, 93, 100, 105, 106, 107, 109, 129, 178, 217, 226
retribution, 28, 178, 247
Revelation, 61, 92, 105, 106, 107, 108, 109, 183
Revelations, 108, 245
revenge, 37, 79, 90, 104, 108, 168, 175, 176, 179, 180, 186, 189, 191, 227, 230, 250
Roeg, Nicolas, 48, 242, 246
Romanticism, 11, 21, 23, 24, 25, 27, 28, 29, 31, 32, 33, 34, 35, 51, 60, 65, 66, 75, 76, 80, 112, 126, 164, 166, 206
Romero, 139, 140, 146, 221, 236, 245
Roux, Maggie, 18, 253
rubber reality, 17, 22, 110, 111, 112, 113, 114, 116, 117, 118, 119, 121, 122, 248
Rumi, 123, 231
Russell, Bertrand, 8, 36, 252, 254

sacred dances, 125, 159, 161, 228, 249
Sacrifice, The, 30, 73, 245
sage, 123
Said, Edward, 194
saint, 16, 73, 133, 148, 183, 222, 230, 248
Saints and Soldiers, 171, 245
Samouraï, Le, 163, 245
samurai, 159, 162, 163, 171, 172, 188, 191
Santería religion, 49, 50
Sartre, Jean-Paul, 8, 34, 233, 238
Saved, 232, 245
savior, 121, 184, 188
Schopenhauer, Arthur, 93, 192, 257

Schrader, Paul, 16, 17, 18, 20, 30, 74, 110, 111, 129, 130, 138, 139, 164, 165, 166, 185, 186, 222, 223, 224, 225, 237, 238, 243, 244, 245, 252, 259, 261, 262, 266, 268
Schuler, Jean, 34, 254
Schwartz, Susan L., 33, 76, 93, 205, 206, 254, 257, 263, 268
science fiction, 21, 59, 119, 225
Scopes, John, 212, 215, 216
Scorsese, Martin, 8, 17, 33, 60, 154, 155, 156, 164, 165, 183, 184, 185, 186, 219, 222, 223, 224, 225, 237, 238, 242, 243, 245, 248, 262, 265
Sea Inside, The, 78, 245
séance, 85
Sebastiane, 165, 245
Secret of Roan Inish, The, 97, 98, 245
secularism, 3, 5, 6, 7, 8, 9, 11, 12, 13, 15, 18, 20, 21, 22, 26, 31, 34, 36, 38, 51, 53, 56, 57, 63, 65, 66, 67, 68, 69, 71, 73, 79, 80, 81, 86, 89, 90, 91, 92, 106, 111, 116, 123, 124, 128, 130, 133, 134, 136, 137, 138, 139, 141, 144, 148, 150, 151, 152, 155, 160, 167, 168, 170, 174, 177, 181, 182, 187, 188, 191, 192, 193, 194, 196, 198, 199, 201, 204, 205, 207, 208, 209, 210, 211, 212, 213, 214, 217, 219, 221, 223, 224, 225, 229, 230, 232, 234, 235, 236, 238, 248, 250
secularist, 9, 23, 36, 65, 91, 106, 112, 137, 149, 153, 205, 219, 238
secularization, 12, 23, 198, 206
Seven, 47, 98, 109, 155, 156, 163, 171, 172, 185, 188, 191, 204, 245, 250
Seven Samurai, 163, 171, 172, 188, 191, 245
Seven Years in Tibet, 47, 98, 109, 155, 156, 204, 245, 250
Seventh Seal, 73, 245, 257
sexual politics, 196, 207, 208, 225, 227
Shadowlands, 68, 70, 90, 245, 257, 266
Shakespeare, 51, 170
shaman, 18, 37, 38, 40, 44, 45, 47, 48, 49, 56, 59, 98, 99, 100, 123, 127, 203
shamanic, 6, 11, 17, 18, 21, 26, 32, 36, 38, 41, 42, 43, 44, 45, 47, 48, 49, 50, 59, 62, 63, 64, 81, 89, 97, 98, 100, 155, 156, 161, 167, 192, 203, 204, 206, 226, 247, 248
Shane, 187, 200, 245, 263
shapeshifting, 98
She, 7, 20, 26, 27, 41, 43, 46, 47, 59, 69, 70, 75, 76, 79, 80, 84, 85, 86, 89, 97, 99, 101, 102, 103, 106, 115, 116, 134, 135, 137, 138, 146, 150, 161, 172, 175, 176, 179, 180, 182, 189, 195, 202, 205, 209, 210, 211, 217, 226, 227, 228, 229, 232, 235, 245
Shinto, 10, 45, 46, 192, 202, 255, 263, 269
shishigami, 45, 46
Siesta, 113, 245

Signs, 36, 61, 62, 68, 70, 84, 245, 255, 266
Silence of the Lambs, 85, 245
Silent Light (Stellet licht), 28, 245
Simon, Stephen, 18, 33, 60, 117, 255, 259
Sioux, 38, 41, 59
Sixth Sense, The, 84, 85, 86, 90, 91, 245, 250
Sluyter, Dean and Sluyter, Ean, 25, 253, 268
Smith, David L., 25, 253
Snow Cake, 13, 73, 74, 245
social activism, 140, 141
socialism, 31, 140, 153, 198, 199, 219, 220, 234, 249
Socrates, 65, 88, 138, 196, 198, 231
Solaris, 30, 245
Somewhere in Time, 60, 245
Son, The, 9, 176, 191, 210, 211, 235, 236, 239, 245, 250
Song of Bernadette, The, 210, 211, 235, 236, 245, 250
Spielberg, Steven, 13, 84, 94, 241, 242, 243, 245
Spirit, Stallion of the Cimarron, 45, 245
Spirited Away, 44, 45, 86, 90, 202, 245, 250
Spiritism, 82
spiritual advisor, 178
spiritual crisis, 10, 22, 33, 110, 111, 116, 118, 122, 123
spiritual intelligence, 13
spiritual practice, 6, 21, 29, 32, 40, 61, 147, 149, 150, 152, 155, 156, 157, 158, 159, 161, 163, 166, 167, 168, 189, 194, 207
spiritual teacher, 7, 22, 57, 58, 59, 98, 104, 123, 124, 132, 133, 138, 146, 147, 148, 153, 196, 202, 238, 249
Spiritualism, 82
Spring, Summer, Autumn, Winter ... and Spring, 28, 35, 77, 125, 132, 157, 159, 167, 181, 245, 250
St. Paul, 50, 69, 73, 107, 116, 127, 138, 143, 144, 152, 221, 224, 247
Stalker, 30, 51, 245
Star Wars, 15, 18, 44, 54, 245
Starhawk, 227, 265, 268
Stone, Oliver, 59, 242
Story of the Weeping Camel, The, 193, 206, 245
Strada, La, 140, 230, 245, 265
Straight Story, The, 177, 245
Stranger Among Us, A, 53, 152, 245
Stranger, The, 198, 245
Sufism, 123, 125, 130, 158, 159, 161, 167, 205, 249
sui generis, 14
suicide, 20, 32, 33, 65, 74, 75, 76, 77, 78, 79, 80, 85, 86, 102, 103, 107, 115, 119, 125, 135, 141, 152, 164, 165, 182, 184, 185, 196, 202
Sukkot (Judaism), 152

supernatural, 16, 20, 23, 27, 29, 33, 36, 37, 41, 43, 57, 58, 60, 61, 62, 63, 71, 80, 84, 85, 87, 112, 114, 130, 171, 175, 213, 224, 236
Surrealism, 112, 234
Swedenborg, 34
Switch, 95, 96, 101, 103, 104, 108, 210, 245
syncretism, 10, 49, 97

Tai Chi, 52
Taliban, 181, 201, 202
Taoism, 10, 11, 45, 89, 158
Tarkovsky, Andrei, 10, 11, 13, 14, 17, 20, 24, 29, 30, 31, 51, 52, 73, 111, 123, 193, 198, 210, 219, 227, 228, 237, 241, 244, 245, 252, 254, 259, 264, 268
Tarnation, 11, 245
Taste of Cherry, A, 78, 245
Taxi Driver, 102, 164, 183, 184, 185, 186, 187, 224, 225, 238, 245
telekinesis, 58, 61
teleology, 125, 206
Temple, Julien, 11, 244
Teresa of Avila, 8
Terminator, The, 245, 253
Terrorist, The, 77, 245
Theatre of the Absurd, 79, 234
theologian, 8, 13, 14, 112, 153, 183, 188
Theorem, 198, 234, 245
Theosophy, 37, 56, 192
They Shoot Horses, Don't They?, 79, 245
Thin Red Line, The, 171, 245
Thirteenth Floor, 111, 121, 245
Thomas, Jolyon Baraka, 255
Thoreau, Henry, 32, 254, 266
Three Colors Blue, 68, 69, 70, 83, 245
Through a Glass Darkly, 72, 73, 245
Thunderheart, 38, 40, 41, 63, 100, 245, 250
thy will be done, 122, 137
Tibet
Cry of the Snow Lion, 155, 220, 245
Tibetan Book of the Dead, 67, 100, 114, 156, 203, 245
Tibetan Buddhism, 67, 98, 99, 155, 156, 167, 193, 203, 204, 220
Tillich, Paul, 14, 15
Time of Favor, 78, 152, 245
Tolle, Eckhart, 7
Tolstoy, Leo, 169, 170, 190, 212, 261, 268
Torah, 52, 149, 150, 152
Touch, 89, 129, 130, 133, 140, 245
Touch of Zen, A, 166, 245
Touching the Void, 66, 245
Traherne, Thomas, 89
transcendent, 1, 2, 16, 18, 20, 21, 29, 43, 51, 59, 66, 67, 74, 110, 112, 116, 138, 139, 164, 166, 186, 225
Transcendental Meditation (TM), 60
transcendental style, 16, 74, 110, 225

transmigration of souls, 104
transmission, 133, 136
Travelers and Magicians, 203, 204, 245
Tree of Life, The, 29, 74, 245
Trial of Joan of Arc, The, 16, 245
Trudell, John, 38
True Confessions, 144, 245
Truly Madly Deeply, 69, 83, 90, 102, 245
Truman Show, The, 111, 245
Trungpa, Chögyam, 98, 257, 268
Tucker, Mike, 17, 18, 44, 111, 127, 253, 255, 259, 263, 269
tulku system (Tibetan Buddhism), 98, 99, 102, 109, 239
21 Grams, 9, 68, 69, 70, 74, 80, 178, 179, 187, 245, 250, 256
2001 A Space Odyssey, 8, 9, 245

Unbreakable, 84, 245
Unforgiven, 187, 246
unitive, 59, 116
Upanishads, 30, 89, 183, 193, 196, 197, 198
Ushpizin, 152, 246
utopia, 30, 193

Vajra Sky Over Tibet, 155, 246
Van Gogh, Vincent, 33
Vanilla Sky, 111, 116, 117, 118, 120, 121, 122, 246, 250
Vatican, 9
Vedas, 198
Verbeek, Marjeet, 24, 253
Vertigo, 101, 102, 103, 165, 246
via negativa, 10, 209, 215
via positiva, 10
vigilante, 175, 178, 183, 185, 189, 238
violence, 12, 13, 14, 17, 18, 19, 22, 36, 42, 62, 63, 111, 120, 121, 127, 139, 145, 167, 168, 169, 170, 171, 172, 173, 175, 183, 184, 185, 186, 187, 188, 189, 190, 191, 212, 220, 234, 235, 236, 247, 248, 251, 262
virgin birth, 27, 136, 248
Virgin Spring, 182, 246
Viridiana, 115, 139, 140, 230, 246, 259, 264
vocation, 88, 135, 136, 139, 140, 141, 154, 247
Vogler, Christopher, 18, 126, 127, 253, 269
Voltaire, 11
Voodoo, 50
VR, 110, 113, 116, 117, 119, 121, 122, 250
vulnerability, 140, 229, 230

wakan, 41
Waking Life, 246
Walkabout, 48, 193, 246
Waltz with Bashir, 172, 246
Warrior, The, 170, 171, 246
Weber, Max, 14, 192, 263, 269
Weil, Simone, 138

Western (film genre), 10, 11, 12, 18, 21, 33, 37, 38, 42, 50, 56, 58, 59, 63, 65, 70, 72, 75, 76, 81, 82, 83, 85, 86, 90, 94, 96, 97, 99, 100, 101, 105, 106, 108, 119, 120, 123, 124, 125, 126, 127, 132, 138, 144, 145, 155, 157, 158, 160, 161, 162, 163, 165, 166, 167, 170, 171, 172, 173, 174, 178, 183, 187, 188, 189, 192, 193, 194, 195, 197, 198, 199, 200, 201, 202, 203, 204, 205, 206, 207, 208, 215, 219, 221, 224, 225, 226, 228, 235, 250, 254, 261, 263, 265, 267, 268
Westworld, 79, 246
Whale Rider, 161, 167, 228, 246, 250
What Dreams May Come, 33, 34, 60, 68, 76, 87, 117, 205, 246, 254, 257, 263, 268
What the Bleep Do We Know?, 61, 246
Where the Green Ants Dream, 29, 246

Whitman, Walt, 26, 32, 66, 114, 214, 231, 254, 256, 259, 263, 269
Why Did Bodhidharma Leave for the East?, 28, 35, 125, 132, 157, 167, 181, 246
Wicker Man, The, 92, 100, 124, 226, 227, 228, 246
Wide Awake, 84, 246
Wilber, Ken, 59
Williams, Robin, 8, 19, 32, 33, 174, 175, 191, 239
Wilson, Colin, 33, 238, 254, 265
Wilson, Eric, 18, 53, 62, 111, 182
Wings of Desire, 88, 89, 91, 238, 246, 251
Winter Light, 72, 73, 141, 246
Wise Blood, 128, 246
witch, 26, 36, 47, 48, 49, 56, 58, 86, 227, 228, 229, 231
witchcraft, 49, 56, 227, 228, 229, 231
Witness, 96, 99, 170, 212, 213, 232, 236, 246, 251

Woolf, Virginia, 75, 76
Wordsworth, William, 11, 31, 61, 75
World of Apu, 246
Wounded Knee, 38, 39, 40, 43, 100
Wright, Melanie J., 15, 252, 263

Yamakage, Motohisa, 45, 46, 255, 263, 269
Yeelen, 48, 112, 246
yoga, 158, 162, 168, 197
Yoga Sutras of Patanjali, 58
Yoruba religion, 49
Yuga Purusha, 96, 246

Zabriskie Point, 79, 246
Zār tradition, 48, 56, 167
Zelig, 187, 246
Zen, 8, 11, 17, 28, 32, 44, 67, 77, 110, 123, 124, 125, 126, 145, 148, 156, 157, 158, 162, 164, 167, 225, 248, 250, 259, 268

www.ingramcontent.com/pod-product-compliance
Lightning Source LLC
LaVergne TN
LVHW081352060426
835510LV00013B/1785